CW00546051

GENDERCIDE AND GENOCIDE

To Judy,

With warm wishes, and admiration for your groundbreaking work on gender and development,

Adam

9 October 2006

GENDERCIDE AND GENOCIDE

Edited by Adam Jones

VANDERBILT UNIVERSITY PRESS
NASHVILLE

First Edition 2004

This book is printed on acid-free paper.
Manufactured in the United States of America
Text design by Ellen Beeler

Earlier versions of Chapters 1–5, 7–8, and portions of Chapter 10 of this volume were published in the *Journal of Genocide Research*, special issue, vol. 4 (1); Taylor & Francis, Ltd. (2002) *www.tandf.co.uk/journals* and are reprinted here with permission: "Gendercide and Human Rights," by David Buchanan; "A Theory of Gendercide," by Øystein Gullvåg Holter; "Gender and Genocide in Rwanda," "Problems of Gendercide," and "Gendercide and Genocide," by Adam Jones; "Gendercide and Humiliation in Honor and Human-Rights Societies," by Evelin Gerda Lindner; "Genetic Engineering and Queer Biotechnology," by Stefanie S. Rixecker; and "Geno and Other Cides," by Stuart Stein. Earlier versions of Chapter 9 and portions of Chapter 10 were published in the *International Journal of Human Rights*, Frank Cass Publishers (London) and are reprinted here with permission: "Beyond 'Gendercide'," R. Charli Carpenter, vol. 6 (4) (2002) and "Response to Carpenter," by Adam Jones, vol. 7 (1) (2003).

Library of Congress Cataloging-in-Publication Data

Gendercide and genocide / edited by Adam Jones.—1st ed.
p. cm.
Includes bibliographical references and index.
ISBN 0–8265–1444–8 (cl : acid-free)
ISBN 0–8265–1445–6 (pb : acid-free)
1. Genocide. 2. Genocide—Sociological aspects
I. Jones, Adam, 1963–

HV6322.7.G452 2004
303.6'6—dc22

2003017646

Contents

Editor's Preface

In the conclusion to my article "Gendercide and Genocide," published in June 2000 in the *Journal of Genocide Research* (Taylor and Francis), I expressed the hope that "other scholars in various disciplines will be prepared to explore" the gendercide framework, and suggested that "there will be much to learn from their contributions." I hardly anticipated that such a scholarly engagement would follow so rapidly, and in such a wide-ranging fashion. Dr. Henry Huttenbach, editor of the *JGR*, offered me the opportunity to prepare a special issue focusing on the theme of gender and genocide, with contributions from an international set of scholars from various disciplines. This was published in March 2002. I extend my deepest thanks to Dr. Huttenbach for his willingness to devote an entire issue to the gendercide theme, and for giving me the opportunity to prepare it.[1]

This volume includes nearly all the recently published scholarly materials on gendercide—all seven essays published in the special issue of the *JGR* (some with minor modifications and updates), together with four others: my original "Gendercide and Genocide" piece; Augusta C. Del Zotto's treatment of black male gendercide in the United States; R. Charli Carpenter's essay "Beyond 'Gendercide'"; and the closing chapter, Terrell Carver's "Men and Masculinities in Gendercide/Genocide."[2] I believe this book represents an important step forward in our understanding of the importance of gender in cases of genocide and mass killing, including institutionalized and "structural" mass killing.

Perhaps the most impressive aspect of this collection is the diversity of disciplines and pursuits represented: psychology (Lindner), sociology (Holter), sociology/social psychology (Stein), human rights activism (Buchanan), environmental/queer studies (Rixecker), political theory (Carver), and international relations (Carpenter, Del Zotto, Jones). Among the issues raised for consideration and further research are the following:

- Does the gender "lens," inclusively applied, help us to understand the dynamics of genocide, and of particular genocides? In my chapter on the Rwandan genocide, I contend that "gendering" the holocaust is in fact indispensable to understanding the social and structural background to the crisis of 1994; the planning and propaganda of the *génocidaires;* the course of the genocide itself; and the social and demographic quandaries of postgenocide Rwandan society. In some respects, the Rwandan case is unusual or exceptional, and the gender variable may be more muted in many other instances of genocide. On the other hand, it may be even more profoundly salient (for example, in Bosnia-Herzegovina, Kosovo, Bangladesh, Burundi, Indonesia in 1965 and 1966, the Congo "rubber terror," and the Nazi slaughter of Soviet prisoners of war).[3]

- Which conflicts, societal settings, and framings of masculinity tend to be most closely associated with gendercidal atrocities? In "Gendercide and Genocide," I proposed a link between "patriarchal" societies and gendercide. Three contributors to this volume expand fruitfully on this line of inquiry. Evelin Lindner suggests a focus on "honor" versus "human rights" societies, indicating that the former, in their construction of both masculine and feminine gender, may bolster gendercidal trends. Øystein Holter, in "A Theory of Gendercide," points to how different stages of genocidal and gendercidal build-up tend to be fueled by particularly murderous, and highly manipulated, gender constructions. He also ties these constructions to deeper "background" transformations in economy and society, in a way that I find very suggestive. Finally, Terrell Carver, in the chapter that closes this volume, expands on concepts of gender and their utility for inquiries into genocide, basing his analysis on the rich literature produced by both feminist scholarship and studies of men and masculinities.
- Can the concept of "gendercide" usefully cover institutionalized discrimination of the type experienced by African Americans in the United States, as Augusta C. Del Zotto contends?[4] If so, one wonders whether elements of the African American male experience also feature in the treatment of minority males in other parts of the world. Parallel arguments might be made for women's experiences of discrimination in the Third World. The project that I co-launched early in 2000, Gendercide Watch (*www.gendercide.org*), includes a case study of maternal mortality —a plague that takes the lives of some 600,000 women annually,

according to UN estimates.[5] In that case study, I argue that governments' refusal to provide adequate prenatal and postnatal care renders them complicit in—indeed, the direct agents of—gendercide.

- Are gendercidal trends and potentials an issue that ethicists and other concerned individuals should be attuned to in evaluating the new biomedical technologies? Stefanie Rixecker presents a strong argument for the possible significance of these technologies in campaigns against bearers of different and dissident sexualities. Her analysis also serves as a reminder that "gender" cannot be equated simply with biological sex. The role constructions and systemic constraints experienced by those gendered "queer," for example, may expose them, no less than those targeted as "embodied" women and men, to gendercidal attack. (Definitions of sex and gender, and debates over whether it is legitimate to conflate the two for certain analytical purposes, also feature in the contributions by Stein, Carpenter, and Carver.)
- Of what relevance might the gendercide framing be to human rights activism? David Buchanan finds the theory a valuable tool in analyzing gender-selective atrocities, and—in particular—in carving out a place in the analysis for male-selective victimization. (A. C. Del Zotto's chapter echoes a number of these claims.) The subject, Buchanan asserts, has been skated over or ignored by most human rights authorities, to the point that "outrageously" discriminatory legislation can be entrenched even by an avowedly progressive body like the International Labor Organization. One wonders, again, whether these arguments can legitimately be extended to the more diffuse and decentralized forms of victimization that women suffer—such as female infanticide and maternal mortality. Similar questions might be posed vis-à-vis institutions that are at times gendercidal in their impact upon males—military conscription, corvée labor, and incarceration prime among them.[6]
- Does the prominence of the gender variable in some instances of mass killing warrant the deployment of the term "gendercide"? Stuart Stein, in "Geno and Other Cides," and Charli Carpenter in "Beyond 'Gendercide,'" express doubt on this point. Their chapters make an enormously useful—even seminal—contribution to

situating the gender-and-genocide debate within the field of genocide studies as a whole. But Stein and Carpenter also provide a forceful critique of the assumptions and stated implications of my gendercide thesis. In my "Problems of Gendercide" chapter, I try to give these two contributions the sustained response that they merit.

I thank all the authors whose work is assembled here. I have indeed learned much from their efforts and hope that other readers will emerge similarly challenged and enlightened. I also thank editor Michael Ames, who oversaw preparation of this volume for Vanderbilt University Press, and the renowned scholar of men and masculinities, Michael S. Kimmel, who offered both moral support and practical assistance in getting *Gendercide and Genocide* published. Lastly, I am grateful to Dariel Mayer of Vanderbilt for her diligent production assistance; Bobbe Needham for her wonderfully rigorous copy editing; and Vancouver artist Miriam Tratt for her haunting cover graphic.

Adam Jones

Notes

1. I am grateful as well to Assia Nakova for her diligent production assistance.

2. My chapter "Problems of Gendercide" is more substantially reworked, incorporating sections of a "Response to Carpenter" as published in the *International Journal of Human Rights,* 7: 1 (spring 2003), pp. 141–47.

3. For case-study treatments of the "gendering" of all these genocides, see the Gendercide Watch website, *www.gendercide.org.*

4. The mechanism of "quasi-morticide" proposed by Jawanza Kunjufu and cited by Del Zotto invites an even more probing question: Can self-destructive behavior that is the product of systematic discrimination also be considered gendercidal? If so, the phenomenon might usefully be linked to the analysis of suicidal behavior by both women and men in Evelin Lindner's fascinating contribution.

5. For the full text of the maternal mortality case study, see *www.gendercide.org/case_maternal.html.*

6. These institutions receive case-study treatment on the Gendercide Watch site.

1

Gendercide and Genocide

Adam Jones

WE ARE BEGINNING TO DETECT A SHORTFALL IN . . . OUR DATA BASE.

—Cable sent by the UN special representative in the Balkans, Yasushi Akashi, on 13 July 1995, two days into the gendercidal massacres at Srebrenica in Bosnia.

From the opening hours of the 1999 war in Kosovo, an overriding tactic was evident in Serb military strategy: the gender-selective detention and mass killing of ethnic Albanian men, especially those of "battle age."[1] Although the Milosevic regime's genocidal assault on Kosovar society swept up all other sectors of the population, killing many and expelling hundreds of thousands to neighboring countries, the most systematic and severe atrocities and abuses were inflicted disproportionately or overwhelmingly upon noncombatant men. The Organization for Security and Cooperation in Europe (OSCE) was emphatic in its recent report, the most comprehensive available:

> Young men were the group that was by far the most targeted in the conflict in Kosovo. . . . Clearly, there were many young men involved in the UCK [Kosovo Liberation Army] . . . but every young Kosovo Albanian man was suspected of being a terrorist. If apprehended by Serbian forces—VJ [Yugoslav army], police or paramilitary—the young men

> were at risk, more than any other group of Kosovo society, of grave human rights violations. Many were executed on the spot, on occasion after horrendous torture. Sometimes they would be arrested and taken to prisons or other detention centres, where, as described afterwards by men released from such detention, they would be tortured and ill-treated, while others would simply not be seen again. Others were taken for use as human shields or as forced labour. Many young men "disappeared" following abduction.[2]

Similarly, although much remains unclear at the time of this writing, a large body of refugee testimony and forensic evidence from East Timor suggests a systematic targeting of younger males for dismemberment by machete, mass execution, and torture to death.[3] A Timorese woman in a camp for refugees/abductees said she was told by a militiaman: "You may have got your country but it will be a land full of widows."[4] As in Kosovo, fragmentary but cumulatively powerful reports have spoken of younger men being pulled from refugee groups and executed or "disappeared," and of a massive underrepresentation of men in refugee communities, this time in the militia-run camps of West Timor.[5]

The present chapter seeks to place such acts of "gendercide" in comparative and global-historical perspective. It argues that gendercide—inclusively defined as *gender-selective mass killing*—is a frequent and often defining feature of human conflict, and perhaps of human social organization, extending back to antiquity. I contend as well that gendercide is a regular, even ubiquitous, feature of contemporary politico-military conflicts worldwide.

A theme of the chapter is that gendercide, at least when it targets males, has attracted virtually no attention at the level of scholarship or public policy. As such, it can be classed as one of the great taboo subjects of the contemporary age. I hold, nonetheless, that an inclusive understanding of gendercide carries powerful implications for the emerging field of comparative genocide studies. For present (not necessarily all) purposes, "gender" can be defined primarily, if not exclusively, in terms of biological sex.

Why "Gendercide"?

The term "gendercide" was first coined by Mary Anne Warren in her thought-provoking 1985 book, *Gendercide: The Implications of Sex Selection*. Warren drew

> an analogy between the concept of genocide and what I call gendercide. The Oxford American Dictionary defines genocide as "the deliberate extermination of a race of people." By analogy, gendercide would be the deliberate extermination of persons of a particular sex (or gender). Other terms, such as "gynocide" and "femicide," have been used to refer to the wrongful killing of girls and women. *But "gendercide" is a sex-neutral term, in that the victims may be either male or female. There is a need for such a sex-neutral term, since sexually discriminatory killing is just as wrong when the victims happen to be male.* The term also calls attention to the fact that gender roles have often had lethal consequences, and that these are in important respects analogous to the lethal consequences of racial, religious, and class prejudice.[6]

Warren gives the analyst a great deal to work with here. There is the gender-inclusive framing of "sexually discriminatory killing"; the normative injunction that all such killing is equally "wrong"; and the sophisticated linking of the gender variable to "racial, religious, and class prejudice." But although she pledges to explore the issue in detail in her chapter on "Gendercidal Precedents," the promise of the theoretical framing is never fulfilled—or rather, it is only partially fulfilled. The chapter concerns itself exclusively with female-selective killing: female infanticide, the witch-hunts in Europe, suttee or widow burning in India, female genital mutilation, "the denial of reproductive freedom" (to women), and "misogynist ideologies." Much of the remainder of her book is devoted to the subject of the sex selection of children as a form of gendercide against women. Whatever the merits of extending the framework this far (or to the genital mutilation of women or men), gendercide, for all practical purposes, is limited in Warren's analysis to "anti-female gendercide."[7]

In fact, however, noncombatant men have been and continue to be the most frequent targets of mass killing and genocidal slaughter, as well as a host of lesser atrocities and abuses. The mass killing of males, particularly of "battle-age" men, has roots deep in the history of conflict between human communities.[8] "From antiquity, [patriarchy] has had an inherent problem with men not covered by the bonds of kinship or culture and has traditionally sought to marginalise them through diverse means," writes the Jamaican scholar Errol Miller in a little-known and stimulating book. "The practices of killing all male captives, of castrating the men whose lives have been spared, and of offering men less opportunities for manumission from slavery, all show that men's domination of men outside the bonds of kinship and community has been more severe and brutal than men's domination of women within or outside the kin or ethnic group."[9]

Gerda Lerner writes of the Middle East in classical times: "There is overwhelming historical evidence for the preponderance of the practice of killing or mutilating male prisoners and for the large-scale enslavement and rape of female prisoners." Citing Lerner, Barbara Ehrenreich speculates that in the gendercide of males may lie, by a curious twist, the origins of misogyny: "In the situation Lerner describes, where enemy males were killed and enemy females enslaved, the only surviving adult representatives of the defeated enemy would of course be female, and the psychological equation would have been established, over time, between femaleness and the enemy 'Other.'"[10]

Such gender-selective strategies were by no means fully consistent or universal, even to the limited extent that historians have been able to test the classical accounts. Leo Kuper agrees that "it was common enough practice to destroy besieged cities and to slaughter their inhabitants, or their male defenders while taking the women and children into slavery." But he implicitly contrasts events such as the classical "destruction of Troy and its defenders, and the carrying off into slavery of the women (as described in the legendary accounts and the Greek tragedies which have come down to us)," with the genus of "root and branch extermination, expressed in the slaughter of men, women and children."[11]

It is nonetheless remarkable how regularly one comes across references, in the literature on modern mass killing, to staggering demographic disproportions of adult males versus adult females—that is, a wildly skewed underrepresentation of adult men. Among the best-documented cases, though their strict designation as "gendercide" is disputable, are the Stalinist purges of the 1930s and 1940s. "As early as August 1937, they were shooting seventy men a day," wrote Robert Conquest in his study *The Great Terror*. In a fascinating addendum, Conquest used 1959 census figures to argue that the Soviet population "was some 20 million lower than Western observers had expected *after* making allowance for war losses." "But the main point," he noted, "arises from a consideration of the figures for males and females in the different age groups." He then unveiled a striking table indicating that whereas age cohorts up to 25–29 displayed the usual 51-to-49 percent split of women to men, from 30–34 the gap widened to 55 to 45 percent. Thereafter, the disparity became massive, reflecting the generations of males caught up in the purges and the Great Patriotic War. From 35–39, women outnumbered men by 61 to 39 percent; from 40–54, the figure was 62 to 38 percent; in the 55–59 age group, 67 to 33 percent; from 60–69, 65 to 35 percent; and 70 or older, 68 to 32 percent. Conquest summarized the findings as follows:

> Many women died as a result of the war and the purges. But in both cases the great bulk of the victims was certainly male. From neither cause should there be much distinction in the figures for the sexes for the under-30 age groups in 1959. Nor is there. For the 30–34 block the[re] . . . is a comparatively small difference, presumably indicating the losses of the young Army men in their late teens during the war. In the 35–39 group, which could have been expected to take the major war losses, we find figures of 391 to 609 women. *One would have thought that these men, in their early twenties in the war, would have had the highest losses. But the proportion then gets worse still,* and for the 40–44, 45–49 and 50–54 [cohorts] remains a set 384 to 616. Even more striking, the worst proportion of all comes for the 55–59 age group (334 to 666: in fact in this group alone there are almost exactly twice as many women as men). The figures for the 60–69 group (349 to 691) and for the 70 and over group (319 to 681) are also much worse than the soldiers' groups. Now all authorities agree that the Purge struck in the main at people "between thirty and fifty-five"; "generally, arrested people are all thirty or over. That's the dangerous age: you can remember things." There were few young or old, most of them being "in the prime of life." Add twenty years for the 1959 position.
>
> Precise deductions are not possible. Older men died as soldiers in the war. But on the other hand, the mass dispatch to labour camps of prisoners of war returned from Nazi hands in 1945 must have led to an extra, and non-military, death rate among the younger males. So must the guerrilla fighting in the Baltic States and the Western Ukraine, which lasted for years after the war; and so must the deportations from the Caucasus and the general renewal of Purge activities in the post-war period. But in any case, the general effect of the figures is clear enough. The wastage of millions of males in the older age groups is too great to be masked, whatever saving assumptions we may make. We here have, frozen into the census figures, a striking indication of the magnitude of the losses inflicted in the Purge.[12]

And, we might add, a striking indication of perhaps the worst gender-specific slaughter in human history. But Stalin has not lacked for competitors among the architects of twentieth-century genocide and mass killing:

> No territory-wide census was taken in the Congo until long after the rubber terror [of 1890–1910] was over. But Daniel Vangroenweghe, a Belgian anthropologist who worked in a former rubber area in the 1970s, found persuasive demographic evidence that large numbers of men had been worked to death as rubber slaves or killed in punitive raids—and he discovered the evidence in the [Belgian] regime's own statistics. No other explanation accounts for the curious pattern that threads through the village-by-village headcounts taken in the colony long before the first territorial census. These local headcounts consistently show far more women than men. At Inongo in 1907, for example, there were 309 children, 402 adult women, but only 275 adult men. . . . At nearby Iboko in 1908 there were 322 children, 543 adult women, but only 262 adult men. Statistics from numerous other villages show the same pattern. Sifting such figures today is like sifting the ruins of an Auschwitz crematorium. They do not tell you precise death tolls, but they reek of mass murder.[13]

> I was . . . told that in Cerewek, Gabus, and Sulur [Indonesia, after the 1965–66 genocide] 70 percent of the population are widows. Some people even said that in Banjardowo it was very hard to find a single adult male. Where could they have gone to?[14]

> All through the liberation war [of 1971], able-bodied young men [in East Pakistan/Bangladesh] were suspected of being actual or potential freedom fighters. Thousands were arrested, tortured, and killed. Eventually cities and towns became bereft of young males who either took refuge in India or joined the liberation war.[15]

> The major long-term demographic result [of Pol Pot's 1975–79 genocide] is the preponderance of women in modern Cambodia. Women, including large numbers of widows, make up 60 to 80 percent of the adult population in various parts of the country, as well as among Cambodians abroad.[16]

That the gender-selective mass killing and "disappearance" of males, especially "battle-age" males, remains a pervasive feature of contemporary conflict is not open to dispute. Indeed, its frequency across cultures and conflict types marks it as a possibly *definitional* element of contemporary warfare, state terrorism, mob violence, and paramilitary brigandage:

> **Kosovo, 1999.** "Shortly before dawn on April 27, according to locals, a large contingent of Yugoslav army troops garrisoned in Junik started

moving eastward through the valley, dragging men from their houses and pushing them into trucks. 'Go to Albania!' they screamed at the women before driving on to the next town with their prisoners. By the time they got to Meja they had collected as many as 300 men. The regular army took up positions around the town while the militia and paramilitaries went through the houses grabbing the last few villagers and shoving them out into the road. The men were surrounded by fields most of them had worked in their whole lives, and they could look up and see mountains they'd admired since they were children. Around noon the first group was led to the compost heap, gunned down, and burned under piles of cornhusks. A few minutes later a group of about 70 were forced to lie down in three neat rows and were machine-gunned in the back. The rest—about 35 men—were taken to a farmhouse along the Gjakove road, pushed into one of the rooms, and then shot through the windows at point-blank range. The militiamen who did this then stepped inside, finished them off with shots to the head, and burned the house down. They walked away singing."[17]

Jammu and Kashmir, 1999. "Since 1990, some 700 to 800 people have 'disappeared' after being arrested by police or armed paramilitary forces. . . . The victims have included men of all ages, including juveniles and the very old, and all professions, including businessmen, lawyers, labourers and many teachers. Many of them appear to be ordinary citizens picked up at random, without any connection to the armed struggle. . . . Their relatives still live in unbearable uncertainty about the fate of their loved ones."[18]

Colombia, 1998. "Rightist militiamen using chainsaws on some of their victims killed 11 peasants and kidnapped 13 others, accusing them of collaborating with leftist guerrillas. . . . Police said the chainsaws were used to torture and behead several of the victims. Others were shot to death. Ten of the victims were men, police reported. The slain woman, a minor, was killed by militiamen seeking her husband, who was not at home."[19]

Rwanda, 1997. "I've been a member of the RPF [Tutsi-dominated Rwandan Patriotic Front] since April 1991. I know a lot about the massacres committed by the Rwandan Patriotic Army [in the course of invading Rwanda and ending the genocide]. The RPF wanted to establish its supremacy, and to do so they had to eliminate any potential rival. In many cases the Army came for men, ages 18 to 55, and took them away by night, never to be seen again. Their families search for them in vain, in the prisons of Rwanda, but they all died at the hands of the Rwandan

Patriotic Army. The general pattern was to select youth and men who were still active, as well as leaders, teachers, farming instructors—anyone who played a role, any community leader was particularly singled out."[20]

Bosnia-Herzegovina, 1992. "They were shelling our village [while] I was in a shelter. Some men got away. Those who were in their homes were beaten, tortured and killed by the Cetniks [Serbs]. . . . We came out of the shelter. They were looking for men. They got them all together. We saw them beating the men. We heard the sounds of the shooting. One man survived the executions. They killed his brother and father. Afterwards the women buried the men."[21]

Sri Lanka, 1991. "Soldiers have searched for rebel suspects in some of the 30 refugee camps that now ring Trincomalee. A leader of one camp, near the village of Nilaveli north of Trincomalee, said that 84 men were detained in a series of Army sweeps last year. One refugee who returned said he was locked in a prison that held about 350 men. 'They tied my hands behind my back and kept a blindfold around my eyes. I hardly ate for two weeks,' he said. 'I was finally released with 15 [men]. We don't know what happened to the others.' The camp leader, who requested anonymity, said only 45 out of the 84 detainees are accounted for. The others 'disappeared or have been killed. We don't know.' "[22]

Peru, 1990. "The Peruvian Army occasionally reacts to ambushes and attacks by invading a community and killing dozens of young and old males, sometimes in full view of relatives."[23]

Delhi, October–November 1984 [following the assassination of Prime Minister Indira Gandhi by her Sikh bodyguards]: "The nature of the attacks confirm that there was a deliberate plan to kill as many Sikh men as possible, hence nothing was left to chance. That also explains why in almost all cases, after hitting or stabbing, the victims were doused with kerosene or petrol and burnt, so as to leave no possibility of their surviving. Between October 31 and November 4, more than 2,500 men were murdered in different parts of Delhi, according to several careful unofficial estimates. There have been very few cases of women being killed except when they got trapped in houses which were set on fire. Almost all of the women interviewed described how men and young boys were special targets. They were dragged out of the houses, attacked with stones and rods, and set on fire. . . . When women tried to protect the men of their families, they were given a few blows and forcibly separated from the men. Even when they clung to the men, trying to save them, they were hardly ever attacked the way men were. I have not yet heard of a case of a woman being assaulted and then burnt to death by the mob."[24]

Iraqi Kurdistan, 1983. "In August 1983, Iraqi security troops rounded up the men of the Barzani tribe from four resettlement camps near Arbil. These people were not engaged in any antigovernment activities. . . . Two of Barzani's sons at that time led the Kurdistan Democratic Party and were engaged in guerrilla activities against the Baghdad government, but only a part of the tribe was with them. The entire area of Barzan had, along with many other parts of Kurdistan, been evacuated by the government, and the Barzanis who had opted no longer to oppose the government had been moved to resettlement camps. All eight thousand men of this group, then, were taken from their families and transported to southern Iraq. Thereafter they disappeared. All efforts to find out what happened to them or where they had gone, including diplomatic inquiries by several European countries, failed. It is feared that they are dead. The KDP [Kurdish Democratic Party] has received consistent reports from sources within the military that at least part of this group has been used as guinea pigs to test the effects of various chemical agents."[25]

What explanations can be advanced for this apparent predominance of males among the victims of genocide and mass killing? Most of the variables are, in fact, fairly intuitive. First, there is a military logic to the destruction of the "battle-age" portion of a targeted community, whether as a sufficient measure in itself or as a prelude to "root-and-branch" extermination of the community. Honig and Both's examination of the gendercidal massacres at the Bosnian city of Srebrenica in July 1995 conveys this military logic well:

> If it is not as simple an answer as "revenge," and if the suggestion of [the victims being] "combat casualties" is patently false, why did the Bosnian Serbs kill the men of Srebrenica in cold blood? Much of it seemed to have to do with the character of the war in Bosnia. Muslim men posed a pointed threat to the Serbs, who were educated in the traditions of people's war and who aimed to create an ethnically pure Serb territory. And, as the police chief of Serb-controlled Banja Luka commented in 1992, "In ethnic warfare the enemy doesn't wear a uniform or carry a gun. Everyone is the enemy." Civilians were considered indistinguishable from soldiers. The long-term success of ethnic cleansing depended on killing off the Muslim men, without whom the population's women and children would have no means of returning to their birthplaces. And since Srebrenica had been one of the main refuge places for Muslims

> from eastern Bosnia, executing the men would give the Serbs a more secure hold over the region. Both the requirements of people's war and the dictates of ethnic purity demanded that potential resistance, now and in the future, be minimised. As many men as possible had to be killed.[26]

As well, many genocides contain strong overtones of "eliticide." Societal elites, like "battle-age" males, may be targeted in isolation or as part of a phased assault on an entire people. And males overwhelmingly constitute the public face, at the very least, of those elite sectors. (The Burundi genocide of 1972, for instance, targeted mainly Hutus who were senior students, prominent church workers, and soldiers. These are all institutions in which the analyst would expect to find a strong male predominance.) Moreover, since most elites are to most appearances mostly male, it is not a great leap to the proposition that male equals elite—just as men's 'potential" as combatants may be enough to secure them death in a typical counterinsurgency sweep.

Lastly, there are the cultural codes and humanitarian biases that have been pervasive throughout cultures. Even many highly warlike societies have chosen to limit the scale of their physical destruction of an opposed population through enslavement, concubinage, or outright freeing of women (and children). Certain ingrained norms have sometimes obtained in dealing with the elderly and infirm, though there is also ample evidence of specific savageries directed against this group. Regardless, and crucially, *the most vulnerable and consistently targeted population group, throughout time and around the world today, is noncombatant men of "battle age,"* roughly fifteen to fifty-five years old. They are nearly universally perceived as the group posing the greatest danger to the conquering force, and are the group most likely to have the repressive apparatus of the state directed against them. The "noncombatant" distinction is also vital. Unlike their armed brethren, these men have no means of defending themselves and can be detained and exterminated by the thousands or millions. The gender of mass killing, moreover, likely extends beyond the age range specified. Elderly males are probably more prone than elderly women to be caught up in the "malestrom" of war; and modern warfare, with its relentless press-ganging and criminality, extends ever farther down the age ladder in the hunt for child soldiers and street thugs—overwhelmingly boys.

In all of these actions there are institutional, material, political, and cultural interests and variables underlying the systematic targeting of males. We are not, in other words, talking about an abstract "hatred of men" as lying at the root of these genocides and genocidal massacres, in the way that Nazi mass murder was clearly founded on an ideological hatred of Jews (and others). But the frequent and often massive correlation between male victimization and the most annihilatory genocidal excesses may merit a fundamental rethinking of the prevailing "gendered" framing of many of these issues.

If gendercide and mass killings of males are to some degree definitional of modern conflict, we may also be able to isolate an essential if not universal ritual of gendercide against men. *It is the physical act of separating men from women as a prelude to consigning men to death.* The ritual is enacted with great frequency the world over, although it is not always explicit in the examples just given. Nonetheless, as Adam Hochschild likened the evidence of gendercide in the grotesquely misnamed Congo Free State to the "ruins of an Auschwitz crematorium" (see the earlier excerpt), we should see in our minds the camp commander and his henchmen on the platform, systematically and dispassionately culling part of a group (here, the male part) and consigning those selected to rapid extermination.

Women and Gendercide

The manner in which women are targeted in genocidal slaughters may also amount to gendercide. There is no doubt that the term should be applied to all cases of mass rape followed by murder. In certain historical circumstances—including relatively recent ones (Bangladesh, Nanjing, Berlin)—women have been targeted en masse for combined rape and killing, or raping to death. This must surely rank among the most excruciating deaths known to humankind, and much the same culling process may be evident as in gender-selective mass killings of men. In the contemporary era, a further deadly element has been added to the mix: AIDS. Most of the current cases of large-scale rape in conflicts are in sub-Saharan Africa (Sierra Leone, the Democratic Republic of Congo, Angola), in areas that also lie at the heart of the "AIDS belt."[27] For women in these conflicts, rape thus carries with it the realistic threat, not only of death on the spot, but also of a lingering and agonizing wasting by disease.

Moreover, the century's best-studied genocides—the holocausts against the Armenians and the Jews—also featured acts of gendercide against women that (like those against males) were analytically significant, if subsidiary. These ranged from individual actions to full-fledged gender-selective policies and institutions. Two examples of the latter in the case of the Jewish holocaust are the female "work" camps and the genocidal death marches from their gates at the end of the war. (In both cases, the agents of the gendercide were also predominantly female.)[28] However, there seem to be very few such cases of women being separated from men and marked off for execution while men are *preserved,* even temporarily. Women (and children and the elderly) tend to be targeted as part of "root-and-branch" exterminations that target all members of the community.

We should by no means limit our framing to the traditional politico-military one. In first deploying the term "gendercide," Mary Anne Warren examined *infanticide* in history, making plain how pervasive and exterminatory toward girl children in particular this policy has been over the ages. "There are very few cultures in which male infants are more apt to be killed than females," Warren writes. She finds evidence across civilizations, from Arab societies where "the birth of a daughter was regarded . . . as a humiliating calamity—and often still is"; to northern Indian tribes "that "killed virtually all female infants at birth"; to nineteenth- and early twentieth-century Western Europe, where the murder of girl children (and sometimes boys) "was publicly condemned but practiced covertly, in ways that made it appear accidental or inadvertent."[29] R. J. Rummel may be not far off in his suspicion that "the death toll from infanticide must exceed that from mass sacrifice and perhaps even outright mass murder":

> In many cultures, government permitted, if not encouraged, the killing of handicapped or female infants or otherwise unwanted children. In the Greece of 200 B.C., for example, the murder of female infants was so common that among 6,000 families living in Delphi no more than 1 percent had two daughters. Among 79 families, nearly as many had one child as two. Among all there were only 28 daughters to 118 sons. In India . . . young girls were murdered as a matter of course. When demographic statistics were first collected in the nineteenth century, it was discovered that in "some villages, no girl babies were found at all; in a total of thirty others, there were 343 boys to 54 girls. . . . In Bombay, the number of girls alive in 1834 was 603."

Rummel adds: "Instances of infanticide . . . are usually singular events; they do not happen *en masse.* But the accumulation of such officially sanctioned or demanded murders comprises, in effect, serial massacre."[30] And though the infanticide phenomenon (like the ritual sacrificing of children or adults) is very far from an exclusively female phenomenon, *specifically female* infanticide seems closely enough identified with the subordination of women and most things "feminine" in history to constitute a gendercide against women. Fortunately, it is a phenomenon that may today have something of the status of slavery: largely eradicated in its classic form, though with lingering traces (China, India) and more muted offshoots still apparent (such as sex-selective abortions for upper-class families in India and elsewhere).

Feminist scholars have frequently cited the trial, condemnation, and slaughter of tens of thousands of women for "witchcraft" in early modern Europe as an example of the gender-selective killing of women. Christina Larner's equation of "witch-hunts" with "woman-hunts" seems well grounded, given that the gender disproportion was of the order of four to one against women, at least in the Scottish data she cites.[31] This "identification of the relationship of witch-hunting to woman-hunting" is necessary, Larner writes,

> to concentrate attention on such questions as why women were criminalized on a large scale for the first time in this period, and whether there is any significance in the simultaneous rise of prosecutions for witchcraft (old women) and infanticide (young women); whether there was any change in the socio-economic position of women in this period; why [the idea of] a female secret society should seem particularly threatening at this juncture, and to what extend the popularization of Christianity, a patriarchal form of religion, was a factor.

"This does not mean that simple overt sex war is treated as a satisfactory explanation for witch-hunting, or that the 20 per cent or so of men who were accused are not to be taken into account," Larner stresses. "*It means that the fact that the accused were overwhelmingly female should form a major part of any analysis.*"[32]

Men: Gendercidal Institutions

But the opposite of Larner's formulation is also true. In fact, I can think of no better defense of a focus on the mass killing of males than a simple paraphrase of her argument: "The fact that those targeted were overwhelmingly male should form a major part of any analysis." Are there areas outside the extermination of noncombatant men in conflict situations that might also be amenable to a "gendercide" analysis?

We must acknowledge first that the line between combatants and noncombatants is often blurred. Consider the fate of press-ganged Ethiopian conscripts flung into battle against Eritrea in early 1999:

> Nearly two months [30 May 1999] after the battle of Tsorona, the bloodiest yet of this desert "border war," Ethiopian soldiers still lie unburied on the baking plain, just metres from Eritrean trenches. . . . The Ethiopian commanders' strategy was simple. Deploying tens of thousands of barely trained recruits along a 5km front, they drove them forward, wave upon wave, with the aim of blowing them up on minefields until they had cleared a path to the Eritrean front line for better trained infantry, mechanised forces and armour. . . . It didn't work: the soldiers hardly raised their weapons, but linked hands in communal solace in the face of certain death from mines, the trenches, perfectly aimed artillery and their own officers, who shot them if they turned and ran. This was the horror of which Ms. Haile [an Eritrean woman soldier] and her companions spoke, of mowing down the horde till their Kalashnikovs were too hot to hold.[33]

The result in the Ethiopian/Eritrean conflict was a slaughter that, if not gendercide strictly viewed, must still be seen as a profoundly gendered atrocity—one of the worst of the post–World War II era, in fact.[34] The "press-gang" trend can be traced back through history. Rummel, for example, gives an estimate of three million Chinese men who died out of some fourteen million conscripted by Chiang Kai-shek's Nationalist forces during the Second World War—"close to the total military battle dead for Germany in all of World War II, and twice the number for Japan."[35]

The mass murder of prisoners of war might also be considered an act of gendercide against noncombatant males. This group has received "particularly lethal treatment . . . throughout history," according to Rummel. "If their lives were spared they were often sent to work as slaves in mines, on galley ships, in swamps, or at other labor that killed them off rapidly. The Mongols used their prisoners in the front ranks when attacking fortified cities and towns, and forced them to fill in moats or prepare catapults close to the dangerous walls. If not turned into slaves, prisoners of war were often simply killed, captured garrisons massacred."[36]

The picture of modern times is distinguished only by the greater scale of the killing. Indeed, the worst gender-selective slaughter in human history—perhaps the most concentrated mass killing of any kind—targeted male prisoners of war barely half a century ago. I refer to the mass liquidation by Nazi forces of Soviet POWs captured or rounded up behind the lines in the first year or so of Operation Barbarossa. Daniel Goldhagen gives a figure of "*2.8 million* young, healthy Soviet POWs" killed by the Germans, "mainly by starvation . . . *in less than eight months*" of 1941–42, before "the decimation of Soviet POWs . . . was stopped" and the Germans "began to use them as laborers."[37] Nor should it be assumed that the POW designation referred to men who had, in fact, seen military service. Nazi policy in the rear areas was very explicit: "Men between the ages of 15 and 65 were to be treated as POWs . . . [and] taken to POW camps." The Eighteenth Panzer Division studied by Omer Bartov had "orders to arrest all men of military age and send them to the rear"; "send them to the rear" rapidly became a euphemism for mass murder by execution, starvation, and exposure. In his detailed study of German occupation policies in the USSR, Alexander Dallin devoted a chapter to the fate of these Soviet prisoners of "war," whatever their particular route to detention and death:

> Testimony is eloquent and prolific on the abandonment of entire divisions under the open sky. Epidemics and epidemic diseases decimated the camps. Beatings and abuse by the guards were commonplace. Millions spent weeks without food or shelter. Carloads of prisoners were dead when they arrived at their destination. Casualty figures varied considerably but almost nowhere amounted to less than 30 percent in the winter of 1941–2, and sometimes went as high as 95 per cent.[38]

Bartov states the consensus view that "some 5,700,000 Russian soldiers fell into German hands [during the entire war], of whom about 3,300,000 died in captivity." This outright genocidal *and gendercidal* assault was a direct result of "the ideological concepts of the Nazi regime, which strove physically to eliminate the 'Bolshevik *Untermenschen*' [subhuman]."[39] The fact that the subhumans specifically targeted for death among the population of the occupied zone were almost exclusively male has tended to pass—as it were—un*menschen*ed.

What of institutions other than the military that target men for genocidal atrocity? Corvée labor is an obvious one, and one of the most time-honored of state-building and empire-building strategies. Rummel estimates that in colonial times, "at a rock-bottom minimum, 10 million . . . forced laborers must have died thusly," and "the true toll may have been several times this number."[40] The estimate is indeed a conservative one: Adam Hochschild claims the death toll in the Congo "rubber terror" *alone* numbered many millions, though male forced laborers were far from the only Congolese who suffered and died.[41] According to Jessica Kraft, "the Congo terror ceased only after the population declined so dramatically that forced labor became unprofitable"; we have already seen demographic evidence for the gender disproportion of that decline.[42] Jonassohn and Björnson place French rule in "their" part of the Congo around this time in the same category of cruelty. French governor-general Antonetti, planning construction of a railway to the coast, was "frank about the human cost" of the project. "Either accept the sacrifice of six to eight thousand men, or renounce the railways," he declared, and later: "I need 10,000 dead [men] for my railways."[43] In general, if such corvée groups across cultures and throughout history were less than 90 or 95 percent male, one would be surprised. The primacy of the gender variable in the equation—the overwhelming tendency of despots to select males for forced labor that leads rapidly to extinction—might reasonably warrant the designation of certain corvée institutions as gendercidal.

Predictably, the historical record shows a considerable overlap between corvée and associated institutions of imprisonment and incarceration—again, a victimization experience that is and always has been a near male monopoly the world over. (In Canada, the federal prison population is 99 percent male.) Integrating this phenomenon properly into a discussion of state-directed mass killing throws surprising light on the "accepted" gendering of historical events. Taking an example already cited, it allows us to set the witch-hunts of early modern Europe against the backdrop of "the harshest period of capital punishment in European history"—knowing what we know of the gendering of capital punishment almost everywhere throughout history. And what happens when we gender the "witch-hunts" and mass incarcerations of the modern era—for example, Stalin's purges, or state crackdowns on "Reds," "terrorists," and "agitators"? These historical and sociological questions have barely been hinted at, let alone coherently framed, in any mainstream discourse; and there is no space or specialist's competence to explore them here. My ambition, as throughout, is simply to "engender" the debate.[44] With this objective in mind, I turn now to consider the implications of the gendercide framework for the field of comparative genocide studies.

Gendercide and Genocide

> In the light of this record, one is prompted to wonder as to why the historical recurrence of a social phenomenon failed to register as a critical social problem, particularly among social thinkers and social scientists.
>
> —Vahakn Dadrian, "A Typology of Genocide"

One of the most promising developments in the academy's engagement with issues of conflict and human rights is the recent emergence of a school of "genocide studies." This dates from Leo Kuper's short, seminal book *Genocide: Its Political Use in the Twentieth Century* in 1981, though antecedents can be traced back through Vahakn Dadrian and Hannah Arendt to Raphael Lemkin, who coined the term "genocide" in 1943.[45] Currently, the school—which includes such scholars as Kuper, Frank Chalk, Kurt Jonassohn, Yves Ternon, and R. J. Rummel—has sought to develop a comparative history, sociology, and typology of genocide, as well as attempted to isolate "early warning" signs and propose ameliorative strategies. Though still in its early stages, the work, now buttressed by genocide-studies institutions worldwide, has produced a flourishing case-study literature that has added inestimably to our understanding of mass killing throughout history.

It is remarkable, though, how invisible or barely visible the gender variable remains in this emerging literature, at least as far as noncombatant males are concerned. One is put in the position of piecing together fragments. Kuper, in his field-defining work, mentions in passing that "While unarmed men seem fair game, the killing of women and children arouses general revulsion"; but it is a specific reference to the Northern Ireland conflict, which has not (in Kuper's view and others') reached a genocidal scale.[46] The obfuscation of the variable in the wider literature may reflect the fact that it is noncombatant *males* who tend overwhelmingly to be the victims of gender-selective mass killing, and this remains a powerful taboo in the feminist-dominated discussion of gender.

Some sense of the theoretical confusion that can result is suggested in Jonassohn and Björnson's analysis of genocides in antiquity. They write: "The Old Testament contains a number of cases that today would be considered as genocides—not because of the casualties of warfare, *but because of the killing of noncombatant women and children.*"[47] Later, they state of the destruction of Sybaris in southern Italy that "*Since the killing was not limited to members of the army,* we can call this a genocidal massacre."[48] What is seeping in here, albeit subtly, is a cultural bias that defines an entire population group by the activities of some of its members—a phenomenon that ought to be of particular concern to scholars of genocide. Jonassohn and Björnson seem to be suggesting, first, that the death of noncombatant *women and children* is definitional to a genocide; and in the second place that the mass killing of *civilians* constitutes a genocide. The strategy, as is so often the case, makes "womenandchildren" coequal with the civilian population, while expunging noncombatant males from the framing. Thus, a group that constitutes a prime target of genocidal assault throughout history, continuing to the present day, drops out of the analysis.

It could be argued that the line between militarized and nonmilitarized males is difficult to draw in many situations of social strife and military conflict. But in many of the cases Jonassohn discusses (such as besieged cities in classical and medieval times), such distinctions would also have been debatable in the case of women, the elderly, and even children. Total wars in microcosm tend to enlist all members of the "civilian" population in military or quasi-military activities—which may explain the determination of many conquerors to engage in "root-and-branch" extermination of the entire city or community. There seems little reason, prima facie, to consign males to the "military" category in this manner—in effect, marking them off as expendable and nondefinitional to genocidal killing—while granting blanket exemption to "womenandchildren," the destruction of whom, it is implied, defines *really* egregious (i.e., genocidal) acts of mass murder.

I have come across just one mainstream definition of "genocide" that accords gender first-among-equals status as a primary category of victims. It is simultaneously so broad and so confining a framework, however, that it cannot be adopted without substantial modification. The definition was proposed by Steven Katz, building on the crucial ingredient of the perpetrator's perception and intention stressed by predecessors like Chalk, Jonassohn, and Dadrian.[49] The term "genocide," Katz argues, can be applied only to "the actualization of the intent, however successfully carried out, to murder in its totality any national, ethnic, racial, religious, political, social, *gender* or economic group, as these groups are defined by the perpetrator, by whatever means."[50]

In one of his Talmudic footnotes, Katz pursues the point further, critiquing the work of Henry Huttenbach for discounting the possibility of sexual—"what I prefer to call gender"—groups being targeted for extermination. Huttenbach contended that this "is an error because empirically neither homosexuals nor women under Hitler were the targets of genocide. I agree with the facts—that is, I concede that neither homosexuals nor women (qua women) were the victims of genocide in World War II—but this empirical argument does not count against *the logical argument that homosexuals or women could, under other circumstances, be the targets of genocide.* Both of these possibilities are logically conceivable."[51]

From an inclusive gender perspective, Katz's definition can be seen as seriously deficient in its inability to comprehend that a group beyond women and homosexuals might be attacked on gender grounds (that is, "qua men"). An overriding problem, though—as Jonassohn and Björnson point out—is that Katz's definition of genocide is so restrictive that not even his main subject, the Jewish holocaust, would qualify: "It is quite clear that Hitler did not intend to murder the Jews in their totality. There were many exceptions to this intent."[52] This brings up the critical debate over necessary scale that preoccupies analysts of mass killing. Can the term "genocide" (and thus "gendercide") legitimately be applied to acts of mass murder that are not total in their effect, or even in their intention?[53]

"Genocide," in common usage, does tend to carry totalizing implications. But it is far from the case that this framing reflects a consensus among scholars, let alone international legal theorists and policymakers.[54] Citing the UN definition of genocide (1948), John B. Allcock carries the argument to the opposite extreme: "It is often assumed that in order to qualify as genocide, killing must take place on a very large scale, with perhaps thousands if not millions of victims. It is important to note, however, that within the terms of the UN Convention, no account is taken of the number of victims. The execution of a handful of villagers for reasons of national, ethnical, racial, or religious identity might be legitimately regarded as an act of genocide."[55] Mary Anne Warren also puts the argument succinctly, in a passage from *Gendercide:*

> The concept of genocide, as it is commonly understood, does not apply only to those actions which result in the complete extermination of a race of people. . . . Sometimes it is appropriate to speak of certain actions as genocidal atrocities, even though many members of the victimized race or culture survive. . . . Furthermore, not all instances of genocide involve direct or deliberate killing. Deaths or cultural disintegration deliberately or negligently brought about through starvation, disease or neglect may also be genocidal. Indeed, some acts of genocide do not involve any deaths at all, but rather consist in the wrongful denial of the right to reproduce.

Accordingly, Warren "suggest[s] that an action, law or policy should be regarded as genocidal if (1) it results in an absolute or relative reduction in the number of persons of a particular racial or cultural group; and (2) the means whereby this result is brought about are morally objectionable for independent reasons—e.g., because they violate certain individuals' right to life, liberty, or security against wrongful assault."[56] All these formulations are useful in constructing a gendered analysis of genocide, even if Warren's exploration is exclusively women-focused, and even if she applies her framework to phenomena (such as female genital mutilation) that detract from the force of her argument.

I join with proponents of the trend in arguing that the partial destruction of a wider group (ethnic, religious, etc.) is sufficient to warrant the designation "genocide," though I share Kuper's view that "the charge of genocide would not be preferred unless there were a 'substantial' or an 'appreciable' number of victims."[57] If this argument is accepted, we can eliminate Katz's requirement of "murder in its totality" from our definition of genocide. This is far from a cosmetic alteration, since it undermines the Jewish holocaust exceptionalism that lies at the heart of Katz's thesis. But I nonetheless choose to rework his definition as follows: "the actualization of the intent, however successfully carried out, to murder *in whole or in substantial part* any national, ethnic, racial, religious, political, social, gender or economic group, as these groups are defined by the perpetrator, by whatever means."

Gendercide against men and women—but particularly men—may be seen in this light as one of the more common forms of genocide. Can we go a step further and hypothesize what *types* of genocide or genocidal massacre are most likely to exhibit a gender-specific and/or gender-selective dimension? Female infanticide, the rape-killings of women through history, and mass murders for witchcraft (of which the European case stands alone in history) should probably be so characterized. On the other hand, mass purges and "politicides," such as Stalin's massacres and the Cultural Revolution in China, could be expected to be weighted disproportionately or overwhelmingly against males. The related phenomenon of "eliticide" could be similarly classed. Finally, the most militarized genocides—those carried out against a backdrop of partisan or rebel activity, or heavily masculinized dissidence—seem to exhibit the most pronounced gendering against male victims. A correlation is often evident with "patriarchal" culture, as this might be manifested in patterns of community organization and family roles. In his richly insightful study of "blood-feud" institutions in Montenegro,

Christopher Boehm gives a vivid picture of the almost surreal lengths to which the gendering of such conflicts can be carried:

> In the old days, women were free to come and go as they chose under feuding conditions, since taking their blood did nothing to help the blood score and also counted as a dishonor, morally speaking. Thus, their normal daily activities could continue. But men were sorely pressed when it came to doing any work other than herding, which allowed them to stay under cover with a rifle ready at all times. In 1965 [at the time of field research] it was for this reason that women still did so much of the heavier work in the fields, so I was told by the slightly apologetic Montenegrin "male chauvinists," who viewed this as a once-necessary custom formed in an earlier era. During the traditional period it also made sense, from the standpoint of economics, for Montenegrin men to go raiding a great deal. By engaging in this activity they were contributing to the household economy, and in a raiding party, whatever its risks, they at least were safe from attacks motivated by blood revenge. But whatever might happen to the men during a feud, the women were always free to keep the household economy going because the rules of feuding were taken so seriously by the opposing party.
>
> With respect to the sanctity of women, it was even possible for them to enter directly into combat during the first stage of a feud, when the killer's clan shut itself in and the victim's clan attacked the fortified stone farmhouse, which had loopholes [for firing rifles] everywhere. With no fear of being harmed, women could carry straw and firebrands up to the house to try to burn it. Also, women of a besieged house could go outside at night carrying torches, to light up the enemy so that their own men could shoot at them. This exemplifies the strength of these particular rules: to shoot a woman was a source of shame (*sramota*) for the entire clan.[58]

That these trends are not historical relics was attested to by an Agence France-Presse dispatch from northern Albania in June 1999. Mihaela Rodina described vendetta killings in the town of Shkoder. When a bar owner refused to pay protection money to local mafiosi and instead killed five gang members, a local villager observed: "Isufu's family knows it will not escape *kanun,* which requires bloodshed to be avenged by bloodshed. The males, even the youngest, will be cowering in their homes, hoping to escape the vendetta that will be mounted by the relatives of the five dead." Rodina added: "According to non-governmental groups, the men of some 25,000 families in northern Albania live thus, never going out of the house for fear of being victims of similar feuding. The women, who are unaffected by the *kanun*, are left alone to provide for the family's needs."[59] In the Middle East, the Caucasus, Colombia, and certain urban zones of the United States, such acts of execution and mass murder similarly display a selective, ritualized, and intricately coded gendering. This framing could be extended as well to children and women, who are overwhelmingly the victims of domestic mass murder, the perpetrators of which are largely (though not exclusively) male.[60] Such acts of extermination possess their own coded and ritualized character (including, frequently, the suicide of the perpetrator), although the assailant acts outside the centrally directed power structure that characterizes standard politico-military genocides and gendercides.

Latent, Retributive, and "Preemptive" Gendercide

A particularly useful set of concepts for the study of gendercide is the typology offered by Vahakn N. Dadrian. Dadrian refers to *latent* genocides, in which genocide is the "unintended consequence" of policies undertaken for other reasons, particularly in the context of military campaigns. He notes that in many cases, "instead of, or in addition to, tackling the armed forces of the opponent or the secessionist or militant revolutionary parties of a minority, the perpetrator *seeks to destroy or emasculate the manpower resources* of these groups as a means of winning the contest." However, Dadrian does not explore the implications of his highly gendered language, limiting the examples of latent genocide to (non-gender-selective) strategic bombing and mass expulsions/removals. Also useful is Dadrian's concept of *retributive* genocide. He depicts "this form of genocide [as] limited in scope insofar as its objective is confined to localized atrocities as a form of meting out punishment to a segment of the minority, challenging or threatening the dominant group." The strategy "possesses the concomitant function of warning and/or intimidating potential challenges and of deterring a recurrence of trouble."[61] This captures quite well the operation of the gender variable in gendercides against men, where the wider collectivity is culled and sifted to isolate a minority considered threatening, according to the blanket application of diverse variables (usually gender and age). Furthermore, the challenge and threat to "the dominant group" captures something of the competitive and belligerent character of intramale politics, the principal challenge of which has always been to suppress perceived male rivals or competitors.

The retributive strategy might also be a preemptive one. Indeed, one line of investigation that offers real promise is the notion of gendercide as a trip-wire or harbinger of fuller-scale root-and-branch genocides. A gendered understanding of the dynamics of genocide throws important new light on key cases of mass killing throughout modern history. The Armenian genocide of 1915–16, for example, is remembered primarily—and rightly—as a full-scale assault on the ethnic Armenian population of Turkey. But the dynamics and development of the genocidal attack exhibited a little-noticed gendering that may be predictable, and thus theoretically useful:

> The first step in the genocidal process was the emasculation of the Armenian population. It was initiated by the disarming of the many soldiers serving in the Turkish army, followed by the disarming of the civilian population. . . . In the early part of 1915, the Armenian soldiers, mostly combatants, were stripped of their arms and transformed into road labourers, and into pack animals, stumbling under the burden of their loads, and driven by the whips and bayonets of the Turks into the mountains of the Caucasus. They were given only scraps of food; if they fell sick, they were left where they had fallen. In many cases, they were dealt with in even more summary fashion, "for it now became almost the general practice to shoot them in cold blood."[62]

Once the "battle-age" Armenian males swept up in military conscription had been exterminated, a similar cull of remaining community males was carried out before the wider program of deportation was effected. Drawing on the work of Arnold Toynbee, Kuper describes "a common pattern of deportation" as starting

> with a call from the public crier that male Armenians forthwith present themselves at the Government Building. This was the usual procedure, though in some cases the warning was given by the soldiers or gendarmes slaughtering every male Armenian they encountered in the streets. When the men arrived, "they were thrown without explanation into prison, kept there a day or two, and then marched out of the town in batches, roped man to man. . . . They had not long to ponder over their plight, for they were halted and massacred at the first lonely place on the road. . . . The women and children were not disposed of by straightforward massacre like the men. Their destiny under the Government scheme was not massacre but slavery or deportation" [Toynbee]. Usually after a few days, the women and children, and the remnant of men who, through sickness,

> infirmity or age, had escaped the general fate of their sex, were ordered to prepare themselves for deportation. For the women, the alternative of conversion to Islam (if available) could only be ratified by immediate marriage to a Muslim and the surrender of children to be brought up as true Muslims. "Deportation was the alternative adopted by, or imposed upon, the great majority."[63]

That it was no alternative at all became progressively clear, however, as the horrors of the march mounted. Toynbee wrote of the deportations that

> Women who lagged behind were bayoneted on the road, or pushed over precipices, or over bridges. The passage of rivers, and especially of the Euphrates, was always an occasion of wholesale murder. . . . The lust and covetousness of their tormentors had no limit. The last survivors often staggered into Aleppo naked; every shred of their clothing had been torn from them on the way. Witnesses who saw their arrival remark that there was not one young or pretty face to be seen among them, and there was assuredly none surviving that was truly old.[64]

Thus, although the element of "gendercide" in the Armenian holocaust is important to an understanding of the Turks' genocidal strategy, it is far less significant in describing or explaining the broader exterminatory impulse toward ethnic Armenians. The destruction of males was a necessary, but not a sufficient, condition for the expression of that impulse. The generalized nature of the severe atrocities inflicted on the entire Armenian population places such genocides in a different category than, say, the Balkan wars of the 1990s—though there are superficial similarities, both in the genocidal massacres of males and the forced deportation of women, the elderly, and children.

The Jewish holocaust under Nazi rule and occupation similarly represented an attempt to eliminate an entire people. Again, though, the gendercide framing sheds new light on Nazi procedures. Daniel Goldhagen has examined *Einsatzgruppen* killing operations on the Eastern Front, which accounted for some two million Jewish lives *before* the main apparatus of death camps and "work" camps was fully operational. He points out in *Hitler's Willing Executioners* how this "up-close," intimate killing of manifestly defenseless civilians was incrementally managed according to gender:

> The *Einsatzgruppen* officers . . . could habituate their men into their new vocation as genocidal executioners through a stepwise escalation of the

> killing. First, by shooting primarily teenage and adult Jewish males, they would be able to acclimate themselves to mass executions without the shock of killing women, young children, and the infirm. According to Alfred Filbert, the commander of *Einsatzkommando 9,* the [execution] order from Heydrich "quite clearly" "included also women and children." Yet, "in the first instance, without a doubt, the executions were limited generally to Jewish males." By generally keeping units' initial massacres to smallish numbers (by German standards) of a few hundred or even a thousand or so, instead of many thousands, the perpetrators would be less likely to become overwhelmed by the enormity of the gargantuan bloodbaths that were to follow. They also could believe that they were selectively killing the most dangerous Jews, which was a measure that they could conceive to be reasonable for this apocalyptic war. Once the men became used to slaughtering Jews on this sex-selective and smaller scale, the officers could more easily expand the scope and size of the killing operations.

In the early weeks of these murder campaigns, the *Einsatzkommandos,* again according to Goldhagen, "were the equivalent of genocidal scouting parties, developing the methods of killing, habituating the perpetrators to their new vocation and, generally speaking, working out the feasibility of the overall enterprise."[65] Acts of gendercide can be seen in such cases as a vanguard for the genocide as a whole, an initial barrier to be surmounted and "threat" to be removed before the remainder of the community is consigned to violent death.[66]

The development of the mass killing of Jews and others on the eastern front by poison gas in specially designed vans was also apparently a response to the reluctance some executioners felt to killing women. Christopher Browning is emphatic on this point: "Faced with the complaints . . . about the psychological burden on the men of killing women and children, Himmler ordered the search for alternative killing methods that led to the development of the gas van."[67] But though they would subsequently be disproportionately targeted for this form of slaughter—less "stressful," as far as the perpetrators were concerned, anyway—women were not the first to be gassed by the Nazis, either in vans or in gas chambers. The victim generally selected for early tests of poison gas was the male Soviet prisoner of war. This seems to have been true both on the eastern front and at the first gas chamber in Auschwitz.[68]

The link between the gendercide against Soviet POWs and the Jewish holocaust may extend further still. In passages that are nothing short of revelatory, Christian Streit has pointed out that the very infrastructure and techniques of the death camps were originally developed to enslave and exterminate Soviet POWs, not Jews:

> Two large groups of Soviet prisoners were involved. The first comprised those prisoners who were selected and executed as "politically intolerable." Before the end of December 1941 at least 33,000 such prisoners had been executed in the concentration camps of the Reich and the General Government [in occupied Poland]. The second group consisted of those Soviet POWs who had been allotted to Himmler as slave laborers in the SS enterprises. The decision to turn these POWs into Himmler's slaves also resulted from the basic decision to brush aside international law in the war against the Soviet Union. . . . Repeatedly during the summer of 1941, and starting with a convoy of several hundred in July, groups of Soviet prisoners of war, who had been selected as "intolerable," had been taken to the Auschwitz concentration camp to be executed there. To ease the mental strain of the shooting squads and to save costs and energies the executors soon started looking for a simpler method. It was probably deputy commander Karl Fritzsch who experimented in early September with a pesticide, Zyklon B, to murder some 600 such prisoners and another 250 camp inmates who had been selected as "unfit for work." After more such "test gassings"—there were at least two more convoys of Soviet prisoners among the victims, one numbering 900 men—the gassings of Jewish victims were started in January or February 1942. . . . Even the infrastructure used in the Final Solution, the Birkenau camp with its rail connection, had originally been intended for 100,000 Soviet prisoners of war who were to be Himmler's allocation of slave labourers for the giant industrial complex at Auschwitz which I.G. Farben and the SS were planning as a joint venture. Soviet prisoners numbering 10,000, who were to build the huge Birkenau camp for 100,000 POWs, had been brought to Auschwitz in October 1941. By the end of November half of them were dead, by February 1942 about 8,000. Only 186 were still alive on 1 May 1942. Those prisoners who had not starved had been tortured to death.[69]

A gender variable clearly underlies the broader development of the concentration camp, the definitive Nazi institution. The first camp, Dachau, created in March 1933, housed only males (including homosexuals). The *Kristallnacht* of 1938, one of the definitive "markers" on the road to the holocaust, was also followed by a gender-selective mass roundup: the Nazis "arrested and sent to concentration camps some 30,000 Jewish men at least."[70]

Two important caveats should be attached to this brief discussion of the Jewish holocaust. First, there is an offsetting—and again secondary—process of extermination that seems to have disproportionately targeted women (and children, and the elderly) ahead of adult males for destruction. This was the prototypical "selection on the railway sidings," in which emphasis was placed on the preservation, usually brief, of those deemed able to work in the factories. All "women in charge of children" were targeted for immediate extermination in these procedures, along with "the old people, all the children, . . . and in general all the people unfit for work," according to Johann Paul Kremer, a Nazi "doctor" at Auschwitz. "[They] were loaded into trucks and taken to the gas chambers."[71] Auschwitz managers reported an "arrival strength" for 21 January 1943 as "2,000 Jews, of whom 418 were selected to be put to work (254 men, 164 women), i.e., 20.9 percent; 24 January 1943, 2,029 Jews, of whom 228 were selected to be put to work (148 men, 80 women), i.e., 11.8 percent; on 27 January 1943, 993 Jews, of whom 284 were selected to be put to work (212 men and 72 women), i.e., 22.5 percent."[72] The gender discrimination against women may have been even more intense than at first appears, since there is evidence of a preselection of males for mass execution *before* the construction of the death-camp system, as noted. I am aware of no overall comparative research on the numbers of men and women killed by the different Nazi mechanisms, however, and must abandon further speculation—which is perhaps appropriate, since gender was far from a dominant consideration in the holocaust overall.

The second caveat is that other variables mentioned in this chapter can also serve as tripwires or harbingers of full-scale genocide. Elite status is an obvious example. One might also point to the selective killing of the elderly, handicapped, or infirm. How many instances one could locate beyond the infamous Nazi case is uncertain. But in retrospect, for the Nazis at least, the destruction of the "useless" and "burdensome" elderly, handicapped, and infirm was clearly an early manifestation of the exterminatory impulse that would later target Jews, Gypsies, Slavic males, and others. It also buttressed the Nazis' penetration of the German professions—so that when medical doctors, for example, were called upon to oversee and inflict atrocities at Auschwitz, many had long since abandoned any fealty to their Hippocratic oaths.[73]

Conclusion

> When doing comparative research it is important to be aware of the cultural and moral imperatives in a society that will lead otherwise reliable sources of data to practice a form of self-censorship that will make the reported data incomplete and therefore less useful. Such "black holes" in our sources of data exist in every culture so that the researcher needs to be alert to what is not there.[74]

The preceding discussion has sought to explore the utility of the "gendercide" framework, inclusively approached, across a broad range of historical and contemporary case studies. It has been found that while the framework varies in its explanatory power, depending upon a host of other variables, it is a powerful aid in understanding the character and dynamics of many if not most acts of genocide and mass killing.

One possible objection to the analysis should be anticipated. Is it legitimate to isolate males as a target of genocide and "gendercide" when the perpetrators are themselves overwhelmingly male? It can be countered that the Hutus who slaughtered Tutsis in Rwanda were also "other blacks"; that the deranged young man who culled and murdered fourteen women at the École Polytechnique in Montreal in 1989 was a "fellow Quebecker." Which ascriptive trait we choose to grant explanatory power may say a great deal about reality. It may also say a good deal about our biases. To dismiss the Rwandan genocide as a matter of "primitive," "tribal" blacks killing "other blacks" would seem the nadir of redneck thinking. But to ignore or dismiss mass atrocities against men because the perpetrators are generally "other men" is an argument—actually, a bigoted and dangerous assumption—that slides down much more easily.

Other examples can be found closer to the heart of feminist scholarship and activism. Is female genital mutilation, for example, a crime against women? Or is it to be dismissed as merely a matter of "women cutting women"? It is not men wielding the knives. Consider also the gendering of witchcraft in early modern Europe—not just the gendering of the accused, but of the accusers. Robin Briggs's research on Lorraine found that

> women did testify in large numbers against other women, making up 43 per cent of witnesses in these cases on average, and predominating in 30 per cent of them. . . . A more sophisticated count for the English Home Circuit, by Clive Holmes, shows that the proportion of women witnesses

> rose from around 38 per cent in the last years of Queen Elizabeth to 53 per cent after the Restoration. . . . It appears that women were active in building up reputations by gossip, deploying counter-magic and accusing suspects; crystallization into formal prosecution, however, needed the intervention of men, preferably of fairly high status in the community.

The witch-hunts, moreover, are best seen as part of a wider campaign to criminalize women's actions, exemplified by "a new punitive attitude towards . . . 'social' crimes," such as infanticide and prostitution. But as Briggs points out, the women denounced and arrested on these charges "with very few exceptions . . . were denounced by other women, without whose participation the legislation would have remained a dead letter."[75] Can these literal and metaphorical witch-hunts be construed as acts and atrocities against women, even though women constituted a substantial or predominant portion of the precipitators, hence of the perpetrators? The events certainly have been so construed in the feminist literature and the wider public debate—apparently without encountering insuperable analytical difficulties. In fact, the witch-hunts are often presented as a paradigmatic instance of "genocide" against women, or in the view of Mary Anne Warren, of "gendercide." Why should the gendering of the genocidal agents be of greater consequence when noncombatant males are the targets?

This chapter has sought to establish the empirical proposition that gendercide exists. It derives two normative propositions from the historical record: first, that the framing should be an inclusive one, encompassing the experiences of both women and men; and second, that recognition and amelioration of the phenomenon is long overdue, and a matter of the highest urgency.

Notes

This chapter is dedicated to Dr. Ferrel Christensen, without whose example and inspiration it could not have been written.

1. Quoted in Mark Danner, "The Killing Fields of Bosnia," *New York Review of Books,* 24 September 1998, p. 69.

2. "Young Men of Fighting Age," ch. 15 in "Kosovo/Kosova As Seen, As Told," Organization for Security and Cooperation in Europe—Kosovo Verification Mission, December 1999, *www.osce.org/kosovo/documents/reports/hr/part1/ch15.htm.*

3. See the materials I have compiled at *adamjones.freeservers.com/timor1.htm* and following.

4. John Aglionby, "Herded, Sifted, and Cut Off," *The Guardian,* 10 September 1999.

5. See, e.g., Paul Dillon and Jeff Sallot, "The Chilling Disappearance of East Timor's Young Men," *Globe and Mail,* 16 September 1999; Doug Struck and Keith B. Richburg, "Refugees Describe Method to Murderous Rampage in E. Timor," *Washington Post,* 14 September 1999.

6. Mary Anne Warren, *Gendercide: The Implications of Sex Selection* (Totowa, N.J.: Rowman and Allanheld, 1985), p. 22 (emphasis added). The inclusive term "gendercide" could usefully be supplemented with a reworked conception of "gynocide"—one that moves away from Mary Daly's eccentric original use of the term in her *Gyn/Ecology*—and "androcide" for the gender-selective extermination of males.

7. "An understanding of some of the forms which gendercide has taken in the past may facilitate a recognition of the forms in which it survives today, and may persist into the future. The material in this chapter will not be unfamiliar to feminist scholars, and may safely be skipped by those who are already aware of the many forms of anti-female gendercide." Ibid., p. 32.

8. I place "battle-age" in quotation marks throughout to problematize a term that rolls off the tongue too trippingly, in my view. The "battle-age" construction implicitly assumes that if a male is of an age that renders him liable to military conscription and combat, his entire identity should be so defined. This renders the analyst complicit with those who would subordinate the destiny of "battle-age" males to this outside demand—akin to defining women by their capacity to be raped ("rape-age" women?), and suggesting as well that "battle-age" men are "asking for it." With this equation of males and combatants completed, the analyst or policy maker can move to the final stage of effacing all noncombatant males from the policy and analytical equation, a phenomenon that is also commonplace.

9. Errol Miller, *Men At Risk* (Kingston: Jamaica Publishing House, 1991), pp. 124–25. Miller adds: "There is every reason to believe that the tradition of tracing one's ancestry through the mother, matrilineal descent, must have emerged partly as a means of increasing the chances of a lineage surviving capture and the killing of all its males. . . . For tracing one's lineage through its captured females allowed the conquered lineage to survive conquest if by some means in the future its offspring were able to separate themselves from or overthrow their conquerors" (p. 125). The institutions of eunuchry and slavery are also examined in this chapter, "Patriarchy's Problem with Alien Men," the strongest and most interesting in *Men At Risk.*

10. Barbara Ehrenreich, *Blood Rites: Origins and History of the Passions of War* (New York: Metropolitan Books, 1997), p. 130. Ehrenreich's short work has many more insights into the gendering of war and communal conflict than I can do justice to here.

11. Leo Kuper, *Genocide: Its Political Use in the Twentieth Century* (London: Penguin, 1981), p. 11. The fall of Carthage in 146 B.C. is an ambiguous case, accord-

ing to Chalk and Jonassohn. "We have narratives indicating that the Romans enslaved survivors of the siege, but none of the classical authors claim that the Romans killed survivors in cold blood or that the annihilation of the inhabitants of Carthage was one of Rome's motives for going to war." Nonetheless, the authors agree that "In the ancient world, killing all the men was often a measure aimed at destroying the military potential of a rival. It seems highly unlikely that the Romans simply released the men who survived the siege of Carthage." Frank Chalk and Kurt Jonassohn, *The History and Sociology of Genocide* (New Haven and London: Yale University Press, 1990), pp. 73, 76.

12. Robert Conquest, *The Great Terror: Stalin's Purge of the Thirties* (New York: Macmillan, 1968), pp. 711–12. What is debatable, I believe, is whether Stalin's purges can be considered a gender-selective slaughter—and therefore a true "gendercide." The primary variable is political affiliation of an obvious kind—holding a party card in a party state. Men composed the annihilated group overwhelmingly, perhaps almost exclusively, a fact that should always be part of the discussion; but there was a real sense in which gender was incidental, in a way that it was not for Serbs executing Kosovar males en masse, for example.

13. Adam Hochschild, *King Leopold's Ghost* (Boston: Houghton Mifflin, 1998), p. 232.

14. Indonesian journalist Maskun Iskandar (reporting in 1969, after a further series of mass killings in the afflicted regions), quoted in Robert Cribb, "The Indonesian Massacres," in Samuel Totten, William S. Parsons, and Israel W. Charny, eds., *Century of Genocide: Eyewitness Accounts and Critical Views* (New York and London: Garland, 1997), p. 261.

15. Rounaq Jahan, "Genocide in Bangladesh," in Totten et al., *Century of Genocide,* p. 298. R. J. Rummel writes: "By November [1971], the rebel guerrillas . . . had wrested from the army control over 25 percent of East Pakistan, a success that led the Pakistan army to seek out those especially likely to join the resistance—young boys. Sweeps were conducted of young men who were never seen again. Bodies of youths would be found in fields, floating down rivers, or near army camps. As can be imagined, this terrorized all young men and their families within reach of the army. Most between the ages of fifteen and twenty-five began to flee from one village to another and toward India. Many of those reluctant to leave their homes were forced to flee by mothers and sisters concerned for their safety." Rummel, *Death by Government* (New Brunswick, N.J.: Transaction Publishers, 1994), p. 329.

16. Ben Kiernan, "The Cambodian Genocide—1975–1979," in Totten et al., *Century of Genocide,* p. 345, citing the associated research of Chanthou Boua ("Women in Today's Cambodia," *New Left Review,* no. 131, pp. 45–61). See also Anne E. Goldfeld, "More Horror in Cambodia," *New York Times,* 4 June 1991: "Cambodia is a land of widows, where women head about 60 percent of the households"; John Pilger, "Playing a Game of Holocaust," *Manchester Guardian Weekly,* 12 November

1989: "Up to 70 percent of adults are women in areas such as this, where the killing was unrelenting. Many of the widows will describe, obsessively, their husbands' violent deaths and the cries of their smallest children denied food; and how they were then forced to marry a man they did not know."

17. Sebastian Junger, "The Forensics of War," *Vanity Fair*, October 1999.

18. Amnesty International Action File (AI Index ASA 20/013/99), 19 April 1999.

19. "Columbian [*sic*] Militia Massacres 11," Associated Press dispatch, 9 November 1998. From a 1995 report on Colombia: Gloria Cuartas, Mayor of Apartado, "attends to many of the widows of an estimated 677 men . . . who have been killed so far this year. 'You have no idea my feeling of impotence when a widow shows up at my office begging for a casket to bury her husband. They have no money and I don't either,' she said. . . . The victims, most of them banana workers, die one by one or in massacres. . . . In this macho society, women are protected and only the men are murdered, leaving about a thousand widows in the region, the Roman Catholic diocese estimates." Ken Dermota, "Workers Caught in Clutches of Fatal Conflict," *Globe and Mail*, 21 September 1995. This area of Colombia, the region of Urabá in the northwest part of Antioquia province, is probably the most violent region in the most violent province in the most atrocity-ridden country on earth. I can think of only parts of northern Algeria that compare—an important counterexample, however, since the Algerian slaughter has in no way been "gendered" as strongly as in Colombia.

20. Seth Sendashonga, ex-minister of the interior in the RPF government, speaking from exile in Kenya; quoted in *Chronicle of a Genocide Foretold*, vol. 3, pt. 3 (video production: National Film Board, Ottawa, 1997).

21. Helsinki Watch, *War Crimes in Bosnia-Herzegovina*, vol. 2 (New York: Human Rights Watch, 1993), pp. 82–83.

22. "Black Shirts in Sri Lanka," *Newsweek*, 25 March 1991.

23. Juan E. Mendez, "US Joins Peru's Dirty War," *New York Times*, 7 May 1990. (Mendez was executive director of Americas Watch.)

24. Madhu Kishwar (a leading light of the Indian women's movement), "Delhi: Gangster Rule," in Patwant Singh and Harji Malik, eds., *Punjab: The Fatal Miscalculation* (New Delhi, 1985), pp. 171–78. Thanks to Hamish Telford for bringing this source to my attention. For a discussion of the "Widows' Colony" in Delhi and the women's activism it spawned, see John Stackhouse, "India Dithers As Sikhs Seek Justice," *Globe and Mail*, 5 November 1994 (referring to the massacre victims as "Sikhs," "people," "family members," "murder cases," and "breadwinners," but not as "men"); also John F. Burns, "The Sikhs Get Justice Long After a Massacre," *New York Times*, 16 September 1996.

25. Martin van Bruinessen, "Genocide in Kurdistan?" in George J. Andreopoulos, ed., *Genocide: Conceptual and Historical Dimensions* (Philadelphia: University of Pennsylvania Press, 1994), pp. 156–57.

26. Jan Willem Honig and Norbert Both, *Srebrenica: Record of a War Crime* (London: Penguin, 1996), pp. 177–78. See also Vahakn Dadrian's account of the

military mobilization of Armenian males in 1915, the prime strategy by which the most "threatening" portion of the Armenian population was concentrated and culled before the wider genocide was implemented (see ch. 6). "Though [the] mobilization had many other objectives, it served a major purpose for the swift execution of the plan of genocide. By removing all able-bodied Armenian males from their cities, villages, hamlets, and by isolating them in conditions in which they virtually became trapped, the Armenian community was reduced to a condition of near-total helplessness, thus an easy prey for destruction. It was a masterful stroke as it attained with one blow the three objectives of the operation of trapping the victim population: a) dislocation through forcible removal; b) isolation; c) concentration for easy targeting." Dadrian, *The History of the Armenian Genocide: Ethnic Conflict from the Balkans to Anatolia to the Caucasus* (Providence, R.I.: Berghahn Books, 1995), p. 226.

27. Colette Braeckman writes of the eastern Congo that "there have been numerous reports of rape by men involved in the fighting, many of whom are HIV positive." Braeckman, "Carve-up in the Congo," *Le Monde diplomatique,* October 1999.

28. See also the discussion of gender-selective exterminations at Auschwitz later in this chapter.

29. Warren, *Gendercide,* pp. 32–41.

30. Rummel, *Death by Government,* pp. 65–66.

31. Robin Briggs, in *Witches and Neighbors: The Social and Cultural Context of European Witchcraft* (New York: Penguin, 1998), gives a figure of 25 percent males among accused witches between the fourteenth and seventeenth centuries. However, in France males accounted for about half the total; in Iceland, 90 percent. For a good overview of the literature on witchcraft and gender, see Steven T. Katz, "Witchcraft and Misogynism," chapter 9 in Katz, *The Holocaust in Historical Context,* vol. 1, *The Holocaust and Mass Death before the Modern Age* (New York: Oxford University Press, 1994), esp. pp. 175–76 (n. 1).

32. Christina Larner, *Enemies of God: The Witch-Hunt in Scotland* (London: Hogarth Press, 1981), p. 3. Steven Katz rejects the idea that the witch-hunts were a "gynocidal" attack on women, primarily because the alleged targeted group was not assaulted on a remotely genocidal scale. "One never arrives at a situation in which more than 1/10 of 1 percent, at a maximum—the actual rate in all probability never exceeding 1/20 to 1/30 of 1 percent at a maximum—of the female population was executed [for witchcraft] in any given decade. That is, even at its peak, 99.9-plus percent of women in Europe were safe from the annihilatory impact of the panic." He compares this to "the over 60 percent death rate for European Jewry as a whole" during the holocaust, "with no compromises having been made for Jewish women and children. Medieval antifeminism, even in its most brutal form, the witch-hunt, simply did not produce, and was not intended to produce, the same level of murderous violence generated by the genocidal project spawned by Hitlerian racial antiseminitism." Or, one might add, by any of the great gendercides against men in human history. See the discussion and computations in Katz, *The Holocaust in Historical Context,* pp. 502–505.

33. David Hirst, "Ethiopia Strikes out for the Sea," *Guardian Weekly,* 30 May 1999.

34. The major perpetrators of the atrocity were, of course, the Ethiopian conscriptors, not the Eritrean troops (a fifth of them women) who did the killing. This is the sort of paradox that regularly clouds an analysis of "gendercide" beyond the gender-selective killing of strict non- (or never-) combatants.

35. Rummel, *Death by Government,* p. 130. Other estimates cited in his chapter "The Depraved Nationalist Regime" more than double the death toll.

36. Ibid., p. 67.

37. Daniel Jonah Goldhagen, *Hitler's Willing Executioners: Ordinary Germans and the Holocaust* (New York: Vintage, 1997), p. 290 (emphasis added).

38. Alexander Dallin, *German Rule in Russia, 1941–45: A Study of Occupation Policies,* 2d ed. (London: Macmillan, 1981), pp. 414–15.

39. Omer Bartov, *The Eastern Front: German Troops and the Barbarisation of Warfare* (Basingstoke: Macmillan, 1985), p. 107. Wrote one Wehrmacht soldier in a letter home: "What would have happened to cultural Europe, had these sons of the steppe, poisoned and drunk with a destructive poison, these incited subhumans, invaded our beautiful Germany?" Quoted in Bartov, "Operation Barbarossa and the Origins of the Final Solution," in David Cesarani, ed., *The Final Solution: Origins and Implementation* (London: Routledge, 1994), p. 18.

40. Rummel, *Death by Government,* pp. 64–65.

41. Hochschild, *King Leopold's Ghost,* pp. 126, 130, 161–62.

42. Jennifer Kraft, reviewing Hochschild in *Current History,* May 1999.

43. Kurt Jonassohn and Karen Björnson, *Genocide and Gross Human Rights Violations* (New Brunswick, N.J.: Transaction Publishers, 1998), p. 242. Hochschild likewise notes that "In France's equatorial African territories, where the region's history is best documented, the amount of rubber-bearing land was far less than what Leopold controlled, but the rape [he apparently means gendercide] was just as brutal. . . . The population loss in the rubber-rich equatorial rain forest owned by France is estimated, just as in Leopold's Congo, as roughly 50 percent. . . . In the 1920s, construction of a new railway through French territory bypassing the big Congo River rapids cost the lives of an estimated twenty thousand forced laborers, far more than had died building, and later rebuilding, Leopold's railway nearby." Hochschild, *King Leopold's Ghost,* p. 280.

44. See Adam Jones, "Engendering Debate," *Review of International Studies,* 24: 2 (1998), pp. 299–303. *adamjones.freeservers.com/engender.htm*

45. "New conceptions require new terms. By 'genocide' we mean the destruction of a nation or of an ethnic group. This new word, coined by the author to denote an old practice in its modern development, is made from the ancient Greek word genos (race, tribe) and the Latin cide (killing), thus corresponding in its formation to such words as tyrannicide, homicide, infanticide, etc." Lemkin quoted in Jonassohn and Björnson, *Genocide and Gross Human Rights Violations,* p. 139.

46. Kuper, *Genocide,* p. 204. Kuper also mentions that in the lesser genre of "genocidal massacres," "the victims may be a selected category, such as the men in a village suspected of sabotage or held as hostages" (p. 191). Quite clearly, however, a substantial gender-selective pogrom of this type could be fitted into Kuper's framing of genocide. He writes at p. 32: "I will assume that the charge of genocide would not be preferred unless there were a 'substantial' or an 'appreciable' number of victims. I would have no difficulty in applying the term to the slaughter of a stratum of the educated of a racial or ethnic group, a common enough occurrence, provided there are 'appreciable' numbers." If such eliticide can be genocidal, even if it does not approach "root-and-branch" extermination, then there is no reason not to include gendercide in the same class.

47. Emphasis added. This is apparently Jonassohn's formulation, since it appears with slightly different wording in Chalk and Jonassohn, *The History and Sociology of Genocide,* p. 61: "The Old Testament . . . contains a number of cases that we would today consider genocides—not because of the casualties of war but because of the extermination of noncombatant women and children."

48. Jonassohn and Björnson, *Genocide and Gross Human Rights Violations,* p. 49 (emphasis added).

49. "It is evident . . . that the understanding of the role of the perpetrator has paramount import; in fact it has primacy over all other consideration[s]. In the last resort, it is that group which preempts the pattern of conflict resolution, directs the course of consummation of the conflict and in doing so, initiates genocide, provocations and other forms of victim contributions to the crime notwithstanding." Vahakn N. Dadrian, "A Typology of Genocide," *International Review of Modern Sociology* 5 (fall 1975), p. 203.

50. Katz, *The Holocaust in Historical Context,* p. 131.

51. Ibid., pp. 131–32 (n. 20).

52. Katz quoted (and rebutted) in Jonassohn and Björnson, *Genocide and Gross Human Rights Violations,* p. 132.

53. "An allied methodological problem refers to the criterion of cost and casualty, [e]specially in relation to the victim group. If genocide implies mass violence, how massive should this violence be to deserve the label?" Dadrian, "A Typology of Genocide," p. 202.

54. W. Michael Reisman and Chris T. Antoniou, eds., *The Laws of War* (New York: Vintage Books, 1994), pp. 84–86.

55. John B. Allcock, "Genocide," in Allcock, Marko Milivojevic, and John J. Horton, eds., *Conflict in the Former Yugoslavia: An Encyclopedia* (Denver, Colo.: ABC-CLIO, 1998), pp. 99–100. The UN definition reads as follows: "Genocide means any of the following acts committed with intent to destroy, in whole or in part, a national, ethnical, racial or religious group, as such: (a) Killing members of the group; (b) Causing serious bodily or mental harm to members of the group;

(c) Deliberately inflicting on the group conditions of life calculated to bring about its physical destruction in whole or in part; (d) Imposing measures intended to prevent births within the group; (e) Forcibly transferring children of the group to another group." Reisman and Antoniou, eds., *The Laws of War,* pp. 84–85.

56. Warren, *Gendercide,* pp. 22–23.

57. Kuper, *Genocide,* p. 32. Elsewhere Kuper has written: "I will assume that 'in part' denotes an appreciable part, while recognizing the imprecision of the phrase." Kuper, "Theoretical Issues Relating to Genocide," in Andreopoulous, *Genocide,* p. 32.

58. Christopher Boehm, *Blood Revenge: The Anthropology of Feuding in Montenegro and Other Tribal Societies* (Lawrence: University Press of Kansas, 1984), pp. 111–12.

59. Mihaela Rodina, "Blood Code Rules in Northern Albania," Agence France-Presse dispatch, 30 June 1999.

60. In the conjugal rather than national sense of "domestic," of course.

61. Dadrian, "A Typology of Genocide," pp. 206–7. Dadrian also captures something of the "harbinger" character of many gendercidal atrocities against "battle-age" males: "[Retributive genocide] may also serve as an effort to test the kind and range of response on the part of the victim group and as a measure to extrapolate future schemes of more encompassing forms of genocide" (p. 207).

In my 1994 article, "Gender and Ethnic Conflict in ex-Yugoslavia," I independently theorized mass killings of men as acts of "retributory or 'pre-emptive' execution" (*Ethnic and Racial Studies* 17: 1, p. 124; text also available at *adamjones.freeservers.com/yugo.htm*).

62. Kuper, *Genocide,* p. 108.

63. Ibid., pp. 109–10.

64. Quoted in ibid., p. 111.

65. Goldhagen, *Hitler's Willing Executioners,* pp. 149–50. Importantly for the analysis of gendercide, Goldhagen notes that "even if . . . the initial order was to kill 'only' teenage and adult Jewish males—the order was still genocidal and clearly was understood by the perpetrators as such. . . . The killing of the adult males of a community is nothing less than the destruction of that community" (p. 153). For another example of such incrementalism around the same time (24 October 1941), see the "curious order of a German army corps before Leningrad [that] provided for use of artillery against civilians trying to break out of the city, so as to prevent German infantrymen from being compelled to shoot at innocent women and children." Dallin, *German Rule in Russia,* p. 79 (n. 4).

66. Jürgen Förster's analysis buttresses Goldhagen's: "The first formal order, to kill immediately 'all male Jews of 17–45 years of age' was issued . . . on 11 July 1941. . . . The necessity of killing male Jews was not justified . . . with any reference to partisan activities but 'resulted from the political situation.' Since the SS was still liquidating selected target groups, the Intelligence Officer of the Kommandostab Reichsführer-SS informed his superiors in his after-action report of 28 July 1941 that 'all persons

involved are in doubt whether the Jewish problem can be brought to a fundamental solution by the multitude of executions of male Jews alone.' While the Einsatzkommando 3 . . . began to include Jewish women and children on 15 August 1941, the Police Regiment Centre only increased the age band for men to be killed to 16–65. Its 3rd Battalion, however, executed sixty-four Jewish women, too, in Minsk on 1 September 1941. The evidence on the practice of liquidating after 22 June 1941 suggests that a second, principal decision was made in the summer of 1941, this time to cleanse the conquered living space more thoroughly from any manifestations of Jewry and Bolshevism, to make it 'free' of Jews and communists." Förster, "The Relations between Operation Barbarossa as an Ideological War of Extermination and the Final Solution," in Cesarani, *The Final Solution,* p. 93.

67. Christopher R. Browning, "Hitler and the Euphoria of Victory: The Path to the Final Solution," in Cesarani, *The Final Solution,* p. 142.

68. Kogon et al. write in their chapter on "Killings in the Gas Vans behind the Front" that "First, trial gassings were conducted, one of them with Russian prisoners of war in the Sachsenhausen concentration camp in the autumn of 1941." Eugen Kogon, Hermann Langbein, and Adalbert Ruckerl, eds., *Nazi Mass Murder: A Documentary History of the Use of Poison Gas* (New Haven and London: Yale University Press, 1993), p. 54. The mass killings of women and men together then began in December 1941 (p. 55).

69. Christian Streit, "Wehrmacht, Einsatzgruppen, Soviet POWs and Anti-Bolshevism in the Emergence of the Final Solution," in Cesarani, *The Final Solution,* pp. 111–12. The appraisal of Theo Schulte, who calls the slaughter "the 'forgotten holocaust'" of World War II, is entirely congruent: "It could be argued that the destruction of millions of Soviet POWs had partly shaped the subsequent escalation of overall annihilation policies. The measures taken to liquidate the captured soldiers had not only established certain techniques of extermination, but had created a value system which facilitated, clarified and formularised implementation of the 'Final Solution.' The radicalisation of policy both by and through the actions of the German Army thus produced an extension of categories for extermination, in what Hans Mommsen has called an 'almost geometrical progression' from the Bolshevik leadership down through the mass of Soviet POWs to the Jewish population. . . . The captured Soviet troops were subjected to systematic and exploitative actions which treated them according to ethnic and racist criteria." He notes that "the mistreatment of captured Red Army soldiers had been a central issue at the Nuremberg War Trials"—but not, I would add, subsequently. Schulte, *The German Army and Nazi Policies in Occupied Russia* (Oxford: Berg, 1989), pp. 180, 182–83. See also Gerhard Hirschfeld, ed., *The Policies of Genocide: Jews and Soviet Prisoners of War in Nazi Germany* (London: Allen and Unwin, 1986).

70. Yehuda Bauer, *A History of the Holocaust,* cited in Chalk and Jonassohn, *The History and Sociology of Genocide,* p. 353.

71. Quoted in Kogon et al., *Nazi Mass Murder,* p. 153.

72. Ibid., p. 159.

73. Outside of the politico-military framework, this phenomenon seems to hold a place in historical human societies somewhat analogous to that of infanticide, though doubtless on a smaller scale. It might also respond to similar environmental variables as infanticide, including population pressure and resource scarcity. Anti-euthanasia activists might see similar thinking behind the growing tolerance in the West for "mercy killings" and doctor-assisted suicides.

74. Jonassohn and Björnson, *Genocide and Gross Human Rights Violations,* p. 157. The authors add two implicitly gendered examples: "Thus, rape was probably part of warfare throughout history; but with rare exceptions, such as the famous case of the Roman rape of the Sabines, it was not considered important enough to be mentioned. [Likewise,] the feeding and housing of prisoners only rarely deserved recording."

75. Briggs, *Witches and Neighbors,* p. 262.

2

Gendercide and Humiliation in Honor and Human-Rights Societies

Evelin Gerda Lindner

Introduction

Why is the concept of gendercide interesting? Why did the definition of the concept of gendercide start with "femicide"—in other words, why was the emphasis placed on women (as opposed to men) when the concept first emerged? Why has the selective killing of men, especially men of "battle age," long been neglected in scientific research? Is it because men are not regarded as sufficiently "worthy" victims, and are therefore discriminated against?

Such questions regarding gendercide will be linked in this chapter to the gendering of suicide: Why do three times more young males than young females commit suicide in Western countries (like Britain)? Why, in contrast, do more young women commit suicide in traditional China? Why are suicide numbers approaching Western levels in the westernized parts of China? And why are numbers of female suicides rising in the West (though they are still lower than the figure for males)?

Many of these questions converge and overlap with the important issues to which Adam Jones has drawn attention in Chapter 1. He has attempted to locate genocide within the broader context of male-female relations, and this has elicited some controversy. This chapter locates not only Jones's insights, but also the controversy his work has produced, within a broader context: that is, the long-term historical transformation under way between the honor code and the ideology of human rights. This transformation from honor to human rights as the standard for evaluating human behavior is itself located within an even broader framework: namely, the part played by humiliation in societal structure and historical change. Humiliation, I will argue, is a force that underlies both the killing of others (for example in war), and the killing of oneself (suicide).

I define humiliation as the enforced lowering of a person or group, a process of subjugation that damages or strips away their pride, honor or dignity. To be humiliated is to be placed, against your will, or in some cases also with your consent, often in a deeply hurtful way, in a situation that is greatly inferior to what you feel you have a right to expect.[1] Humiliation entails demeaning treatment that transgresses established expectations. It may involve acts of force, including violent force. At its heart is the idea of pinning down, putting down, or holding to the ground. Indeed, one of the defining characteristics of humiliation as a process is that the victim is forced into passivity, acted upon, made helpless. However, the role of the victim is not necessarily always unambiguous. A victim may feel humiliated in absence of any humiliating act—as the result of a misunderstanding, or as the result of personal and cultural differences concerning norms of what respectful treatment ought to entail—or the "victim" may even invent a story of humiliation in order to maneuvre another party into the role of a loathsome perpetrator.[2]

My object is to scrutinize societal structures in their historical contexts by using the concept of humiliation. I hope, in this way, to shed more light on both gendercide and gender-specific patterns of suicide. In both cases, my concern is equally with patterns of causation (Why does the phenomenon occur?) and patterns of evaluation (What is its significance?).

In Chapter 1, Jones introduces the term "gendercide" and reports that it was first coined by Mary Anne Warren in her 1985 book *Gendercide: The Implications of Sex Selection.* Jones praises Warren's book for attending to the basic idea, but criticizes Warren for gender discrimination: namely, that much of her book "concerns itself exclusively with female-selective killing: female infanticide, the witch-hunts in Europe, suttee or widow burning in India, female genital mutilation, 'the denial of reproductive freedom' (to women), and 'misogynist ideologies.'" Jones reports further: "Much of the remainder of her book is devoted to the subject of the sex selection of children as a form of gendercide against women." Continuing with his critique, he writes: "Whatever the merits of extending the framework this far (or to the genital mutilation of women or men), gendercide, for all practical purposes, is limited in Warren's analysis to 'anti-female gendercide.'"

Jones then reminds the reader that "noncombatant men have been and continue to be the most frequent targets of mass killing and genocidal slaughter, as well as a host of lesser atrocities and abuses." He states further "that gendercide, at least when it targets males, has attracted virtually no attention at the level of scholarship or public policy. As such, it can be classed as one of the great taboo subjects of the contemporary age." He concludes: "I hold, nonetheless, that an inclusive understanding of gendercide carries powerful implications for the emerging field of comparative genocide studies."[3]

The present chapter has two anchoring points, namely the gender-selective killing of others (gendercide), and the gender-selective killing of oneself (suicide).[4] Recent research on suicide carried out at the University of Southampton by Colin Pritchard shows that typically in Britain more men than women kill themselves, the ratio being 3 to 1. Five times more young men than young women between fifteen and twenty-four die in this way, and more die in urban than in rural areas. However, Pritchard's research on patterns of suicide in China shows that "their suicide is the very opposite of that in the West: Chinese women kill themselves more than do men. Young women die at double the rate of young males, and more people die in rural than in urban areas." Significantly, the research "also found that in 'westernized' Chinese societies, such as Hong Kong, Singapore, and Japan, patterns of suicide followed trends in the rest of the developed world, which points to social factors as key determinants of suicide."[5]

Pritchard's research gives plausibility to the suggestion that patterns of suicide (and, perhaps, by implication, patterns of gendercide) alter as societal structures change over time. I want to add another dimension by proposing that one of the key transmitting agents that communicates the pressures leading to gendercide and gender-specific suicide is humiliation. As patterns of humiliation change in the course of the transition from the honor code to the human-rights code, so patterns of gendercide and suicide may also be transformed, although the lines of causation are neither simple nor one way.

The reasoning presented in this paper draws upon evidence collected in two contexts. The first is a research project conducted at the University of Oslo entitled *The Feeling of Being Humiliated: A Central Theme in Armed Conflicts,* and subtitled: *A Study of the Role of Humiliation in Somalia, and Rwanda/Burundi, between the Warring Parties, and in Relation to Third Intervening Parties.*[6] A total of 216 qualitative interviews were carried out from 1998 to 1999 in Africa (in Hargeisa, capital of "Somaliland"; in Kigali and other places in Rwanda; in Bujumbura, capital of Burundi; in Nairobi, Kenya; and in Cairo, Egypt), and from 1997 to 2000 in Europe (in Oslo, various places in Germany, Geneva, and Brussels).[7] The topic has been discussed with about four hundred researchers working in related fields. The chapter also draws upon my experience as a clinical psychologist and consultant in Germany (1980–84) and Egypt (1984–91).[8]

The Historic Transition from Honor Societies to Human Rights Societies

During the past two hundred years, and especially during the last half-century, the spread of the ideology of human rights has popularised the principle that all human beings should expect to receive respectful treatment solely on the grounds of their humanity, without reference to gender, ethnicity or other "secondary" criteria. Human rights are, for example, oriented to the principle of equality between males and females, unlike the honor code that assumes a fundamental inequality between them.

The principles of human rights with their strong egalitarian emphasis have become so omnipresent, especially in the West, it is easy to overlook that they developed in reaction to a traditional honor code. Dov Cohen and Richard Nisbett examine honor-based societies in their research and writings. The honor to which Cohen and Nisbett refer is the kind that operates in the traditional branches of the Mafia or, more generally, in blood feuds. Adam Jones has also cited other evidence relating to the blood feud.[9]

William Ian Miller in *Humiliation and Other Essays on Honor, Social Discomfort, and Violence* examines honor as understood in the *Iliad* or Icelandic sagas. He explains that these concepts are still very much alive today, despite a common assumption that they are no longer relevant. Miller suggests "that we are more familiar with the culture of honor than we may like to admit. This familiarity partially explains why stories of revenge play so well, whether read as the *Iliad*, an Icelandic saga, *Hamlet*, many novels, or seen as so many gangland, intergalactic, horror, or Clint Eastwood movies. Honor is not our official ideology, but its ethic survives in pockets of most of our lives. In some ethnic (sub)cultures it still is the official ideology, or at least so we are told about the cultures of some urban black males, Mafiosi, Chicano barrios, and so on. And even among the suburban middle class the honor ethic is lived in high school or in the competitive rat race of certain professional cultures."[10]

I am familiar with all shades of the traditional honor/blood-feud scenario as a result of my work as a psychological counselor in Egypt. It was here that I learned about the role of humiliation and its significance for the key difference between the honor/blood-feud scenario and the scenario associated with human rights. Within a blood-feud culture, it is honorable, perfectly legitimate, and highly "obligatory" to "heal" humiliation by killing a targeted person. The opposite is true in a society where universal human rights are recognized; "healing" humiliation means restoring the victim's dignity by empathic dialogue, sincere apology, and finally reconciliation.[11]

The Link between Honor, Dignity, and Humiliation

The notion of humiliation links the concepts of honor and human rights in an enlightening way, providing a framework both for ideologies and for the transition between them. "The idea of humiliation contains three elements, which entered the cultural repertoire [of humankind] in three phases that coincided, approximately, with advances in technological and organisational capacity and shifts in the balance of power between humankind and nature and between human groups. During the first phase, the idea of subjugating nature entered the repertoire. In the next phase, the idea of subjugation (or 'putting/keeping/striking down') was extended to human beings. During the third phase, the idea became widespread that subjugating human beings was illegitimate, morally wrong."[12]

The introduction of agriculture extended the previously existing technology of making small tools to the production of the digging stick and the plough. But agriculture did not stop there. The surplus produced by agriculture provided the material means for subjugating not just nature but also people. The instrumentalization of some human beings (the "slaves") by others (the "masters") was "invented."

The pyramid of power that evolved over the next centuries gave everybody a rank and a certain definition of honor attached to it:

> For example, in medieval and early modern Europe, armed combat among members of the most "honourable" class, the aristocracy, was a means of defending or enhancing family honour. Defeat in a duel lowered the loser's rank in the scale of honour. Small humiliations could be borne by those who had fought bravely. However, a cowardly response to a challenge could mean that all honour was lost. Furthermore, it was not possible to accept defeat by an opponent one did not respect. In extreme cases where no road back to honour existed, suicide was preferable. The main point is that within "honour societies," humiliation and violence were regarded as normal means of managing tensions. For the most part, people accepted them and got on with their lives. Violence did not have the strong connotation of "violation" it has since acquired.[13]

In his book *Getting to Peace: Transforming Conflict at Home, at Work, and in the World,* anthropologist William Ury argues that the transition to hierarchy from the relatively egalitarian social structures of hunting-and-gathering societies occurred around ten thousand years ago, and that humankind is currently "returning" to egalitarian nomadic structures in the specific form of the global information society. It may be hypothesized that the egalitarian notion of human rights, with its acceptance of equal dignity for every human being, is one aspect of this transition.

Changes in international relations theory also reflect the transition.[14] "Classical and Structural Realism saw the world as being guided by 'anarchy'—anarchy as the 'state of nature' (Hobbes)—with an ensuing 'Security Dilemma' within which only states are actors. Liberalism, on the other hand, considers firms, NGOs, and international organizations as also being actors and proposes that through cooperation the 'Security Dilemma' may be overcome."[15]

Human rights introduce a fundamental turning point in the chain of social changes. They transform "normal" traditional practices into illegitimate abuses. They place followers of the old code in direct confrontation with adherents to the new code. People from the human-rights camp in the international community, for instance, are appalled by the practices of dictators who believe in honor codes. However, regimes that gain from the old code hesitate to let go of it and find reasons to keep it alive. International criticism of human-rights abuses, for example in Southeast Asia, may be opposed as intrusive, humiliating, and arrogant breaches of Asian sovereignty in the name of alien Western values.[16]

How does the mechanism of humiliation present itself within a human-rights context as compared to an honor context? Dennis Smith writes in "Organisations and Humiliation: Looking beyond Elias": "The human rights revolution—especially the core principle that all human beings are equally worthy of respect—has a dramatic effect upon the experience of humiliation. Once this revolution has occurred, the casual blows and insults . . . that used to serve as a routine proclamation of the hierarchical status quo become transformed in the mind of the victim into an outrageous forced expulsion from the community of equals. . . . ('How dare you deprive me of my freedom?,' 'how dare you make me less than I am?')." Smith continues: "In a human-rights society people still get scorned, spat upon, ignored, turned away and forced to kow-tow to authority. Humiliation is present whenever someone is made to feel fundamentally inferior and less worthy of consideration than others. Human rights do not abolish humiliation. On the contrary, they intensify the experience. In a human-rights society, we do not accept humiliation as a 'normal' mechanism built into the bone and muscle of society. Instead, we reject its legitimacy."[17]

In other words, humiliation, already hurtful in an honor society where it is used routinely as a means to put people down or keep them down, becomes many times more hurtful when it occurs in a human-rights society. In a human-rights context, humiliation acquires an explosive potential. Along with Suzanne Retzinger, Thomas Scheff has studied the part played by "humiliated fury" in escalating conflict between individuals and nations.[18] Retzinger and Scheff show that the suffering caused by humiliation is highly significant, and that the bitterest divisions have their roots in shame and humiliation.[19]

Definition of "Male" and "Female" in Honor Societies and in Human Rights Societies

In an honor society, the man is defined as the principal actor, no matter how functionally important female activities might be. He is the "subject," she is the "object."[20] He is the defender of honor against humiliation. He is defined as being responsible, self-reflexive, and rational. He is expected to protect "his" women, at least as long as he values them as a "resource," for example, as prizes and symbols of his honor, or as mothers of "his" children.

A woman who lives in an honor society learns either that she is not regarded as a human being at all, or that she is a lowly human being. In the first case, she is perceived as a passive recipient of male actions, as "material" to be either used or thrown away by him; she is on the same level as household items or domesticated animals. In the second case, she is also seen as a passive recipient, but also as a human being whose rank is lower than a man's; in this case, she is on the same level as children or slaves.

To illustrate the argument, it may be mentioned that some honor cultures in the Arab world and in Africa regard the woman's hymen as a symbol of the family's honor, and for this reason they practice female genital mutilation—on the grounds that in this way the family's honor (in which she shares) is being "protected." In many traditional honor societies, a female is a token, or representative, of the family or group to which she belongs; daughters are needed for marriage into families "her" males want as allies.[21] In Latin American "macho" cultures, the "conquest" of many women is taken as a proof of male prowess. In honor cultures, where property is inherited by the owner's male offspring (and where the male is informed of the basic biological facts that his genes live on in his children), the male will value the bearer of "his" children, their mother. In all these cases women will be "protected" by "their" males.

On the other side, however, a father will resent having to "invest" in a daughter who later will contribute only to another man's household and future: China and India come to mind. Furthermore, in all militaristic cultures, where the male is trained to be tough and fearless when facing death in battle, he may resent women because they remind him of desires that he deems unmale or female: for example, his desires to be cared for, to be emotional, or to be weak. In all such cases, women will be in danger of receiving hostility rather than protection from "their" males.

Another context for male hostility toward women is war. Women are captured, raped, and/or killed. As argued previously, masculine ferocity is functional for the male role as warlike defender of the group in the "anarchic" world described by Hobbes, whose global model became the basis for classical realism in international relations theory. It is evident that an honor society encourages its men to be aggressive in war situations—an aggression that includes a sexual element. This means also that the same society may have problems controlling this fierceness when the soldiers come home, giving rise to "protective institutions" such as gender segregation or veiling.

However, rape was not necessarily *part* of war. For example, in Somalia and other blood-revenge societies, women traditionally are not systematically raped or killed in wars or periods of violent reprisals, a fact noted by the International Committee of the Red Cross Somalia Delegation.[22] Wars and blood revenge are carried out between men, and women can move around freely. They are, so to speak, "invisible." According to Kari H. Karamé of the Norwegian Institute for International Affairs, during the years of fighting in Lebanon there was a kind of contract between the warring parties not to rape each other's women. She recounts: "It just happened twice, when fighters from 'outside' came, for example Palestinians. But a lot of sexual violence happened in connection with men; they were castrated, died of that, et cetera."[23]

The recent upsurge in war rape may very well be a new phenomenon. War rape, especially rape in public, draws women into the "game" more than previously. During my fieldwork in Somalia and Rwanda (1998–99), I learned that rape in front of husband, children, and neighbors during genocidal onslaughts was perceived as the "atomic bomb for emotions," the very peak of humiliation and thus the most "efficient weapon." This represents, so to speak, an evil "democratization" of war—a transition from combat among a select group of honorable warriors to torturing, raping, and slaughtering everybody. It is possible that leaders who want to create the conditions for spontaneous mass mobilization for war might see war rape as a cheap way to minimize the cost of getting willing soldiers, because in populations that have humiliated each other enough, for example, through rape in public, the divisions and hostilities run so deep that war fever infects the whole population.

Rape of women in an honor context, especially when committed publicly, may well be aimed primarily at humiliating the enemy's males, who are forced to watch helplessly, unable to protect "their" women. Somali men explained to me that they could not live with their raped wives, precisely because they could not stand being reminded of their humiliation. This means that the humiliation does not last only as long as the incident, but lingers on in the memory of the humiliated men (and, of course, women). The utmost embodiment of this humiliation within the honor code is the creation of children of rape. The author monitored a pledge from women in Sierra Leone that Western women should adopt their rape babies, since they could not take them to their villages, as much as they loved them as mothers —or more accurately, *because* they loved them.[24]

Helen Smith has written about the same tragedy in Kosovo in the UK *Guardian;* her article is entitled "Rape Victims' Babies Pay the Price of War."[25] Such children are a living reminder of utmost humiliation, as understood in an honor framework—of the enemy males' inability to protect "their" women. The article includes the statement that Serb rapes in Kosovo were "about power and control, humiliation and revenge. And what better way to damage the enemy's morale than to hit at his family? 'Our society is a traditional one where Albanian men are brought up to see themselves as breadwinners and protectors,' [Sevdije] Ahmeti points out. 'Once you touch the woman, you touch the honour of the family and you provoke the man to react. The Serbs knew this. Belgrade had, for years, put out propaganda that the only thing Albanian women could do was produce like mice. So daughters were gang-raped in front of their fathers, wives in front of their husbands, nieces in front of their uncles, mothers in front of their children, just to dehumanise, just to degrade.'" Another quote describes Kosovar Albanian women as "the property of men, to be bought, sold and betrothed before birth" and "sacks to be filled."

To summarize, in an honor society women are "material" for demonstrations of the male "power play." By contrast, in a human-rights society, males and females are actors in the social world, and keen defenders of their personal dignity against humiliation. Both are defined as being responsible, self-reflexive, and able to combine rationality with mature emotions. Both are seen as endowed with an inner core of dignity on the grounds of belonging to humanity, without reference to gender, ethnicity, or other "secondary" criteria.

The Incompatibility between Human Rights and Honor Codes

Males may be found both as advocates of traditional honor codes and as promoters of human rights. The same can be said for females. However—and this is a key difference between males and females—men and women make the transition to the new egalitarian human-rights code from different starting points. Males "come down" to the level of equality, from their previous level of superiority within the pyramid of power, while women rise up.

That males traditionally inhabited the higher ranks within hierarchies and thus were the "dominators" makes them easy targets for the "risers," namely the women who want to liberate themselves from unwanted domination. Some women may commit the error of confounding biological maleness with social maleness. In other words, they may forget that not all males dominate, and that males may also be victims of domination. It may be quite understandable, psychologically, that during a hard-fought struggle to rise up, the "enemy" may be painted in very stark terms without making subtle distinctions. But this does not contribute to accurate analysis, and it does not lead to a fair representation of the nature of the struggle or its desirable outcome. Men—Adam Jones, for example—may quite justifiably tell women that they do not enjoy being overlooked as victims just because they happen to share the same biological makeup as some of the unjust masters against whom women rightly protest.

In a society ruled by an honor code, a male is "worthy" when he can defend his own and his people's honor against the threat of humiliation. This is well expressed in the ideal of knights who successfully defend fortresses and slay dragons, as related in the innumerable fairy tales that still form children's view of the world to a great extent. The fearless, brave, and glamorous prince who undergoes difficult trials and wins the hand of the princess at the end remains the blueprint for male success, even today. However, in an honor society, a male is liable to be cast out or killed if he fails to meet the "knightly" standards just described. The unsuccessful warrior faces humiliation and death, perhaps by his own hand.

It is important to realize how strong an influence these traditional values were on a leader such as Hitler, who presented himself as someone seeking "honorable" vengeance for the insults that the German people had been forced to endure in the past. As is well known, when his failure became impossible to deny, Hitler committed suicide. He paid the price for his dishonor. Similarly, in a very traditional honor context, all men of "battle age" lose their right to live if they are incapable of defending themselves. This is because to be a male is to be a warrior; the concept of the noncombatant male does not exist in such societies.

Adam Jones, in "Gendercide and Genocide," Chapter 1 of this volume, rightly deplores the behavior and attitudes just described, since they cannot be defended in terms of his human-rights point of view. But he may not realize how tightly people may hold onto such structures of meaning. In my practice in Egypt, I had clients—young Palestinian men and women—who showed signs of severe depression because they had been sent by their families to study in Egypt. What they strongly wished to do instead was to take up arms and die for their people—many males thought this a most holy duty, not to be neglected—or to get married and give birth to as many future warriors as possible, which many females felt to be their equally holy duty. They felt that they were utterly betraying their people by enjoying life far away from danger, accumulating knowledge as if nothing was amiss. Their only consolation was the hope that they were safeguarding the traditions and interests of their families and helping them to survive into the future.

In an honor society, a female is "worthy" with reference to the interests of her male protector, her husband. Her task is to give birth to "his" children, and serve as symbol and prize for "his" male honor. This is the traditional ideal of the "proper" woman. It was an ideal nourished not only by the men, but also by the women themselves. As Jones reports in Chapter 1, those who accused women of being witches, in other words of failing "proper" standards, were often other women: In the last years of Queen Elizabeth I up to 53 per cent of all cases fell into this category.

As a consequence, in an honor society a female is regarded as "unworthy" and of little account if she cannot give her husband children or otherwise enhance the honor of his family. There are many variants of this theme. For example, Chinese families, especially those in rural areas with traditional belief sets, hope for sons because only a male heir is able to perform the rites that give honor to ancestors. This is a serious problem especially under current circumstances, in which China seeks to limit birth rates and fertility is restricted by government fiat. In such a context, the birth of a girl may be seen as a heavy burden. Such considerations may lie behind many cases of infanticide or suicide and help to answer the question asked in the beginning of this chapter about why so many more girls than boys in rural China commit suicide. A girl who "understands" and internalizes that she is a burden on the family, and that her mere existence may deprive her family of a much-yearned-for son, may conclude that she must relieve her family of her existence.

Turning to human-rights societies, all human beings, male or female, are considered "worthy" if they have the capacity to work and live as mutually respectful and supportive members of creative teams or networks consisting of equals. This standard is applied both at work and in the home. To be able to function in such a team is the ideal of the modern human being, as presented in modern management seminars and therapies for personal growth.

However, males and females are "unworthy" in a human-rights society, and consequently at risk from the hostility of others or themselves, if they cannot meet or fail to acknowledge the standards just set out. Uneducated young men in the West have particular problems with the transition to the new ways and find themselves without a respectable role. They are humiliated in terms of both the honor code and the human-rights code. They feel humiliated in the old context because they cannot earn a living, care for a family, and be a worthy patriarch. They feel humiliated in the new context because their male prowess, their bodily abilities, their capacity to frighten people, are all of little worth in a global information society. They may despise the "geeks" who achieve success, but they cannot emulate them. Unless such a young man manages to become a sports star, few careers are open to him. In extreme cases, he may become a hooligan, a member of a violent gang, an alcoholic, a drug user—or suicidal.

Turning to the female case, uneducated young women in the West also have specific problems related to the transition to the new ways and, like their brothers, find themselves without a respectable role. They, too, are humiliated in both the old and new contexts. An uneducated young woman may choose to become a mother, even at a very young age (witness the high numbers of pregnancies of very young girls in England, for example), but this will consign her to the margins of society, with little money or recognition, since the old role model of the "protected" woman loses its credibility in a human-rights society. As the honor code weakens its grip, fewer people are prepared to give a young woman acknowledgment and praise for her dutiful motherhood. However, lacking education and self-confidence, she is not prepared to make her way successfully in the new context of human rights. As in the case of her brother, she finds that the old way to gain respect is disappearing, while the doors to the brave new world remain closed. For some, suicide may seem the only way out.

In fact, the situation is even more complicated, since a person (or group of persons) may be defined differently by her relatives, neighbors, and friends than she defines herself. A Turkish girl living in Germany, for example, may want to live like German girls and have a boyfriend, while her family is appalled because they conceive of her in a very different way. A similar dilemma is confronted by a man who advocates human rights while his family expects him to defend their honor. I became familiar with such cases in Egypt, where blood feuds from the home village may reach men who live in Cairo, are highly educated, and have almost forgotten about their background.

A brief example: Dr. Hamza (the name is changed) came to me in 1988. He had been studying abroad, led a cosmopolitan life, wore Western clothes, spoke English perfectly, and was very much a member of the international elite. His family background and roots were in Upper Egypt, south of Cairo. This is the area of Egypt that has the strongest Arab-nomadic influence, as opposed to the broad Nile delta in the north where time seems to have stood still since the pharaohs disappeared some two thousand years ago. The north is felt by many to be more "Egyptian," while the south is perceived as more Arabic, with the Nubians even farther south at the point where Egypt merges into Africa.

Upper Egyptians are said to be fiercer than those in the north. Northerners think of themselves as more civilized, better able to talk and reconcile conflicts by using sophisticated communication strategies. They look down upon the southerners and ridicule them in innumerable jokes that express the cliché that the Upper Egyptian does not talk much but is ready to shoot fast.

Upper Egypt is a land of blood feuds. The blood feud has a simple logic: The next male in line has to be killed by the opposing family, which has the duty of avenging the murder of one of its own men, who previously may also have died as part of the cycle of revenge. Such cycles may go on for centuries and decimate the males of entire families.

Dr. Hamza was a little element in one such long-lasting cycle. One day he received unexpected visitors wearing long galabiyas, the dress of the villagers, in his fancy urban apartment. They informed him that he was the next one due to be killed. Dr. Hamza had grown so distant from such practices, so accustomed to another world that he initially did not take their words seriously: "Stupid hopeless villagers," he thought. He knew that long peace negotiations with the dishonored family who sought satisfaction were a possible way out. He also knew that his own family was the one most opposed to such negotiations. However, he did not even bother to think about this until the first attempt to kill him. The end of the story is not relevant to the main point, which is that Dr. Hamza confronted a deadly serious dilemma. He was caught between two worlds: the world of honor and the world of human rights.

The same dilemma affects whole groups, even nations. For example, few people with political power in Europe during the 1930s were prepared to believe that Hitler actually aimed at archaic domination, a form of dominion legitimized by the honor code and hostile to human rights. Germany's neighbors, tired of war and longing for continued peace, chose to believe that he as well wanted peace and cooperation.

Jones recognizes that "patriarchal" culture, the culture of the honor code, may play a role also in gendercide. He writes in Chapter 1 of this volume:

> Gendercide against men and women—but particularly men—may be seen in this light as one of the more common forms of genocide. Can we

> go a step further and hypothesize what *types* of genocide or genocidal massacre are most likely to exhibit a gender-specific and/or gender-selective dimension? Female infanticide, the rape-killings of women through history, and mass murders for witchcraft (of which the European case stands alone in history) should probably be so characterized. On the other hand, mass purges and "politicides," such as Stalin's massacres and the Cultural Revolution in China, could be expected to be weighted disproportionately or overwhelmingly against males. The related phenomenon of "eliticide" could be similarly classed. Finally, the most militarized genocides —those carried out against a backdrop of partisan or rebel activity, or heavily masculinized dissidence—seem to exhibit the most pronounced gendering against male victims. A correlation is often evident with "patriarchal" culture, as this might be manifested in patterns of community organization and family roles.

In effect, Jones belongs to the camp of male human-rights advocates who assert the need to treat all human beings as having an equal claim to justice and dignity. In the concluding paragraph of chapter 1, he states that he has "sought to establish the empirical proposition that gendercide exists." He "derives two normative propositions from the historical record: first, that the framing should be an inclusive one, encompassing the experiences of both women and men; and second, that recognition and amelioration of the phenomenon is long overdue, and a matter of the highest urgency."

In an earlier article, "Engendering Debate," Jones responds to a critique of his work by Terrell Carver and others entitled "Gendering Jones."[26] Jones makes it clear that he wished to "entrench" the subject of gender within the mainstream of the international relations discipline. He writes: "I am trying to incorporate feminism's basic theoretical perspectives and normative concerns, while giving balanced consideration to both sexes." Then he explains to the reader how he suffered unfair treatment from his adversaries, Carver and others.

> Even so, after assailing me for my "odious and otiose" arguments and my "obvious immaturity," Carver *et al.* acknowledge that I have come up with "a dozen or so important topics that might be investigated in IR." Not an unpromising start in the four pages of text they cite, I would have thought. Perhaps next time, the authors will set aside their reflexive hostility towards my project, and engage with a few of these "important topics" from their own vantage points. . . . This could only promote the more "stimulating and supportive" environment for such investigations that they, and I, desire.[27]

This little duel shows how an advocate of feminism—a man, Adam Jones—may be perceived as being on the wrong side, or at least this reaction may be hypothesized, since his opponents react with what he calls "reflexive hostility." A sociologist who now writes on gender issues has told me about his own experience of being ostracized from "proper" sociology in 1997. It seems to him that he is getting the message: "A man does not engage in gender research!" Thus, both men and women seem to have great difficulties in dealing with a man "on the wrong side."

This indicates that the most significant fallacy, one that hampers clear analysis and increases misunderstandings, is the confounding of categories. During my fieldwork in Africa, I met Rwandan Hutu who had suffered greatly when they opposed the genocide that was carried out against Tutsi in 1994 by Hutu extremists. Many moderate Hutu were killed; I spoke with some of the survivors. They gave accounts of the bitter incidents of humiliation that they faced throughout Africa, simply because they were Hutu. The word "Hutu" had acquired the connotation of "*génocidaire.*" So a Hutu who actually opposed the genocide, and suffered greatly for it, was accused of perpetrating the act he had painfully opposed. The resulting bitterness was great and profoundly disempowering.

The same fallacy happens when maleness is equated with the old honor code, and women "occupy" the new normative stance of human rights in an exclusive manner, not allowing males to be a part of it. Wherever this happens, it means that men are locked in their role as dominators in oppressive patriarchal systems and are not allowed to be victims, since women have claimed a monopoly in this sphere.

Many of the difficulties and dilemmas just described illustrate the particular stage in which the human-rights revolution currently finds itself. The former "underlings," women, have dared to raise their heads and develop what was called "feminism." The social environment started opening up for such a number of years ago. In my piece "Women in the Global Village: Increasing Demand for Traditional Communication Patterns," I argue that the driving agent of the human-rights revolution, including women's rights (see the Fourth World Conference on Women in Beijing in 1995), is the formation of a global village consisting of neighbors, not enemies. The trend toward turning enemies into neighbors is breaking down the earlier division between "male warriors" and "female carers." In a global village of neighbors, this division, together with strictly gendered pyramids of power, is becoming dysfunctional, and egalitarian relations between men and women become functional. This fact is gradually being understood by humankind—at first only by a few male and female feminists, and only now also by advocates for men's need to change their position.

More egalitarian relations mean that women may rise, while men must descend from unequal power positions. However, rising is perhaps easier than descending. A woman who raises her head and becomes a feminist has little to lose, but much to win—at least as long as she avoids having her head chopped off, although even that fate might not make her so much worse off than she was previously. By contrast, a man like Adam Jones who argues that the gendercide of "battle-age" men should be acknowledged, bemoaned, and stopped may be accused of selling out on traditional male superiority without good cause. This is because the killing of "battle-age" males is a sign of respect for *males in a traditional honor society:* These men are treated as "dangerous" and therefore "worthy" enemies within an honor context.

So the response dictated by an honor code is: "A real 'man' should take defeat without whimpering! This Jones is crying like a woman!" This would be the comment of a traditional male who has difficulties understanding that Jones rejects honor codes altogether and claims the status of victims for men as much as for women within an opposing code, namely the human-rights code. Here Jones finds himself in a similar situation to the westernized Egyptian lawyer in Cairo, who at first laughs when being informed that he is the next male on the list of blood feud in his village. He stops laughing after the first attempt to kill him. To be more explicit, it is slightly shocking for a man who demonstrates his thorough commitment to the principle of equality in a human-rights code to experience the emotional force of residual honor-bound thinking among colleagues.

As mentioned, it is comparatively easy for women to become feminists, because they are rising from a lowly position to the level of equality. Not surprisingly, it is much more difficult for a man to "descend" from a position of superiority to the level of equality. His move may be interpreted, within an honor context, as an attempt to humiliate malehood altogether. And women may misunderstand his move as the shrewd attempt of a male to weep about victimization in order to hide his factual domination.

Now the first question posed in this chapter can be revisited in conclusion. Why is the concept of gendercide interesting? My answer is that gendercide—especially as emphasized by Jones, namely the selective killings of males—is a concept that is only likely to emerge when the human-rights revolution has been accepted and understood by a sufficiently large number of people. Or, put the other way around, its arrival marks a certain advance of human rights—namely, a change in the self-image of people, in this case especially Western scholars. It is a self-image that has for a long time remained relatively untouched, and perhaps did not expect to ever come in conflict with human rights.

The concept of maleness that Jones addresses may not have been scrutinized sufficiently in the light of human rights. Its first advocates, those who have already understood its fuller implications, have a heavy task of explaining to do. Jones is such an advocate. He has raised the cry "But don't you see!" and has been met with silence or hostility. But his advocacy is, perhaps, more important than many a feminist's endeavor.

Notes

The reasoning presented in this paper draws partly upon evidence collected in a project supported by the Norwegian Research Council and the Royal Norwegian Ministry of Foreign Affairs. I am grateful for their support and also thank the Institute of Psychology at the University of Oslo for hosting it. I extend my warmest thanks to all my informants in and from Africa, many of whom survive under the most difficult life circumstances. I hope that at some point in the future I will be able to give back at least a fraction of all the support I received from them. I thank Reidar Ommundsen at the Institute of Psychology at the University of Oslo for his continuous support, together with Jan Smedslund, Hilde Nafstad, Malvern Lumsden, Carl-Erik Grenness, Jon Martin Sundet, Finn Tschudi, Kjell Flekkøy, and Astrid Bastiansen. Michael Harris Bond, Chinese University of Hong Kong, helped with constant feedback and support. The project would not have been possible without the help of Dennis Smith, professor of sociology at Loughborough University (UK). Without Lee D. Ross's encouragement my research would not have been possible; Lee Ross is a principal investigator and cofounder of the Stanford Center on Conflict and Negotiation. I also thank Pierre Dasen, Professeur en approches interculturelles de l'éducation, Université en Genève, Département de Psychologie, for his most valuable support. The project is interdisciplinary and has benefited from the help of many colleagues at the University of Oslo and elsewhere. I would especially like to thank Johan Galtung. Regarding topics of gender I benefited greatly from communication with Beverly Crawford, Øystein Holter, Adam Jones, Michael Kimmel, Ruth Lister, Susan McKay, and Claudia von Braunmühl.

1. See Stoller's work on sado-masochism: R. J. Stoller, *Pain and Passion: A Psychoanalyst Explores the World of S&M* (New York: Plenum Press, 1991).

2. Margalit defines humiliation as the "rejection of persons of the Family of Man,"

as injury of self-respect or, more specifically, as failure of respect combined with loss of control. Avishai Margalit, *The Decent Society* (Cambridge: Harvard University Press, 1996). His position is disputed, however, for example by Quinton, who argues that self-respect "has nothing much to do with humiliation." A. Quinton, "Humiliation," *Social Research* 64: 1 (1997), p. 87.

3. See Adam Jones, "Gendercide and Genocide," Chapter 1 in this volume.

4. Jones defines gender in Chapter 10 of this volume as "a continuum of biologically given and culturally constructed traits and attributessex and socially constructed gender." He defends this approach against criticism that accuses his gendercide definition of not distinguishing clearly enough between gender and sex.

5. The description of the research, issued by the public affairs office of the University of Southampton in August 1996, can be found at *www.soton.ac.uk/~pubaffrs/1996/suicide.htm.*

6. This article is one in a series that builds on this research. See Evelin Gerda Lindner, "Love, Holocaust, and Humiliation: The German Holocaust and the Genocides in Rwanda and Somalia," *Medlemsbladet for Norske Leger Mot Atomkrig, Med Bidrag Fra Psykologer for Fred* 3 (November 1999), pp. 28–29; Lindner, "Hitler, Shame, and Humiliation: The Intricate Web of Feelings among the German Population towards Hitler," *Medlemsblad for Norske Leger Mot AtomvDpen, Med Bidrag Fra Psykologer for Fred* 1 (February 2000), pp. 28–30; Lindner, "Women in the Global Village: Increasing Demand for Traditional Communication Patterns," in Ingeborg Breines et al., eds., *Towards a Women's Agenda for a Culture of Peace* (Paris: UNESCO, 1999); and the following manuscripts by Lindner, all dated 2000: "The Anatomy of Humiliation," "The 'Framing Power' of International Organizations and the Cost of Humiliation," "Globalisation and Humiliation: Towards a New Paradigm," "How Humiliation Creates Cultural Differences: The Psychology of Intercultural Communication," "Humiliation and How to Respond to It: Spatial Metaphor in Action," "Humiliation, Rape, and Love: Force and Fraud in the Erogenous Zones," "What Every Negotiator Ought to Know: Understanding Humiliation." For these manuscripts, please contact the author.

7. The title of the project indicates that three groups had to be interviewed, namely both conflict parties in Somalia and Rwanda/Burundi, and representatives of third intervening parties. These three groups stand in a relationship that in its minimum version is triangular. In cases of more than two opponents, as is true in most conflicts, it acquires more than three corners.

Both in Somalia and Rwanda/Burundi representatives of the "opponents" and the "third party" were interviewed. Those who have not yet been interviewed are the masterminds of genocide in Rwanda, those who planned the genocide. Many are said to be in hiding in Kenya and other parts of Africa, in Brussels and other parts of Europe, or in the States and Canada. Some are in the prisons in Rwanda and in Arusha, Tanzania. The following categories of people were interviewed:

- Survivors of genocide, that is, people belonging to the group targeted for genocide. In Somalia this was the Issaq tribe, in Rwanda the Tutsi, in Burundi also the Hutu. The group of survivors consists of two parts, namely those who survived because they were not in the country when the genocide happened—some of them returned after the genocide—and those who survived the ongoing onslaught inside the country.
- Freedom fighters (only men). In Somalia these were the SNM (Somali National Movement) fighters who fought the troops sent by the central government in Mogadishu; in Rwanda these were the former Tutsi refugees who formed an army, the RPF (Rwandan Patriotic Front), and attacked Rwanda from the north in order to oust the Hutu government that carried out the genocide in Rwanda in 1994; in Burundi these were also Hutu rebels.
- Some of the many Somali warlords who have their retreat in Kenya, interviewed there.
- Politicians, among them people in power before the genocide whom survivors secretly suspected of having been collaborators or at least silent supporters of perpetrators.
- Somali and Rwandan/Burundian academicians, who study the situation of their countries.
- Representatives of national nongovernmental organizations who work locally with development, peace, and reconciliation.
- Third parties, namely representatives of UN organizations and international nongovernmental organizations who work with emergency relief, long-term development, peace, and reconciliation.
- Egyptian diplomats in the foreign ministry who deal with Somalia; Egypt is a heavyweight in the OAU.
- African psychiatrists in Kenya who deal with trauma and forensic psychiatry. In Kenya many nationals from Somalia and also Rwanda/Burundi have sought refuge, not only in refugee camps, but also on the basis of private arrangements.

8. From 1980 to 1984, I worked as a clinical psychologist in collaboration with the Department of Psychiatry of the University of Hamburg, employing Carl Rogers's nondirective methods. I also led sessions with groups of women with oral problems, for example anorexia nervosa and obesity, at the university's Institute of Psychology. From 1984 to 1987, I was a psychological counselor at the American University of Cairo. My clients included students of all nations and teaching staff, and their languages ranged from English through French, German, and Norwegian to Egyptian Arabic. Most of the clients were young Egyptian students who had problems either with their parents or with their studies. These cases gave me strong insights into Egyptian culture as it related to gender issues.

Between 1987 and 1991, I had a private psychological practice in Cairo, in collaboration with the German embassy physician. Clients came from Europe, the Middle East, and Africa. They were Egyptians (some Western-oriented, others more traditional) and non-Egyptians of all nations, including members of Western embassies, institutes, and schools; managers of Western companies; partners in mixed marriages and their children. Many Western women are married to Egyptian husbands, and together with their children they embody a meeting point between cultures, especially cultural views on gender. Also, my doctoral thesis in medical psychology addressed related questions, comparing the definitions of quality of life in Egypt and Germany. See Evelin Gerda Lindner, *Lebensqualität im Ägyptisch-Deutschen Vergleich. Eine Interkulturelle Untersuchung an Drei Berufsgruppen (Ärzte, Journalisten, Künstler)* (Hamburg: University of Hamburg, 1994). My cross-cultural work as a clinical psychologist, counselor, and researcher in social psychology gave me insights into the intense conflicts engendered by the transition from traditional honor codes to the modern human-rights code, especially with respect to the way male and female roles and relationships are defined.

9. See Richard Nisbett and Dov E. Cohen, *Culture of Honor: The Psychology of Violence in the South* (Boulder, Colo.: Westview Press, 1996); Christopher Boehm, *Blood Revenge: The Anthropology of Feuding in Montenegro and Other Tribal Societies* (Lawrence: University Press of Kansas, 1984); Noel Malcolm, *Kosovo: A Short History* (London: Papermac, 1998); Mihaela Rodina, "Blood Code Rules in Northern Albania," *Agence France-Presse dispatch*, 30 June 1999. See also the Gendercide Watch case study, "Honour Killings and Blood Feuds," at *www.gendercide.org/case_honour.html.*

10. William Ian Miller, *Humiliation and Other Essays on Honor, Social Discomfort, and Violence* (Ithaca: Cornell University Press, 1993), p. 9.

11. Mention should also be made of Avishai Margalit's much-discussed argument that the distinguishing characteristic of a "decent society" is that its institutions "do not humiliate people" (Margalit, *The Decent Society*, p. 1). Margalit's work sparked a debate reflected in the special issue of *Social Research* (64: 1 [1997]) devoted to a consideration of his approach to the "decent society." See, for example, the articles by Lukes, Quinton, Ripstein, and Schick, all of which take up the theme of humiliation. The present chapter also draws upon the conceptualization of long-term social processes advanced by Norbert Elias in his explorations of the "civilizing process" (see Norbert Elias, *The Civilizing Process*, 2 vols. [Oxford: Blackwell, 1994]), especially as revised by Dennis Smith in his work on the "humiliation process" (see Dennis Smith, "Organisations and Humiliation: Looking beyond Elias," *Organization*. 8: 3 [2001], pp. 537–60).

12. Evelin Lindner, "Humiliation and the Human Condition: Mapping a Minefield," *Human Rights Review*, 2: 2 (2000), pp. 46–63.

13. Lindner, "What Every Negotiator Ought to Know," p. 12. To put it another

way, honor-humiliation regards "structural violence" (see Johan Galtung, *Peace by Peaceful Means* [Oslo and London: PRIO and Sage, 1996]) as legitimate.

14. See, for example, Unni Wikan, "Shame and Honour: A Contestable Pair," *Man,* 19: 4 (1984), pp. 635–52.

15. Beverly Crawford at the Sommerakademie für Frieden und Konfliktforschung, Loccum, Germany, 20–25 July 1997. See also Lindner, "'Framing Power,'" p. 7.

16. Mohamad Mahathir, the Malaysian prime minister, is one of the advocates of this view.

17. Smith, "Organisations and Humiliation," p. 8.

18. T. J. Scheff, *Emotions, the Social Bond, and Human Reality* (Cambridge: Cambridge University Press, 1997), p. 11. See also Scheff and S. M. Retzinger, *Emotions and Violence: Shame and Rage in Destructive Conflicts* (Lexington, Mass.: Lexington Books, 1991); and Scheff, *Bloody Revenge: Emotions, Nationalism, and War* (Boulder, Colo.: Westview Press, 1994).

19. See also Anatol Rapoport, *The Origins of Violence: Approaches to the Study of Conflict* (New Brunswick, N.J.: Transaction Publishers, 1995); Vamik D. Volkan, *Bloodlines: From Ethnic Pride to Ethnic Terrorism* (New York: Farrar, Straus and Giroux, 1997); Ervin Staub, "The Evolution of Caring and Nonagressive Persons and Societies," *Journal of Social Issues* 44 (1988), pp. 47–64; Staub, *The Roots of Evil: The Origins of Genocide and Other Group Violence* (Cambridge: Cambridge University Press, 1989); Staub, "Moral Exclusion, Personal Goal Theory, and Extreme Destructiveness," *Journal of Social Issues,* 46 (1990), pp. 47–64; Staub, "The Psychology of Bystanders, Perpetrators, and Heroic Helpers," *International Journal of Intercultural Relations,* 17 (1993), pp. 315–41.

20. See the classic work by Simone de Beauvoir, *The Second Sex* (London: Jonathan Cape, 1953).

21. On the practice of exchanging women between groups, see Marcel Mauss, *Sociologie et Anthropologie* (Paris: Presses Universitaires de France, 1950); Claude Lévi-Strauss, "Reciprocity, the Essence of Social Life?" in Lewis A. Coser and Bernard Rosenberg, eds., *Sociological Theory* (New York: Macmillan, 1957); and Lévi-Strauss, *Les Structures Élementaires de la Parenté,* 2d. ed. (Paris: Mouton, 1968). I was confronted with this practice during my fieldwork in Somalia in 1998, where the exchange of women between clans was widely regarded as the last step on the way to solving the current divisions. See Lindner, "Humiliation and the Human Condition."

22. See International Committee of the Red Cross Somalia Delegation, *Spared from the Spear: Traditional Somali Behaviour in Warfare* (Nairobi: International Committee of the Red Cross, 1997).

23. Kari H. Karamé, personal conversation, 1997.

24. "Verden på lørdag," Norwegian radio program, 5 May 2000.

25. I owe this reference to Adam Jones. See *www.guardianunlimited.co.uk/Kosovo/Story/0,2763,1943666,00.html.*

26. See Terrell Carver, Molly Cochran, and Judith Squires, "Gendering Jones: Feminisms, IRs, Masculinities," *Review of International Studies,* 24: 2 (1998), pp. 283–97, and Jones's response, "Engendering Debate," *Review of International Studies,* 24: 2 (1998), pp. 299–303. Carver et al., in turn, were responding to Jones's original article, "Does 'Gender' Make the World Go Round? Feminist Critiques of International Relations," *Review of International Studies,* 22: 4 (1996), pp. 405–29.

27. Jones, "Engendering Debate," p. 303.

3

A Theory of Gendercide

Øystein Gullvåg Holter

Introduction

Over the last ten years, there has been an increase in reports of the gender-selective use of terror in war—much of it scattered, but possibly indicating a new and very serious historical pattern. At least, its scale is new. What is the background of this seeming "genderization" of war?

Reports also indicate that civilian boys and men are increasingly targeted. An "able-bodied male" becomes a legitimate object of aggression regardless of his civilian status. Boys and men have been systematically separated from women and children and killed. Most recent wars display this pattern, including the wars in Bosnia, Kosovo, Timor, Rwanda, and Chechnya. Across very different local scenarios, two common patterns emerge—increased genderization and targeting of boys/men.

In order to investigate these themes, recent gender research and analyses are presented, including research on men and masculinities. Two masculinity-related themes are discussed in particular: "men are expendable" and "men do not care." A reactive combination of gender factors and inequality structure is seen as the main sociological background trait of gendercide, together with a breakdown of democracy and a "total" or inclusive form of war.

Perspective and Hypotheses

My argument is based on a distinction between *inequality structure* (centered on class, "race," and sex stratification) and *gender culture* (also called "sex differentiation" or the "gender system"). Gender culture is seen as a system of social differentiation, although often transformed by stratification. Gender identity is a "compromise formation," created as a mixed response to the existing social conditions and inequalities.[1]

Sex stratification is often called "patriarchy" in the literature. This essay does not enter substantially into the debate over this concept, but it does highlight two main points of recent patriarchy theory—namely, the changing character of patriarchal structures over time, and the connections between sex stratification and other forms of stratification. These views may allow for the development of new lines of research.

"Gendercide" cannot be seen simply as a result of gender culture, for example, as a general element of male aggression. Nor is it only a result of inequality structures. Rather, gender cultures that remain mainly peaceful in most circumstances can, in some contexts, be mobilized as parts of an aggressive policy, usually by being linked to other forms of oppression. Gender becomes racist gender or classist gender. We know that this process may have disastrous consequences—a nation with some private-life violence and battering can become a violent, battering state. Gender culture and social structure can be linked in a particularly negative way.

Gendercide is usually a component of other terror processes (genocide, ethnocide). A theory of gendercide cannot, therefore, address gender in isolation, but must highlight the gender relations that also exist in these other processes. The theory will, necessarily, cover some of the same ground as its counterparts in genocide studies, but from a different perspective. A main point is the way in which gender conflict contributes to other forms of conflicts, and is present within them.

The following elements seem to be typical of the buildup of aggression that leads to gendercide.

(a) a process of devaluation—a breakdown of normal political outlets and democracy combined with poverty, exploitation, or perceived humiliation, as well as sex stratification;

(b) reactive reevaluation through gender, "race," and other social mechanisms, usually together with increased victimization;

(c) a buildup of aggression;
(d) antagonistic conflict and war.

Although some of these points resemble models of genocide buildup, there are also specific gendered traits. The process of perceived devaluation, for example, extends to gender as well. The level of sex stratification is usually high or fairly high, but may also undergo a process of transformation where patriarchy or male power in the traditional sense is challenged. This can lead to specific gender reactions, not only among men but also among women, as described later. In turn, these reactions are exploited and incorporated into a policy of aggression, so that an enhanced sense of gender identity and patriarchal order becomes part of the social basis of the regime. Typically, this reactive reevaluation is created through a linking of gender and "race," combined with a process of victimization.

The gender element of the buildup may be subdued in the initial stages, and it is part of the logic of the process that it tends to be hidden or placed in the background. Gender is seldom a main issue in an aggressive ideology, although there are often attempts to present repression as if it favored gender equality. Later, however, as conflicts become violent, gender conflict is often an early warning signal—as with mass rape, for example—that exemplifies the underlying connection. And as war or persecution turns into gendercide, sex stratification, the race-gender link, and the victimization aspect all become manifest.

In this perspective, gendercide is interpreted as an outcome of civil-life processes, as well as conflict and war events. Gendercide is an extreme that also says something about normal conditions. For example, the evidence on gendercide shows that gender is more closely tied to the social body, to nationalistic notions of people, "race," and motherland, than is usually assumed.

The Evidence

The devaluation, regression, and aggression model presented here may be useful for understanding some main developments leading to gendercide, especially gender terror as part of an aggression and war strategy. Sometimes there seems to be little planning or strategy behind the terror. This is often a camouflage tactic to hide the overall strategy, but it may also represent a reality—for example, in mob and riot-like situations. I shall discuss gendercide mechanisms in such cases later.

The main evidence examined here consists of journalistic reports, media coverage, and literature on recent wars. In many cases, there are no statistics on the sex proportion (or adult/child proportion) of the killings. In most of these contexts, however, a main terror pattern and series of events can be established through the reports.

Often, what happens may be clear, while the wider meaning is not. As an example, consider an event in East Timor:

> We were taken to an open space, women, children, old people and men, including me. . . . There were about fifty of us then, all men, just picked up at random. All able-bodied men. . . . Then the soldiers, there were three of them, started spraying us with bullets.[2]

The men were separated from the rest and shot at; only a few survived. What was the strategic target in this situation? Were the Indonesian soldiers killing anyone "able-bodied" because the commanders could face protests if they had ordered the soldiers to shoot everyone? Often, there is an element of cover-up or camouflaged genocide. Shooting only the men may serve to hide the broader pattern of ethnic cleansing, for example, in Bosnia. The slaughter of men can more easily be portrayed as legitimate combat.

When we look at the wider pattern, however, such answers do not suffice. Gendercide is more than a cover-up for genocide. Although usually not stated, there is little doubt that an element of gender-related motivation is also present—an attempt to destroy the gender of the enemy, to use gender-selective murder as a means of terror, to make a particularly effective example of the victims.

Seen as a whole, the strategic cases, the more incidental cases, the camouflage type of cases, and those cases where gendercide is the first step in genocide, all convey a common meaning. They entrench a very masculinized image of the enemy. Any male is potentially dangerous. Commonly, civilian men and older boys are separated off from women and small children and killed. When this becomes a general pattern, the gender dimension cannot be seen as incidental; the evidence speaks for itself.

Gendering Conflicts

How can we say a conflict is gender related? When is gender a useful angle for understanding conflicts and wars? Often, gender makes sense only as a relationship between that which is stated and that which is not, or as a pattern of discourse shifting between the gendered and the neutral.

When Russian leaders left 118 men aboard the sunken submarine *Kursk* to die in the Barents Sea in August 2000 by not calling for international help until it was too late, there was no reference to gender. Yet the event concerned men, and not only as incidental male individuals. It happened in an all-male environment, an important arena of Russian masculinity. The accident and the way it was treated and announced were gendered also in a cultural and symbolic sense, conveying a more general message. The men were expendable. It was possible not to care—or not to care enough to act quickly.

Some signals about gender are open; some are not. In the modern view, gender seems more relevant when women are involved. If 118 women had been killed, alarm bells regarding discrimination against women would probably have gone off around the world. Yet these were men, and men are more commonly seen as neutral, nongendered.

It is true that the accident was not about gender in the direct sense. Very few gender conflicts are! As we start applying a gender perspective to conflicts, we should be careful not to jump to conclusions or attribute gendered motives. In this case, neither the accident nor the political handling of it was predominantly dictated by the fact that the personnel involved were men. Rather, this was part of the scenery, positioned in the background.

As gender research has advanced, however, this kind of "mute gender" situation has been recognized as quite typical, especially where males are concerned. Gender differs from sex. It is a changing social construction that often operates without anyone announcing its presence; it does not walk around carrying a sign.

How, then, do we decide whether a conflict is gendered or not? Or more precisely, recognizing that *some* gender aspect usually comes into play in social conflict, when is this important or dominant?

A subjectivist answer is that a conflict is gender related whenever the participants declare gender to be important. It starts with intentions. An objectivist answer instead starts with consequences. Regardless of ideology or subjective references to gender (which may vary), what counts is the actual behavior, the objective results. Do the actions of the participants contribute to gender segregation and discrimination in society as a whole, or not? Do they contribute actively (directly), as opposed to passively (indirectly)? If the answer to such questions is yes, gender is indeed of primary importance in understanding what occurs. If the answer is no, gender may be relevant, but not of primary importance.

Consider the situation of a Jewish girl like Anne Frank hiding in a loft in Nazi-occupied Amsterdam. Was the Nazi aggression gendered? Yes, partly. Did it target men first? Yes, often. A typical Nazi response to partisan action in occupied Europe was to burn down the nearby village and either kill the men outright or send the men to death camps in Germany. This happened even in "mildly" treated occupied areas, like Norway (the village of Telavåg).[3] But if Anne Frank had taken this gendered and anti-male aspect of Nazi *tactics* to be their main *strategy* and emerged from hiding, she would not have survived. Whatever the gender situation, she would have been killed as a Jew, due to the racist (or regressive-political) character of Nazi aggression, which overrode the gender aspect.

Analyzing gender and conflicts therefore usually means understanding how gender and other forces *interact.* In the Nazi case, gender was secondary to politics and race. Gender issues were reformulated by being taken on board as part of an extreme anticommunist and racist strategy.

Note, however, that gender is often *subordinated* (or sublimated) as a minor matter in the ideology. It may be of much greater importance in real life, including war, than it appears. Although racism reorganizes gender, as happened in Germany in the 1930s, there are also gender conflicts and developments that may *precede* other and more visible parts of the conflict buildup. The causal chain runs in both directions. Sexism and gender ideology may help to create racism and sharpen class differences. The gender perspective is therefore especially important for early conflict prevention.

In a psychodynamic view, modern forms of terror are of the ersatz or surrogate type. The sadistic Nazi leaders had not been assaulted by Jews or Bolsheviks in their childhood (but they often were by their own parents). Stalin had not been harmed by Trotsky. The selection of objects of hatred came later, as a means of revenge. We may thus consider gendercide and genocide to be effects of social psychoses with a background and dynamics of their own, although one should be careful not to oversimplify the picture. Social inheritance of psychological or psychosomatic trauma, especially experiences of war in preceding generations, has some explanatory power in many cases (e.g., Yugoslavia), but other factors are also important.[4]

Consider the submarine accident once again. Only a muted gender dimension was evident, even if all victims were men. The gender system appeared as something neutral, peripheral, as it often does in male contexts. However, this surface of silence was broken on one important point. A gender relation emerged, but a relation between men, not the male-female relation that we often spontaneously think of as lying at the core of gender, especially in a Western or "masculinist" view. Instead, gender emerged in a more paternalistic and classlike setting—a male-male relation between the men in the submarine and their commanders on land. Gender appeared in the form of men in power who did not really care for their followers, even if a claim to care had been central to their image building.

We may argue, therefore, that the gender system itself contains information about the underlying patriarchal (sex stratification) content, although it is often hidden or twisted. It needs careful analysis. In the Russian case, there was a conflict between the gender ideology of the manly leader, and the patriarchal logic that men are expendable and men don't care. The latter overrode the former, which in turn partially eroded the power base of the leaders. The example also illustrates the behind-the-scenes power of gender on opinion formation.

Enlisting All Men

Many discussions of the development of modern war are also gender discussions. The totalization of war, the tendency to include more and more of society and the population, is a prime example.

In traditional society, manliness often meant the ability to *avoid* war, through cleverness, strength, or prowess, and to fight only if need be. The man should prove his courage—but wars were primarily fought between lords and their trained followers, not between men as such. An army without officers was therefore worthless to a lord, and often quite dangerous—as in the late Roman Empire, where emperors were replaced as the result of soldiers' coups.[5] One should not exaggerate the "limited" character of premodern war (for example, the Middle Ages rules that war was not allowed on church days, outside designated areas, and so on), for in some contexts most of the population did participate in the warfare. Yet the modern "everyman" definition of the soldier did not dominate; nor did a "masculinity" as the common discipline of all men.[6] Ordinary men fought mainly to survive.[7]

The massive social gap between lords and commoners that still existed in the early modern world is illustrated in the following example. The Swedish historian Peter Englund describes how the officers of the Swedish army of Karl XII, after the defeat at Poltava, feasted with their Russian opponents. The year is 1709:

> In the middle of the corpse-filled battle ground and in front of the positioned troops, a camp church was raised, as well as a couple of huge,

> richly decorated tents. . . . After the highest Swedish officers had ceremoniously given over their weapons, signaling defeat, the Tsar invited them along with the Russian generals to a grand feast. . . . The battle ground looked terrible. Around 9000 dead and many wounded were lying or crawling around, in a fairly small area. . . . From a distance, the ground seemed to move, as if alive. The air was filled by a terrible pulsating sound of the crying and weeping of the thousands of wounded.[8]

Nevertheless, in this paternalistic order of society, the "heads" could wine and dine, whatever the state of the "bodies," the ordinary men. Englund describes the short-lived Swedish claim to European hegemony as a mixture of robber-baron capitalism and authoritarian feudalism. There was a systematic attempt to discipline the soldier in terms of Protestant religion and make him believe that King Karl was acting out God's will. Each grade in the army was in on the looting, although with a very low proportion of the spoils set aside for the common men. We can see how attempts were made to make the men into soldiers in more self-motivated, modern ways; yet they were still partly treated as serfs, or even waste material comparable to inanimate things. The feast was perceived as a scene of honor, and the cries went unheard, although a few of the younger officers may have been sickened.

The development of dominant masculinity as a semi-militarized role can be understood only in view of long-term global aggression. Many cultures became masculinized in negative ways through their contact with the Europeans. Native North American hunter-gatherer cultures, for example, had long emphasized manliness in the figure of the warrior. Now, however, the aggression was no longer symbolic or limited but emerged as the only means of survival, with the victims increasingly forced to fight according to the premises of their oppressors, by adopting "white" notions of manliness and gender. Since the colonizing power in this and other ways also acted indirectly *within* the culture under attack, the latter not only lost the wars but also ended up with long-term social trauma.

The European sense of a gendered self was also created on the basis of slave trade. The European man was potentially a white master overseas. Elsewhere in this book, Augusta C. Del Zotto writes:

> Their observations of early Caribbean (and South American) slave plantations . . . led northern U.S. planters to establish the practice of "breaking" African families and controlling interactions between the genders. . . . This form of social engineering was informed by both economism and the positivist philosophy of man's control over nature itself; in this case, human

> nature. . . . The black male became the focal point of this ambitious project. The public spectacle of the ritual flogging, burning, castration, and execution of male slaves became an important and enduring method of discouraging leadership and group cohesion within the slave population.

This treatment was typical of reactionary forms of paternalism, like the slave society of the U.S. South before the Civil War. Increasingly, however, modern society turned from paternalistic to masculinist inequality forms, a development associated with the factory system and the need to discipline, but also invest in, the working class. Often, the transition period was accompanied by authoritarian nationalism.

The principle of the enlistment of all adult able-bodied men as soldiers was a product of the bourgeois revolution—or, more accurately and typically, the first tyrannical versions of it, as in Napoleonic France. It became tied to competing universalistic visions of European nationalisms. The creation of the "total war" kind of soldier can be further traced through the nineteenth and twentieth centuries, although I cannot do so here.

With the introduction of social class to the public mind, Northern European and North American industrial society became self-reflective in a new way, and it is not surprising that many subsequent conflicts were tied to the appreciation of this kind of self-insight. The transition from paternalist to masculinist forms of gender inequality was accompanied by emerging working-class political movements. This created a wave of reaction and eventually, in the mid–twentieth century, a new conflict paradigm between authoritarian and democratic forces. Paternalistic principles resurfaced in authoritarian masculinist regimes. Enlistment in the army was democratized, but in a total and totalitarian sense. Eventually, even the professional barrier was broken; any person, or at least any man, could be "rationally" treated as an enemy soldier, whether he was military or not.

Yet gendercide is more than a spillover effect of total war, or a side effect caused by a lack of professionalism. We must look more closely at the creation of modern gender and its connection with war.

The Motherland

The increasingly inclusive aspect of soldiering on the male side was connected with a feminine formation on the other side. I do not write "women's side," since this formation was the creation, mainly, of the men in power.

In midindustrial Europe—in hindsight, a latent holocaust society—the woman was to become the moral elevator, sheltering men from the jungle law of competition. Atop the gender system that emerged in the Victorian period was the upper-class, attractive woman—the (male) ideal of beauty and sexuality, with the corset its appropriate symbol (a woman in a cage). Long before this, in medieval and early-modern times, women had been used as icons of war. But this symbolic form of inclusion, usually part and parcel of the mobilization of lower-rank men, was now extended, intensified, and given a more systematic character. There was a deep symbolic genderism derived from, or accompanying, notions of the parental-motherly homeland and its "naturally entitled" empire.[9]

The homeland became more feminine in part because the old fatherland had been symbolically beheaded. Heads had literally fallen in the French Revolution. It had become a fatherless homeland; and as the figure of man gradually merged with that of the universal soldier, the figure of woman began to resemble the universal parent-mother. Women were disciplined for reproduction, men for production. Older, more externally controlled forms of intimacy were replaced by a more uniform hetero/homosexual orientation system, with the "wrong" role orientation resembling the "wrong" race.

In the early phase of industrialism, however, women's (and child) labor had dominated in the factories. It may be argued that this contributed to later anxiety as a more masculine industrial bastion was established, and remained as a continued basis for regressive politics and race-gender notions. This hypothesis is strengthened by the fact that when regressive politics emerged in the late 1920s and the 1930s, they did so in a way that was closely connected with breadwinner notions and efforts to return women to the domestic sphere.

War was *for* something; it should *involve* any man; and its goal was expressed in terms of nation, race, and gender. To be a gentleman was to protect women and children, in the rather specialized form of colonial and imperialist wars.

It has often been noted that the father became increasingly absent in modern culture, and that there was a transition, in the late nineteenth and early twentieth century, from fatherly to leaderlike (or big brother–like) figures of power. One might also say that wars were increasingly fought over mothers or, to be more precise, a maternal-feminine social body. This was given other names, of course, such as the Nazi *Lebensraum* (living space), terms that can also be interpreted in view of sublimated parental loss. According to Max Horkheimer and other critical theorists, father absence (and noncaring male roles) helped to create a climate for political demagogy. The mythology of fascism is relevant here. If we kill all, the "mother" will still be there; a great parental figure, now more feminine, will cleanse the social body, our wider sense of self. Men should make war not just to protect women and children, but on a symbolic level, to become mother's white knights.[10]

What was "nuclear" about the nuclear family was the construction of destructive-productive capability as the other side of a loving-reproductive capability—a segregation mechanism comparable to apartheid, although described by sociologists like Talcott Parsons as a refined form of work division ("complementary specialization"). In the gender mirage called sexuality, the utmost specialization was associated with the highest genital pleasure. The sex object of the market, transformed into the motherly feminine figure at home, was defined as the shelter of the masculine fatherless—the woman as power wielder, so long as she followed rules of gender, race, and class. The result, among other things, was a more annihilative, uncaring, and emotionally empty form of masculinity. In Norway, where nationalism arrived late and to some extent stood at odds with economic development, male writers expressed a new sense of melancholy and alienation in the face of this development.[11]

World War I can be seen as a last catastrophic act of paternalistic aggression—a "generals' war" that would have earlier been resolved through limited wars. The new masculinist, mass-directed society, however, turned the war into a slaughter of millions of young men. In Germany, the sense that all this was for nothing was especially bitter. Reactive, ersatz personal-authoritarian forms of politics have been mapped, especially on the male side, beginning in the Bismarck period. The failure of democratic social development before the 1920s contributed to the growth of authoritarian nationalism later.

This is important also for the current genocide debate, especially Daniel Goldhagen's thesis that most, or many, Germans contributed to the Nazi holocaust.[12] I think Goldhagen exaggerates somewhat (taking participation as agreement), but he has a genuine point. Many Germans actively participated in the Nazis' aggression, more than has been acknowledged, and more than one would "normally" think, if approaching the phenomenon from a rational power, class, or exploitation perspective. The combination of revanchist groups and semi-military, paternalistic institutions may explain some of this.[13] Forces eager to reactivate inequality could mobilize a large part of the existing gender culture.

The Role of Women

Let me return to the main argument. Earlier, I found reasons to believe that racism and other regressive politics create the basis of renewed sexism, which in times of conflict and war may lead to gendercide. Now we consider the opposite relation, wherein gender creates race—or, more precisely, where gender culture is linked to inequality structure in a way that creates racism. Gender developments, often latent, may *precede* more manifest race (or class) developments.

The events leading to World War II illustrate this "gender-first" tendency. Many historians have been busy shifting guilt between the Allies and the Axis, but few have recognized that there was a common tendency of repression against women that led up to the power conflict. There was a global tendency to close or disband women's independent organizations in the years immediately preceding the aggression build-up phase, and an attempt, in many countries, to remove women from wage work.[14]

Also, many processes that lead up to geno- and gendercide are characterized by the cooptation of women, as well as by the active support of some women, especially in the early phases. Gender culture developments and changing feminine ideals can contribute to aggressive development. This is evident, especially, in the rise of Nazism to state power.

Recent research has highlighted how gender stereotypes hide the real role of men and women. Men have been more unwilling to participate in, and more harmed by, war than stereotypes suggest, while women have been more active. The victim status of men has been underreported along with the aggressor status of women, since these areas do not fit the notions of warlike manhood and peaceful womanhood. So, for example, the participation of women in the genocide in Rwanda is not as rare as it might seem; women have participated more actively in wars than the textbooks say and have also been more instrumental in the background. We should be very skeptical of superficial statistics claiming that 99 percent of the world's violence is done by men—the average distribution through time is probably more like 70 percent. In ancient Sparta, the landowning and fairly powerful women would rather have had their sons brought honorably home on their shields than receive them as weaklings fleeing from battle. In the Middle Ages, aggression was sometimes associated with femininity, and it did not have the fixed masculine connotation it has today.[15] Similar evidence exists for many cultures, such as that of the Vikings. On the other hand, men's nonviolence has been overlooked, and the effects of the victimization of men and boys have been downplayed. For example, studies of sexual abuse and rape of boys and men have uncovered a process of collective denial: "Men cannot be raped."[16]

Finally, from a more theoretical point of view, we have no reason to assume that a persistent and manifold structure of inequality involves one gender only, or that it should fail to use the oppressed in power roles whenever profitable. A main sociological tendency of dominance structures is to seek to transfer the costs of the arrangement to the oppressed. Let them oppress themselves—as far as possible. The Roman "divide et impera" policy is an early example.[17] Much theory points to the same mechanism as regards gender inequality structures, although again I cannot do justice to this theme here.

In the Nazi case, gender issues were reformulated by being taken on board as part of a race strategy. The Nazi view of women illustrates this point: "*To be a woman means to be a mother,* it means affirming with the whole conscious force of one's soul the value of being a mother and making it a law of life." A woman has a "*duty intrinsic to her gender of conserving her race,*" argued Nazi women leader Paula Siber.[18] Griffin notes: "It should be remembered when reading such reactionary texts that fascist leaders claimed to be revolutionizing traditional womanhood and motherhood by making them vital to the creation of the rejuvenated national community."[19] The whole ensemble of gender relations was reoriented in terms of racist ideology.

At the same time, and in the background, some of the racism may have been an outcome of changing gender relations. Raffael Scheck writes:

> Radical feminists have tended to see Nazism as an entirely male phenomenon and, more basically, denied that women in patriarchal societies are fully liable for their actions. Yet historians have been astonished by the sudden success of the NSDAP among women in the three Reichstag elections of 1932 and 1933. The Nazi party was most reactionary on women's issues; whereas all other parties, even the conservative DNVP, had sponsored female representatives in parliaments since the passage of female suffrage in 1918/19, the Nazis had declared that politics would debase women and draw them away from their "precious" work as mothers and housewives. No woman ever sat in a Nazi parliamentary group or an important party committee. It was clear that Hitler's coming to power would mean the loss of achievements in women's rights made during the Weimar Republic.

Initially the Nazis, like the communists, had received far more votes from men than from women. This changed dramatically in 1932. With its promise to restore law and order and to turn the economy around, the Nazis seem to have appealed to many women voters earlier deterred by Nazi brutality. The Nazis now got even more votes from women than from men. This had its precedents. Women tended to vote more to the Right than men (though until 1932 not for the extreme Right) throughout the Weimar Republic. The majority of German women held different priorities than the feminists. Women, they felt, should be educated to pursue their traditional roles in the greater service of the nation. This rhetoric sometimes abounded with racism, as when female politicians saw German women as responsible for preserving a "pure" race. The Nazis' call may also have sounded good to many women disappointed with how little their greater legal opportunities since 1918 had benefited them in a generally depressed period.[20]

In 1932 and 1933, Hitler's rise to power was accompanied by emotional outbursts among large groups of nationalist women, making some historians speculate about the sexual image projected by Hitler as a man driven by a higher cause. That Hitler played on "family feelings" is clear:

> The average woman began to look at the three K's (Kinder, Kirche, Kuche) in a more favourable light. It was in this situation that Hitler—with a unique blend of cynicism and psychological insight—assured a delegation who had come to discuss women's rights with him that in the Third Reich every woman would have a husband.
>
> Nor must it be thought that women's organisations themselves were necessarily opposed to the three K's. Some of the most powerful feminist lobbies were closely linked to the National Party and the Lutheran Church . . . and their particular opposition to the modernizing tendencies of the Weimar era only differed in degree from that of the Nazis.[21]

Elections and public events were only part of the picture. Behind the scenes, there was a breakdown of democratic rules:

> Hitler . . . was not "elected" prime minister. He was admitted in by the coterie of an anti-liberal nobility that hated the SPD and thought they could crush democracy and yet neutralise Hitler by offering him some power. Their contempt for a state governed by law and their pandering to right-wing populism became the tragedy of Europe.[22]

The female majority of the Hitler electorate in 1933 is not the rare exception that many believe. In the current context of new and more "legitimate" forms of racism, such as in Europe, similar trends can be found. If gender issues are mostly proactive for women, they turn reactive when they become gender-race issues.

In a symbolic analysis, Irina Novikova argues that Russian women today want to "forget their activism," to erase their war memories (e.g., of Afghanistan), "another silenced zone of the maternal." Instead women "want to play the virtuous role of wife and mother, and eventually become the staunchest proponents of male domination, neo-patriarchalism and the image of a powerful man," Novikova claims.[23] At the least, one should be careful not to confuse ideologies of the motherly, the peaceful, and the domestic with a culture of peace—since these ideologies may in fact be part of a more aggressive, militarized society.

The Breakdown of Politics

Some of the cases of genocide and gendercide belong to an "aggression abroad, oppression at home" pattern, and such a tendency also appears more weakly in many, perhaps most, cases. The conflicts of this type have three principal parties—the aggressors, the external victims, and the internal opponents.

In some of these cases, a traumatic internal conflict, like the mass killings of suspected opposition, precedes the external aggression. The Indonesia/East Timor conflict is an example. In the United States, the Vietnam/Watergate connection displayed the same link in a weaker form, revealing the inner authoritarianism behind the external aggression. Gendercide has also often been part of a context where the aggression shifts back and forth—with internal and external violence both being used to reinforce the regime.

In many recently independent countries, like Congo in the early 1960s, political leaders were killed and replaced by generals or gangsters, sometimes with Western support as a supposed barrier against communist influence. Again, this is a major dimension, though I can mention the Cold War dynamics and their social costs only in passing. "Creating an enemy" is an important and related element. Studies of the social construction of enemy images have shown, for example, how "the Muslim" could take the place of "the Communist" in the so-called free world imagination.[24]

Authoritarianisms and the breakdown of democratic politics are not to be reduced to a left/right political matter, even if most of them, over the last century, have arisen on the Right. Some Western "academic Marxists" (now a rare species), like Hans Jørgen Schantz in Denmark, have argued that Karl Marx was no more responsible for Stalin than Adam Smith was for Pinochet.[25] Yet the broader historical connection between left radicalism and authoritarianism cannot be denied, and one cannot understand right-wing reaction without taking this link into account.

Part of the breakdown of democracy, therefore, typically occurs within the opposition, and this may precede authoritarian changes in the regime itself. In the case of "scientific socialism," its authoritarian political cadre, with secrecy and couplike maneuverings, clearly paved the way for the authoritarian communist state and the great purge of the 1930s. We find the same tendency in the Northern Ireland and Israeli/Palestinian conflict. The higher the level of aggression, the smaller the chances for the forces of democracy—not just among the dominant force, but among oppressed and weaker parties as well.[26]

The most extreme breakdown of democracy on the Left was undoubtedly Stalin's purge in the 1930s. Robert Conquest argued that the purge was distinct in three main respects—"above all, its immense scale, in which millions perished and every member of the population was held under immediate threat; secondly, its methods, and in particular the extraordinary device of the confession trial, with the ruler's leading critics publicly denouncing themselves for treason; and thirdly, its secrecy."[27] The purge was not an effect only of masculine dynamics, Stalin's personal paranoia, or similar factors—themes that have been exaggerated in some Western analyses. What was involved was a conflict-filled variety of modernization in which many repressive mechanisms and patriarchal structures from old Russia were "reformed" and refined so as to become means, supposedly, for working-class ends.[28]

"The Stalinist terror was not a punishment—so many of those taken were innocent of any crime. Its main goal was education. . . . Stalin was a real man in the old Russian sense of the word," having learned how "to inculcate the desired behavior through fear."[29] Some have described the purge, and this type of fanaticism in general, as "fratricidal": a brotherly system that turned cannibalistic, with brother eating brother. Sinelnikov instead describes Stalin as a father figure in the more paternalistic setting of Russia, "teaching mother Russia how to be a perfect wife."[30] The mixture of paternalism and masculinism is perhaps the main point, and it is especially notable that the trend was an international one, not restricted to Russia. The suppression of women's independent agenda was followed by harsh political repression that took many forms, including the "Night of the Long Knives" in Germany

(1934), when working-class and socialist-minded leaders in the National Socialist movement were killed in their beds.[31]

Let me now attempt to connect this evidence to the main line of argument. As we saw, racism is often an important part of gendercide conflicts, but not necessarily the main element. Racism can also be a secondary projection, arising from an earlier sequence of regressive-political developments. Here, a certain type of politics comes *before* (or exists in the shadow of) the projective fixation called race.

I return to Anne Frank as example. She might have been half-Jewish or purely "Aryan," white as snow, and yet killed as a suspect spy or radical. The Nazis killed "Aryans" when needed. The strategy was politically reactive, not racist as such—although the two were already tightly bound in *Mein Kampf.* It is important to distinguish between the core political purpose, and its link to scapegoating and victimization processes with massive projection of social problems. The core purpose was popularized and institutionalized as a profitable matter for all Germans through the scapegoating mechanism, with the Jews as primary victims, via the racist-hierarchical policy of *Lebensraum.*[32]

The typical first target of this type of strategy is dissidents and opponents in one's own ranks. The first inmates of the Nazi camps were the radicals and communists of Germany; the Jews came later. Racism served a political purpose, yet it is in the nature of regressive-authoritarian politics to get out of hand, and in the worst case, to lead to a holocaust.

The Build-up Phase

In Germany, Hitler's men set fire to the Reichstag and blamed the communists. The next day, 28 February 1933, a special-powers decree on the "need to protect people and state" ("Notverordnung zum Schutz von Volk und Staat") was declared, dismantling most of the Weimar constitution. The election a week later gave Hitler 44 percent of the votes.[33] In the following months, thirty thousand Germans—communists, social democrats, and trade unionists—were arrested and consigned to provisional concentration camps. On 21 March 1933, the police president in Munich, Reichsführer SS Heinrich Himmler, announced: "Close to Dachau, Germany's first concentration camp will be opened. Here, Communists, Marxists and others that represent a danger to the Reich's security will be collected." Further, Himmler declared that the prisoners would be "set free after a period of reschooling' "(pp. 178–79; my translation). After Rohm and the SA had been suppressed in 1934, Himmler and the SS oversaw the building-up of the camp system, which had six permanent concentration camps in 1939, five for men, one for women.

"The first prisoners were the political opponents of the regime. Later, the prisoner criteria were extended to include other categories: criminals, antisocials, 'bible researchers' [Jehovah's Witnesses, who were pacifists], homosexuals. The transfer of criminals from prisons to concentration camps was an especially important part of the attempt to destroy solidarity in the concentration camps." Besides their political functions, "the concentration camp system also had a clear economic goal. Through unpaid and often highly educated labour, the concentration camps came to represent a considerable economic resource for the SS" (p. 41; my translation).

Not only was politics the core of the camp system. It is often overlooked that it continued to play a main role in the holocaust:

> In the years 1939–42, seven new concentration camps (Auschwitz, Neuengamme, etc.) were created. Some of the camps now got a new function as extermination camps (*Vernichtungslager*). There were two categories that were to be exterminated. One was Jews, the other was political commissars among the Russian prisoners of war. Even if the formal political basis for systematic extermination of Jews in Europe first came on paper in 1942, it had in reality started right after the invasion of Poland in autumn 1939. In order to carry the liquidations through, several new camps were established in the years 1940–43. . . . The other category to be liquidated was, as mentioned, a special group among the Russian prisoners of war, the so-called political commissars. This decision was made by Hitler himself. Although he met resistance from the military, he decided that Russian prisoners who were members of the Communist Party and had a political function in the armed forces should be killed at once after imprisonment. The basis for this action was in the well-known Commissar decision (*Komissarbefehl*) made by Hitler and his close co-workers in winter and spring 1941. It was put into effect after the attack on the Soviet Union on June 22, 1941. . . . The extermination of Jews and Russian prisoners of war did not only take place in the concentration camps. To a large extent, especially in 1939–41, [it occurred] through the so-called SS-*Einsatzgruppen*, of which there were five. They moved in the wake of the Wehrmacht and did their bloody deeds in bestial ways and on a very large scale. (pp. 42–43; my translation)

Elements of the Buildup of Genocidal Aggression

I have discussed devaluation, regressive reevaluation, and buildup leading to aggression. The model can be useful for understanding the major lines of development, but it does not explain all. In the last part of the chapter, therefore, I outline some other important elements, most of them closely connected to masculinity dynamics and what happens between men themselves.

Humiliation and Shame

A sense of humiliation and shame, discussed elsewhere in this volume (see Evelin Lindner, Chapter 2), is often part of the background of conflicts that create genocide. In patriarchal and especially in paternalistic circumstances, when the head "loses face," the body—the dependents, the followers, et cetera—will have to suffer. A "shame culture" creates shame-related violence.

Modern society, however, is also (and I think primarily) a "guilt culture," with a more internalized form of control. Shame and guilt often work together, but the guilt element is central to most of the conflict phenomena. If the Nazi holocaust had been driven by shame principles, there would be no need to kill millions of Jews. The symbolic loss of face and targeting of selected persons as examples, along the lines of traditional anti-Semitism, would have been sufficient. Instead, the industrialized killing of six million people through extreme inhumanity disguised as rationality points to a much more self-inclusive or egocentric power system than those typical of paternalist societies and shame cultures. In this logic, there is no moderation, only a final solution.

Gendercide and Masculine Hysteria

Hysteresis is Greek and originally meant being behind, being late, and being deficient as a result. In psychological terms, it can be seen as an acute anxiety-rigidity positioning—a condition creating hysteria, an "uncontrollable outburst of emotion or fear," according to *Webster's Dictionary.*

When we regard masculine forms of hysteria, a neglected subject (for many traditional gender reasons), we should recognize that common terms associated with femininity—like "uncontrollable" and "irrational"—may not fit. We would not expect hysteria to take the same forms among men. "Outburst," for example, might better translate to "controlled outburst," as suggested by studies of domestic violence.[34]

Masculine hysteresis and divergent, underrecognized forms of hysteria may be more important in wars and aggressive conflicts than is usually conceived. This line of inquiry is especially interesting as regards "pathological machismo" and similar hyped-up, aggressive masculinity processes, as well as the more calculated uses of men as "uncontrollable" in war.[35]

There is a psychological level where an *inner* killing is going on through external terror. One interpretation is that the male hysteric has to kill himself again and again, following the masculine line of "acting out." He kills some of himself, or averts something in himself, through the death of others.

This is often reflected in authoritarian propaganda. There is a feeling of pollution; the man must cleanse himself. In the words of race ideologist Hans Gunther: "This act of *overcoming ourselves* is rewarded by the knowledge of participating in a spirit which . . . determines the course of natural selection."[36] This action/reaction can be seen as a low-key, background process in most "normal" masculinity of the twentieth century, not just as a particular feature of some men in certain contexts. It is when this process becomes personally extreme *and* sociologically encouraged, that is, when this masculinity is provided with power, money, and weapons, that the consequences of the syndrome become extreme. Men's blood lust in modern wars has mainly been the product of extreme circumstances, either incidentally among normal soldiers under dehumanizing conditions and bad officers, or in more institutional forms like specialized terror troops.[37]

A pattern of anxiety, rigidity, and aggression is found also in civil life studies of men's violence against women. One type of violent man is described as rather more passive or weak than the male ideal, even too kind—until he hits a woman, usually his partner or spouse. There are also more traditional masculine variants, but these may be in the minority.[38] Further, "kind" men seem to hit women in quite specific situations, usually those that create a sense of panic. Most typical is a situation of acute sexual jealousy. The panic is associated with a feeling of loss of self or intense reification. It is as if the man freezes before he hits—shrinking into an absolute zero. The phenomenology of wife battering can be associated with the anxiety/rigidity just described.

Men may experience an *acute negative positioning* (hysteresis) not just individually, but collectively. Susan Faludi's term "stiffed" is relevant here. At this point, different research traditions have described similar phenomena; these include the "double-bind" research originating in psychic war trauma, and the "authoritarian personality" research. Basically, the man becomes numb, lost to himself, and this numbness is part of the reason he can kill—not just in desperation, or to reach a calculated goal, but as an end in itself.

Victimization (Mobbing) and Scapegoating

Like the link between racism and sexism, victimization and scapegoating are so common that they can be seen as intrinsic to genocidal and gendercidal conflicts. Civil life research into mobbing processes is therefore relevant. If hysteresis, sociologically speaking, creates a tremendous pressure toward projection—getting rid of, "cleansing," "giving birth through death"—it becomes more understandable why aggressive but still "rationalist" strategies like Nazism and Stalinism were also constantly linked to civil life and military mobbing and scapegoating processes. There was widespread anti-Semitism even in the U.S.Army in World War II. The projective system is a central part of the aggression itself. It may appear in seemingly senseless ways, like neighbors who become incoherent and start shooting at each other in war-torn Sarajevo, but this is often camouflage.[39] One cannot, for example, reduce Serbian "cleansing" in Bosnia and Kosovo to groups of men acting out old male hunting roles.[40] There is a strategic purpose at the core, and if it can be hidden behind notions of age-old warrior masculinity or other metaphysics, so much the better. The victimization process serves to give a policy of aggression its populist mask—a notion that all who support the policy will profit, great and small, as with the appeal to all Germans to share the confiscated Jewish property.

The victimization process, then, serves at least three main purposes: (a) to function as a terror weapon, (b) to widen the basis of support, and not least (c) to *hide* the political purpose of the regime. In the Nazi dream Reich, class difference would no longer be a problem; all Aryans would be powerful and free. Killing the Jews was the mobbing logic's answer to the problems of Germany and capitalism. As the victimization process escalates, participation is ensured by force. For example, prisoners are turned into informers. Many Nazi camp survivors carried a burden of shame.[41] Mobbing principles serve as inner control mechanisms in aggressive regimes, destroying democracy and solidarity. Studies of mobbing in civil life show how the victim is positioned as a target of projections, leading to a destruction of the sense of self. This indirect aggression is a primary cause of long-term psychological harm.

Creating Race-Gender

If gendercide is caused by a combination of power and masculinity processes, we may look at the intermediate positions. What are the links between the two? How are power imperatives translated into gender system terms, mobilizing men?

The early writings of Joseph Goebbels, to take one example, are filled with a mixture of socialist sentiment and reactive anxiety formations. "One class has fulfilled its historical mission and is in the process of withdrawal in favor of another. The bourgeoisie must yield to the working class," he writes, in the authoritarian, machinelike conception of capitalism that was typical of the period. This is a merciless, anxiety-provoking development. He clings to the past and has "childish" fantasies. For example, he writes of how "a real woman loves the eagle." The outlet is through scapegoating: "There are absolutely no Jews here, that is a blessing. Jews make me physically ill." Goebbels even claims, "Jesus cannot have been a Jew."[42]

Goebbels was able to give the impression of a great rationality compressed into simple, strong imagery, and he was therefore the ideal Nazi propaganda minister, although his quirks and increasing tendency toward paranoia diminished his propaganda impact, at least outside Germany. Goebbels's writings display the extent of the male embodiment of race-gender ideology; he becomes physically ill.[43]

Humor is a way to defuse anxiety, and in parts of occupied Europe folk humor was an effective weapon against local fascist leaders, like Quisling in Norway.[44] Yet the German hysteresis position seems not to have allowed this development. The German people's sense of humor was mobilized against Hitler only at the end of the war.[45]

Although gender images and metaphors often appear in the research on authoritarian regimes and aggressive leaders, the masculine side of this has not been systematically investigated. For example, Roger Griffin argues that "the mythic core" of fascism contains a "vision of the (perceived) crisis of the nation as betokening the birth pangs of a new order."[46] He does not ask whether this core contains an element of masculine hysteria, with "birth pangs" and similar expressions. In a context of hysteric masculinity, the leader must give birth to the new nation.

Global Gender Culture and the "Sex-Violence Syndrome"

Global gender culture and media exposure play a role in conflicts and may be more important than recognized. Westernized entertainment often directly links violence to sexuality. The idea of using gender as a means of aggression, surrounded by pervasive imagery, is central in commercial culture; the message "Kill the (gendered) enemy" plays a background role in gendercide. Terms like "terminator masculinity" seem relevant, at least, in contexts where large population groups, young men especially, participate in terror and killing.

Also, successful gender is constantly linked to money and power. Most gendercides occur in the poorer parts of the world, where the majority of men lack the means of gender success in the media sense and therefore, with increasing media exposure, become all the more invisible. Impoverished male roles, including the absence of symbolic gender, the inability to achieve successful manliness according to rich-world ideals, are an important underlying feature of many conflicts, for example in Africa.[47] Poverty is increasingly contrasted to a media-exposed, culturally hegemonic and (also) locally imagined gender, with hyper-masculinization as the only way out. The sex/violence content and the contradiction between imagined gender success and real-life situation are both likely to increase the chance of gender-related aggression.

Consider the background of the Rwanda genocide/gendercide, seemingly peripheral to the rich-world problematics discussed earlier. Clearly, poverty was a main background theme. "In view of this identity crisis and the feelings of being socially and economically downgraded, the majority of African men turn more and more to revolutions and bloody ethnic and religious conflicts, swelling the ranks of the military. . . . War is the sole remaining domain of men, at least in sub-Saharan Africa, which makes them feel powerful and strong and offers them the intoxicating cocktail of masculine superiority."[48] Masculinity and poverty should be considered together with social structure. Historically, "the system of social relations which emerged in Rwanda were more completely hierarchical and feudal than in most other parts of Africa."[49]

Men Caring

The exclusion of men from caring roles and the construction of breadwinner/soldier masculinities form a common background pattern in the phenomena described so far. Genocides have many causes, but a common element is dehumanization, an extreme practice of noncaring and treating other people as things.

The noncaring of men—"breadwinner" masculinity and its converse, homemaker femininity—are still often presented as eternal and natural institutions. Their historical origin is more recent than most people realize. Early- and pre-modern male roles and masculine forms generally combined authoritarian relations with caring relations. Men's lives were less separated from those of children (and other groups in need of care), since people of various ages often worked together, and so looking after others was more of a common responsibility.[50]

Wage labor and industry created the new breadwinner/homemaker economic tie, a "contract gender."[51] Although woman and man had worked partly in different, sometimes separate, roles and specializations, often with men in more mobile work and women in more house-bound tasks, and although these societies had often stressed obedience on the part of women, women's economic activities had not been seen as "support services" for men's labor.

Pre-modern societies offer a rich display of political and religious masculinities, but not breadwinner masculinities.[52] This form of male dominance was modern, based on a combination of a "whip" and a "carrot"—an offer of breadwinner status and discipline for men; an offer of a child, and a monopoly on caring, to women. The exclusion of men from caring roles developed as work life became mechanized and industrial, and with the fall of paternalist patriarchy it also emerged as a political process. "Enlightened" law makers at the turn of the twentieth century designated the new divorce laws that excluded men from contact with their children, supposedly to protect women.

Total war is also often totally hidden war: It no longer has an objective beyond the killing process. It becomes generalized and obscured at the same time. The Russians in Afghanistan, like the Americans in Vietnam (as at My Lai), had no "rational" purpose. The top commanders perhaps did not really "mean to" bring about, or even allow, the atrocities that took place. Often, middle management is involved—that is, the men caught between the inequality structure and the gender culture. It seems as if the war machinery itself somehow runs off the rails. Why do such things happen?

Again, an important perspective is to examine the noncaring aspect of men's situation, and how this is made into something that men can identify with, define as masculine, and feel proud of. In times of war, this sense of masculinity is brought out and used as a hammer against the enemy; but inside, among participant men themselves, it tends to break down. Soldiers develop a great deal of compensatory caring to survive the war, some of it in opposition to their officers.[53]

As we have seen, pre-modern societies had many different gender arrangements, but none of them made one gender into a service function of the other. This was mainly established in industrial society. Modern economy started from a patriarchal basis, and if men and women had been differently placed in society, the results might well have been different. It is not obvious, for example, why fluid, flexible equivalent value, developing into capital, should ally with old-time patriarchy, except in an early period. Femininity and economy had often been associated in pre-modern patriarchal ideology; women were seen as capital-like, like Eve, representative of sin in the form of "knowledge capital." Women were burned as witches as Europe was modernized. The emergence of European genocide and gendercide can be seen as a reaction against capital, taken out, primarily, on the "inner differentials," women and Jews.

A unique relationship was created with a "she" in service to a "he." It is true that industrial societies never grew into full breadwinner societies, with every man a wage earner and every woman a homemaker. But the tendency is clear. In principle, women became "producers of the relations of production," creating human resources, while men became producers of other resources. The economic polarization created a new sense of "she" as a "not-he," and "he" as a "not-she." In turn, this created dramatic cultural changes, for example, regarding conceptions of the body, from placid paternalist unisex bodies to dual-sex bodies.[54]

These changes also affected the military. Until World War I, recruitment philosophy was based on relations between men; certain types of men were fit to become soldiers, others were not. This was expressed through body types. Later, however, the main criterion shifted toward men's relation to women. A man fit for war was a man who did not resemble a woman.[55] Not only were men offered a new semi-militarized, gradually democratized breadwinner masculinity, but also they were excluded and hindered from taking on caring roles.

Many societies have "balancing" arrangements of socialization and reproduction (e.g., couvade).[56] Caring for the young, the elderly, and the ill is a common concern. Societies may allow extensive work divisions between men and women and yet emphasize norms of sharing. This sense of caring as a common concern tended to disappear, however, in the new breadwinner/homemaker gender constellation and the nuclear family that emerged from the splitting of business and home.

In civil life, a by-product of noncaring is technicism. This is typical of some major cases of genocide also. In speeches to concentration guards, holocaust architect Heinrich Himmler talked about their "civilizing duty" of exterminating Jews and Bolsheviks. He claimed they should think of it as technical work.

If we combine the evidence from the new studies of men, feminist research, and the research on genocidal and holocaust-producing conflicts, it becomes clear that the marginalization and devaluation of men's caring potential, including the attempt to erase men's caring and emotional sensibility in wars, have been much more costly to society than is ordinarily assumed.

Conclusion

Gendercide and genocide have many causes. Some are more common and significant than others. Research on the best-known and main cases, like the Nazi holocaust, shows the following nine-step pattern: (1) A core political purpose; (2) early and/or background gender dynamics; (3) a victimization connection and, gradually, a system; (4) creation of an aggressive ideology; (5) mythic core formation; (6) breakdown of democracy; (7) buildup; (8) conflict; and (9) genocide and gendercide. Some concluding comments on these follow.

(1) Core political purpose. The purpose may be complex, but it has an antidemocratic kernel. In the case of authoritarian variants of Marxism, the purpose was to dismiss the bourgeois-democratic rights of the capitalists and their supporters; in fascism, to head off workers' movements; in Nazism, to quash the Bolsheviks and their "capitalist and Jewish agents." In ex-Yugoslavia, the aggression served to eliminate any "third way" of workers' democracy and national and religious tolerance; a main purpose was the death of the cosmopolitical society exemplified by Sarajevo.[57] Early warning signals included gang rapes of Western tourists.[58]

(2) Early and/or background gender dynamics. In the case of Germany, women supported the Nazi idea of women as masters in a separate domestic sphere that would be fed by Germany's "naturally greater role in the world," to the extent that women became the majority of Hitler's voters. In research, there is a tendency to downplay this sort of evidence, reminiscent of the tendency to downplay women's role in violence—which in turn is sometimes countered by reactionary notions of "women behind it all." The point is that even if men are, on the whole, more involved than women with aggression, there is usually a *relation* between the two genders and a shared understanding that underpins the violence. The "who does most" debate tends to overlook this element, which is often tacit or implicit. A reactive turn in the gender system may precede other developments and is often an early sign of problems to come.

(3) A victimization connection and, gradually, a system. In the build-up process there is a point, sometimes clear and in the open, where largely

"internal" victim problematics (like the would-be Nazi leaders, troubled young men dreaming of cleansing and revenge) are externalized (e.g., by throwing stones at Jewish shops). This change often happens through a gangster or criminal connection. A link to victimization, which at first may be hidden, now emerges and is magnified and transformed as part of a power system.

There is some support for the idea that leaders and participants in genocide and gendercide are the products of problem childhoods, but it is also a sociological fact that many men and women with "normal" backgrounds participate. A system of victimization is based not only on trauma and anxiety, but also on greed and control. For example, Ottosen relates how an "ordinary German," a low-class young maid in Furstenberg (known as a "merry girl with an attraction to men"), took a job as a "bat" (female guard) in the women's concentration camp of Ravensbrück in 1939. She soon became attracted to her new power over other women, turning into a torturer.[59] An extension or enlargement of gender identity is usually important in such processes. Michael Kimmel argues that masculinity may become a feeling that one is entitled to something bigger, better, an entitlement to power—power not just over women, but over everyone.[60] While this may be a "slumbering" trait in normal circumstances, it can be brought out and enlarged through victimization.

(4) Creation of an aggressive ideology (often disguising 1–3). I have discussed a number of traits, including masculine violence and hysteria, that may be termed *neotraditionalist,* but in the specific sense of masking political purpose and modernist maneuvering. Compare, for example, Hitler the propagandist and vote collector, promising death to Jews and capitalists, to Hitler the interlocutor with German industrialists and the backstage gangster ordering the death of the SA leadership.[61] In Germany, religious fundamentalism also played a background role. In other parts of the world, like Iran and other Islamic areas, or Ireland, it became a main springboard of neotraditionalism. Although these contexts differ, the neotraditionalist component is similar.

(5) "Mythic core" formation, including race-gender.[62] The gendercide evidence is in line with a social constructivist view, wherein modern gender is tightly connected to "race" both in its historical origin, as a modern system combining differentiation and stratification, and in many of its patterns today, so that we might better speak of a "race-gender." The mythic core is created by a vicious mix. In Yugoslavia, for example, neonationalist leaders

mobilized public opinion against free ("provocative," "Western") women, and then made the media portray rapes as ethnic attacks. "Women-prey were defined by class and race; . . . the taboo prey was Serbian women," Slapsak argues in a discussion of the buildup to war in Yugoslavia. "These groups, especially 'Muslim women,' were invented by Serbian and Croatian nationalists" in the 1980s. There was a "cruel game of traditional behavior, ideological constructs, media manipulations and clashes of political interest." In Croatia, five feminist authors were attacked by the media as "witches," condemned for "'raping Croatia' because they pointed to the fact that women in general were being raped, not primarily Croatian women (in a short initial period) or 'Muslim' women (the secondary, but then permanent version)."[63]

The basic mythic core consists of motherland and soldier, as an alternative to worker and democratic citizen. Before the war, "the Yugoslav political structures had strict laws and local rules protecting the principle of equal ethnic representation at all levels . . . which earlier also included gender and age representation (1950s and 1960s)."[64] The mythic core is a regression from a democratic everyday problem-solving approach, which it replaces with the idea that troubles can be avoided by exploiting, dominating, or killing other people.

I have mainly discussed the first five phases of a larger process. The later, more well known phases include (6) the rise to power of authoritarian leaders and the breakdown of democracy; (7) the buildup, including a reorganization of gender; (8) conflict; and (9) genocide and gendercide. Considering this nine-step model as a whole, we should note that some of the phases are perhaps better understood as elements; they tend to play a more permanent role. Further, the phases, in any concrete case, may not follow the exact sequence of the model.

Does the model give the misleading impression that politics precedes all? I do not think so. Perhaps, as Wilhelm Reich argued, sexuality comes first. Authoritarianism is a complex entity. But there are reasons to emphasize the destruction of politics as a major aspect. War, Clausewitz argued, is politics by other means. Yet Clausewitz referred to restricted forms of war, rather than the total warfare later introduced by figures like Erich Ludendorff, the notorious First World War general who became a key Hitler supporter. One may argue, therefore, that gendercide and genocide are consequences not mainly of politics, but rather of attacks on the social "body politic." The terror can develop when democratic political processes have been corrupted and the leaders eliminated. Politics becomes an arena of victimization rather than of association and negotiation.

In this context, gendercide is often a first step toward genocide, but also important in itself. For example, the Nazi killing of male Soviet POWs should be interpreted as not only a political move, but also a gender statement showing the superiority of the Aryan "superman" (although in the most cowardly way possible). From this vantage point, genocides are the outcome of a twisted, "racialized," regressive politics. The stronger the gender component, the greater the chance of gendercide or the use of gender terror as part of genocide.

What are the bases of the social reaction and "reactive" tendencies that create the build-up process? Researchers have pointed to factors like the European heritage of absolutism and authoritarianism that became part of the industrial world; to anxiety in rapidly changing (modern) circumstances; and to other patterns that cannot be addressed here. Apart from political and historical matters, an element of inflated expectations and greed is typical of the buildup. It is not only that social class and other political matters take on a regressive form by being cloaked under "race" and "gender." There is also an economic side—the use of victimization for plunder or slave labor. Race-gender becomes part of a context of more severe class exploitation, but this does not appear within the privileged race- and gender-defined group. Instead, the regime creates an ideology of a "cleansed" motherland area, the basis of the master state, and a wider periphery (the *Lebensraum* in the Nazi case, legitimated by notions like the "drive toward the east").[65] This "sub-human" periphery is created with the goal of making the servant population work for the master state, and/or extinguishing it through inhuman work methods.[66] The spoils from this undertaking can be used domestically, to buy off the public or corrupt the opposition. There is a *bigger* class, a more totalitarian politics, hidden in the language of race and nation.

A main point, therefore, is that conflicts become genocidal and gendercidal when other and more normal options—sexual, moral, social, political—are stalled. If economic differences, power conflicts, and class issues cannot be openly resolved, they will reappear in more reified, socially costly forms, beyond class and political repression. A "mythic core" mechanism linking racism and sexism will arise and take on a life of its own.[67]

When one investigates their social and psychological roots, various fundamentalisms and authoritarian policies show similar tendencies. Gender segregation and noncaring masculinity (father absence) are typical traits, together with the political construction of an aggressive "male nature."

These traits also point to new ways to *reduce* gender terror and gendercide. First, research can contribute by developing a gender relations view on conflict and war beyond the simplistic identification of masculinity and power. The gender system and the power structure are partly independent and in some respects opposed. This provides potential for practical efforts at peace building. As long as an aggressive leader is seen as merely aggressive, it is often possible to avoid further buildup. It is the linking of aggression to successful gender (e.g., through the motif of the leader as a national symbol of manliness) that worsens the prognosis. One preventive strategy, therefore, is to deconstruct this new reactive gender, also in "traditional" or conservative terms, in order to reduce the support for aggression. For research, a first step is to identify the different processes at work and determine why outcomes can be so dissimilar. In some situations, the dangerous mixture of patriarchal power politics and masculine aggression succeeds. In others, it does not: Men's sense of manliness is instead turned against aggressive leaders and victimizing politics. Today we know little about the conditions that create either a reactionary or a democratic response, but we do know that there is much more *variation* than conventional wisdom acknowledges. Developing a gender perspective that helps to analyze conflicts and prevent aggression means disassembling the "masculine mystique" and recognizing that most men do not participate in atrocities; and many who do, do so only under severe pressure.

Second, the link between gender and power is itself closely connected to other forms of stratification, mainly class and "race"; and the tension described here, wherein the gender system either enhances or counteracts the buildup, depends upon these other connections. For example, a social situation of increasing racism in daily life may, in turn, create negative gender developments. These interconnections are often mentioned in research, but "process knowledge" is lacking. We do not know much about how changes in one power structure lead to changes in the others.

A third important step is to delve further into masculinities—the problems of caring and conflict problems discussed in this chapter—thereby avoiding the idea that a "culture of peace" can be narrowed down to a women's issue. What are the processes in civil life, including politics and the economy, that promote gender segregation and noncaring masculinity? How are they connected to victimization and the other processes of the buildup to large-scale aggression? These are huge and important areas for new research, as well as for more practical measures to prevent aggression.

The expendability of men is closely related to an ideology of noncaring masculinity. It is also often the reality that men confront in conflicts and wars, underlying the surface ideology. This is an important element, a "reality gap" that many men may be unaware of before it is too late. Again, evidence of this can be found, in more moderate forms, in civil life. In fact, a likely social explanation of the shorter average life span of men compared to women is the "breadwinner cost" of the male role—a one-sided adaptation that does not work well in health terms. Many ideological moves that are typical of aggressive buildup can also be found in less extreme variants, like an attribution of aggression to boys in the school system.

Improving knowledge in these areas depends on a better integration of gender and equal- status research with peace studies and genocide studies. A main point is the need to recognize men as gendered, and to reexamine conflicts and peace possibilities from a gender-and-equality perspective. This is an important task for the United Nations and other organizations that seek to promote peace. Involving men is a "cide" issue, not a "side" issue.[68]

Reducing the likelihood of genocide and gendercide involves many peacetime changes as well. Men are carers and caring persons and should receive greater recognition in these roles than they generally do today—not just in their role as fathers, but in other respects as well. Improving women's career opportunities and reevaluating men's caring roles can be seen as part and parcel of a consistent policy to dismantle gender-related discrimination. Further, men need to be seen as valuable, not expendable; peace efforts must address local questions of masculine self-worth in more positive ways, if this terrain is not to be left to authoritarian forces.

Notes

1. See Øystein Gullvåg Holter, *Gender, Patriarchy, and Capitalism: A Social Forms Analysis* (Ph.D. diss., University of Oslo, 1997). For previous conceptualizations of "gendercide," see Mary Anne Warren, *Gendercide: The Implications of Sex Selection* (Totowa, N.J.: Rowman and Allenheld, 1985), especially ch. 2; and Adam Jones, "Gendercide and Genocide," this volume.

2. John Taylor, *East Timor: The Price of Freedom* (London: Zed Books, 1999), pp. 68–69.

3. In the small fishing village of Telavåg, near Bergen, two Gestapo officers were killed in 1942. In order to set an example, the Germans burned down the houses, destroyed the boats, and sent the men to Sachsenhausen, where thirty-one died.

4. On Yugoslavia, see Roger Cohen, *Hearts Grown Brutal: Sagas of Sarajevo* (New York: Random House, 1998).

5. In some recent wars, soldiers have again become more unruly. In the Vietnam War, "the ratio of violence against officers was believed to be fifteen times as high as

in the grim trench warfare in World War 1." See Michael Maclear, *Vietnam: The Ten Thousand Day War* (London: Thames-Methuen, 1981), p. 372.

6. I am forced to simplify. Indeed, there was a sense of masculinity common to all men, since this is a part of gender culture in all known societies. It belongs to gender as a differentiation system. The point is that it did not operate like, or really resemble, the modern sense of masculinity. Men were primarily subject not to gender as an economic abstraction (hegemonic masculinity, abstract masculinity norms, etc.), but to more open and concrete forms of patriarchal authority. Social status (king, lords, serfs, etc.) was the main issue, and definitions of manhood varied accordingly.

7. Joanna Bourke shows that this rule applies to twentieth-century wars also. Most men are in practice unwilling to fire at the enemy, at least at close distance, despite training and orders. Also, many participants develop posttraumatic illness. The attempt to create obedient killers on the basis of "masculine aggression" has met much greater opposition from men than is commonly recognized. Although the development of twentieth-century "he-man" masculinity widened the recruitment base, there was also increasing conflict between this gender logic and the reality of war. See Bourke, *An Intimate History of Killing* (London: Granta Books, 1999).

8. See Peter Englund, *Poltava—Berättelsen om en armés undergång* (Stockholm: Atlantis, 1988), pp. 278–79.

9. Historical sources on the change from eroticism to sexuality are discussed in Øystein Gullvåg Holter, "Seksualitet og historie," *Materialisten,* 3 (1982), pp. 50–77, which also features a critique of Foucault. For deep symbolic gender analysis see Jorun Solheim, "Shelter from the Storm," in Tordis Borchgrevink and Øystein Gullvåg Holter, *Labour of Love: Beyond the Self-Evidence of Everyday Life* (Aldershot: Avebury, 1995), and Solheim, *Den åpne kroppen* (Oslo: Pax, 1998).

10. Since father absence is sometimes used as a catchall explanation in social science, we should be clear that the children might be father's knights, too. Authoritarianism, or misuse of authority, has traditionally been associated with the father, rather than the mother. Also, masculine authoritarianism has been more visible. In a society that leaves caring and socialization to women, however, authoritarianism in early life will often be feminine. The mother as primary authoritative (bonding) figure was what the Frankfurter researchers found, much to their surprise, doing research on continental European family forms in the 1920s and '30s. They had expected to find the father in this role (M. Horkheimer et al., *Studien über Autorität und Familie.* Orig. Paris 1936, Lüneburg: Dietrich zu Klampen Verlag, esp. pp. 306–7). For a recent study that highlights that mothers can have authoritarian roles, cf. Mogens Nygaard Christoffersen, *Opvækst hos fedre. En sammenligning av 3–5-årige børns opvekst hos fædre og mødre* [Growing up with the father: A comparison of 3–5-year-old children's upbringing by fathers and mothers] (Socialforskningsinstituttet, Report 96: 23, Copenhagen), showing that single mothers more often than single fathers use violence against children.

11. See Jørgen Lorentzen, *Mannlighetens muligheter. Om mannlig under, erfaring og etikk i det moderne gjennombrudds litteratur* (Ph.D. diss., University of Oslo, 1996).

12. See Daniel Jonah Goldhagen, *Hitler's Willing Executioners: Ordinary Germans and the Holocaust* (London: Little, Brown, 1996).

13. See Klaus Theweleit, *Male Fantasies* (Cambridge: Cambridge University Press, 1987).

14. Øystein Gullvåg Holter, "Gender as Forms of Value," in H. Holter, ed., *Patriarchy in a Welfare State* (Oslo: University Press, 1984).

15. See Barbara Tuchman, *A Distant Mirror* (Harmondsworth, UK: Penguin, 1980).

16. See Ruth Almedal and Laila Danielsen, *Voldtekt på menn* (Hovedoppgave, Psykologisk Institutt, Universitet I Oslo, 1994). The denial occurs in the courts and the media as well: See, e.g., Gunnar Rasi Larsen, "Mann utsatt for massevoldtekt nektes voldsoffererstatnig," *Osloposten,* 7 June 2000, pp. 6–7.

17. For this and other principles of "patriarchal strategy" see Holter, *Gender, Patriarchy and Capitalism.*

18. Quoted in Roger Griffin, ed., *Fascism* (Oxford: Oxford University Press, 1995), p. 137 (emphasis added).

19. Griffin, *Fascism,* p. 136.

20. Raffael Scheck, Associate Professor and Chair, History Department, Colby College (Maine, USA). Abridged quote from an Internet text at *www.colby.edu/personal/r/rmscheck/GermanyD7.html* (emphasis added).

21. Richard Grunberger, *A Social History of the Third Reich* (London: Penguin, 1971), p. 252.

22. Professor Bernt Hagtvedt, Department of Political Science, University of Oslo (in the Norwegian daily *Aftenposten,* 18 October 1993, p.13; my translation).

23. Irina Novikova, "Soviet and Post-Soviet Masculinities: After Men's Wars in Women's Memories," in Ingeborg Breines, Robert Connell, and Ingrid Elde, eds., *Male Roles, Masculinities, and Violence: A Culture of Peace Perspective* (Paris: Unesco Publishing, 2000), p. 128.

24. See Rune Ottosen, *Mediestrategier og fiendebilder I internasjonale konflikter—norske medier I skyggen av Pentagon* (Oslo: Universitetsforlaget, 1994).

25. Hans-Jørgen Schanz, "Tilbakeblikk på Marx (from Har det moderne menneske blevet voksent, Modtryk 1993)," *Sosiologi i dag,* 1 (1995), pp. 19–47.

26. On the "siege mentality," see Uta Klen, "'Our Best Boys': The Making of Masculinity in Israeli Society," in Breines et al., *Male Roles, Masculinities, and Violence.*

27. Robert Conquest, *The Great Terror: Stalin's Purge of the Thirties* (Harmondsworth: Penguin, 1971), p. 11.

28. See Holter, "Gender as Forms of Value."

29. Andrei Sinelnikov, "Masculinity à la Russe: Gender Issues in the Russian Federation Today," in Breines et al., *Male Roles, Masculinities, and Violence,* p. 204.

30. Ibid.

31. The "first-warning" gender conflicts have been ignored in other cases too. In Yugoslavia, feminists drew attention to increased oppression of women in the middle of the 1980s, a neopatriarchy that was "more pervasive and domineering than the old, traditional form" (see Barbara Jancar, "Neofeminism in Yugoslavia: A Closer Look," *Women and Politics,* 8:1 (1988), pp. 1–30. This was not heeded, however: See Ivan Siber, "Review of Research on the 'Authoritarian Personality' in Yugoslav Society," *Politics and the Individual,* 1:1 (1991), pp. 21–28; Sergej Flere, "Explaining Ethnic Antagonism in Yugoslavia," *European Sociological Review,* 7:3 (1991), pp. 183–93. The treatment of democrats is another typical early warning sign, for example, in Nazi Germany. See Kristian Ottosen, *Natt og tåke. Historien om Natzweiler-fangene* (Oslo: Aschehoug, 1989), p. 154.

32. The "mobbing/scapegoating" character of Nazi society is another important element in Goldhagen's findings that many ordinary Germans participated in the holocaust. It also seems to be a typical companion tendency of genocide/gendercide.

33. Ottosen, *Natt og tåke,* p. 39. Succeeding quotations from this work will be cited in this section by page number in the text.

34. See Kristin Skjørten, *Voldsbilder I hverdagen* (Oslo: Pax, 1994). In order to create a similar, but now sociological, sense of hysteria, the Nazis in 1939 started what they thought would be a limited takeover of Poland (in fact starting World War II) by mounting a mock attack on Germany by the Polish army, represented by Germans in Polish uniforms. When in doubt, fabricate a bigger lie—the classic Goebbels trick.

35. Probably this should be related not just to masculinity dynamics; it concerns patriarchal structure also. For example, one might consider the uncontrollability and increasing irrationality of a patriarchal structure like the Nazi high command in the last years of World War II.

36. Griffin, *Fascism,* p. 125 (emphasis added).

37. See Bourke, *An Intimate History of Killing.*

38. Based on unpublished material from the Alternatives to Violence Center, Oslo, and other sources.

39. On Sarajevo, see Cohen, *Hearts Grown Brutal.*

40. Svetlana Slapsak, "Hunting, Ruling, Sacrificing: Traditional Male Practices in Contemporary Balkan Cultures," in Breines et al., *Male Roles, Masculinities, and Violence.* On hunter/warrior rationalizations, see Bourke, *An Intimate History of Killing.*

41. See Ottosen, *Natt og tåke;* Kristian Ottosen, *Liv og død. Historien om Sachsenhausen-fangene* (Oslo: Aschehoug, 1990).

42. See Heinrich Fraenkel and Roger Manvell, *Goebbels. Hans liv og død,* translation of *Joseph Goebbels, His Life and Death* (Oslo: Aschehoug, 1960), pp. 36–37.

43. "Body fascism" is not well studied (after the early empirical research of Wilhelm Reich before he became an "orgone philosopher"), but see Theweleit, *Male Fantasies,* and more recently Frigga Haug and other feminist researchers' work on body memories.

44. See Øystein Gullvåg Holter, "Masculinities in Context: On Peace Issues and Patriarchal Orders," in Breines et al., *Male Roles, Masculinities, and Violence.*

45. See Grunberger, *Social History of the Third Reich,* p. 339.

46. Griffin, *Fascism,* p. 3.

47. Constantina Safilios-Rotschild, "The Negative Side of Development Interventions and Gender Transitions: Impoverished Male Roles Threaten Peace," in Breines et al., *Male Roles, Masculinities, and Violence.*

48. Ibid., p. 88.

49. Walter Rodney, *How Europe Underdeveloped Africa* (London: Bogle-L'Ouverture, 1983), p. 139.

50. John Boswell documents the broader male roles regarding sexuality (in a more empirical vein than Foucault's); John Gillis shows that early modern fathers took their caring and reproduction roles seriously; Clas Ekenstam and others show how men's legitimate emotional range was narrowed in the modernization process. See Boswell, *Christianity, Social Tolerance, and Homosexuality* (Chicago: University of Chicago Press, 1980); Gillis, "En reise gjennom faderskapets historie: er vi på feil spor?" *Kvinneforskning,* 1 (1995), pp. 14–31; and Ekenstam et al., *Rädd att falla: studier I manlighet* (Stockholm: Gidlunds, 1998).

51. See Carole Pateman, *The Sexual Contract* (Oxford: Polity Press, 1988) for a political analysis of the contractual element; I investigate current "market gender" from a similar perspective in Øystein Gullvåg Holter, *Raggning, kärlek och kønnsmarknad* (Stockholm: Hammarstrøm and Åberg, 1983).

52. Breadwinning meant so little in antiquity that a free man might well be the employee of a slave, or a slave might own the property used by a free man. It was held that work and economy should not "disturb" the politically oriented society of antiquity. See Moses Finley, *Ancient Slavery and Modern Ideology* (Harmondsworth: Penguin, 1983).

53. There is a large literature on how men in the terrible conditions of war go "beyond gender," no longer recognizing power and authority, trying to be fair and caring even in the most unlikely circumstances—and on how the military apparatus tries to coopt men's alienation as soldiers and redirect it toward murdering enemies (see Bourke, *An Intimate History of Killing*).

54. See Thomas Laqueur, *Making Sex: Body and Gender from the Greeks to Freud* (Cambridge: Harvard University Press, 1992).

55. Bourke, *An Intimate History of Killing.*

56. Studied mainly by anthropologists, couvade is a ritual or institution whereby women's pregnancy becomes a shared concern for men and women; local rituals often depict men as pregnant too.

57. The core political purpose is often brought out in political murders, like the murder of democratic leaders in newly independent states like Congo or Algeria—or even in the West, as with the murders of Robert Kennedy in the United States and

Olof Palme in Sweden. It is precisely those who combine democracy with social justice that cannot be tolerated. In the context of a culture of peace, these may serve as early warning signals.

58. See Slapsak, "Hunting, Ruling, Sacrificing."

59. Kristian Ottosen, *Kvinneleiren. Historien om Ravensbruck-fangene* (Oslo: Aschehoug, 1991), pp. 30–41.

60. Michael Kimmel, "Reducing Men's Violence: The Personal Meets the Political," in Breines et al., *Male Roles, Masculinities, and Violence.*

61. Hitler also held discussions with international industrialists like Henry Ford. Usually, the core political purpose is disclosed in the way big business is linked to the aggressive strategy.

62. The mythic core is identified by Roger Griffin, as discussed earlier. A mythic core is an agent that depends upon the use of in-depth symbolism, including such gender symbolism as mapped by some feminist researchers like Jorun Solheim. "I am afraid that a Bolshevik-Jew might rape my daughter—therefore I vote Hitler."

63. Slapsak, "Hunting, Ruling, Sacrificing," pp. 133–34.

64. Ibid., p. 132.

65. The Germans in the 1930s discussed the "Drang nach Osten" as a genetic trait of the Aryan superman. The core political purpose of quashing radical workers movements, the Bolsheviks and their agents, coincided with the dream of German empire.

66. The reactive segregation targets anyone in peripheral positions, as the peace theorist Johan Galtung's center/periphery model argues, and it may also be traced in "care chains," e.g., in the form of Filipino nannies in the United States, as Arlie Hochschild has recently argued.

67. This is why closing off "the class struggle" may not be such a good idea for the health of capitalism, even as we recognize that the antagonism of class and authoritarian variants of Marxism have often been partly responsible for this closure.

68. See Stuart Stein, "Geno and Other Cides," this volume.

4

Gender and Genocide in Rwanda

Adam Jones

Introduction

The gendering of the Rwandan genocide is perhaps more intricate and multifaceted than that of any holocaust in history. The claim is a bold one, but it can be sustained by considering the combination of factors specific to the events in Rwanda between April and July 1994:

- the enormous stress that traditional gender roles, especially masculine ones, were under when the genocide erupted;
- the prominence of women in perpetrating the genocide (a historically unprecedented feature, in terms of the scale and directness of the involvement);
- the bluntness of the *génocidaires'* appeals to gendered expectations and aspirations, again including women as active agents of the slaughter;
- the complex evolution of the genocide—from a tradition-bound gendercide targeting predominantly adult and adolescent males, as well as young and even infant boys (with many horrifically indiscriminate massacres as well), to a chronologically progres-

sive and culturally transgressive targeting of Tutsi women, elderly, and girl children;
- the substantial gender imbalance among those Rwandans who survived the holocaust, and the social, economic, cultural, and epidemiological implications of the gender-selective slaughter of males; and
- the pronounced gendercidal character of reprisals during and after the genocide by Rwandan Patriotic Front [RPF] forces and their allies and agents (also apparently contributing to the gender disproportion just noted).

Perhaps only the dimension of women's complicity is truly unique to Rwanda. Many of the other features have been evident in other genocides of the modern and pre-modern world: the Jewish and Armenian holocausts, for example, have also been powerfully "gendered" from the viewpoint of both the tormented and the tormentors.[1] But in its representation of *all* these characteristics, the Rwandan genocide cries out for a sustained analysis and an attempt, however preliminary, at synthesis.

Most of the following account is based on the five most significant human-rights reports on the Rwanda genocide published thus far in English: *Leave None to Tell the Story: Genocide in Rwanda* (1999) and *Shattered Lives: Sexual Violence during the Rwandan Genocide and Its Aftermath* (1996), both by Human Rights Watch; *Rwanda: Death, Despair and Defiance* (revised edition, 1995) and *Rwanda—Not So Innocent: Women As Killers* (1995), both by the UK organization African Rights; and the Organization of African Unity report *International Panel of Eminent Personalities to Investigate the 1994 Genocide in Rwanda and the Surrounding Events* (July 2000).[2] Until the truth and reconciliation commission established in 1998 by the Organization of African Unity delivers its findings and testimony, these are likely to be the most extensive accounts on record of what occurred during the terrible hundred-day bloodbath of April–July 1994. All make for agonizing reading. The 1200-page *Death, Despair and Defiance,* in particular, is relentless in its up-close depiction of the genocide (the reader who manages to make it through the chapter on "A Policy of Massacres"—some 300 pages long—is then confronted by another 300-page chapter entitled "Genocidal Frenzy"). In large part *because* of its detail and specificity, however, this African Rights report, above all other accounts of the Rwanda genocide, is foundational to our understanding of the events—and of their complex "gendering" in particular.

Gender and Crisis in Rwanda

The onset of renewed civil war in the early 1990s, and a prolonged drought, exacerbated Rwanda's far-reaching economic and social crisis. "Fragile at the start, the Rwandan economy had crumbled under the burden of the costs of war," writes Human Rights Watch:

> In 1990 war-related expenses accounted for 15 percent of the budget, but by 1993, they consumed some 70 percent of the operating expenses of the state. In 1993, agricultural production, the mainstay of the economy, declined 15 percent, partly because hundreds of thousands of displaced persons were no longer able to work their fields, partly because of poor weather conditions. Foreign assistance increased nearly 100 percent from 1989 to 1993, when it amounted to US $334 million, to which was added some US $130 million in direct emergency aid in 1993. The additional support notwithstanding, living conditions worsened dramatically, as per capita income that stood at US $320 in 1989 (nineteenth poorest in the world) fell to US $200 in 1993.[3]

This economic decline combined with a continuing crisis over available land to produce a *gender* crisis for younger Hutu men. The best appraisal of this phenomenon I have found is in the African Rights report *Death, Despair and Defiance,* which points out that "in Rwandese society, there were previously a number of options open to poor young men. These included (1) acquiring land from the older generation of farmers, (2) clearing new farmland on the hills, (3) migration to Uganda or Zaire to find work or land, (4) becoming a client of a wealthier or more powerful man and (5) obtaining formal employment, usually in the civil service." The authors note that "by 1990, most of these options were rapidly disappearing, or had gone altogether." The parceling of land resulted in smaller and smaller plots, or none at all, being distributed to male offspring; migration onto the agricultural frontier was progressively closed off by the expansion of tea plantations and other cash crops, which "deprived farmers of potential land for cultivation"; work in the bureaucracy, or for a patron, was increasingly sparse as a result of structural-adjustment programs imposed by the International Monetary Fund and World Bank.[4] "In 1991, there was a burst of recruitment into the expanding army, which absorbed twenty-five thousand young men, but this represented only a fraction of the unemployed, frustrated young Rwandese looking to the state to fulfil their aspirations for a job, and being disappointed."[5] It was also a measure that was prone to being rolled back under the terms of the 1993 Arusha peace accords, which would have forced both the Rwandan army and national police "to demobilize at least half their military personnel."[6]

I do not wish to suggest that the subsistence crisis generated by these factors and measures was unique to males. Rwanda in 1994 was one of the poorest countries in the world, with some 86 percent of its population living below the poverty line, and this situation affected women (and children, and the elderly) no less than young men. But for younger Rwandan males, the crisis was additionally an *existential* one: "Without land or employment, young men cannot advance in life, they cannot marry or achieve the social status of their parents."[7] When the genocide erupted, the temptation for Hutu men to kill their Tutsi counterparts and seize their land, cattle, money, and belongings must have been irresistible.

One might even argue that the genocide represented, to some extent, an attempt by Rwanda's "Hutu Power" extremists to solve the gender crisis of young Hutu men by making available resources (land and other property, positions in higher education, work in the bureaucracy and private industry, etc.) that the government itself could not otherwise provide for them. This would simultaneously bring about a "final solution" to the "problem" of the Tutsi minority in Rwanda, bolster the fragile legitimacy of the governing authorities, and diminish the threat posed to all Third World regimes by disenchanted young men.[8]

The gender crisis certainly helps to explain the type of propaganda and rhetoric directed toward the Hutu population by the regime and its genocidal allies in the mass media. It is probably no coincidence, for example, that the task of genocide was "sold" to the young men who would be its main implementers by referring to it as "work"—harkening back to "the communal work parties of the 1970[s] and '80s" that had perhaps fortified the self-esteem of the men involved even if they did little to line their pockets. "The word 'interahamwe' [the genocidal militia] itself was previously used for communal work parties; 'clearing the brush' originally referred to clearing land for cultivation and has subsequently been used for killing Tutsi; and the word 'work' itself has been used for the work—and often very physically demanding labour it is too—of killing."[9] One is not surprised to learn that the genocidal killers of April–June 1994, according to Human Rights Watch, "included many young men who had hung out on the streets of Kigali or smaller commercial centers, with little prospect of obtaining either the land or the jobs needed to marry and raise families. They included too thousands of the displaced who focused their fear and anger on the RPF and defined that group to include all Tutsi"[10]—or at least all Tutsi males.

Propaganda was also directed toward heightening the martial sensibilities of young Hutu males. "I know you are men . . . who do not let themselves be invaded, who refuse to be scorned," stated Hutu Power leader Léon Mugesera in his famously vitriolic speech of 1992. A hard-line military officer, "Commandant Mike Tango," followed Mugesera by calling for each commune to establish a battalion of "robust young men" to receive military training. "Hutu Power was to be implemented by [a] 'popular army of strong young men.' " Especially sought after were married males "who have something to defend," according to notes written by Théoneste Bagosara, perhaps the leading architect of the genocide, in September 1993.[11]

The organization and strategy underlying the genocide itself similarly played on younger-male aspirations and fears. Men who refused to participate were denounced as cowards: an official visiting one commune that was "negligent" in its genocidal duties asked "if there were no more men there, meaning men who could deal with 'security' problems themselves."[12] Hutu men seeking to flee combat with the RPF were scapegoated little less than ordinary Tutsis: "If you see deserters, arrest them wherever they are, even on roadblocks, and send them back to their barracks," demanded an announcer on Hutu hate-radio. "What are those *sons of dogs* fleeing from? . . . Let them save their country. They ought not to escape. Beat them up, refuse them food, drinks, take them to the authorities so that they can go back to the battlefield. . . . They have to fight and fight the enemy. . . . To flee is out of the question."[13]

The all-consuming emphasis on killing Tutsis presented significant opportunities for upward mobility to those within the armed forces and national police who were willing to serve as diligent *génocidaires*. Underlings at the prefectural and subprefectural levels could similarly rise above their superiors, establishing a primacy that "depended more on commitment to the killing than on formal position in the hierarchy. . . . This flexibility encouraged initiative and ambition among those willing to purchase advancement at the cost of human lives."[14] Even the power of *bourgmestres* (burgomasters) and other senior officials could be "trumped" by the newly empowered *interahamwe* militiamen who possessed superior weaponry and were key to the actual perpetration of the genocide. The new opportunities associated with the genocide extended to men at the very bottom of the social and economic chain. Gérard Prunier points out, in a powerful and implicitly gendered passage, that

> [the] social aspect of the killings has often been overlooked. In Kigali the *Interahamwe* and *Impuzamugambi* [militia] had tended to recruit mostly among the poor. As soon as they went into action, they drew around them a cloud of even poorer people, a *lumpenproletariat* of street boys, rag-pickers, car-washers and homeless unemployed. For these people the genocide was the best thing that could ever happen to them. They had the blessings of a form of authority to take revenge on socially powerful people as long as these were on the wrong side of the political fence. They could steal, they could kill with minimum justification, they could rape and they could get drunk for free. This was wonderful. The political aims pursued by the masters of this dark carnival were quite beyond their scope. They just went along, knowing it would not last.[15]

On many occasions, the mere promise of free beer—with its overtones of male bonding—was sufficient to draw men into the hunt. The organizers of the killing in Musebeya in Gigonkoro prefecture "went around from sector to sector to organize people. . . . They would buy drinks for everyone who helped them. Other people were told that if they joined in, they could get drinks bought for them as well. They said, 'You can get free beer. Come with us tomorrow [to kill Tutsis] and then you can join us at the bar.' Every evening there was a meeting there at the bar to expand their group."[16] Human Rights Watch notes that "the need for 'refreshments' was so important that the prefect of Kibuye requested a police escort for a boat bringing beer from the BRALIRWA brewery in Gisenyi to remedy 'the scarcity of drinks' in his prefecture."[17]

To summarize, the construction of the genocidal policy can be seen as deeply and intimately influenced by the desire to head off the threat that younger males, above all other demographic groups, pose to Third World regimes worldwide. The fear, moreover, seems to have been solidly grounded, as indicated by the increasing disorganization and indiscriminate violence and venality of the last stages of the genocide, in June–July 1994 (discussed further hereafter).

One final piece of evidence for this thesis can be cited: the choice of weaponry used in the genocide. For most observers, the machete became the very symbol of the Rwandan horror (at least two works—Human Rights Watch's *Leave None to Tell the Story* and Fergal Keane's *Season of Blood*—include the image on their front cover). In the 1993–94 prelude to the genocide, more than half a million machetes were imported, "or one for every third adult Hutu male in Rwanda."[18] Why were machetes supplied, rather than more efficiently destructive firearms? One reason was surely expense—but the fear of a well-armed younger-male population may have been equally significant. "The militias had been armed—but crudely," notes Prunier. "It was clear that if their masters had succeeded in their scheme, there would have been a law-and-order problem after the successful conclusion of the genocide and then a disarmament period. *Men with machetes are easier to disarm than men with firearms.*"[19]

April–July 1994: Genocide and Gendercide

In a passage from her provocative study of the witch-hunts in early modern England, *Malevolent Nurture*—it is in fact the concluding passage of the book—Deborah Willis develops her sophisticated gendering of the hunts with an important digression on "some of the most virulent of the twentieth-century 'witch-hunts,'" in which "violence has been directed against symbolic 'fathers' or other figures of authority." The trend is especially prominent "in countries where newly emergent but precarious ruling elites needed 'others' to blame for the serious economic or other problems they faced." The example she chooses is Stalin's purges in the USSR:

> During the 1930s and 1940s in Stalin's Soviet Union, leadership fractured at all levels, not only within Stalin's "inner circle" but also within local and regional party machines (paralleling in some ways the neighborly quarrels and religious controversies that divided early modern communities). As power oscillated between different factions, purges were carried out in the name of Stalin, "Father of the Country," "the Great and Wise Teacher," "the Friend of Mankind," against the antifathers and betraying sons who had perverted the socialist program, the "enemies with party cards." Underlying the psychology of the purges may have been, among other things, the magical beliefs of the Russian peasantry, still lively in the late nineteenth and early twentieth centuries, translated after the Revolution into the language of "scientific socialism." Rather than the female witch, however, it was the male possessed by evil spirits who anticipated the typical target of persecutory violence—the "evil spirits" of foreign, class-alien, or counterrevolutionary ideas. Demystified, secularized, stripped of his supernatural power, the great demonic adversary no longer needed to seduce a weaker [female] vessel but could walk among the elect as one of their own.[20]

Willis's comments are the only treatment I have found of the gendering of modern "witch-hunts," which in the twentieth century have overwhelmingly targeted adult males. (Indonesia in 1965 and 1966, East Pakistan/Bangladesh in 1971, Punjab/Kashmir, the Kurds in Turkey and Iraq, and the Balkans wars of the 1990s are just a few of the cases that could be added to the list.)[21] Willis's analysis also draws out a number of the key variables (social class, political affiliation) that typically combine with gender to produce gendercidal outcomes.

The demonization of adult Tutsi males, prior to and in the earlier stages of the Rwanda genocide, is precisely comparable. The insurgency of the Rwandan Patriotic Front spawned a climate of fear and vengefulness among both the Hutu Power elite and the Hutu population at large: all Tutsi men, and many Tutsi women, were viewed as a traitorous and counterrevolutionary "fifth column" (to the extent that Hutu Power saw itself as a "revolutionary" force securing the majority Hutu population against Tutsi attempts to reestablish their pre-1959 hegemony in Rwanda). "Search everywhere in the commune for the enemy," wrote the subprefect of Busoro, "because *he* is clever and can sneak in like a snake."[22]

The panic thus engendered—in both senses of the term—was critical not only to drawing the bulk of the Hutu population onto the side of the génocidaires, but also to determining how and against whom the genocidal rampage would be directed during its initial and most virulent stages. In short, the extermination of males, both Tutsi and oppositionist Hutu, served as a kind of "vanguard for the genocide as a whole, an initial barrier to be surmounted and 'threat' to be removed, before the remainder of the community is consigned to violent death." I am quoting here from comments I made on the Jewish holocaust as instigated on the eastern front during World War II.[23] In Rwanda as in the Nazi-occupied territories of the east, gendercidal atrocities against males served to acclimatize the killers to the killing: "Authorities first incited attacks on the most obvious targets—men who had acknowledged or could be easily supposed to have ties with the RPF—and only later insisted on the slaughter of women, children, the elderly, and others generally regarded as apolitical."[24] Implicit in this passage is that *all* males from groups deemed "oppositionist" were deemed ipso facto to be political, and therefore "fair game" for genocide: the apocalyptic witch-hunt that swept Rwanda in 1994 was, to repeat Deborah Willis's insight, gendered male. In the Nazi-occupied territories, as Daniel Jonah Goldhagen demonstrates in *Hitler's Willing Executioners,* the extension of the genocide from adult men to other population groups was accompanied by significant trauma on the part of the killers, leading eventually to the development of poison-gas technologies to reduce the culturally induced stress of murdering women, children, and the elderly. I will show later that much the same cultural constraints existed in the Rwanda case, resulted in similar stress to some of the killers, and may have played a role in blunting the genocidal impetus in the later stages of the slaughter.

It is certainly the case that when the genocide first erupted, Tutsi males —and many Hutu men of an oppositionist bent—understood immediately that they were at greatest risk. "As soon as I heard that [Rwandan President Juvénal] Habyarimana had been assassinated, I knew they would go for all Tutsis, especially Tutsi men," one survivor, Emmanuel Ngezahayo, told African Rights. Particularly vivid in the memory of Rwanda's Tutsi men was the pogrom of October 1990, which began—as did the 1994 genocide—with the imposition of a curfew. "I got scared as soon as I heard the word curfew" on the first day of the slaughter, recalled one young man, a student at the University of Butare who was in Murabi, Kibungo prefecture, at the time. "The curfew in October 1990 had been a disaster for Tutsi men. Thousands of them were arrested and thrown into prison. Some died. I feared the same thing would happen again." "It was simply not safe for a Tutsi man to be visible," another survivor, William Rutarema, recalled.[25]

To enter into a discussion of the gendering of the holocaust's victims is both a painful and a difficult exercise. The pain and difficulty alike arise from the widespread accounts of massacres in April 1994 that were both gargantuan in scale and largely indiscriminate in targeting Tutsi men, children, and women. One of these massacres, in fact, may qualify as the worst ground-level slaughter of the twentieth century, with another not far behind.[26] "On 20 April, at the Parish of Karama in Butare, between thirty-five and forty-three thousand people died in less than six hours"—a higher death toll than the Nazis' two-day slaughter of some thirty-three thousand Jews at Babi Yar in September 1941, and higher than the highest single-day extermination spree in the gas chambers of Auschwitz-Birkenau.[27] An even greater toll was exacted, though over a much longer period, in the weeks-long carnage on Bisesero Mountain in southwestern Rwanda, where "more than fifty thousand people . . . lost their lives" amidst heroic scenes of resistance. A number of other massacres, particularly in Cyahinda prefecture, claimed "ten thousand or more at one time."[28] In nearly all cases, the carnage seems to have been utterly indiscriminate—save, of course, for the overriding ethnic variable. ("They encircled the whole hill," recalled one survivor of Bisesero. "They shot and shot and shot. There was no distinction. Everyone died—adult men and women, young men and women and children.")[29]

And yet, the general thrust of the human-rights reportage suggests that, on balance, males were overwhelmingly targeted in the genocide's earliest and most virulent stages. The African Rights report *Death, Despair and Defiance* makes it clear that the early and most exterminatory weeks of the holocaust included both mass killings of the type just described, which left thousands or even tens of thousands of dead men, children, women, and the elderly strewn about the terrain; and a more selective and *gender-selective* targeting of males, notably those with wealth and education:

> The primary target of the hunt [for survivors of the opening massacres] were Tutsi men, particularly what extremist propaganda portrayed as the "ultimate" enemy—rich men, men between their twenties and forties, especially if they were well-educated professionals or students. Most hated of all were well-educated Tutsi men who had studied in Uganda (and to a lesser extent Tanzania and Kenya) who were immediately suspected of being members or supporters of the RPF.
>
> Within days, entire communities were without their men; tens of thousands of women were widowed, tens of thousands of children were orphaned.[30]

Many of these men and boys were killed in classic gendercidal massacres, such as the one in the parish of Mibilizi, Cyangugu prefecture, beginning on 20 April.[31] African Rights describes hundreds of interahamwe militia arriving at the church, where they "began the macabre 'favourite' game of the killers, selecting Tutsi men and boys for the slaughterhouse." Catherine Kanyundo, a sixty-year-old Tutsi woman, described what followed:

> They took all the men and boys, everyone masculine from about the age of two. Any boy who could walk was taken. They put them on one side. They were particularly interested in men who looked like students, civil servants, in short any man who looked as if he had education or money. They left only very poor men, those who were already wounded and tiny babies. Not even the very old were spared. They were all killed with machetes, spears and swords. They were killed nearby.

Kanyundo related the testimony of a peasant observer of the killings, who "told Catherine and the other female survivors that boys of thirteen to fifteen were killed by boys of their own age. The others were killed by groups. The first group beat them with sticks and clubs, the second group undressed them, the third group continued to torture them and the fourth group finished them off. The victims numbered about two thousand men and boys."[32]

At Sovu, Butare prefecture, at the local health center, some seven thousand refugees were assaulted on 23 April. In the words of one survivor, Domatile Mukabanza:

> At about 8:00 A.M., there was the final attack of the genocidal killers.... They shot and threw grenades until about 5:00 P.M. We saw that above all, the criminals were looking for men. The gendarmes arrived [around 5:00 P.M.] and stopped the killing. They grouped us together, saying that they were going to assure our security. But when we arrived on the Butare-Gikongoro road, they forced us to sit down on the grass. Some of them wanted to finish us off. There was not a single man amongst us. I don't think a single Tutsi man had escaped. They obliged us to go back to Sovu Health Centre where we spent the night in the middle of the corpses.[33]

At the Collège St. André in Kigali, "a string of massacres" occurred from 9 to 13 April, also ruthlessly gendercidal in their targeting of adolescent and elderly males, along with those of "battle age."[34] Likewise, refugees who arrived in early and mid-June at St. Paul's Church in Kigali found that it "was not a safe haven for Tutsi men.... On 14 June, a large group of militiamen arrived in search of Tutsi men to kill, particularly businessmen, professionals, students and any able-bodied male who they thought would join the RPF. They did not look at ID cards but took anyone who 'looked Tutsi,' in the process killing three young Hutu men who were tall. They killed fifty-nine Tutsi men." At Kamarampaka Stadium in Cyangugu prefecture, "the killers would periodically come with a list of refugees who were taken and killed nearby. The victims that were sought after were men, particularly educated or wealthy men." A survivor of the killings at the Kabgayi detention camp, where some thirty thousand terrified Tutsis congregated, described "the interahamwe [who] came and took people away to be killed, especially young men." "Men and young boys were killed regularly just behind the toilets," one survivor remembered. "After they had killed nearly all the young Tutsi men and boys, they started looking for young Tutsi women to rape. Four other young men and I survived because we were working with the Red Cross and others in the kitchen. But altogether, few able-bodied Tutsi men were left.... No young women were killed."[35]

In the case of children, males were again at particular risk: "The extremists were determined to seek out and murder Tutsi boys in particular. They examined very young infants, even new-borns, to see if they were boys or girls. Little boys were executed on the spot. Sometimes they ordered mothers to kill their children. . . . In what can only have been a horrific unending nightmare, older boys were relentlessly hunted down. Many mothers dressed their little boys as girls in the hope—too often a vain hope—of deceiving the killers. The terrified boys knew exactly what was happening." The boys were particularly targeted, according to African Rights, "on the basis that they will be tomorrow's RPF soldiers. 'Paul Kagame [then-RPF rebel leader, now Rwandan president] was also three when he left the country' is the phrase that preceded the cold-blooded murder of thousands of little Tutsi boys. Little Tutsi girls were spared with the comment that 'they can be married off to our boys.'"[36] Indeed, the opening blast of the genocide was accompanied by an injunction not to repeat the "mistake" of the 1959 revolution, when male children had apparently been spared, only to return later as guerrilla fighters.[37]

One of the best indicators of the special vulnerability of men and boys is the frequency with which relatives and friends sought to disguise them in women's clothing. The African Rights report *Death, Despair and Defiance* cites a number of examples of such procedures, which are reminiscent of similar practices followed in the Bosnian and Kosovan conflicts of the 1990s. One such account comes from Kamarampaka Stadium, where, as at all the "death camps, the favourite occupation of the soldiers and militia guarding the stadium was to select Tutsi men to be killed." On 12 May, a group of army officers and gendarmes arrived at the stadium "with a list indicating the men that were to be taken away that day. No one answered to the names." One occupant, Théodore Nyilinkwaya, recalled a typical gendercidal massacre at the stadium:

> Since they did not know the faces of the people they wanted, people were able to hide. Women concealed men by lending them their clothes. Absolutely no one responded to the names they called out. They became furious. They called for all men to come out and form lines. So the men had no choice. They asked them to show their identity cards. This was just theatrics since there were only Tutsis in the stadium. They looked closely at the faces, seeking out educated men and those who "looked" wealthy. They asked between twenty and thirty men to step aside. No one could refuse because the orders were given at gun point. They were taken

> to Gatandara, about one kilometre away, and killed by the militia with machetes.[38]

The gender-selective tradition of corvée labor in Rwanda assisted the génocidaires in targeting Tutsi males. It allowed them, first of all, to round up Hutu men for "work" at the infamous barricades that sprang up everywhere in the first hours and days of the genocide. "All men worked at the barriers," noted a resident of Musebeya, Gikongoro prefecture. "This was required. It was organised by the councilor of the sector who compiled a list of those who would work. He would go to the families and write down the name of the head of the family and all those boys over eight years old. . . . Anyone . . . who did not do patrols was an enemy." Anyone displaying noncompliance "will have shown that *he* is an enemy and *he* will be prosecuted by the authorities," noted a *bourgmestre* in Butare.[39]

Tutsi males were also instructed to turn out to "man" the barricades. This was nothing more than an "effort to lure Tutsi men to their deaths. . . . Many Tutsi men who were not warned in time were murdered at the very checkpoints where they had been assuring the security of their communities." "From the evening of the 7th [of April], interahamwe would come to your home and say, 'Let's go. You are going to man the roadblock,'" recalled Angelo Nkurunziza, an employee with the Kigali office of the U.S. Agency for International Development. "A few steps away from your house, they would kill you."[40]

Likewise, gendered role expectations dictated the behavior of Tutsis who sought safety in numbers on hilltops, or at churches and other centers (or who were channeled there by those who would later annihilate them). Numerous eyewitness testimonies record the sieges of such communities, in which younger males were thrust to the forefront of the fighting and died en masse. Often—perhaps usually—this was merely the prelude to a root-and-branch extermination of all the occupants of the facility in question. On some occasions, the killers may have been satisfied with slaughtering the male defenders, at least for the time being. In any case, the men were nearly always attacked first.[41]

A subject that deserves closer investigation is the possibility that men were overrepresented among the populations that gathered on strategic hilltops, where many of the worst genocidal massacres took place. The evidence for this is extremely sparse, but there are interesting fragments of testimony from Sovu in Butare prefecture, where one of the largest gendercidal massacres took place at the local health center on 23 April, as mentioned earlier. The men targeted in that assault had not originally sought sanctuary in the health center. Rather, as the genocide erupted, "adult males and young men decided to stay on the hill and obliged us, the women, girls and children, to go and take refuge toward the Health Centre of Sovu."[42] As noted, the gendercidal slaughter in this case took place at the health center, not on the hilltop. But, again given gendered role expectations, it is perhaps intuitively likely that other such scenes occurred in Rwanda, as Tutsi menfolk (recognizing themselves to be the prime targets of the génocidaires) placed themselves in the firing line, while seeking to ensure that other members of the population found at least temporary refuge. We must set against this the extensive testimony from Bisesero and other sites, which certainly suggests a sizable representation of children, women, and elderly among the hilltop populations. But if the decisions taken at Sovu were, in fact, repeated elsewhere, they may help to account for the some of the gendercidal atrocities against men, and the resulting disparities in the death toll.

Women were also far more likely than men to receive "mercy" from the killers, though often at the price of surrendering themselves sexually to their captors, as we will see. Marie Leimalda Munyakazi described a house-to-house search during the killing campaign in Kigali. "One of the Presidential Guards . . . said I had to die. He took me and other women hiding in the house outside. A soldier from Butare who I knew happened to pass by. He asked what the fuss was about. The Presidential Guard replied 'These women are rebels and must be killed.' The soldier looked at him and asked 'How can these women be a threat to you? If you want rebels, go and fight the RPF. They are in Gikondo and Rebero [districts in Kigali].'" Reflecting the patrilineal character of Rwandan society, Tutsi women were frequently viewed as "less" Tutsi than their men—or capable of being "liberated" from their ethnicity by rape and forced concubinage. At the St. Famille Church, scene of repeated gendercidal massacres, interahamwe told the duplicitous Abbé Wenceslas "to separate the Tutsis from the Hutus. They also told him that next time it would be the women's turn. Wenceslas told them that the women were not a problem as they did not have an ethnicity. He said the bad ones were the men."[43] In Gikongoro prefecture, meanwhile, "killers . . . told a woman that she was safe because 'sex has no ethnic group.'"[44]

I conclude this section with a brief polemic. The clear evidence of a gendercidal targeting of males casts into severe disrepute the many subsequent attempts to rewrite history and depict women as the principal targets of the genocide. Leading the way in this regard was the UN special rapporteur on Rwanda, René Degni-Ségui, who stated in January 1996 that women "may even be regarded as the main victims of the massacres, with good reason, since they were raped and massacred and subjected to other brutalities."[45] Here the "good reason" for passing an untenable comparative judgment is the fact that women suffered enormously; there is no serious attempt to evaluate the scale of their suffering by comparison with men. Christopher Taylor, in his important work *Sacrifice As Terror*, goes so far as to claim that "Tutsi women were killed during the 1994 genocide in numbers equal to, if not exceeding, those of men."[46] Aloysia Inyumba, in her analysis "Women and Genocide in Rwanda," offers up a truly spectacular self-contradiction, in consecutive sentences no less: She claims that "The genocide in Rwanda is a far-reaching tragedy that has taken *a particularly hard toll on women.* They now comprise 70 percent of the population, since *the genocide chiefly exterminated the male population.*"[47] Such comments typify the general trend in discussions of "gender" and human rights, which tend to take women's disproportionate victimization as a guiding assumption, indeed as a virtual article of faith.

Men: Willing and Unwilling Executioners

As noted earlier, the reporting on the Rwandan genocide is full of vignettes of men who saw the holocaust—as they had been encouraged to—as an unprecedented opportunity to claim power and property. Their preening swagger rapidly came to terrify even the Hutu general population and the extremist leadership. It typified the pathological machismo that is usually central to the perpetration of genocide, and that the authorities, well aware of its murderous potential, had hoped to channel and control:

> A failed student turned killer, Shalom [Ntahobari] became a big man in Butare once the slaughter began. He swaggered around town with grenades hanging from his belt, often armed with a gun which he once aimed in insolent jest at a local burgomaster. One witness asserted that even military officers saluted Shalom. He controlled his own barrier in front of the family house near the university campus where he bullied his militia subordinates as well as passersby. One witness who had known Shalom as a fellow student witnessed him killing a man in order to rob him of his cattle. This was only one of numerous murders Shalom was said to have committed.[48]

Other men seem to have been motivated by a genuine fear that the RPF/Tutsis were about to seize control in Rwanda and implement a genocide of their own—a fear bolstered by the massive slaughter of Hutus (overwhelmingly males) in Burundi in 1972, and the new round of killings there at the hands of the Tutsi-dominated army in 1993. In Butare, "the authorities had no difficulty recruiting men for the self-defense training. According to one participant, people [men] fought for the opportunity to participate. Some no doubt were motivated by real fear and desire to protect their homes from the threat so dramatically depicted by the government."[49]

In many other cases, men participated only reluctantly, as numerous accounts from the barricades make clear. Adolescent males—sometimes even younger boys—were also coerced into killing. A ten-year-old named Ndayambaje described being ordered by a local councilor to murder another young boy: "The councillor was holding a machete and a *masu* [nail-studded club]. He beat a boy with the flat part of the machete. Then he said to me 'Either you kill him or you will fuck your mother.' Still, I did not understand what I would have to do. The person he was beating was a boy slightly older than me. He had already clobbered him and wanted me to finish him off. He gave me a *masu* and told me to kill him after insulting me."[50] Ndayambaje complied, later confessed, and was interviewed in the central prison of Butare.

As younger men were the vanguard of the victims, acclimatizing the killers to the task of genocide, they were also—perhaps uniquely—the vanguard for other population groups, including women, to join in the genocidal mayhem. "Soldiers taught hesitant young people to kill on the streets of Kigali," notes Human Rights Watch; "When the young people balked at striking Tutsi, soldiers stoned the victims until the novices were ready to attack." "In the commune of Shyanda on April 22, as the burgomaster and councilors were holding a meeting in one place to persuade people to remain calm, soldiers were passing over the next hill ordering others to burn, pillage, and kill. . . . Several returned to Shyanda a few days later to threaten men at a barrier for not having killed enough Tutsi. The civilians responded to the intimidation by seizing several Tutsi for execution."[51]

I argued earlier that, in both its aims and its logistics, the genocide against Tutsis and moderate Hutus displayed an overriding fear of the threat posed by younger Hutu males to the autocratic and, eventually, extremist-dominated government. That this danger was not chimerical was shown in the final stages of the genocide, when "the more stable and established citizens withdrew" from their assigned duties, and "the militia and young men from the 'civilian self-defense' program increasingly dominated the barriers and the patrols":

> They sometimes were armed with guns and grenades and had received enough training in military skills to intimidate others. With far fewer Tutsi to be caught, they spent more time harassing, robbing, and killing Hutu passersby. The minister of [the] interior asked those at the barriers and on patrols to "use better judgment and not confuse the guilty with the innocent." Several days later, the prefect of Kibuye reported to him that young people [men?] at a barrier tried to help themselves to the beer and tobacco from passing trucks that belonged to an important government official. The prefect had intervened to protect the goods, but, he commented, the incident showed "that there are people [men?] who still do not understand the role of the barriers." Burgomasters and members of the councils of several communes expressed their anger at the abusive young men who controlled the roads and paths of their communities. One critic remarked later, "It is a good thing that the RPF arrived when it did. The thugs were beginning to take over."[52]

Clearly, the gendered gamble of the génocidaires—that they could discipline and exploit younger men's frustrations and aspirations as long as was necessary to perpetrate the slaughter, then rein them in—was proving a losing one as the genocidal impetus petered out. It is possible that, had the RPF not succeeded in taking power when it did, Hutu rule in Rwanda might have degenerated into the situation familiar to us from images of life and death in Somalia, Sierra Leone, and Liberia: armed gangs of young men taking direction only from local or regional "warlords," and inflicting violence and intimidation indiscriminately on the civilian population.

Women as Victims

All authorities who address the matter agree that one of the defining features of the 1994 genocide in Rwanda was the removal of previous restrictions on killings or severe abuse of Tutsi women. There is thus a strong consensus that "in the past Rwandans had not usually killed women in conflicts," as Human Rights Watch phrased it, though they were by no means invulnerable to slaughter on these earlier occasions.[53]

The genocidal atrocities meted out to Tutsi women during the holocaust reflected the intricate gendering of these targets in the period prior to 1994.

As with male victims, a class variable was prominent. Tutsi women had long been depicted, by both Hutus and Tutsis, as a female "elite" on the grounds of their average greater stature, education, and alleged physical beauty. At the same time, they were depicted as a population of potential Mata Haris, ready to use their supposed sexual advantage to subvert the nation. Christopher Taylor argues in *Sacrifice As Terror:*

> Hutu extremists harboured enormous psychological ambivalence toward Tutsi women. On one hand Tutsi women were despised for their potential subversive capacity to undermine the categorical boundary between Tutsi and Hutu. On the other hand, many Hutu extremist men were unable to completely shed feelings of attraction toward Tutsi women. Of colonial origin, the representation of Tutsi women as superior in intelligence and in beauty to Hutu women appears to have plagued the psyches of Hutu extremists. Envy and resentment are perhaps the most social of emotions. When these emotions concern traits like intelligence and physical beauty, they are not easily expunged.[54]

Tutsi women's vulnerability was heightened by the claimed linkage between their sexual charms and the desires of the foreign, notably Belgian, troops stationed in Rwanda under the terms of the Arusha accords. Hutu Power propaganda cartoons, for example, regularly depicted Tutsi women embracing Roméo Dallaire, commander of UNAMIR, the UN Assistance Mission in Rwanda ("General Dallaire and his army have fallen into the trap of fatal women"), or sexually servicing Belgian paratroopers (often in culturally transgressive ways).[55]

As Taylor has also pointed out, something of a "gender crisis" existed in male-female relations at the time of the genocide, mirroring on a lesser scale the crisis of younger Hutu males. "To many Rwandans gender relations in the 1980s and 1990s were falling into a state of decadence as more women attained positions of prominence in economic and public life, and as more of them exercised their personal preferences in their private lives. Complex sexual politics preceded the genocide and were manifest in it."[56] This may help to account not only for the lifting of taboos against the mass murder of women, but also for Hutu women's conscription and (frequently) ready participation in the slaughter—a reflection, in its macabre way, of women's greater independent agency in the Rwandan social equation. The added element of Hutu women's "subordination" to Tutsi women was doubtless a powerful motivation for the atrocities these Hutu women would inflict on other women, a point addressed further later in this chapter.

Most of the women (and girl children) who perished in the genocide appear to have been killed in four major contexts: (1) they were family members of Tutsi or Hutu men targeted from lists, especially during the opening wave of "eliticide";[57] (2) they were swept up in the root-and-branch genocidal massacres that consumed Rwanda in the first weeks of the genocide; (3) they had separated themselves from, or been separated by, male members of the community in the tragically mistaken belief that they would be spared;[58] or (4) they were annihilated, along with girls and the elderly, as the only Tutsis remaining after the gendercide against males had been largely completed (and after they themselves had experienced protracted rape and sexual servitude as the price of their temporary survival; see "Genocidal Rape" later in this chapter). Of these different contexts, by far the largest number of women and child victims perished in root-and-branch slaughters. But large numbers were also murdered in locales where they had sought sanctuary while men fled to the hills or heroically faced their attackers. A young housewife, Claudine Muteteyimana, described one such slaughter to African Rights investigators in May 1994, as the genocide was still raging. Muteteyimana had taken refuge at the St. Joseph's School in Rwamagana, Kibungo prefecture:

> I was in a room with many other women and children. They [the interahamwe] shattered the windows and walked in. They started firing at us. I was immediately hit by a bullet in my right leg. Dozens of women fell down dead around me. They dragged the survivors through [*sic*] the floor, beating them as they did so with *masus*. Others they did not even bother to drag. They just hacked them to death. This was done right in front of us. While some interahamwe were busy with the killings, others were looting everything in sight.
>
> After this scene of butchery, they went to the private residences of the religious people who run the school[,] some of whom had already fled. There were two other women who had been badly wounded but were still alive, though in agony. They came back and finished them off with machetes. That left me.[59]

An important unanswered question is whether, and when, an official decision was made to target women, along with the elderly and children. The Human Rights Watch report *Leave None to Tell the Story* claims that "in many communities, women and children who had survived the first weeks of the genocide were slain in mid-May. . . . The number of attacks against women, all at about the same time, indicates that a decision to kill women had been made at the national level and was being implemented in local communities."[60]

It is certainly true that in the early stages of the genocide, a degree of official exemption was frequently granted to women. "The law for killing Tutsi women has not yet been passed," one interahamwe told a female survivor, Patricia Musabyemariya, in April. "But the law for killing Tutsi men and boys has been passed."[61] Moreover, the vast number of gender-selective killings of males in the early stages of the genocide attests to centralized and localized policies aimed at consigning Tutsi males to mass slaughter, and at exempting other community members for the time being. But there are difficulties with the idea of a mid-May campaign against women. The most obvious is that, whatever the "official" policy might have been, a blanket exemption was hardly granted to females in the first five or six weeks of the genocide. In fact, they were killed by the tens of thousands. Moreover, the Human Rights Watch researchers acknowledge that the evidence for a mid-May order is only "indicat[ive]." African Rights, meanwhile, records the testimony of one female survivor that the *bourgmestre* of Gikongoro prefecture "in May . . . declared that there was *no longer* a need to kill women."[62]

It is at least possible that the evolution of the genocide depicted in *Leave None to Tell the Story* and several other sources is mistaken: that in terms of centralized policy, the opening blast of the genocide—which all accounts suggest was overwhelmingly targeted at Tutsi and Hutu males—was in fact followed by a stage in which attempts at root-and-branch extermination of Tutsis were pursued, although authorities at the prefecture, commune, and cell levels may have inhibited or countermanded this program to some extent.[63] This second stage, in which tens of thousands of women, the elderly, and girl children were killed along with a disproportionate number of men and boys, may then have given way to a "lull" in which gendercidal strategies against remaining males were hotly pursued. This, in turn, may have been followed by a fourth stage, the renewed killing campaign of May–June, in which Tutsi survivors—who by this time included very few adult and adolescent males—were targeted.

There are intriguing indications that attempts to exterminate women, girls, and the elderly eventually encountered significant popular opposition—that, in fact, it was *this element* of the campaign that largely gave rise to increasing disorganization and disorientation among the forces of genocide. "In the later part of May and in June," notes Human Rights Watch, "administrators found ordinary people were deserting the barriers and refusing to do the patrols. . . . In permitting or directing the slaughter of the weak, the elderly, women, and infants, who posed no threat to anyone,[64] authorities discredited the justification that killing was an act of self-defense. Prefects pressed burgomasters who pressed councilors who pressed the citizens to carry out their assigned duties, but with shrinking success." In Butare, "the decision by the interim government to push the genocide ever deeper into the community undermined its authority. People found it hard to believe that women, children, and the elderly and infirm posed the same threat as *armed soldiers* [unarmed men]. . . . The authorities found that the legitimacy which they had used at the start to cover the genocide had been consumed during the course of the killing campaign and that they no longer had the authority to control the assassins whom they had armed."[65]

Genocidal Rape

In recent years, the phenomenon of the mass rape of women in ethnic and other conflicts has attracted a flood of attention from feminist scholars. The inquiry, which arguably began with Susan Brownmiller's discussion of mass rapes in East Pakistan/Bangladesh during the genocide of 1971,[66] was substantially deepened with the onset of the wars in the former Yugoslavia and the rape of tens of thousands of women, mostly Bosnian Muslims assaulted by Serbian regular and irregular forces.[67]

The rapes of Rwandan Tutsi women were on a vastly greater scale than those in the former Yugoslavia. Both in their murderous dimension—with rape frequently followed by killing, either immediately or after a period of forced sexual servitude—and in the element of savage mutilation, they bear comparison with the genocidal rampage of the Japanese army in Nanjing in 1937 and 1938.[68] The UN special rapporteur on Rwanda, René Degni-Ségui, noted that in atrocities against Tutsi women, "rape was the rule and its absence the exception"; he offered the staggering estimate of 250,000 to 500,000 rapes committed during the twelve weeks of the genocide.[69] "Again and again, rape is reported as an act of extreme brutality," notes Elenor Richter-Lyonette. "Objects are said to have been used to cause extra pain, and rapes with objects are said to include among others rapes with stones, with branches from trees of bushes, with weapons. Rape accompanied by mutilation is reported to include: the pouring of boiling water onto the genital parts and into the vagina in order to create pain and ordeal, the opening of the womb to cut out the unborn child before the killing of the mother, the cutting off of breast(s) and the mutilation of other parts of the female body." Even rapes of female cadavers were not unknown.[70]

In many cases, rape and forced sexual servitude were accepted, or desperately sought, as the price of evading slaughter. The male (and sometimes female) perpetrators of this sexual slavery generally fed off stereotypes of Tutsi women as uniquely seductive and desirable. There was clearly an element of "class revenge" involved for the "uneducated thugs [who] had moved into villas surrounded by televisions, videos and nice furniture," and who now "wanted a beautiful woman to complete their victory." "It is terrible to see highly educated girls, some of them university graduates or at university, being forced to go with such specimens of the human race," lamented a Hutu man in Kigali who had helped Tutsis attempting to escape the genocide.[71] One Tutsi woman who survived, "Juliana," related the accounts given by a Hutu family that had witnessed women being "taken to the roadside and forced to watch the killing of Tutsi men, after which they would be given lectures by one of the key killers, one Karaguye":

> They said he told them, "You Tutsi women, you have no respect for Hutu men. So now, choose between death and marriage to a Hutu interahamwe." . . . Then they went looking for the most filthy-looking vagabonds, jigger-infested and God knows what else. They looked for the kind of man who was least likely to get a woman under normal conditions. There were so many women that they could not find enough of these dirty men. But so intense was the fear of being killed that the women would plead and ask these men to take them.[72]

As feminist scholarship has increasingly grappled with rape as a tool of "ethnic cleansing," the term "genocidal rape" has achieved considerable currency. The justification offered is that, even if rape does not lead or is not intended to lead to death, it aims to undermine the security and cohesion of the targeted community (in part by shattering the self-confidence of community males who are unable to protect "their" women from the atrocities). This, in turn, terrorizes entire communities into leaving their homes; and the bonds among community members may be further undermined when women bear the ethnically mixed offspring of rape at the hands of men from other ethnic communities.

Some have bridled at this direct equation of rape with genocide.[73] Rape, it may be contended, must involve killing (as at Nanjing) in order to qualify as "genocidal." Against such an argument, it can be proposed that the prevailing usage is fully in line with the UN Convention on Genocide (1948), which does *not* require deaths among members of the targeted community: genocide can involve "causing serious bodily or mental harm to members of the group," "deliberately inflicting on the group conditions of life calculated to bring about its physical destruction in whole or in part," and "imposing measures intended to prevent births within the group." All of these may be facilitated or implemented by the rape of community women.[74]

In the Rwandan context, moreover, rape frequently *was* followed by killing, or was the means of bringing it about. Here we must attend to a regularly overlooked aspect of the mass rapes: the threat of AIDS associated with them. "It appears that at least some 35% of Rwandese soldiers were HIV-positive before the genocide of 1994," a figure that "seems to be very much in line with . . . other African armies,"[75] and which may have held true for the interahamwe killers and other men who participated in genocidal atrocities.[76] The testimony of women survivors is replete with expressions of concern about the possibility of having contracted AIDS from the rape and sexual servitude to which they were exposed.[77]

Acts of genocidal rape may thus bring about the death of victims many years after the genocide itself has "ended." I have argued elsewhere that this phenomenon is likely to become ever more prominent in cases of mass killing and genocide, given that "most of the current cases of largescale rape in conflicts are in sub-Saharan Africa (Sierra Leone, the Democratic Republic of Congo, Angola), in areas that also lie at the heart of the 'AIDS belt.'"[78] In the Rwandan case, the risk is compounded by the apparent heavy underrepresentation of males in the country after the 1994 events. I return to this issue later in discussing the aftermath of genocide and gendercide in Rwanda.

Genocidal Women

"I had seen war before, but I had never seen a woman carrying a baby on her back kill another woman with a baby on her back," said a UNAMIR officer, interviewed in 1996.[79]

As noted in the introduction to this chapter, the Rwandan holocaust is unique in the annals of genocide for the prominent role that women played as organizers, instigators, and followers. The major source on this phenomenon is the African Rights report *Rwanda—Not So Innocent: When*

Women Become Killers, published in August 1995. The organization—bravely, it must be said—countered the standard trend of portraying women as inherently or automatically the "main" victims of the genocide. This stereotype, it claimed, had contributed to "obscuring the role of women as aggressors."[80]

It is clear that many women were coerced into participating in the genocide by the "wide array of policies [developed by the extremists] . . . to cajole and frighten the population into a killing frenzy." But as the African Rights investigators noted, "When it came to mass murder, there were a lot of women who needed no encouragement."[81] Indeed, one can speculate that *a greater proportion of women than men participated voluntarily in the killings,* since it was men, almost exclusively, who were forcibly conscripted into the "work" of the roadblock killings, and who were exposed to suspicion or violent retribution if they did not take part. Evading direct participation was probably much easier for Hutu women (and children) than for Hutu men.

Perhaps the most notorious case of a female génocidaire is Pauline Nyiramasuhuko, who, in a grotesque twist, served as minister for women and family affairs in the Hutu Power regime. Nyiramasuhuko "regularly visited places where refugees had been congregated and personally supervised the selection of hundreds of Tutsi men for the slaughterhouse." Among the other female architects of the genocide were:

> **Rose Karushara**, a councilor in Kigali, who "took an extremely active role in the genocide, wearing military uniform throughout. A tall and physically strong woman, she used to beat up the refugees herself before handing them over to her interahamwe for the final kill. . . . At least five thousand people were killed, all thrown into the Nyabarongo river under orders from Karushara."
>
> **Odette Nyirabagenzi**, "the terror of Rugenge" (a sector of Kigali): "As soon as the genocide began, Odette sent her militia in pursuit of the Tutsi men of Rugenge. Her thugs hunted for Tutsi men in St. Famille and St. Paul's [parishes], as well as the missionary language centre of CELA. She was physically present on every occasion when men were taken out of these churches and CELA and massacred. She took an active part in selecting the men who were to die."
>
> **Athanasie Mukabatana**, "a teacher at the School of Nursing of Kaduha [Gikongoro prefecture]. . . . When this girl saw the attack arrive near the hospital, she quickly jumped over the gate of the hospital to get into the

compound. She didn't even wait for the gate to be opened. You [could] see the enthusiasm this girl had for finishing off these sick Tutsis. She had a machete and went into the hospital with the other assassins. She made all the sick Tutsis go out, often dragging them out. And once outside, she killed them with a strike from the machete. She made several trips and all the dead were on the hospital grass."

Sister Julienne Kizito, one of a number of nuns who played key roles in genocidal atrocities. She was "accused of working directly with the killers [in Butare], standing in their midst while they massacred refugees, handing out jerrycans of petrol which were used in her presence to burn people alive."[82]

These cases of female leaders represent only a small part of the story of women's participation in the genocide. At the grassroots, "very often, groups of women ululated their men into the 'action' that would result in the death of thousands of innocent men, women and children, many of them their own neighbours." Their role was dominant in the postmassacre looting and stripping of bodies, which often involved climbing over corpses (and those still alive and moaning in agony) piled thigh-high in the confined spaces in which many Tutsis met their end. Frequently these women assisted in administering the coup de grâce to those clinging to life.[83] Women (especially, it seems, prostitutes) were also prominent as spies, denouncing Tutsis and moderate Hutus in hiding to the interahamwe; according to African Rights, Hutu women were no more likely than men to grant refuge to those seeking to flee the holocaust.[84] They participated in the street-level gauntlets that terrified Tutsis had to run: "Anyone who felt like hitting me, hit me with whatever they had in their hand," recalled one male survivor, François Régis Jabo Bugwiza. "I was even beaten by women on their way to fetch food." And they helped to keep interahamwe and government forces suitably drunk for their genocidal activities, as at the Kabgayi death camp, where "there was a woman permanently outside the camp who sold beer and other things to the soldiers," in the words of one survivor.[85]

Women additionally played an important role in pressuring younger Tutsi women to accept their designated fate as sex slaves and concubines for Hutu militia members and other men. Pauline Nyiramasuhuko, for example, kept "the daughters of Bihira, a Tutsi businessman from Butare, . . . at her house for [her son] Chalôme to rape."[86] One woman survivor, "Juliana," described her capture by a young man named Marcel, after which she faced a "court of women" in which "all his female relatives became involved." Marcel's mother "brought some elderly women to the house to insult and intimidate me. These women accused me of being childish. One of them said 'Many women of your kind have been taken by dog-like vagabonds. And here you are, rejecting this nice young man. . . . What are you waiting for?' "[87]

It is far from clear whether these genocidal women directed the majority of their atrocities against Tutsi women; but to the extent that they did, there appears to have been a kind of gendered jubilation at the "comeuppance" of Tutsi females, who had for so long been depicted in Hutu propaganda as Rwanda's sexual elite. Otherwise, the motivations for women's involvement as genocidal killers frequently paralleled those of Hutu men: bonds of ethnic solidarity ("it was as if all the men, women and children had come to kill us," recalled one Tutsi survivor from Sovu);[88] suasion and coercion by those in authority (including other women); the lure of material gain; and the intoxicating pleasure of untrammelled sadism, "liberated" from the normal constraints of one of the most tightly managed and micro-administered societies on earth.[89]

Aftermath of Gendercide

"Rwanda has become a country of women," Human Rights Watch contended in its 1996 report *Shattered Lives: The Aftermath of Sexual Violence in Rwanda.* "It is currently estimated that 70 percent of the population is female and that 50 percent of all households are headed by women."[90]

There are three important points to note about this claim that the genocide resulted in a staggering demographic disproportion of men versus women. First, the statistic has usually been presented as evidence of *female disadvantage*—i.e., to call attention to the fact that the overwhelming majority of survivors are females. This would appear to require that some attention be devoted to the gendercidal atrocities against Rwandan males; but the focus of the Human Rights Watch report is violence against women, and the targeting of males is skated over in a vague and rather shameful fashion: "*As a result of the genocide,* many women lost the male relatives on whom they previously relied for economic support and are now destitute." Second, it is intriguing to note that in some commentary, the claim that the Rwandan population is 70 percent *female* has been subtly transformed into the assertion that it is 70 percent *women*—clearly a demographic impossibility, but not one that has troubled certain authors.[91] Lastly, no commentator citing these estimates (and here I must regretfully include myself) apparently bothered to ask an obvious question: How could such a skewed demographic pattern possibly be explained by genocidal atrocities against Tutsi males, when the Tutsi minority constituted between 8 and 12 percent of the total population in 1994?[92] Even a total extermination of Tutsi males, and the corresponding survival of the entire Tutsi female population, could not produce a postgenocidal society that was 70 percent female, or anywhere close.

The explanation appears to be fairly straightforward: The estimate was exaggerated, and a substantial proportion of the males presumed dead were, in fact, only temporarily absent from the country. According to Heather Hamilton:

> Shortly after the genocide it was estimated that 70 per cent of the Rwandan population was female, reflecting the greater number of men killed in the genocide and the large number of ex-FAR [Rwandese Armed Forces] and militia men who had fled the country. That figure is still sometimes quoted today, although it is quite out of date. Thanks to the return of millions of refugees and those living in the diaspora, the figure today is closer to 54 per cent. If we focus on economically active women (by subtracting the young and old) the telling figure is that more than 57 per cent of the population is female. But even this figure does not tell the complete story, since some 150,000 men are in the army or in jail awaiting trial.[93]

This depiction is more in keeping with a genocide that predominantly targeted Tutsi males. It also suggests a substantial underrepresentation of *Hutu* men. This is a point that cannot be addressed in detail here but is worth considering briefly, since the disparity may derive in part from the RPF's apparent duplication of Hutu Power's gendercidal strategies, both during the rebel invasion of Rwanda and in the immediate aftermath of the 1994 holocaust. The atrocities inflicted by the vengeful, predominantly Tutsi forces of the RPF included a number of indiscriminate slaughters, such as the mid-April attack on a "mixed group of hundreds of civilians and militia at the hill Kanazi [which] killed all except three persons," and neighborhood sweeps at Murambi (Byumba prefecture) where the RPF "killed seventy-eight persons, of whom forty-six were listed as children."[94] But gender-selective massacres of adult males (including prisoners of war) appear to have predominated.[95] And the gendercidal component, if anything, seems to have become more prominent during the subsequent period, in which the RPF sought to consolidate its newly won national power: "The RPF wanted to establish its supremacy," recalled ex-RPF minister of the interior Seth Sendashonga, "and to do so they had to eliminate any potential rival. In many cases the Army came for men, ages 18 to 55, and took them away by night, never to be seen again. Their families search for them in vain, in the prisons of Rwanda, but they all died at the hands of the Rwandan Patriotic Army."[96]

Whatever the precise extent and underlying causes of the demographic disparity in post-1994 Rwanda, however, it is clear that it is substantial. According to the important "International Panel of Eminent Personalities" report issued in 2000 by the Organization of African Unity,

> By 1999, 34 per cent of households were still headed by women or minors (usually female), an increase of 50 per cent over the pre-genocide period. The great majority of those women had been widowed by the war or the genocide. . . . Soon after the genocide ended, more than 250,000 widowed victims registered with the Ministry of Family and Women in Development. Most had lost not only their husbands, but also their property. By 1996, the government was faced with about 400,000 widows who needed help to become self-supporting. Since the new regulations of post-genocide Rwanda made it impermissible for government operations to ask about ethnic identities, it is not known how many of these women were Tutsi and how many Hutu.[97]

The yawning gender gulf will have a long-term social, cultural, and epidemiological impact. Two specific effects can be noted: transformations in patterns of marriage and cohabitation, and the further exacerbation of the AIDS crisis in the country. On the first score, Judy El-Bushra states: "A major issue of concern to women in Rwanda is the impact of the demographic imbalance on marriages. Polygamy, which is not legally permitted in Rwanda, is often suggested as a means of solving the problem of the large number of widows and younger women whose prospects of marriage have become drastically reduced. Rivalry between women over potential husbands has become common, and an issue which sparks off heated debate."[98] And David Gough of the UK *Guardian,* reporting from Gitarama prefecture ("scene of some of the worst excesses in 1994"), points out that the demographic deficit of males in Rwanda—like the genocidal rape of women—has important implications for the spread of AIDS. "With so many men killed during the genocide, or later imprisoned for their part in it, . . . the practice of sharing men, known as *kwinjara,* has become so widespread . . . that health officials say that it represents the greatest challenge to their efforts to combat the spread of AIDS. 'If a woman has land and maybe some money then she can attract the services of young men,' said Jerome Ndabagariya of CARE. 'He does some work for her in the field and then some more work in the bedroom.' A more affluent woman will give a man some food, maybe some beer or, in rare cases, money. In return he may well give her the AIDS virus."[99]

Conclusion: Rwanda in Comparative Perspective

> Focusing solely on ethnicity has tended to obscure sex and gender. In examining Rwandan attitudes and representations of gender, it becomes clear that gender psychology, gender politics, and gender symbolism played a more important role in preparing the terrain and in shaping the violence than . . . has heretofore been suspected.[100]

The Rwandan holocaust offers important evidence that "gendering" genocide can provide powerful insights into the outbreak, evolution, and defining character of genocidal killing. For this approach to bear full fruit, however, the "gendering" must be both *methodical* and *inclusive.* In particular, any investigation that implicitly equates "gender" with "women" is likely to leave a vast analytical terrain untouched or poorly explored. This is not to say that specific inquiries into women's plight and experience are to be abandoned. They may provide a wealth of useful information and policy recommendations, especially given that women/females are likely to constitute the majority or large majority of a genocide's survivors.[101] But if such analyses are not accompanied by others that consider gender-specific and gender-selective aspects of the *male* experience, they can tell us at best half of the story. Moreover, such commentary as exists on gender and genocide has tended to *actively suppress* the male experience, with the aim, in most cases, of increasing the sympathy and policy attention extended to female victims. Such an approach should be seen as a betrayal of the spirit of human-rights work, which is based on the fundamentally equal worth of all those targeted for abuses and atrocities.

The gendering of genocide in Rwanda bears comparison with many of the worst atrocities of the twentieth century. In the Armenian and Jewish holocausts; the annihilation of Soviet prisoners of war during World War II; the massive slaughters in East Pakistan/Bangladesh and Indonesia; and the gendercides in Bosnia and Kosovo, a pattern of *initial* targeting of males is inescapably evident. The role of antimale gendercide as a "tripwire" or "onset phase" of genocide should be one of the most powerful analytical weapons of anyone seeking to predict, confront, and end genocides. However, the Rwandan genocide, as we have seen, cannot be integrated into this framework without qualification: the elderly, children, and women were all swept up in the slaughter from its very first hours, though much less systematically than adult and adolescent males.

If the pronounced "gendering" of the Rwandan slaughter is nonetheless to be surveyed for the analytical and policy-relevant insights it may offer, so too should the gendering of the killers be considered. We have seen that the period leading up to the genocide was characterized by government policies aimed both at mobilizing younger males to become genocidal killers, and at *defusing* the potential threat to the regime from this same demographic group. Scholars of genocide should be extraordinarily sensitive to the kind of gendered propaganda, rhetoric, and public policies that emanated from the Rwandan regime between late 1990 and early 1994. Both the fear of younger-male "volatility" in the face of such a crisis, and the attempt to harness this volatility for genocidal ends, may have broad comparative relevance.

The extensive role of women in perpetrating the Rwandan genocide is apparently unique in recorded history, which makes it difficult to derive many comparative insights from the phenomenon. Nonetheless, the prominence of genocidal women may have a certain *predictive* value, one that is profoundly relevant to the ongoing debate over women, peace, and conflict.[102] The evidence presented here suggests that when women are provided with positive and negative incentives similar to those of men, their degree of participation in genocide, and the violence and cruelty they exhibit, will run closely parallel to those of their male counterparts. One must ask, in fact, whether "the Rwanda test" does not substantially refute the equation of women and peace that has dominated much of the aforementioned debate. If women anywhere can participate in genocide on such a scale, and with such evident enthusiasm and savagery, then it seems a valid prima facie assumption that they are capable of such participation everywhere. The search then becomes one not for some essential "difference" in women's approach to war and peace, but for the range of cultural and policy mechanisms that either allow or, more frequently, inhibit the expression of women's aggressive and genocidal potential. Useful additional evidence for this inquiry may be sought in other cases where women have participated significantly in genocidal or proto-genocidal activities—as in the Armenian[103] and Jewish holocausts, and the Hindu extremist movement in India.[104]

If males tend to be disproportionately targeted in genocide, then women tend to be disproportionately the survivors, and this opens up a host of important questions and subject areas in the fields of humanitarian intervention and international human-rights policies. Feminist and human rights scholarship has done much to draw our attention to the gender-specific needs and concerns of women survivors, but it has standardly ignored or skated over the gendercides against males that produce such situations.[105] Systematic attention to the male experience is clearly called for and seems no less policy-relevant. Humanitarian interventions, for example, must supplement their attention to the special vulnerabilities of women and girls with a recognition of the particular vulnerabilities of men and boys. Memories are still fairly fresh of the UN debacle at Srebrenica, when UN soldiers actively colluded with Serb forces to evacuate children and women to safe havens in Muslim-controlled territory, leaving thousands of Bosnian men to be rounded up and executed en masse.[106] The Rwandan case offers a glaring example of the failure to incorporate an inclusive gender analysis in such interventions. At the St. Famille Church in Kigali, refugees ostensibly under the protection of UNAMIR (the UN Assistance Mission in Rwanda) were systematically harassed and decimated by interahamwe raids. Finally, in early June, the UN organized an evacuation; but as a female refugee, Gorette Uwimana, reported, the UNAMIR forces "put the names [of the refugees] in alphabetical order and when they came to evacuate they did so in this alphabetical order." This approach failed to take into account the fact that "there were some refugees who were more at risk than others, particularly Tutsi men and boys who should have been evacuated first," something that "was out of the question for UNAMIR." On 17 June, after the first evacuation convoy had left, "more than one hundred Tutsis," nearly all male, were selected out of the crowd and executed nearby. Thereafter, "almost all the Tutsi men were finished."[107]

It is my hope that this chapter has contributed to a more balanced appraisal of the gendering of the Rwandan holocaust than has predominated so far. There seems a great deal to be learned not only by applying the gender variable in the Rwandan case, but by applying it *inclusively*—that is, by extending the framing to males as well as females. This judgment would seem to hold, as well, for most other genocides in history. Only when a gender-inclusive approach is adopted, it seems, can this important variable in mass killings worldwide be properly understood, and integrated into an overarching analysis of one of humanity's greatest and most enduring blights.

Notes

I am grateful to the following people for comments on an earlier version of this chapter: David Buchanan, R. Charli Carpenter, Øystein Gullvåg Holter, Jo and David Jones, Christopher Taylor, and colleagues in the Division of International Studies at the Center for Research and Teaching in Economics in Mexico City.

1. See the case studies of the Armenian and Jewish holocausts on the Gendercide Watch website at *www.gendercide.org/case_armenia.html* and *www.gendercide.org/case_jews.html.*

2. African Rights, *Rwanda: Death, Despair and Defiance,* rev. ed. (London: African Rights, 1995); African Rights, *Rwanda—Not So Innocent: Women As Killers* (London: African Rights, 1995); Human Rights Watch, *Leave None to Tell the Story: Genocide in Rwanda* (New York: Human Rights Watch, 1999); Human Rights Watch, *Shattered Lives: Sexual Violence during the Rwandan Genocide and Its Aftermath* (New York: Human Rights Watch, 1996), *www.hrw.org/hrw/reports/1996/Rwanda.htm;* Organization of African Unity, "International Panel of Eminent Personalities to Investigate the 1994 Genocide in Rwanda and the Surrounding Events," 7 July 2000, *www.oau-oua.org/Document/ipep/ipep.htm.*

3. Human Rights Watch, *Leave None to Tell the Story,* p. 122.

4. These structural-adjustment measures exacerbated the employment problem still further, especially for men: They "not only choked off any possibility of new recruitment into the bureaucratic pyramid, but threatened the jobs of those who were already there. Low-ranking officials in the villages—including administrators, teachers, agricultural extension workers, health workers and policemen—saw their prospects of promotion vanish, and even faced the possibility of losing their jobs altogether. Employees in parastatals who had thought that they were guaranteed a position for life were similarly overcome by uncertainty." African Rights, *Death, Despair and Defiance,* pp. 20–21.

5. African Rights, *Death, Despair and Defiance,* pp. 19–21.

6. Human Rights Watch, *Leave None to Tell the Story,* p. 125. "Many soldiers were angry that Habyarimana had yielded to foreign pressure [at Arusha] when the army had not been decisively defeated," write the authors. "Soldiers disavowed the accords for personal as well as for political reasons. With the planned demobilization, many would lose the chance to live relatively well—from exactions if not from salary"

(ibid.). The organization also notes that talk of "using demobilized soldiers in economic development projects, such as draining marshes to obtain new land for cultivation," only "incensed the soldiers further; it was just such menial labor that they thought they had left behind in their new military careers" (p. 60).

7. African Rights, *Death, Despair and Defiance,* p. 20. Elenor Richter-Lyonette points out that the "landlessness frequent among young men . . . [made] them vulnerable to taking compensatory action. . . . The hope for a redistribution of wealth in one's favour was a distinct incentive for the commitment of acts of genocide, particularly with the landless, unemployed youth." "Women after the Genocide in Rwanda," in Richter-Lyonette, ed., *In the Aftermath of Rape: Women's Rights, War Crimes, and Genocide* (Givrins: Coordination of Women's Advocacy, 1997), p. 106.

8. Human Rights Watch hints at such a strategy when it notes that "in a clear effort to divert the resentment otherwise directed towards Hutu from Habyarimana's region, propagandists argued that it was Tutsi, not other Hutu, who occupied the jobs which southern Hutu wanted and failed to get. They also accused the Tutsi of having taken a disproportionate share of places in secondary school and university and, because of their educational advantages, of having dominated the professions and government." *Leave None to Tell the Story,* p. 74.

9. African Rights, *Death, Despair and Defiance,* pp. 55, 76. It is also interesting, in this context, that as numerous survivors reported, the "work" was carried out according to a strict regimen, imitating the clock time that governed labor in the formal economy: "They came exactly at 7 A.M. each morning, just like government employees. They worked until 5 P.M. and then came back the next morning at 7 again." Witness to the killings at Cyahinda, quoted in Human Rights Watch, *Leave None to Tell the Story,* p. 390.

10. Human Rights Watch, *Leave None to Tell the Story,* p. 261.

11. Ibid., pp. 84, 139, 104–5.

12. Ibid., p. 459.

13. Quoted in African Rights, *Death, Despair and Defiance,* p. 82 (emphasis added).

14. Human Rights Watch, *Leave None to Tell the Story,* p. 222.

15. Gérard Prunier, *The Rwanda Crisis: History of a Genocide* (New York: Columbia University Press, 1997), pp. 231–32.

16. Survivor's testimony cited in Human Rights Watch, *Leave None to Tell the Story,* p. 343.

17. Ibid., p. 244. African Rights also reports that numerous broadcasts of Radio-Télévision des Mille Collines (RTLM) during the genocide "refer to the use of drugs" in an approving way—certainly one of the few instances in the history of broadcasting in which a station has proselytized for the use of narcotics, but another indication of how integral was organized intoxication to the successful perpetration of the genocide. *Death, Despair and Defiance,* p. 83 (n. 38).

18. Human Rights Watch, *Leave None to Tell the Story,* p. 127.

19. Prunier, *The Rwanda Crisis*, p. 243 (n. 53; emphasis added).

20. Deborah Willis, *Malevolent Nurture: Witch-Hunting and Maternal Power in Early Modern England* (Ithaca, N.Y.: Cornell University Press, 1995), pp. 244–45.

21. For detailed treatments of these case studies, see the Gendercide Watch website, *www.gendercide.org*.

22. Human Rights Watch, *Leave None to Tell the Story*, p. 419 (emphasis added). The report draws out some of this paranoia, with its overtones of deeply ingrained superstition: "The 'enemy' who was everywhere was extraordinarily cruel, according to the [Hutu Power] propagandists. . . . [Valérie] Bemeriki [an announcer on RTLM] charged the RPF with cannibalism, saying they killed people by dissecting them and cutting out their hearts, livers, and stomachs. On the air and in public meetings, officials and political leaders also contributed to this sense of a people besieged by a heartless enemy. In an April 15 broadcast, the minister of defense charged the RPF with 'extreme cruelty,' saying that it had massacred 20,000 people and had burned people with gasoline at Nyamirambo in Kigali." On 16 May 1994, as a new round of genocidal atrocities was being prepared, an announcer on RTLM "introduced the novel allegation that RPF soldiers ate the hearts of their victims" (ibid., pp. 255, 643).

23. See Adam Jones, "Gendercide and Genocide," this volume.

24. Human Rights Watch, *Leave None to Tell the Story*, p. 11.

25. African Rights, *Death, Despair and Defiance*, pp. 587, 385, 646.

26. That is, a slaughter not caused by aerial bombing.

27. African Rights, *Rwanda—Not So Innocent*, p. 26. Human Rights Watch gives a death toll of forty thousand at Karama (*Leave None to Tell the Story*, p. 488). "The highest 'output' attained by Auschwitz was 34,000 bodies, in one continuous day and night shift." Eugen Kogon, *The Theory and Practice of Hell* (Berkeley: University of California Press, 1980), p. 241.

28. Human Rights Watch, *Leave None to Tell the Story*, p. 488.

29. African Rights, *Death, Despair and Defiance*, pp. 662–64. "The very first massacre of the genocide" was similarly indiscriminate, at least from a gender perspective: it occurred at the Centre Christus, Kigali, at 7 A.M. on 7 April, an hour after the official announcement of President Habyarimana's death. "The victims were priests, seminarians, visitors and staff." Of the seventeen people killed, eight were "young women belonging to the order Vita and Pax who were on retreat; four diocesan priests who had been meeting there; a visiting social worker; three Jesuit priests and the cook" (ibid., p. 863).

30. Ibid., pp. 597–98.

31. One of the most detailed and disturbing accounts of gendercidal atrocities against Tutsi males was provided by Liberata Mukasakindi, a resident of Musambira commune in Gitarama prefecture; it is too long to quote here. See African Rights, *Death, Despair and Defiance*, pp. 625–26.

32. Ibid., p. 522.

33. African Rights, *Rwanda—Not So Innocent,* p. 165. The attack was supervised by Sister Julienne Kizito of the Sovu monastery.

34. Eyewitness testimony of Hamidou Omar, cited in African Rights, *Death, Despair and Defiance,* p. 561. Another survivor, Eugène Byusa, said: "Looking at the bodies, we understood that they decided to kill the men only. There were male bodies everywhere—bayoneted, macheted, speared and knifed to death" (p. 564).

35. African Rights, *Death, Despair and Defiance,* pp. 587, 603, 455, 717.

36. Ibid., pp. 815, 798.

37. Ibid., p. 39.

38. Ibid., pp. 725, 729. See also pp. 613, 625, 738.

39. Human Rights Watch, *Leave None to Tell the Story,* pp. 324, 528, 508 (emphasis added).

40. African Rights, *Death, Despair and Defiance,* pp. 603–4.

41. Sample testimony to this effect in *Death, Despair and Defiance* includes the following: "The men who had put up the resistance were the first to be exterminated. Women and children sat on the ground. All they could do was to pray" (Nyamasheke parish, Cyangugu, p. 466).

42. Survivor's testimony cited in African Rights, *Rwanda—Not So Innocent,* p. 158. Two other survivors provide identical accounts (pp. 170–71, 173). See also Human Rights Watch, *Leave None to Tell the Story,* p. 537: "On April 17 and 18, women in the area had taken refuge in the Sovu health center, while men had stayed on the hills to fight off attackers."

43. African Rights, *Death, Despair and Defiance,* pp. 676, 692.

44. Human Rights Watch, *Leave None to Tell the Story,* p. 296. See also the testimony from Gashora refugee camp, where the genocide began relatively late: "The first targets were rich Tutsis, but also able-bodied young men. Initially they were not interested in women[,] saying that women did not have an ethnic group." African Rights, *Death, Despair and Defiance,* p. 648. Likewise, at the monastery in Sovu, one woman who watched her husband and children hacked to death was told by one of the killers "that it was man who gave birth and not woman, to confirm that my children were Tutsi." African Rights, *Rwanda—Not So Innocent,* p. 181.

45. Quoted in Richter-Lyonette, "Women after the Genocide," p. 106.

46. Christopher Taylor, *Sacrifice As Terror: The Rwandan Genocide of 1994* (Oxford: Berg, 1999), p. 154. The assertion is repeated in slightly different form on p. 176. In neither case is supporting evidence supplied.

47. Aloysia Inyumba, "Women and Genocide in Rwanda," in Richter-Lyonette, *In the Aftermath of Rape,* p. 49 (emphasis added). Considering the postgenocide situation of women, Swiss researcher Elenor Richter-Lyonette conjures a similarly dramatic absurdity: "After the genocide, the vast number of women and girls reaching marriage age have no legal chance to marry. The tremendous number of widows of

all ages compounds the problem. It is not the women who are the problem, the problem lies with the promiscuity of men"—not with the *extermination* of men, apparently. Richter-Lyonette, "Women after the Genocide," p. 108. Jeanne Kadalika Uwonkunda recognizes that "the [Rwandan] massacres specially targeted men" but nonetheless alleges that "it is women in particular in Africa who feel the terrible consequences of genocide, massacres, and war. They are largely unprepared to assume all the new responsibilities that fall on their backs"—again, as a result of the disproportionate extermination of males, a point which might lead one to conclude that it is *men* in particular "who feel the terrible consequences." In John A. Berry and Carol Pott Berry, eds., *Genocide in Rwanda: A Collective Memory* (Washington, D.C.: Howard University Press, 1999), pp. 159–60. For another example, in a different context, of such "thinking," see the comments by then U.S. first lady Hillary Clinton: "Women have always been the primary victims of war. Women lose their husbands, their fathers, their sons in combat." "First Lady Hillary Rodham Clinton, First Ladies' Conference on Domestic Violence, San Salvador, El Salvador, November 17, 1998 (As Delivered)," at *www.whitehouse.gov/WH/EOP/First_Lady/html/generalspeeches/1998/19981117.html.*

48. Human Rights Watch, *Leave None to Tell the Story*, p. 508.

49. Ibid., p. 519.

50. African Rights, *Death, Despair and Defiance*, p. 852.

51. Human Rights Watch, *Leave None to Tell the Story*, pp. 224, 503.

52. Ibid., pp. 297–98. In Nyakizu commune, Butare prefecture,

> the young people at the barriers "attacked anyone if he looked like he had money." The young people took identity cards from those whom they assaulted, tore them up and then killed the victims. Older members of the community complained that young men who had been trained in the use of arms were "so undisciplined that they have become completely ungovernable." Even when not working at the barriers or on patrol, they hung about on the roads, playing cards and looking for someone to victimize. At a meeting of the security committee in early June, participants complained that at Nyagisozi these men "profit from the situation to create disorder, above all by stopping passersby and taking from them whatever they have on them." . . . The young men also pillaged crops in the fields left by the Tutsi and sometimes vandalized crops that were not yet ripe. (pp. 426–27; see also pp. 572–73).

53. Ibid., p. 296. See also Taylor, *Sacrifice As Terror*, pp. 154, 176. Much more research needs to be done on the "gendering" of the violence in these previous genocidal outbreaks; available sources in English are sparse.

54. Taylor, *Sacrifice As Terror*, p. 177. As Taylor also points out (pp. 174–75), the first three of the infamous Hutu "Ten Commandments," promulgated in 1990, addressed themselves to the lure of Tutsi women and the dangers they posed to Hutu men: "1. Every Muhutu [Hutu male] should know that wherever he finds Umututsikazi [a

female Tutsi], she is working for her Tutsi ethnic group. As a result every Muhutu who marries a Mututsikazi, or who takes a Mututsikazi for a mistress, or employs her as a secretary or a protégéé [*sic*] is a traitor. 2. Every Muhutu should know that our Bahutukazi [female Hutu] are more worthy of, and conscious of their roles as woman, spouse, and mother. Are they not pretty, good secretaries, and more honest! 3. Bahutukazi, be vigilant and bring your husbands, brothers, and sons back to the path of reason."

55. See the examples reproduced in ibid., pp. 172–73.

56. Ibid., p. 157; see also the discussion at p. 161, describing "a wave of repression against young urban Rwandan women who either dressed too stylishly or had European boyfriends."

57. In some cases women were considered "significant" targets in their own right and were killed at the same time as oppositionist males and their families. The best-known case is that of Rwanda's prime minister, Agathe Uwilingiyimana, who was viewed as "having morally and materially demobilized" the Rwandan armed forces in their struggle against the RPF (in the words of the leading architect of the genocide, Col. Théoneste Bagosora). She was killed in the first hours of the genocide, and the ten Belgian peacekeepers who had been dispatched to protect her were disarmed, tortured, and murdered shortly afterward. See Human Rights Watch, *Leave None to Tell the Story,* pp. 187–92.

58. At the Adventist Church in Ngoma, "the men's plan to save women and children by placing them in the church" failed; the attackers killed them all. At the parish of Nyundo, "The women and the children stayed in the chapel," according to a male survivor. "The men stayed outside. . . . But then the bandits attacked us unexpectedly and we dispersed. They did not pursue us but went directly to the chapel. Without any hesitation, and in a cowardly fashion, they killed all our women and children." African Rights, *Death, Despair and Defiance,* pp. 446, 550. It appears also to have been true that males thrust to the forefront of the fight against attackers, in general a position that exposed them to disproportionate risk, could sometimes more easily *escape* from confined areas than the women, children, and elderly moved to the rear; or that males, being fleeter of foot, had a better chance in general to evade the killers. See, for example, the description of the mass killing at the church of Cyahinda, where one male survivor reported: "It was easier for us at the front who had been fighting to escape because we could see better what was happening. The overwhelming [number of] victims were those at the back—elderly people, women and children. They had no chance of escape." At the commune office in Gishari: "Most of the victims were women and children. They could not run as well as the men and were not able to avoid the grenades so well either." Quoted in ibid., pp. 341, 380.

59. Ibid., p. 388.

60. Human Rights Watch, *Leave None to Tell the Story,* p. 296.

61. Quoted in African Rights, *Death, Despair and Defiance,* p. 641. See also the

account of "Catherine," a Tutsi woman who survived rape and incarceration. She describes a "law" being passed by a bourgmestre, apparently as early as mid-April (the timeline of her testimony is not fully clear), "that men who had 'married' Tutsi women since the recent events should hand them over to be killed. . . . This law was passed because there were no more Tutsis to be killed except the Tutsi women who were being kept" (p. 773).

62. Ibid., p. 299 (emphasis added).

63. See, for example, the account of the massacre at the Nyakanyinya primary school: "On Friday the 15th, the interahamwe of the sector of Cyato came, looking for women and girls of their sector. They said that in their area, there was a decision to spare females." Ibid., p. 487.

64. The statement appears to accept the rationale of the génocidaires that unarmed Tutsi males *did* pose a threat.

65. Human Rights Watch, *Leave None to Tell the Story,* pp. 297, 555 (emphasis added).

66. See Susan Brownmiller, *Against Our Will: Men, Women, and Rape* (New York: Bantam, 1975).

67. The best single source is Alexandra Stiglmayer, ed., *Mass Rape: The War against Women in Bosnia-Herzegovina,* trans. Marion Faber (Lincoln: University of Nebraska Press, 1994).

68. For a summary of the Nanjing events, including their gendercidal component against both women and men, see Gendercide Watch, "Case Study: The Nanjing Massacre, 1937–38," *www.gendercide.org/case_nanking.html.* For a more detailed treatment, see Iris Chang, *The Rape of Nanking: The Forgotten Holocaust of World War II* (New York: Penguin, 1998).

69. Cited in Richter-Lyonette, "Women after the Genocide," p. 107.

70. Ibid.

71. Testimony of Emmanuel Sagahutu, cited in African Rights, *Death, Despair and Defiance,* p. 750; the preceding quotes in this passage are also from Sagahutu's account.

72. Ibid., pp. 753–54. African Rights investigators provided pseudonyms to all women who recounted their testimonies of rape and forced concubinage.

73. See, for example, Rhonda Copelon, "Surfacing Gender: Reconceptualizing Crimes against Women in Time of War," in Lois Ann Lorentzen and Jennifer Turpin, eds., *The Women and War Reader* (London and New York: New York University Press, 1998), p. 64: "The elision of genocide and rape in the focus on 'genocidal rape' . . . [is] dangerous. Rape and genocide are separate atrocities. Genocide—the effort to destroy a people—[*sic*] based on its identity as a people evokes the deepest horror and warrants the severest condemnation. Rape is sexualized violence that seeks to humiliate, terrorize, and destroy a woman based on her identity as a woman. . . . To emphasize as unparalleled the horror of genocidal rape is factually dubious and risks

rendering rape invisible once again." Stuart Stein expresses similar skepticism in his contribution to this volume (see Stein, "Geno and Other Cides").

74. See the discussion in R. Charli Carpenter, "Forced Maternity, Children's Rights, and the Genocide Convention: A Theoretical Analysis," *Journal of Genocide Research*, 2, 2 (June 2000), esp. pp. 224–27.

75. Richter-Lyonette, "Women after the Genocide," p. 107.

76. Since the Rwandan army did not fight outside its borders, there is no reason to assume that its members were more likely to be exposed to the HIV virus than were other Rwandan men.

77. See African Rights, *Death, Despair and Defiance*, pp. 761, 781, 795.

78. Jones, "Gendercide and Genocide," this volume.

79. Human Rights Watch, *Leave None to Tell the Story*, p. 261.

80. African Rights, *Rwanda—Not So Innocent*, p. 4.

81. Ibid., p. 27.

82. Ibid., pp. 2, 11, 50–51, 117–18 (the passage following the ellipses is a survivor's testimony), 126, 157.

83. Ibid., pp. 72, 81.

84. "There is no evidence that women were more willing to give refuge to the hunted than men. . . . Scores of Tutsi women and young girls . . . were rescued or assisted in their hiding places by men who had been family friends, neighbours or acquaintances. Many of them were turned out of Hutu homes by women who often threatened to inform the interahamwe if their husbands continued to shelter these women or took any additional steps to assist them." Ibid., pp. 2, 73.

85. African Rights, *Death, Despair and Defiance*, pp. 713, 716. See also African Rights, *Rwanda—Not So Innocent*, p. 219.

86. African Rights, *Rwanda—Not So Innocent*, p. 92.

87. African Rights, *Death, Despair and Defiance*, pp. 92, 754–55.

88. African Rights, *Rwanda—Not So Innocent*, p. 174.

89. "When one looks at Rwanda, one should forget about images of easygoing tropical confusion. . . . Administrative control was probably the tightest in the world among non-communist countries." Prunier, *The Rwanda Crisis*, p. 77.

90. Human Rights Watch, *Shattered Lives*, p. 2.

91. See, for example, the quote from Aloysia Inyumba on page 112; also Judy El-Bushra, "Transforming Conflict: Some Thoughts on a Gendered Understanding of Conflict Processes," in Susie Jacobs, Ruth Jacobson, and Jennifer Marchbank, eds., *States of Conflict: Gender, Violence, and Resistance* (London: Zed Books, 2000), p. 73.

92. I cited the *Shattered Lives* estimate without critical comment in my article "Gendercide and Genocide" as originally published in *Journal of Genocide Research;* I have removed it for publication in this volume.

93. Heather B. Hamilton, "Rwanda's Women: The Key to Reconstruction," *Journal of Humanitarian Assistance*, January 2000, p. 1.

94. Human Rights Watch, *Leave None to Tell the Story,* p. 704.

95. See, for example, ibid. pp. 705, 707, 715, 717–18, 720–22.

96. Quoted in *Chronicle of a Genocide Foretold,* vol. 3, pt. 3 (Video production, Ottawa: National Film Board of Canada, 1997).

97. Organization of African Unity, "International Panel." The quoted passages are drawn from chapter 16, "The Plight of Women and Children," *www.oau-oua.org/Document/ipep/report/rwanda-e/EN-16-CH.htm.*

98. El-Bushra, "Transforming Conflict," p. 74.

99. David Gough, "Husband-hiring Hastens the Spread of AIDS in Rwanda," *The Guardian,* 8 February 2000.

100. Taylor, *Sacrifice As Terror,* p. 184.

101. There are notable exceptions, most prominently the Jewish holocaust. See the discussion in Jones, "Gendercide and Genocide," this volume, and the Gendercide Watch case study at *www.gendercide.org/case_jews.html.*

102. The African Rights report *Rwanda—Not So Innocent* explicitly positions itself in this debate; see p. 7. A good recent contribution, which includes a review of the literature, is Mark Tessler et al., "Further Tests of the Women and Peace Hypothesis: Evidence from Cross-National Survey Research in the Middle East," *International Studies Quarterly,* 43 (1999), pp. 519–31.

103. I am thinking here of the prominent role played by Kurdish tribeswomen in attacking and looting the caravans of dispossessed Armenians.

104. For an excellent overview of women's role in the Hindu extremist movement, see Parita Mukta, "Gender, Community, Nation: The Myth of Innocence," in Jacobs, et al., *States of Conflict,* pp. 163–78.

105. In the Rwandan context, the most detailed treatment is the Human Rights Watch report *Shattered Lives.*

106. The definitive account of the Srebrenica massacre is David Rohde, *Endgame: The Betrayal and Fall of Srebrenica* (New York: Farrar, Straus and Giroux, 1997).

107. African Rights, *Death, Despair and Defiance,* pp. 694, 701. Earlier, on 15 April, "interahamwe accompanied by members of the Presidential Guard entered the church. They selected a hundred and twenty Tutsi men and boys, one by one, took them outside, and promptly executed them by shooting them. They were clearly working from a prepared list—most of the victims were political activists, businessmen, students and young men who 'looked Tutsi.' Only one man is said to have survived this massacre" (p. 689). "Sixty Tutsi men and boys" were also "snatched from the neighbouring church of St. Paul's on 14 June" (p. 698). For an in-depth treatment of this subject, see Adam Jones, "Genocide and Humanitarian Intervention: Incorporating the Gender Variable," *Journal of Humanitarian Assistance,* February 2002, *www.jha.ac/articles/a080.htm.*

5

Gendercide and Human Rights

David Buchanan

Reformers have the idea that change can be achieved by brute sanity.

—George Bernard Shaw

Introduction

Certain fundamental individual rights—the right to not be killed, the right to not be tortured, the right to not be raped, the right to not be imprisoned for your beliefs—are now seen as so important that they have been raised to the status of *human rights:* rights that belong to every member of the human species anywhere, anytime, under any circumstances. Universal moral outrage over violations of these rights of personal security—*blue rights* as they are sometimes called—led to their codification into international law in the International Covenant on Civil and Political Rights, which came into force on 23 March 1976 and has now been ratified by some 140 countries. (Its sister treaty, the International Covenant on Social, Economic, and Cultural Rights, the other pillar of the so-called International Bill of Rights, deals with the more unwieldy economic rights—*red rights*—and has been ratified by a similar number of countries.)

The governments of the states that are party to these covenants agree to occasionally stand before a UN committee and give an account of their alleged human-rights violations. Organizations, most notably Amnesty International and Human Rights Watch, have been formed to advocate the observance of these human rights. That these organizations still fill volumes documenting torture, summary executions, and political imprisonments is a testament to the savagery of our species; Amnesty International tells us that people were tortured or ill treated in 111 states in 2002.[1]

Human rights are individual rights. They belong to every human being, whether the person is red, yellow, black, or white, male or female, Jew or Gentile, Hindu or Muslim, Tutsi or Hutu, Serb or Albanian. So is there any purpose in discussing human-rights violations that target specific groups of people, rather than individuals? In particular, does it make sense to analyze the large-scale killing of men and women, gendercide, in the context of human rights?

Clearly there are times when groups of people suffer human-rights violations *because they are members of a particular group.* Genocide is the best-known example of this phenomenon. The Nazis did not violate the human rights of just anyone; they targeted Jews, Gypsies, and anyone else they did not consider Aryan *because* they were not Aryan. (Some have said that the Jewish holocaust was largely responsible for the modern human-rights movement.)

This paper will concentrate on the issue of large-scale human-rights violations when they are directed against women qua women or men qua men. I hope to draw attention to inequities in the current analysis of sex-selective mass murder.

Female Gendercide

That human-rights violations can target those of a particular gender is widely recognized. The Convention on the Political Rights of Women came into force on 7 July 1954, binding signatories to allow women to vote and hold public office. The Convention on the Elimination of All Forms of Discrimination against Women, often called a bill of rights for women, came into force on 3 September 1981. With 165 state parties as of 20 March 2000, the latter treaty is more widely ratified than is the International Bill of Rights. These two conventions represent part of a concerted and commendable effort to recognize and remedy the systematic discrimination that women have faced throughout history.

The principle of rape as a crime of war has been enshrined in international law for some time. In handing down the first-ever conviction for genocide by an international court to Jean-Paul Akayesu, the International Criminal Tribunal for Rwanda at the same time convicted him of a count of crimes against humanity (rape) and had this to say:

> It should be noted that during the Tokyo trials, certain civilian authorities were convicted of war crimes. . . . Hirota, former Foreign Minister of Japan, was convicted of atrocities—including mass rape—committed in the "rape of Nanking," under a count which charged that he had "recklessly disregarded their legal duty by virtue of their office to take adequate steps to secure the observance and prevent breaches of the laws and customs of war."[2]

In the same ruling, the Trial Chamber stressed that rape in Rwanda in 1994 was an integral part of genocide:

> With regard, particularly, to the acts described in paragraphs 12(A) and 12(B) of the Indictment, that is, rape and sexual violence, the Chamber wishes to underscore the fact that in its opinion, they constitute genocide in the same way as any other act as long as they were committed with the specific intent to destroy, in whole or in part, a particular group, targeted as such. Indeed, rape and sexual violence certainly constitute infliction of serious bodily and mental harm on the victims and are even, according to the Chamber, one of the worst ways of inflict [*sic*] harm on the victim as he or she suffers both bodily and mental harm. In light of all the evidence before it, the Chamber is satisfied that the acts of rape and sexual violence described above, were committed solely against Tutsi women, many of whom were subjected to the worst public humiliation, mutilated, and raped several times, often by more than one assailant. These rapes resulted in physical and psychological destruction of Tutsi women, their families and their communities. Sexual violence was an integral part of the process of destruction, specifically targeting Tutsi women and specifically contributing to their destruction and to the destruction of the Tutsi group as a whole. The rape of Tutsi women was systematic and was perpetrated against all Tutsi women and solely against them. A Tutsi woman, married to a Hutu, testified before the Chamber that she was not raped because her ethnic background was unknown. . . . Sexual violence was a step in the process of destruction of the Tutsi group—destruction of the spirit, of the will to live, and of life itself.[3]

That same tribunal has issued the first-ever indictment against a woman for war crimes. Pauline Nyiramasuhuko, the former Rwandan minister for the family and women's affairs, has been indicted for genocide and crimes against humanity alongside a charge of responsibility for rape "as part of a widespread and systematic attack against a civilian population on political, ethnic and racial grounds."[4]

Over the past decade or so the human-rights community has been assiduous in documenting the patterns of horrors faced by women during armed conflict. A superb example of this came from Human Rights Watch after the hostilities in Kosovo. This report painstakingly details sexual violence against women in Kosovo, not only during the time that NATO bombs dropped, but in the ten years leading up to that, including the year-long battle between the Kosovo Liberation Army and Yugoslav forces. It was at the highest level of the Serbian leadership that hatred of ethnic Albanian women began, according to the report:

> Official state propaganda in Yugoslavia in the decade preceding the war served to dehumanize and stereotype Kosovar Albanian women. Serbian propaganda contrasted Serbian women, viewed as "cultured, strong, and worthy of motherhood," with Albanian women, portrayed as "indiscriminately fecund." . . . The nationalistic propaganda also exploited fears of Albanian population growth. . . . Some young women victims of rape expressed fear that they could not expect to marry following the attack. One purpose that rape in the war may have served was discouraging women from reproducing in the future.[5]

The salient point here is that the sexual violence against women was not simply the result of a few misogynist soldiers; it was a thoroughgoing policy of the state and its agents.

An Amnesty International report dealing with this issue discussed sexual violence against women during the conflagration in Sierra Leone. That report lists a litany of horrors committed against the women of this devastated country, including sexual slavery, where women were held indefinitely and raped repeatedly by members of the armed forces and rebels. Again, the large-scale systematic nature of rape is apparent:

> On 8 January 1999 in the Cline Town area in the east of Freetown a rebel commander ordered that all girls who were virgins report for a physical examination by a woman colleague. Those confirmed to be virgins, mostly aged between 12 and 15 years, were ordered to report each night

> to the rebel commander and other combatants who raped or otherwise sexually assaulted them.

Amnesty then goes on to make recommendations to the authorities to safeguard the civilian population. Oddly, the report implores the Revolutionary United Front, one of the rebel forces, to "order the immediate release of all girls, women, and other captured civilians who remain held."[6] Whom, one wonders, might the authors have had in mind as the "other captured civilians"?

Amnesty also mentioned that it may not be only women who are victimized by the large-scale rape that so often happens during wartime: "The terror wreaked by rebel forces on civilians has also included men being forced to rape members of their own family under threat of being mutilated by having their hands or arms cut off." This point is relevant as well to an understanding of male gendercide, which I address next.

Male Gendercide

The evidence that men are also targeted for large-scale human-rights violations *because they are men,* particularly in the context of armed conflict, is now ubiquitous. A quick review of the horrors of the 1990s brings a number of male-selective atrocities into focus. At the conclusion of hostilities in Kosovo, the Organization for Security and Cooperation in Europe (OSCE) published a detailed report on that war. One chapter was devoted to sexual violence during the war,[7] while another discussed the large-scale human-rights violations perpetrated against women in Kosovo.[8] Chapter 15, "Young Men of Fighting Age," carefully documented the selective targeting of young ethnic Albanian males. An excerpt from that chapter states:

> young men were the group that was by far the most targeted in the conflict in Kosovo; . . . every young Kosovo Albanian man was suspected of being a terrorist. If apprehended by Serbian forces—VJ, police or paramilitary—the young men were at risk, more than any other group of Kosovo society of grave human rights violations. Many were executed on the spot, on occasion after horrendous torture. Sometimes they would be arrested and taken to prisons or other detention centres, where, as described afterwards by men released from such detention, they would be tortured and ill-treated, while others would simply not be seen again.

> Others were taken for use as human shields or as forced labour. Many young men "disappeared" following abduction.[9]

What we have here is not the odd crazed Serbian soldier going on a rampage, not just a My Lai massacre committed against men here or there, but the entire Serbian state juggernaut, the armed forces, the police, the paramilitaries, the militias, all aligned in their efforts to root out and punish ethnic Albanian men, *because they were men.*

A report from the American Association for the Advancement of Science also alluded to this male-specific targeting during the carnage in Kosovo: "Yugoslav forces executed groups of Kosovar Albanians, *primarily men,* in retaliation for KLA [Kosovo Liberation Army] attacks or because the victims lived in villages or towns thought to be KLA strongholds."[10] Human Rights Watch saw the trend as well: "On many occasions, groups of Albanians were systematically executed by Serbian special police or paramilitaries. *Most of the victims were military-age men,* apparently an attempt to eradicate the KLA."[11]

A time-honored prelude to gender-selective human-rights violations is the ritual separation of the men from the women and children. And this was evident in Kosovo. The US State Department wrote that "*Serbian forces systematically separated military-aged men from the general population* as Kosovars were expelled. These men were detained in facilities ranging from cement factories to prisons. Many of these detainees were forced to dig trenches and were physically abused."[12]

Human Rights Watch issued a report titled "Serb Forces Separating Men from Women and Children in Malishevo" that contained the following passage:

> Interviews with refugees arriving in Albania today established that *Yugoslav forces were systematically separating adult males from women, children and elderly men* in the Malishevo area of Kosovo, in the southern part of the province. According to the refugees, thousands of mostly unarmed ethnic Albanian men in the area have fled into the mountains, fearing arrest and possible summary execution; . . . the refugees from the Malishevo area were almost exclusively women, children, and elderly men.

The report goes on to note: "In a number of earlier incidents in the Kosovo conflict, and in the Bosnian conflict, the Yugoslav army and Serb police were responsible for the summary execution of unarmed, fighting-aged men."[13]

Amnesty International had this to say about a Serbian attack on Izbica in Kosovo:

> Witnesses described how scores of men, including the young and elderly, were separated from the women and shot. Some 150 people were believed to have been killed, although it was impossible to confirm whether all were non-combatants.[14]

As refugees poured out of Kosovo, Doctors without Borders reported that in Montenegro there was "a 13% lack of males in the 15–55 age group." Why? Regarding refugee convoys, "all along the route, men were picked out of the convoy of deportees and executed."[15] At the border crossing into Albania, UN aid worker Laura Boldrini lamented that she was witness to a "planet without men, only women and children. It was unbelievable. The old men were there, but I'm talking about young men, between 17 and 45."[16]

Earlier, in July 1995, the Bosnian city of Srebrenica had witnessed the worst massacre in Europe since World War II. There it was not just the Bosnian Serb troops but also the good guys, officials with the United Nations, who must share some of the blame. At this UN-declared safe area, the Dutch peacekeepers pleaded in vain for air strikes (at one point the Dutch commander was told he had submitted the request on the wrong form), while the marauding Serbs separated the men from the women and children, and set about slaughtering more than seven thousand boys and men. The UN report on the fall of Srebrenica provides some grisly details:

> The mortal remains of close to 2,500 men and boys have been found on the surface, in mass graves and in secondary burial sites. Several thousand more men are still missing, and there is every reason to believe that additional burial sites, many of which have been probed but not exhumed, will reveal the bodies of thousands more men and boys. The great majority of those who were killed were not killed in combat: the exhumed bodies of the victims show that large numbers had their hands bound, or were blindfolded, or were shot in the back or the back of the head. Numerous eyewitness accounts, now well corroborated by forensic evidence, attest to scenes of mass slaughter of unarmed victims.[17]

Just as sexual violence against women can also harm men (when they are made unwilling perpetrators of rape, for instance), gendercide against men can be devastating to the women left behind. The former UN special rapporteur of the Commission on Human Rights said in his report following

Srebrenica: "The fate of the menfolk is a cause of great anguish for their relatives and friends. The disappearance of such a huge number of men poses particular problems in a male-dominated society where the women are almost wholly dependent on men for their livelihoods. One woman was reported to have committed suicide by jumping into a lake with her two children because her husband was missing."[18]

Lest it be thought that large-scale enormities occur only during the heat of battle, consider the Indian state of Jammu and Kashmir. On 20 March 2000, unknown thugs entered the village of Chithisinghpora, separated the men from the women, and murdered thirty-five Sikh men. Following this mass murder, Amnesty issued a report that addressed the situation of Sikhs in Kashmir, stressing the religious identity of the victims of this crime and noting that this was the first attack on Sikhs in the decade-long hostilities between Muslims and Hindus in Jammu and Kashmir. But the gender of the victims was only mentioned in passing.[19] (A subsequent Urgent Action from Amnesty relegated the victims to the category of "Sikh civilians.")[20] Five days later, state agents killed five men in the village of Panchalthan-Pathribal, allegedly because the five were "foreign militants" responsible for the Sikh massacre, according to the official government version of events.[21] In an orgy of violence in the summer of 2000, the age-old pattern emerged once again:

> On Tuesday evening, guerrillas swooped down on the Mir Bazar village near Anantnag, forcing people out of their homes and separating women and children from the men, said a police spokesman in Srinagar, the state's summer capital. The men—brick factory workers who had migrated from other Indian states—were lined up and shot, police said. They said 19 people were killed.[22]

With this tsunami of empirical evidence of "gender cleansing" in the Balkans and elsewhere, one would think that human-rights lobbyists, already sensitive to the horrors that state authorities dish out to their citizens, would be clamoring for the grand-scale victimization of males to be brought to everyone's attention. But when that very issue, that of men being targeted qua men in huge numbers, was formally brought to the membership of the English-speaking Canadian section of Amnesty at an annual general meeting, the response was resistance, even hostility. Despite the rather tame final wording of the decision-making clause of the resolution ("DECIDES that Amnesty International will condemn all large-scale gender-selective human rights violations of men and women within the Amnesty International mandate and will highlight the gender-selective nature of these human rights violations"), the resolution was soundly defeated. (For the full text of the resolution, see the chapter appendix.)

Several concerns about the resolution were raised. They supply a microcosm for the general debate about the issue of large-scale male victimization.

Identity-based Human-rights Violations

When the draft resolution was circulated, Amnesty International (AI) mandate expert David Matas wrote:

> Victimization of men is no more or less regrettable than victimization of women or children. I question whether it is appropriate for a resolution to ask AI to highlight the victimization of any one group of victims, whether it be women or men or children. Once you are killed or disappeared, you are equally dead or gone whether you are a man, woman or child. It minimizes one person's tragedy and aggrandizes another's to highlight one set of killings or disappearances and cast a low light on another set.[23]

But does reporting that Tutsis were hacked to death in Rwanda in 1994 *because they were Tutsis* "cast a low light" on the sufferings of moderate Hutus (who were also killed in the genocide)? Or does reporting that ethnic Albanians were forced out of their homes, raped, tortured and killed in 1999 *because they were ethnic Albanians* cast a low light on the sufferings of Kosovar Serbs (some of whom were victims of the Kosovo Liberation Army)?

Surely people would be up in arms if human-rights organizations or the media declared that one million people were forced out of their homes in Kosovo and did *not* mention that they were ethnic Albanians, or if nothing was noted about the ethnicity of the victims in Rwanda. Members of these ethnic groups were targeted simply because they happened to have been born with a particular ethnicity. Just as no one would think that the victimization of Tutsis is more regrettable than that of Hutus upon learning that Tutsis were the principal targets of the 1994 Rwandan genocide, no one would suggest that the victimization of Hutus is more regrettable than that of Tutsis when told that Hutus were the main targets of a genocide in Burundi in 1972.

Or consider the case of Marc Lépine. In December 1989, Lépine walked into Montreal's École Polytechnique, separated the men from the women, and killed fourteen women, wounding thirteen others. This was an exception to the general rule of gender-selective mass murder, in that the men emerged with their lives to mourn their female compatriots. Does noting that Lépine specifically went after women *because they were women* somehow cast a low light on the sufferings of men?

What holds true for Tutsis, ethnic Albanians, and women also holds true for men, when they are tortured and killed *because they are men.* The evidence from many conflicts confirms that simply being born male is a potential death sentence. Indeed, it is hard to conceive of more convincing evidence of the targeting of a particular group than the separation of that group from the rest of the population and its subsequent slaughtering—as happened to the female victims of Marc Lépine, and as happened to groups of men time and again in the Kosovo conflict.

When, in January 2000, the Russian authorities issued an order forbidding any male Chechen refugee between the ages of ten and sixty from entering or leaving Chechnya, Human Rights Watch was unequivocal: "It is fundamentally unacceptable to deny civilian males, including children as young as ten, the right to flee from heavy fighting. And it's against international standards."[24] Worthy sentiments. Would anyone suggest that this casts a low light on the sufferings of female Chechens? (Since Human Rights Watch saw this incident as obviously unconscionable, one might expect it to be all the more outraged when virtually the entire male population is targeted not just for the prevention of freedom of movement, but for death, torture, forced servitude, and disappearance, as in Kosovo. But no report on that subject was forthcoming from Human Rights Watch.)

In any event, no large-scale human-rights violation, be it the marauding of Alexander the Great or any of the four wars started by Slobodan Milosevic, involves a random targeting of people. Serial killers may spontaneously choose their victims, but death machines on the order of Stalin and Hitler know who the "enemy" is and are meticulous in conducting their slaughter.

What is crucial here is that human-rights reporting is not a zero-sum game in which every word written on male victimization automatically leads to one less word written on female suffering or vice versa. As the OSCE report on Kosovo aptly demonstrated, large-scale abuses of both men *and* women during armed combat can be discussed in a fair and balanced way in the same source.

Moreover, Amnesty International has a long history of identifying human-rights violations that affect particular groups—even when the discrimination is much more subtle than in the foregoing examples. In a news release that announced a report on systematic racial discrimination in the application of the death penalty in the United States, Pierre Sané, Amnesty's secretary general, said: "Today, whether you live or die in the USA as a result of your crimes appears to be largely determined by the colour of your skin and the race of your victim." The report added that when it comes to the U.S. death penalty, it is not just blacks who are discriminated against: "Prejudice also applies to Latinos, Native Americans, Asian Americans, Arab Americans and others."[25]

So Amnesty speaks to discrimination based on race and ethnicity (and gender, when women are the victims[26]). Given this, is it reasonable to think that extending the analysis to boys and men would catastrophically tip the scales away from fairness? (While we are on the subject of capital punishment, it is worth asking which identity correlates most strongly with a place on death row in the United States. Skin color? Race? Ethnic origin? IQ? None of the above: The answer is biological sex. The Justice Center of the University of Alaska–Anchorage says, "Of the 19,000 confirmed executions since 1608 in what is now the United States, only 515, less than three percent, were executions of women."[27] But this is a subject on which human-rights organizations are notably silent.)

One question that kept coming up in the deliberations over the Amnesty International resolution was: "Doesn't Amnesty already condemn the killing of male civilians during armed conflict?" Up to a point, yes. It addresses *individual cases* where men are subjected to horrendous human-rights violations (examples from Kosovo have already been cited). Other clear examples come from an Amnesty report on the ongoing Sudanese bloodbath:

> male villagers were killed in mass executions. . . . Reports from other villages claim that soldiers slit the throats of children and killed male civilians who had been interrogated by hammering nails into their foreheads.[28]

Yet the two major international human-rights watchdogs, Amnesty International and Human Rights Watch, have flinched from clearly documenting *large-scale patterns* of male-specific violence during armed conflict. Despite a number of reports from these two groups on patterns of sexual violence against women during wartime, no accompanying report has been issued on the widespread arrest, incarceration, torture, killing, and disappearance of civilian men. In my address to the Amnesty gathering, I even suggested two chapters of the OSCE report, Chapter 15, "Young Men of Fighting Age" and Chapter 16, "Women," as a blueprint of how Amnesty could fairly deal with large-scale gender-selective human-rights violations after or—better—during future armed conflicts, and I reminded the membership that identity-based violations were one of the current focuses of Amnesty International's worldwide movement.

Another question heard repeatedly from fellow Amnesty members was: "Are civilian men killed during armed strife in large numbers because they are men, or is it because they are possible conscripts for the opposing side?" First of all, it is hard to see what difference it makes as to *why* boys and men are tortured, killed, and jailed en masse. (Do human-rights advocates wring their hands over the motives behind the gang rapes of women during armed conflict, honor killings, female genital mutilations, cases of torture, political imprisonments, or even something as controversial as capital punishment? No, they condemn all these as inherently evil, plain and simple.) If a pattern of large-scale killing of civilians is evident, be they men, women, or children, shouldn't human-rights organizations point this out and condemn it, regardless of its underlying causes? And if all or almost all of the victims happen to be men or women, isn't this worthy of mention?[29]

More searching analysis reveals that gender is never the only dimension that enters into sex-specific human-rights violations. Ponder the example of the large-scale rape of women in armed conflict. When women are raped by soldiers, members of paramilitaries, and secret policemen during war, it is not just because they are women. It is also because they happen to be members of the opposing side. (During the Bosnian war, Serbian troops did not rape Serbian women, nor did Bosnian Muslim soldiers rape other Muslims.) It also comes as little surprise to find that in most cases the women who are raped are the younger and attractive ones. In a trend eerily reminiscent of men and boys dressing as women and girls during the genocidal frenzy in 1994 Rwanda,[30] Human Rights Watch reported that in Kosovo:

> Rumors of rape circulated wildly as families attempted to flee their homes. Older women often dressed their daughters in loose clothing and headscarves in an attempt to disguise young girls as grandmothers. Other mothers smeared dirt and mud in their daughters' faces to render them unattractive.[31]

Or take the example of witch-hunts in Europe during the Middle Ages. It was not exclusively women who were the targets; some men were also accused and condemned. But the victims were, in the main, women, so it makes sense to consider this a gender-selective violation; the gender dimension was clearly important. And it was not just any women who were singled out as witches. Steven Katz writes that:

> statistical evidence . . . makes clear that over 99.9-plus percent of all women who lived during the three centuries of the witch craze were not harmed directly by the police arm of either the state or the church, though both had the power to do so had the elites that controlled them so desired.[32]

In general, only those women who were perceived as "strange" or "threatening" were targeted as witches.

During the deliberations around the resolution, I was reminded over and over again that the vast majority of AI cases have concerned themselves with men and that the current trend of highlighting violence against females is simply an attempt to remedy the putative imbalance. And I strongly support the attention that feminism has focused on the unique human-rights violations faced by women—female genital mutilation and honor killings being two of the most prominent.[33]

But Amnesty International has also adroitly refused to rank human-rights violations or violators. In this spirit, I was not trying to suggest that there are more male than female victims of gross human-rights violations. (With so much inhumanity committed behind closed doors, there is no way of ascertaining the real numbers, but what is known is that the preponderance of Amnesty cases have focused on men.)

Instead, I was simply asking for equal treatment when violations based on gender are examined. Just as Amnesty has thrown the spotlight on the far-reaching human-rights violations carried out against women during armed conflicts and elsewhere, a similar analysis would be appropriate in those cases where males are sought out and slain, most obviously during military campaigns.

Amnesty International began when English lawyer Peter Benenson was able to channel his indignation over the seven-year jail sentence of two students for raising their glasses in a toast to freedom in Portugal.[34] If it is outrageous to deny elementary human rights to one or two people, then isn't it that much more contemptible to violate the basic human rights of an entire population of men, as in the case of Kosovo?

Gendercide as Overture to Genocide

Nowadays, human-rights groups desperately want to do more than just produce laundry lists of the human-rights indignities that people in our world suffer. They want to try to head off such abuses, particularly if massive infringements are anticipated. The title of the press release from Amnesty International that announced the release of its 2000 annual report was *Human Rights Crises Are Never Inevitable: They Can, and Must, Be Prevented.*

So what are the signs of incipient genocide? One of the surest tocsins is the selective liquidation of men. A particularly egregious historical example is Operation Barbarossa, the Nazi invasion of the Soviet Union during World War II. Daniel Goldhagen, author of *Hitler's Willing Executioners,* tells how this preliminary slaughter toughened up the Nazis for what was to come.

> The *Einsatzgruppen* [armed forces] officers . . . could habituate their men into their new vocation as genocidal executioners through a stepwise escalation of the killing. First, by shooting primarily teenage and adult Jewish males, they would be able to acclimate themselves to mass executions without the shock of killing women, young children, and the infirm. According to Alfred Filbert, the commander of *Einsatzkommando 9,* the order . . . "quite clearly" "included also women and children." Yet "in the first instance, without a doubt, the executions were limited generally to Jewish males."[35]

Nor is it just the activities of the soft targets—the world's governments, militaries, and armed opposition groups—that can be scrutinized for warning signs of atrocity and genocide. Read this shocking passage from the International Labor Organization's "Convention Concerning Forced or Compulsory Labor," adopted in 1930 and now ratified by 153 countries—an agreement intended as a step along the road to ending forced labor:

> *Only adult able-bodied males* who are of an apparent age of not less than 18 and not more than 45 years may be called upon for forced or compulsory labour; . . . the regulations provided for in Article 23 of this Convention shall fix the proportion of the resident adult able-bodied males who may be taken at one time for forced or compulsory labour, provided always that this proportion shall in no case exceed 25 per cent.[36]

This is so outrageously discriminatory that perhaps it is best to let sleeping dogs lie and not even raise the subject, lest some tyranny decides to use this clause as justification for the widespread use of men for forced labor—an institution that has killed tens of millions of men throughout history. But states continue to ratify this treaty; it was Eritrea's turn on 22 February 2000.

So deeply entrenched is this blind spot for male victimization that the UN General Assembly passed the "Declaration on the Protection of Women and Children in Emergency and Armed Conflict" on 14 December 1974, stating with no supporting evidence that "women and children . . . are the most vulnerable members of the population." The resolution added: "All efforts shall be made by States involved in armed conflicts, military operations in foreign territories or military operations in territories still under colonial domination to spare women and children from the ravages of war."[37]

Which leaves one wondering: *Why shouldn't civilian men also be spared the ravages of war?* Are they not just as vulnerable as civilian women and children, or even more so? ("The monitoring by the OSCE-KVM Human Rights Division confirms that *young men were the group that was by far the most targeted in the conflict in Kosovo,*" affirmed the OSCE report.)[38]

If the ethnic bloodletting of the 1990s (Croatia, Bosnia, Kosovo, Rwanda, Kashmir, and on and on) should have taught the human-rights community anything, it is that when it comes to modern warfare, both men and women face gender-specific threats, as well as less discriminate ones. Civilian men confront conscription, imprisonment, torture, murder, and disappearance; women confront rape (with the associated threat of AIDS and other venereal diseases), sexual servitude, and sometimes outright slaughter as well. Human-rights organizations have acted quite commendably in addressing the large-scale violations meted out against women. The time is ripe to broaden the focus and acknowledge that, particularly in armed conflicts, men are also profoundly at risk. We have been sensitized to the special problems faced by women as well as those experienced by certain minorities, notably blacks, Asians, indigenous peoples, and homosexuals. Now is the time for such sensitization to be extended to men, especially the large-scale killing of men in wartime, as happens so often in our violent world.

Human-rights work is always difficult. It is made that much more harrowing when one encounters entrenched resistance from like-minded human-rights sympathizers.

Appendix

The text of the resolution submitted to the Amnesty International Canadian Section (English-Speaking) annual general meeting in June 2000:

Large-Scale Gender-Selective Human Rights Violations

WHEREAS AICS(ES) has taken a special interest in gender-based human rights violations, particularly in light of its recent publication, "A Methodology for Gender-Sensitive Research," Be It Resolved that AICS(ES) propose and endorse the following to the 2001 International Council Meeting:

The International Council,

1. considering that the Troia Action Plan calls for Amnesty International to focus on "violations based on identity,"
2. considering that Amnesty International has long been a leader in raising awareness of human rights violations,
3. considering that Amnesty International has made a concerted effort to highlight gender-selective human rights violations against women,
4. considering that Amnesty International has failed to take a gender-inclusive approach to large-scale gender-selective human rights violations,

DECIDES that Amnesty International will condemn all large-scale gender-selective human rights violations of men and women within the Amnesty International mandate and will highlight the gender-selective nature of these human rights violations.

Notes

My heartfelt thanks go to Adam Jones, executive director of Gendercide Watch (*www.gendercide.org*), whose article "Pity the Innocent Men," published in *The Globe and Mail* on 20 February 1999, awakened me from my slumbers. His indefatigable efforts have brought the subject of male victimization to a wide audience. I would also like to thank John Argue, Anil Bhatia, Tanya Bhatia, A. C. Del Zotto, Dan Fass, Victoria Gazeley, John Leslie, Wayne Liebau, and Jane MacKimmie for comments on drafts of this paper, and David Matas for comments on the draft resolution.

1. Amnesty International, *Annual Report 2002* (London: Amnesty International, 2002).

2. International Criminal Tribunal for Rwanda, "Judgement on Akayesu, Jean Paul (ICTR-96–4)," 1998, *www.ictr.org/ENGLISH/judgements/AKAYESU/akay001.htm*

3. Ibid.

4. International Criminal Tribunal for Rwanda, "Pauline Nyiramasuhuko Facing Fresh Charges of Encouraging Sexual Violence (ICTR/INFO-9–2–196)," 1999. *www.ictr.org/ENGLISH/PRESSREL/196.htm.*

5. Human Rights Watch, *Gender-Based Violations against Kosovar Albanian Women* (New York: Human Rights Watch, 2000), *www.hrw.org/reports/2000/fry/Kosov003–02.htm*

6. Amnesty International, *Sierra Leone: Rape and Other Forms of Sexual Violence against Girls and Women* (London: Amnesty International, 2000), *www.amnesty.ca/library/afr5103500.html.*

7. Organization for Security and Cooperation in Europe, "Sexual Violence," in "Kosovo/Kosova As Seen, As Told," OSCE, 1999, *www.osce.org/kosovo/reports/hr/part1/ch7.htm.*

8. "Women," in ibid., *www.osce.org/kosovo/reports/hr/part1/ch16.htm.*

9. "Young Men of Fighting Age," in ibid., *www.osce.org/kosovo/reports/hr/part1/ch15.htm*

10. American Association for the Advancement of Science, *Policy or Panic? Patterns of Kosovar Albanian Refugee Flow, March–May 1999* (AAAS, 2000) (emphasis added), *shr.aaas.org/kosovo/policyorpanic.*

11. Human Rights Watch, *Federal Republic of Yugoslavia: Human Rights Developments* (New York: Human Rights Watch, 2000) (emphasis added), *www.hrw.org/hrw/wr2k/Eca-26.htm.* Physicians for Human Rights also noticed this trend when it related this testimony from an anonymous interviewee from Kosovo: "TL said that Serb forces entered his village in early May, [and] went from home to home, ordering all villagers to gather in a square near the school. There, they separated the men from the women and children. They ordered the men to walk away from the group, divided them up, and then killed 143 of them." Physicians for Human Rights, "Kosovo Update #12," 1999, *phrusa.org/past_news/kos12.html.*

12. U.S. Department of State, *Ethnic Cleansing in Kosovo: An Accounting* (Washington, D.C.: Department of State, 1999) (emphasis added). *www.state.gov/www/global/human_rights/kosovoii/homepage.html*

13. Human Rights Watch, *Serb Forces Separating Men from Women and Children in Malishevo* (New York: Human Rights Watch, 1999) (emphasis added), *www.hrw.org/hrw/campaigns/kosovo98/flash2.shtml#13*

14. Amnesty International, *Amnesty International Report 2000* (London: Amnesty International, 2000), *www.web.amnesty.org/web/ar2000web.nsf/europe.*

15. Doctors without Borders, "Kosovo: Accounts of a Deportation," April 1999, *www.doctorswithoutborders.org/reports/kosovo.htm.*

16. Alan Freeman, "Missing: Kosovo's Young Ethnic-Albanian Men," *Globe and Mail,* 6 April 1999.

17. United Nations, "Report of the Secretary-General pursuant to General Assembly Resolution 53/35: The Fall of Srebrenica," 1999, *www.un.org/peace/srebrenica.pdf.*

18. United Nations, "Final Periodic Report on the Situation of Human Rights in the Territory of the Former Yugoslavia, Submitted by Mr. Tadeusz Mazowiecki, Special Rapporteur of the Commission on Human Rights," 1995, *www1.umn.edu/humanrts/commission/country52/9-yug.htm.*

19. Amnesty International, *India: A Trail of Unlawful Killings in Jammu and Kashmir: Chithisinghpora and Its Aftermath* (London: Amnesty International, 2000), *www.amnesty.org/ailib/aipub/2000/ASA/32002400.htm.*

20. Amnesty International, *Fear for Safety. India: Population of Jammu and Kashmir.* AI Index: ASA 20/38/00 (London: Amnesty International, 2000).

21. Amnesty International, *India.*

22. Canadian Press, "Wave of Attacks in Kashmir Leave More Than 90 Dead," 2 August 2000, *www.canada.com/cgi-bin/cp.asp?f=/news/cp/stories/20000802/world-1428046.html.*

23. David Matas, personal communication.

24. Human Rights Watch, *Russia Closes Chechnya Border to Male Civilians* (New York: Human Rights Watch, 2000). *www.hrw.org/press/2000/01/chech0112.htm*

25. Amnesty International, *Death by Discrimination: Skin Colour Influences Who Lives and Dies in the US Judicial System* (London: Amnesty International, 1999), *www.amnesty.org/news/1999/25107599.htm.*

26. Amnesty International, *End Secrecy: End Suffering* (London: Amnesty International, 2000), *www.amnesty.org/ailib/aipub/2000/MDE/_235700.pdf.*

27. Justice Center at University of Alaska Anchorage, "Focus on the Death Penalty," *www.uaa.alaska.edu/just/death/index.html.*

28. Amnesty International, *Sudan: The Human Price of Oil* (London: Amnesty International, 2000), *www.amnesty.ca/library/news/afr54C040.htm.*

29. Upon hearing of the U.S. plan to detain asylum seekers from Iraq and thirty-three other unnamed nations, on 30 March 2003 Amnesty International scolded the American authorities that "this presumes guilt by association and does so on the basis of nationality." True enough. Now substitute "gender" for "nationality" in the quote, and one arrives at similar grounds for condemning the policy of arresting and violating the human rights of young men during armed conflict. This presumes guilt by association, and does so on the basis of gender. Surely, this represents a crystal-clear case of discrimination on the basis of identity. Amnesty International, *Iraq: In the Shadow of War: Backlash against Human Rights* (London: Amnesty International, 2003).

30. See Adam Jones, "Gender and Genocide in Rwanda," this volume, citing the African Rights report *Rwanda: Death, Despair, and Defiance.*

31. Human Rights Watch, *Gender-Based Violations against Kosovar Albanian Women* (New York: Human Rights Watch, 2000), *www.hrw.org/reports/2000/fry/Kosov003–02.htm.*

32. Steven Katz, *The Holocaust in Historical Context,* vol. 1 (New York: Oxford University Press, 1994), pp. 502–505.

33. The mirror image of female genital mutilation—eunuchry, the castration of boys—is conspicuously absent from the human-rights literature. A petition filed with an Indian court in 1998 stated that there are about 500,000 forcibly castrated men in India and went on to detail the widespread horrors of the kidnapping, drugging, and castration of innocent boys on the subcontinent. See Vinod Behl, "Eunuchs Cry for Justice," *Rediff on the Net,* 20 October 1998, *www.rediff.com/news/1998/oct/20hijra.htm.*

34. Appeal for Amnesty, 1961, the forerunner of Amnesty International, was kicked off by Benenson's article "The Forgotten Prisoners" in *The Observer* (London) on 28 May 1961.

35. Daniel Goldhagen, *Hitler's Willing Executioners: Ordinary Germans and the Holocaust* (New York: Knopf, 1996), pp. 149–50.

36. International Labor Organization, "Convention Concerning Forced or Compulsory Labour (28 Jun 30) As Modified by the Final Articles Revision Convention, 1946" (emphasis added), *www.mtsu.edu/~baustin/forclabr.html.*

37. UN General Assembly, "Declaration on the Protection of Women and Children in Emergency and Armed Conflict," 1974, *www.unhchr.ch/html/menu3/b/24.htm.*

38. Organization for Security and Cooperation in Europe, "Young Men of Fighting Age" (emphasis added).

6

Gendercide in a Historical-Structural Context

The Case of Black Male Gendercide in the United States

Augusta C. Del Zotto

Introduction

In his article "Gendercide and Genocide," revised for this volume, Adam Jones presents a richly detailed and often horrific historical account of genocidal practices targeted at males under diverse sociopolitical conditions.[1] One of his most striking references is to the work of Errol Miller, a Jamaican scholar, who posits that "men not covered by the bonds of kinship or culture" were targeted with genocide to a wide degree and within numerous historical settings.[2] Miller's statement serves as a point of departure for this inquiry into the role of gendercide in the African American population. I use a historical-structural analysis to trace how a complex, historically rooted system of control and punishment impacts upon the lives of African American males today.

Unlike many instances of gendercide, where practices involving the systematic elimination of males are situated within specific events involving warfare and political persecution, the practice of gendercide against African American males follows a long historical continuum and is contingent upon an unspoken de facto war involving race and class. Central to this sociopolitical condition is the systematic dismantling of kinship and cultural ties over time, making the African American male vulnerable to various forms of gendercidal targeting. This practice, which I will henceforth label as black male gendercide, has evolved through a series of power-relation regimes embedded within the United States' economic and sociopolitical order. It began with cruder forms of control and punishment informed by a slave-based agrarian economy and later became a more complex, indirect system of male selective genocide under the ideology of globalization. Conversely, traditions of resistance have also existed within each historical phase of black male gendercide. However, exploring this theme in detail is beyond the parameters of this chapter. I will mention only briefly some instances of resistance, and I encourage the reader to explore the issue further through other sources.

Historical Structure and Understanding

In order to understand the targeting of young African American males today, we must understand the genealogy of these practices within a wider historical context. I identify various stages of control and punishment (rooted in ideologies, institutions, and disciplinary forms), each sharing certain common features that have withstood the test of time. These features include: (a) A preoccupation, on the part of cultural/political elites, with economic institutions and identifying the black male as an indirect threat to these institutions; (b) the need to implement modes of social engineering that preserve and expand socioeconomic interests; and (c) the need to impose harm (discursive, social, and physical) upon black males as a central feature of the social-engineering schema.

The Slave Economy: Breaking the Family / Breaking Men

Beginning in the late 1600s, a large segment of the U.S. economy relied on the use of humans as property. This historical fact is widely understood. What is less understood about the slave industry, outside of African

American scholarship, is that the control of slaves for maximum productive use was contingent upon a deliberate and precise system of social engineering. Part of this process involved the dividing and conquering of the genders. As Eugene Genovese posits in his seminal work *Roll Jordan Roll: The World the Slaves Made,* while slave traders could conveniently view their "products" as virtual beasts of burden, slave owners were eventually forced to look upon their "property" as human beings, equipped with the complex sociocultural dynamics common to all humans.[3] This human factor became a problem for their production interests.

North American slave owners (and, later, slave-trading middlemen) observed that the early Caribbean slave plantations were prone to rebellion. Indeed, there were hundreds of documented cases of social *jacqueries* and banditry among slave populations in that region. Anglo merchants and planters in the north identified an important "mistake" that their Latin counterparts in the south were committing in their selection of African slaves.[4] Justo Gonzalez adds to this analysis by identifying specific social practices that led to widespread unrest in both the Caribbean and South America. Spanish and Portuguese (and, to a lesser degree, French) landlords purchased and maintained whole families from West Africa or, at least, whole communities of men, women, and children who belonged to the same ethnolinguistic group. The rationale was that such arrangements made slaves easier to manage (no multiple translations, no rivalry between ethnic groups, etc.). In reality, these familially and/or culturally compatible individuals, maintaining their ties in spite of bondage, were better equipped to conduct coordinated acts of rebellion.[5]

It was their observations of early Caribbean (and South American) slave plantations that led northern U.S. planters to establish the practice of "breaking" African families and controlling interactions between the genders.[6] This form of social engineering was informed by both economics and the positivist philosophy of human control over nature itself; in this case, human nature.[7] The black male became the focal point of this ambitious project. The public spectacle of ritual flogging, burning, castration, and execution of male slaves became an important and enduring method of discouraging leadership and group cohesion within the slave population. Additionally, the male-to-female ratio within the plantation system was carefully kept in check. While males were needed for the more rigorous types of manual labor, it was common to "weed out" males as they reached adult age, either by selling them to other plantations or by indirectly killing them through overwork.[8]

From these early historical/social practices in U.S. society, a bifurcated view of African Americans was created. Through discursive and symbolic cultural mechanisms, the black woman became the strong, independent helpmate of white society (the stereotypical "Aunt Jemima"), while the black male became the weak, shiftless, and dangerous threat to white society (the stereotypical "Jim Crow"). Such stereotypes, constructed along gender lines, inform the popular culture to this day and, in turn, shape U.S. public policy, as we shall see. Preoccupation with controlling and punishing the black male survives within this historical context.[9]

Picnics of Death: The Post-slave Era

Despite the atrocities of slavery and its gendercidal practices, African American families persevered and sought to reconstitute themselves after the Civil War. This period witnessed the growth of self-sufficient African American communities throughout the United States, the development of an African American intellectual class, and early efforts to obtain civil rights and labor rights. These endeavors were often met with violent responses on the part of white populations, in the industrial South as well as the agricultural North. The public spectacle of targeting and eliminating the black male off the plantation was a common feature in U.S. society and lasted into the early 1960s.[10] Lynchings, in particular, were in some communities as commonplace as sporting events. White men, women, and even children gathered with food and beverages to witness the summary execution of black males. Music played and people cheered.[11]

As with the earlier breaking and controlling of slave families, these horrifying events were the indirect result of social engineering. As Mathew Ray rigorously describes it in his book *White Trash* (a critical archeological analysis of the social construction of "whiteness" in the United States), blacks and whites on the lower rungs of society exhibited a high degree of positive social interaction during the early period of U.S. history.[12] Both immigrant European laborers and freed African slaves in the North, as well as indentured whites and enslaved blacks in the South, maintained a substantial degree of contact. Interestingly, in keeping with the "problem" of slave rebellions in the Latin world, blacks and whites who shared common economic and sociospatial realities frequently joined forces in acts of social unrest and banditry.[13] Early on, white elites in the United States identified the black/white social nexus as producing "partners in crime" and consciously sought to divide the country through a socially constructed color line.[14] Segregation policy was the result. Additionally, in terms of furthering the project of gendercide, poor white and black males were pitted against each other through new masculinist identities. Prior to institutionalized segregation, landless males of both races were viewed as less than human (recall that landless white men could not vote because they were seen as cognitively inferior). However, the new segregation system required that poor white males be elevated to the status of full human beings, while black men remained discursively and institutionally in the realm of the animals.

A major means by which the poor white male could assert his "humanness" in U.S. society was by playing a role in the control and punishment of black men on behalf of the white elite. This was done by acquiring one of three poor white male identities—the cracker, the cop, or the good ol' boy.[15] Within plantation society, the cracker cracked the whip, castrated the black man, and even killed him. He continued in this role, albeit with certain modifications, in the postslave U.S. agrarian economy. The cop maintained law and order, oversaw chain gangs, "shook down" black drivers and pedestrians found wandering in the wrong side of town, and so on. The poor white man as cop still plays an important and socially esteemed role in controlling poor black men, a subject that will be examined in greater detail later. Finally, the good ol' boy takes the law into his own hands and orchestrates lynchings and other hate crimes to assert his "whiteness" within an economically competitive society. While the early slave era in the United States broke bonds between black males and their families, the later slave and postslave eras broke bonds between black males and their white counterparts, continuing to control the black man's alleged "dangerousness" by controlling his sociospatial and physical integrity.

Marginalizing the Black Vet: European, Pacific and Inner-City Theatres

The social construction of the inner city can be understood through two historical phases: the red-lining phase that followed the Second World War, and the containment phase that began in the post-civil-rights era of the mid-1970s. Kofi Hadjor, in his book *Another America,* gives an excellent and detailed analysis of the complex factors that led to the construction of what was once termed the "black ghetto" and is today termed the "inner city." I will highlight some of Hadjor's findings here to illustrate how the cultural construction of the black male as a dangerous entity in need of control evolved in the modern context. I also use Hadjor's findings as a point of departure to illustrate how young men and boys today have inherited the so-called 'hood mentality as a form of internalized colonialism.

Hadjor maintains that, unlike immigration in the late nineteenth and early twentieth centuries, the next significant demographic shift in the United States was internal.[16] It involved the northern migration of impoverished black sharecroppers in the period between 1930 and 1960. Many went to work in both unionized and nonunionized industrial centers. Additionally, during World War II, many African Americans migrated to the West Coast in search of high-paying military industry jobs, giving rise to communities such as South Central Los Angeles.[17]

During this period, "inner city" meant literally the central portion of an urban area, and not necessarily a center of high crime and poverty. Additionally, many inner cities remained culturally diverse until after the Second World War. This later era was marked by the "white-flight phase in U.S. demographic history, highlighted by red-lining, institutionalized housing segregation. However, as Hadjor argues, white flight is often misinterpreted as a massive racist "conspiracy" on the part of urban ethnic whites. In reality, the racist context of suburbanization did not necessarily exist within urban ethnic white society. Indeed, there is no empirical evidence or anecdotal data to back this claim. Instead, Hadjor contends, racist ideals existed within the public and private institutional policies of the U.S. housing industry itself.[18]

After the Second World War, both the U.S. Veteran's Administration and the Federal Housing Authority pumped millions of dollars into suburban development, offering good-quality, low-mortgage homes—but in general only to white GIs and their families. The tens of thousands of black servicemen who fought in the Second World War were largely deprived of this privilege.[19] Hadjor cites thousands of records involving black servicemen who applied for both federal and private loans to purchase or improve inner-city property or invest in a local business enterprise as early as 1948. Most, if not all, of these loans in the burgeoning, undesirable "Negro" districts were denied.[20] The combined sociospatial and economic restrictions, over time, contributed to the manufacturing of a new kind of poverty—the ghetto.[21]

By the 1950s, the state's prescription for this problem was (once again) informed by the construct of the dangerous, untrustworthy black male. Welfare policy (although created at an earlier time) reinforced the need for families to break up as a criterion for giving children food, health care, and housing assistance. The black woman had to show "just cause" for such assistance, and in the most degrading way imaginable. She was expected to show that she was unattached to a male partner (and preferably did not know the identity of the child's father), or that the partner, if present, showed no initiative in raising the children. Evidence of a competent male presence (marriage, a male partner seeking work and/or education) was punished by depriving women and children of assistance.[22]

Less than a decade after the Second World War, then, the black family—after struggling to stay alive amidst the legacy of slavery—was once again broken down in many areas of the country, this time through more subtle forms of social engineering overseen by political institutions.[23]

Cosmo Men and Little Men: 'Hood Boys versus Global Elites

While the civil rights movement attempted to reinvigorate the inner city through programs of social investment, the entire concept of the state encouraging the growth of human capabilities became an anachronism by the 1980s. The era of globalization involved a two-pronged ideological framework, one that vilified the welfare state and one that embraced the notion of the hypermasculine "cosmo-man," a kind of affluent "ubermensch" in the Nietzschean sense, one who would demonstrate through wealth his superiority over lesser men.[24]

Today, urban black communities not only are the poorest communities in the United States but also represent a section of the poor that is blamed for creating its own poverty and for threatening the social order of an upwardly aspiring nation. This view of African American society, reproduced and reinforced through popular culture, political policy, and private-sector practices, is linked to the larger discursive framework of global elites. The new economic elitism, under the aegis of "cosmo-man," purports to defend a new kind of patriarchal order, whereby the privileged male "haves" summarily target the male "have-nots."[25] On an international level, it is no coincidence that the number of street children (mostly male) who are killed by police has escalated throughout the world. In the streets of Sao Paulo, Delhi, and even Moscow, an undeclared war against the unwashed male "other" is underway.[26]

In the United States, the systematic objectification and control of poor, particularly black, males likewise play an important role in maintaining the desired social order. In this case, it is informed by the long historical tradition of objectifying black males. While the black female as threat (e.g., the stereotypical welfare queen) can be controlled through policies of manipulation (for example, being thrown into work without adequate training or child-care, or forced into sterilization), the black male as threat requires the implementation of policies of direct force to keep him at the margins, and policies of containment to ensure that he does not encroach upon the serenity of growing industrial parks and gated communities.[27] Here, the image of the dangerous black male, culturally constructed through media, political, and academic discourse, plays an important role in informing such practices.[28] These practices I identify as gendercidal in scope and nature. I also argue that they take on two concrete, overlapping forms: direct gendercide through overt force and indirect gendercide through psychological coercion.

Direct Gendercide through Overt Force

Constructing the criminal. Crime is a grim reality in U.S. life. However, the notion that there is an ever-rising tide of violent crime is a myth.[29] Indeed, crime rates have dropped dramatically over the past two decades. Nevertheless, this myth is strong and has led to billions of dollars being poured into both law enforcement and the prison industry.[30] With regard to crime perpetrated by African American males, TV crime shows and entrepreneurial entertainers from the African American community itself help to perpetuate the myth that the gangsta lifestyle is a far-reaching phenomenon that affects the majority of young black males.[31] The cultural notion of the black male as a criminal has given rise to a significant gap between blacks and whites arrested for the same types of crime. The nature and duration of punishment is often different for blacks than for whites, and the frequency with which the death penalty is meted out to blacks, compared with whites who have committed similar crimes, shows an equally wide discrepancy. Furthermore, black males in the United States are targeted as *potential* criminals far more frequently than are white males. Amnesty International, in its 2000 report on the United States, illustrates these problems quite clearly. African Americans make up 80 percent of death row inmates; approximately 15 percent of black males executed are minors as young as sixteen. Each major city in the United States commits two to six thousand acts of (reported) police brutality per year, 92 percent of which are directed at males of color. Up to 20 percent of these cases involve the death of black males through shooting, beating, excessive restraint, and even torture. The number of African American children, particularly males, who have become the fatal victims of police violence has quadrupled since 1990.[32] Indeed, in its report on the United States, this international human rights organization has a category found only in the U.S. section of its annual human rights world prospectus—"Driving While Black," which lists instances of the beating, torture, and even killing of black (overwhelmingly male) motorists who have committed no crime, or who have committed minor violations such as speeding.[33]

Categorizing the baby criminal. Direct gendercide by force is also upheld by academic institutions and the public and private sectors that support them.[34] Psychologists, sociologists, and even political scientists construct intellectual, seemingly empirical, arguments that reinforce the image of the dangerous black male. An excellent example of this is the $2.7 billion project proposed by Dr. Frederick K. Goodwin of the Alcohol, Drug Abuse, and Mental Health administration in 1994. The U.S. government and the National Science Foundation came close to funding his project, which would have involved identifying a hundred thousand young black boys and monitoring them over a period of time; extracting their DNA to monitor genetically embedded "social pathologies"; and then implementing various programs to redirect their allegedly inherent pathological behaviors. Systems of reeducation, spatiocultural control, psychotherapy, and chemical therapy would have been applied to the target population, making this one of the nation's most ambitious medical projects—a combination of hi-tech futurism and Joseph Mengele–like nostalgia.[35]

Goodwin's project was cut short by the intervention of concerned citizens, both within and outside the African American community, as well as by several concerned members of Congress. While Goodwin's project appears bizarre in its scope and vision, it nevertheless reflects a well-documented trend in U.S. society's preoccupation with black males, and the way in which important and diverse institutions establish a complex social, political, and economic nexus to address the perceived "problem."

Indirect Gendercide: Black-on-Black Violence and the Killing of the Self

A more subtle, though pervasive, form of black male gendercide in the United States is articulated by Jawanza Kunjufu, a respected child psychologist who has acted as advisor to agencies such as the Center for Disease Control. Through extensive quantitative and qualitative research, Kunjufu identifies a psychosocial phenomenon that is prevalent among many young black males, a phenomenon that he calls "black male seasoning." This encapsulates the multiple ways in which the contemporary culture (institutions, the media, political discourse as it informs teachers, police officers, social workers, etc.) bombards the young black male with the ongoing message that he is both dangerous and worthless. As Kunjufu states: "A happy and curious boy is 'seasoned' (e.g., symbolically raped), so that by age seven or eight he is embittered, cynical and expects to die young."[36]

As products of both contemporary social forces and specific intersecting historical events, many young African American boys internalize these conditions, which in turn evolve into acts of self-destruction. It is not a condition that is usually examined at the political level. While labeled a problem for social workers (lacking the intellectual rigor of higher academic enterprises such as political science and political economy), I identify the internalized oppression of young African American males as, indeed, a political issue that requires sustained intellectual analysis. Indeed, the current condition of "male seasoning" in U.S. inner cities in many ways parallels Frantz Fanon's analysis of internalized colonialism. Some of the traits "male seasoning" and internalized colonialism have in common include:

> A belief in the dominant culture's representation of the self;
> Hatred toward those most like oneself;
> Direct or indirect destruction of the self.[37]

A common internalized coping mechanism that many African American boys acquire is what Kunjufu calls "macho posing," as compensation for a feeling of powerlessness. Displaced anger, resulting from a lack of information about the factors that have led to one's sociospatial condition, uncritical acceptance of media images of the alleged "self," and low expectations on the part of immediate authority figures often lead to black-on-black male violence—the first phase of indirect gendercide. This negative view of the self, coupled with a limited, closed, and hostile sociospatial environment, creates a situation in which boys try to outdo other boys in their level of "maleness"—the only possession they feel they truly own, given their limited view of masculinity. Kunjufu posits as follows: "We need to show young African American males how they can preserve their manhood without having to kill someone because their shoes were stepped on." Indeed, the level of black-on-black violence has risen dramatically over the past decade, coinciding with drastic cutbacks in educational, vocational, and recreational expenses for children on the part of both federal and regional governments in the United States.[38]

Self-destruction is the second phase of indirect gendercide, and the most insidious. While black male suicide is on a par with white male suicide, "quasi-morticide," or self-destruction through deliberately dangerous action, is highest among young black males. Indeed, because suicide is viewed as "sissy" in many cultural communities, including African American communities, exposure to conditions that will inevitably lead to an early death may be a more honorable, culturally acceptable way of committing de facto suicide. Kunjufu states: "Of all African American males who OD on heroine or cocaine, how many should be officially registered as 'accidental' deaths?" He cites high rates of HIV through unprotected sex, the use of alcohol or drugs while driving, and instigating altercations that would almost guarantee being killed by one's rival as other widespread manifestations of quasi-morticide.[39]

The murder of the self is, for many young black males, the annihilation of a male self rejected by society. It is a nihilistic condition prevalent among many African American youths.[40] Yet this nihilistic condition, like other phases of black history and its legacy of gendercide, is met with resistance. Programs that embrace a philosophy of discovering one's hidden, more vital identity, and of more critically examining the array of harmful cultural messages, are being implemented—albeit with limited funding—in many African American communities. For example, DeWitt Hoard, a psychologist in San Francisco's juvenile justice system, has worked closely with Brazilian psychologists who utilize Paulo Freire's system of combining psychological treatment with critical sociopolitical analysis.[41] Other efforts have included addressing structural violence (e.g., factors contributing to poverty) in a more direct manner, and identifying the sociopolitical regimes of control that impose structural violence. Other initiatives have employed cultural, religious, and entrepreneurial strategies.

Some programs have been accused of offering mere band-aid solutions to complex problems, and others have been accused of feeding into the same cultural stereotypes they seek to challenge, in order to obtain government and/or corporate funding. Such efforts nevertheless represent vigorous forms of resistance to the pervasive culture of nihilism, and to the institutional, political, and intellectual practices that allow such a negative culture or "life-world" to exist. Especially valuable are programs that employ a transnational model of community work, including an acknowledgment of practices that target young males. Examples include Hoard's Freire model, the Simba program in Atlanta that addresses male-on-male violence, and intellectual projects such as FairTest, which draws together scientists and statisticians of color to deconstruct institutionally sanctioned but ideologically distorted data on minority youth. These efforts and others represent a multifaceted response to a problem that is both old and new.

Conclusion: Black Male Gendercide in the Global Context

Gendercide in the United States is unique in that it is expressed within the context of an ongoing historical project of controlling males within a specific ethnic group. U.S. gendercide does not occur within a narrow time frame or under specific conditions of war or political repression, as does gendercide in many other regions of the world, such as Kosovo, Rwanda, and Kashmir. An analysis of black male gendercide in the United States helps us to frame new questions about gendercidal events and trends in other regions. For example, it is conceivable that many of the acts of gendercide occurring within an atmosphere of warfare and political unrest may, in reality, be rooted in more hidden and ongoing forms of gendercide. A historical-structural approach to gendercide, as presented here, may be a significant analytical tool in understanding these other cases. More importantly, an analysis of black gendercide in the United States helps us appreciate that not only male-to-female oppression is historically and culturally embedded in most societies, but also male-to-male oppression, through historical institutions and repressive cultural mechanisms.

Notes

1. Adam Jones, "Gendercide and Genocide," *Journal of Genocide Research,* 2: 2 (June 2000), pp. 185–211.
2. Miller cited in ibid., p. 187.
3. Eugene Genovese, *Roll, Jordan, Roll: The World the Slaves Made* (New York: Random House, 1976).
4. Ibid.
5. Justo L. Gonzalez, *MaZana* (Austin: Abdingdon Press, 1996).
6. Despite these forms of sociospatial control, families would still find covert ways of maintaining contact over generations. See W.E.B. DuBois, *The Souls of Black Folk* (New York: Penguin, 1903).
7. Richard B. Norgaard, *Development Betrayed* (Berkeley: University of California Press, 1995).
8. Herb Boyd and Robert Allen, *Brotherman: The Odyssey of Black Men in America* (New York: Ballantine Press, 1995).
9. Interview with Dionne Bensonsmith, professor, Department of Political Studies, Cornell University, 20 August 2000.
10. James Allen, *Without Sanctuary* (Santa Fe, N.M.: Twin Palms, 2000).

11. John Hope Franklin and Alfred A. Moss, *From Slavery to Freedom* (New York: Knopf, 2000).

12. Mathew Ray, *White Trash* (Berkeley: University of California Press, 1994).

13. Slave rebellions occurred in North America, but were not as common. See Eric Wolf, *Europe and the People without a History* (Berkeley: University of California Press, 1992).

14. Ray, *White Trash,* pp. 57–59.

15. Ibid.

16. Kofi B. Hadjor, *Another America* (Boston: South End Press, 1997).

17. Augusta C. Del Zotto and Timothy Fong, "The Changing Face of California," National Public Radio, October 1989.

18. Hadjor, *Another America,* pp. 89–93.

19. Although African American servicemen died in the line of duty at a rate proportionately equal to that of white GIs, their true numbers have only recently been documented. From the Civil War up to the Korean War, most African American servicemen were officially documented as performing "service"-type work (e.g., janitor, cook), rather than combat duty. Additionally, African American servicemen were frequently beaten and even killed by white members of their own troop, as well as by enemy units. After the First and Second World Wars, a number of black GIs chose to remain in Europe rather than return to the United States because they faced less discrimination there. See David Maxwell and Thomas Dupont's chronology of African American military service at *www.redstone.srmy.mil/history/integrate/CHRON3.html.*

When the U.S. military was finally integrated in the mid-1950s under Eisenhower, de facto racism was still prevalent. While the rate of African American GI deaths in combat equaled that of whites (Latinos and Native Americans suffered a much higher toll, accounting for some 20 percent of the names on the Vietnam memorial wall), African Americans and other minorities were subjected to longer periods of combat duty without leave. The result was that African American Vietnam veterans have a 40 percent higher rate of posttraumatic stress disorder and are more likely to commit suicide than are their white veteran counterparts. See Matthew Friedman, "Matsunaga Vietnam Veterans Project—Final Report" (Washington, D.C.: National Center for Post Traumatic Stress Disorder, 2000).

20. Hadjor, *Another America,* pp. 38–44.

21. Informal interviews with friends and relatives who served in the Second World War offer a glimpse of how other minorities dealt with housing discrimination. Many Latino veterans overcame these policies by registering as "White," as did Filipino veterans on the West Coast. Southwestern Latinos could not manipulate the racist policy as well, because people with Hispanic surnames were automatically denied access to the suburbs. Men with Jewish surnames were given access to certain suburbs and not others. Some Jews changed their surnames to take advantage of the GI Bill's housing programs.

22. Bensonsmith interview, 1 October 2000.

23. Cornel West, *Race Matters* (New York: Routledge Press, 1993).

24. Lily H. M. Ling, "Global Passions within Global Interests: Race, Gender, and Culture in our Postcolonial Order," in R. Palan and J. S. Rowen, eds., *Global Political Economy: Contemporary Theories* (London: Routledge, 2000).

25. Ibid.

26. Jean Theurauf, *Deprived of Dignity: Children of the Streets* (London: St. John's Press, 1997).

27. Michael Katz, *Improving Poor People* (Princeton, N.J.: Princeton University Press, 1993).

28. Earl Ofari Hutchinson, *The Assassination of the Black Male Image* (New York: Simon and Schuster, 1994).

29. Farai Chideya, *Don't Believe the Hype* (New York: Penguin, 1995).

30. Ibid., pp. 250–52.

31. West, *Race Matters*, pp. 54–57.

32. Amnesty International, *Amnesty International 2000 Annual Report* (London: Amnesty International Headquarters, 2000).

33. Ibid. While President Bill Clinton signed the Police Accountability Act, which would require that the attorney general investigate and document all acts of police brutality, Congress has for the past four years denied funding for this measure (*HRREC Annual Report*, 1999).

34. Public sectors include the Department of Health and Human Services and the Department of Education, which use scholarly data that exclusively targets young black males to implement social policies, usually of a disciplining nature. Private sectors that use similar data to bolster their enterprises include pharmaceuticals, such as Lily and Roche, which contracts with government to dispense drugs used in controlling "violent" black youth (and other minorities), and Lockheed-Martin, which creates elaborate new prison and home-arrest systems paid for by government agencies. See Daniel Burton-Rose, *The Celling of America: An Inside Look at the U.S. Prison Industry* (Monroe, Me: Common Courage Press, 1998). In this last example, DeWitt Hoard, psychologist for San Francisco's juvenile justice system, maintains that one-half of home surveillance systems (e.g., ankle alarms for home arrest) are issued to males of color under sixteen years of age who have committed petty crimes or acts not considered criminal if committed by adults. A recent, much-publicized case involved an eleven-year-old who stole ice cream from a liquor store. Interview with DeWitt Hoard, psychologist, City and County of San Francisco Juvenile Justice Department, 10 December 1999.

35. Chideya, *Don't Believe the Hype*, pp. 191–92.

36. Jawanza Kunjufu, *Countering the Conspiracy to Destroy Black Boys* (Chicago: African American Images, 1999), p. 135.

37. Frantz Fanon, *Black Skin, White Masks* (New York: Grove Press, 1967).

38. Kunjufu, *Countering the Conspiracy,* p. 136.

39. Ibid., p. 126.

40. West, *Race Matters,* p. 115.

41. Hoard interview. See also Paulo Freire, *Pedagogy of the Oppressed* (Chicago: University of Chicago Press, 1989).

7

Genetic Engineering and Queer Biotechnology

The Eugenics of the Twenty-first Century?

Stefanie S. Rixecker

> Of one thing, I have no doubt. The growing use of reprogenetics is inevitable. For better *and* worse, a new age is upon us—an age in which we as humans will gain the ability *to change the nature of our species.*
>
> —Lee M. Silver, professor, Departments of Molecular Biology, Ecology, and Evolutionary Biology, Princeton University

Introduction

The Human Genome Project is the most recent endeavor of biomedical cartography. It is a project dedicated to mapping the entire human genome in order to better understand the genetic heritage and attributes of the species *h. sapiens sapiens.* The significance of the Human Genome Project, and the science involved in decoding the genome, cannot and should not be underestimated. Ultimately, it will impact upon the scientific, medical, economic, political, and cultural futures of all living and future human beings.

As President Clinton heralded, the map of the human genome is "one of the most important, most wondrous maps ever produced by humankind."[1] As wondrous as this map may be, its ability to alter the way medicine and science explore and chart the human body depends upon the older social and cultural maps used to navigate its consequences. These sociocultural "maps," such as ethics, law, policy, justice, and human rights, have received some attention, especially since World War II. But they are not sufficiently mature to handle and address the immediate (and long-term) consequences of the Human Genome Project and its spin-off technologies and programs. As such, future biopolitics will be contentious, economically driven, politically fraught, and potentially catastrophic for minority peoples and cultures around the globe.

Although much of the public relations surrounding the HGP, and genetic engineering generally, focuses upon the potential medical and human benefits—for example, an understanding of and possible cure for diseases such as cystic fibrosis and Alzheimer's—the more insidious and problematic consequences of the science and technology are addressed superficially, ignored entirely, or left to others to contest after completion of the biotechnological innovation. In this way, biomedical researchers, practitioners, and investors have the means to divest themselves of responsibility for their actions. The lack of accountability increases the potential for harm because few sociocultural mechanisms, such as professional censure, financial levy, or prison terms, exist to restrict or constrain certain types of behavior. Thus, the processes and outcomes of biomedical research primarily depend upon internal moral mechanisms, such as research ethics committees and the researcher's own moral code, and societal norms and mechanisms, including policies and laws regarding genetic engineering. In many cases, these are insufficient for protecting people who cannot defend themselves.

The vicissitudes of biopolitics become even more complex because the researchers themselves have a variety of motivations for engaging in their respective field or research. Rarely is it possible to label research as purely "good" or purely "evil." Indeed, as has already been mentioned, the consequences of any given research are ultimately arbitrated through existing sociocultural mechanisms, thereby further removing the researchers themselves from the penultimate consequences of their exploits. Nevertheless, it is important and necessary to deliberate the complexities of genetic technologies and programs, such as the Human Genome Project, due to the potentially profound effects the various research endeavors can yield. This chapter focuses upon the possible consequences of genetic technologies in relation to marginalized and minority populations, with a particular focus upon homosexuality.

Since the desire to understand how humans function drives much of the research into genetics, it should come as no surprise that one focus of research is human sexuality. The research into sexuality focuses on different types of sexuality, and a considerable amount of research has been undertaken with regard to homosexuality. Partly, this is driven by a belief (by researchers and others alike) that proving homosexuality is biological, as opposed to cultural or social, will necessitate social policy and legislation to acknowledge the equality—and "normality"—of homosexuals. In other words, the biological innateness of homosexuality means gays and lesbians could not be discriminated against. Such a conclusion requires two assumptions (or beliefs): first, homosexuality is an innate biological (and hence genetic) trait; and second, proving the genetic innateness of homosexuality is sufficient to secure safe and equitable sociopolitical environs for homosexuals (and others of "queer" persuasion).

Current research has not located one single, specific genetic marker, despite the research focusing on Xq28, yet many researchers remain sufficiently secure in their belief that homosexuality, like all sexuality, is genetically imprinted.[2] Knowing where markers are located, however, does not mean it is possible to remove that characteristic or genetic predisposition in an already fully formed individual. At present, biomedical science is unable to genetically alter a living human being without damaging the person overall. Instead, the focus of most genetics and genetic engineering requires a commingling with reproductive biology, thereby establishing the significance of reprogenetics. The focus of the research in genetic alteration and "enhancement," including with humans, necessitates changing the genetic makeup of embryos or discarding those that carry deadly diseases or other unwanted characteristics.

Such scenarios may sound futuristic, but they are already underway with regard to certain fertility problems and genetically inherited diseases. In the case of homosexuality, for example, the creation of a diagnostic tool would detect whether the characteristic of "homosexuality" was present in a fetus. Then, the prospective parents, or anyone else authorized to decide, could determine whether to allow a fetus with a positive test to be aborted. Alternatively, through the use of preimplantation genetic diagnosis (PGD) and in vitro fertilization (IVF), individuals could preselect for certain traits, including the lack of homosexuality, and thereby circumvent the issue of abortion because none of the embryos (or pre-embryos as they are called at this stage) would be within the woman's womb.[3] Thus, by using current technological knowledge and skills, the eradication of homosexuality in small cultural groups or on a global scale is *theoretically* feasible. The main argument of this paper is that contemporary biopolitics yields the *potential* for the termination of the homosexual population, approximately 3 to 10 percent of the human population. Such elimination is a form of genocide, a genocide enabled through a millenarian form of eugenics. Most likely, this would be targeted initially at male homosexuals, due to current research patterns and greater "success" with male subjects, and thereby constitutes a form of gendercide, as conceptualized by Mary Anne Warren and elaborated by Adam Jones. In unpackaging the contemporary biopolitics scene, I investigate the extent to which current scientific research and contemporary cultural interpretations intersect to create a possible future scenario of queer genocide.

Unravelling Life's Mysteries: Genetic Engineering and the Biotech Industry

The contemporary biopolitics that propel the sciences of genetic engineering and reproductive technologies are dynamic, complex, and fast paced.[4] Like many specialized scientific fields today, the science has actually developed from hundreds of years of research.[5] For many, the advent of the modern era of genetics began with the "discovery" of the DNA double helix by James Watson and Francis Crick in 1953. When this date is used, genetics and genetic engineering can be regarded as young advances in a long history of human innovation. For this reason, amongst others, genetic engineering receives both admiration and disdain, because people (researchers and the public alike) simultaneously relish and deride how this "novel" understanding of life can be used to alter, modify, and improve genetics and reproduction.

Despite the recent dawn of the "Biological Age" and the "Biotech Century," the ideas and activities associated with genetics and genetic engineering are quite old.[6] Humans have used their knowledge of plant variation, as well as of animal husbandry and breeding, to construct or direct the lineage and characteristics of a variety of plants and domestic animals across millennia. Indeed, this is an activity that has been used across cultures, geographic space, and human time. These subtle interventions can also be regarded as contributing to the formation and ongoing changes of life on planet earth, and in this sense they contribute to the processes of evolution.

Nevertheless, the current knowledge of genetics, its ability to be used as a means of changing organisms (hence the use of the term "engineering"), and the added innovations of biological and reproductive technologies (such as embryo selection and cloning) means that the processes of evolution have been ruptured, sped up, or fundamentally altered through further human intervention. For many, the rapidity of change, the risk or uncertainty of such changes, and the lack of useful ethical frameworks makes the newfound technology problematic, if not repulsive, deplorable, and immoral.[7] For others, the new technologies' ability to ignore and circumvent "natural" barriers to breeding and reproduction suggests that humans are tinkering with life processes and systems in ways that are high risk, spiritually corrupt, culturally inappropriate, and imperialistic.[8] Irrespective of these criticisms and concerns, however, the science and research continue and enable the production of technologies, diagnostics, and other tools, whereby the constitution of species, including humans, is being transformed.

The Human Genome Project (HGP) marks a major milestone in genetics because of its immense contribution to the knowledge of how the human genetic infrastructure and its trillions of minute components are arranged and ultimately yield particular effects and characteristics in a given individual. The HGP was initiated in 1990, and it was then estimated that it would take fifteen years to complete, marking a completion date in 2005. A publicly funded consortium of international research institutes, the National Institutes of Health in the United States and the Wellcome Trust in the United Kingdom being the two largest contributors, worked collegially and steadfastly to complete the HGP. However, in an example of postmodern biopolitics exemplified through professional rivalries and economic incentives, a new corporation, known as Celera Genomics, entered the race to sequence the human genome. In 1998, Dr. J. Craig Venter, president of Celera Genomics, announced that his company would be first to complete the sequencing and would bring forward its completion to 2000. This deadline increased the speed with which the publicly and privately funded teams worked on their goal, and the accelerated timetable ultimately yielded a "first draft" of the sequenced human genome heralded by the joint announcement by Drs. Collins and Venter on 26 June 2000.

The race to map the human genome was basically a race to create a standard format for organizing and using the various components of the genome.

Nevertheless, it was still conveyed within the boundaries and discourses of older sociocultural concepts and frameworks. Although less emotive language regarding the genome can be found, the majority of media discussions use (and misuse) metaphorical examples to make sense of the new science and its abilities. Popular science authors, such as Mark Ridley, provide non-comparative descriptions of the genome where the genome is described as "the complete set of human genes . . . packaged in twenty-three separate pairs of chromosomes."[9] Even Ridley, though, requires a familiar metaphorical grounding for his more "neutral" discussion of the human genome. He compares the twenty-three human chromosomes to book chapters, and this is most explicitly represented in his book's title and subtitle, *Genome: The Autobiography of a Species in 23 Chapters.* He is certainly not alone in using familiar language and metaphors to describe new biological and technological concepts. Indeed, the majority of commentators find it necessary to liken the genome to some other familiar entity—be it a map, text, or book. For example, the news media described the genome as "the sum of all genetic material encased in nearly every cell of the human body . . . [which] is very long—at least 3 billion chemical letters long, as many letters as . . . 10,000 copies of the Sunday *New York Times.*"[10]

Such metaphorical allusions to text and books were also common amongst scientific researchers and politicians. On 26 June 2000, when Dr. Collins and Dr. Venter made their joint announcement, the language of the announcement highlighted the views and symbols often associated with this project and genetics generally. For example, Dr. Collins remarked, "Today, we celebrate the revelation of the first draft of the human book of life," and President Clinton extended the metaphor by making a direct link with God and the Bible when he said, "Today we are learning the language with which God created life."[11] These examples illustrate how the products of science and technology remain encoded, interpreted and communicated within older social understandings, discourses, and metaphors.[12] It is exactly this overlay of the old sociocultural maps on new (genetic) maps, and vice-versa, that creates the subsequent issues and problems related to how such technology and scientific possibilities will be used, regulated, and extended. The need to use the old familiar lexicon to explain new concepts is further complicated when another sociocultural layer is overlaid on this complex political landscape. In particular, discussions of "normality" and "nature," especially with regard to human sexuality and reproduction, create a whole new series of questions and conundrums.

Psychobiological Maps of the Self and Other: Normality through Variation

Sexuality in mammals, including humans, is regarded as a natural, normal, and (often) necessary component of a healthy, functioning individual. Procreation, in particular, is regarded as fundamental to continuation of the species, so it is not surprising that modern social frameworks—whether religious, statutory, or scientific—have focused upon heterosexuality and deemed it *the* norm. In casting heterosexuality in this light, it has also become regarded as not only the norm, but the *normal* and *natural* way of behaving sexually and intimately. Although this seems explicit in the older religious mores within the Judeo-Christian framework, it is also evident in the sciences, where any form of sexuality other than heterosexuality became regarded as not only outside the norm in a statistical sense, but outside the norm in terms of being healthy and normal.[13] Even this, though, requires some clarification and qualification.

The term "homosexuality" is a relatively new one, apparently coined by Karl Maria Kerbetny in a letter on 6 May 1868 to Karl Heinrich Ulrichs. Both men were sex reformers in Germany, and in 1869 Kerbetny used the term publicly in a petition to challenge German law "criminalizing 'unnatural fornication.'" Similarly, the term "heterosexual" was used in a pejorative and stigmatized way within the medical profession in the late 1800s and early 1900s. "Heterosexual" during this time was used as a term to describe "erotic intercourse between men and women." In other words, this meant sexual relations between the opposite sex that were not for the purpose of reproduction were also sanctioned as a medical condition requiring some form of medical intervention. The change from heterosexuality as perverse to normal and the distinctions between heterosexuality and homosexuality changed over time. As Jonathan Ned Katz explains,

> Only in the first quarter of the twentieth century . . . did heterosexuality's doctor advocates succeed in constructing and distributing it as a signifier of sexuality's Standard Brand. Their regularization of eros paralleled contemporary attempts to standardize masculinity and femininity, intelligence and manufacturing. The doctors' heterosexual category proclaimed a new erotic separatism, a novel sex orthodoxy, that forcefully segregated sex "normals" from sex "perverts," and set "hetero" over "homo" in a hierarchy of superior and inferior eroticisms. But only gradually did the idea that there were such creatures as heterosexuals and homosexuals emerge

> from the narrow realm of medical discourse to become a popular, commonplace notion.[14]

The shift toward a hierarchy of sexuality popularized by social and biological experts coalesced with a similar (but older) hierarchy between the sexes. Although this sexual hierarchy, known as patriarchy, has been critiqued and reconstructed by feminist activists and theorists since Simone de Beauvoir wrote her treatise *The Second Sex*, the power of social, political, economic, and scientific forces combined to perpetuate the notion that anyone who did not fit the mold of the white, male, propertied heterosexual was an "other."[15] Throughout the twentieth century, the majority of scientific and social scientific research supported and promulgated these hierarchies, resulting in the practice that humans could be categorized according to preset essential characteristics that were deemed biologically manifest, even when socially and culturally promulgated. Thus, dichotomies and various systems of oppression became defined within and around such categories as sex, race, class, sexuality, and ability.[16] Some of the oppressive forces used to police the differences across people became so violent and hate filled that they led to incidents of persecution, including acts of genocide such as those experienced by Jews, gypsies, and homosexuals during National Socialism in Germany from the 1930s through the mid-1940s.[17]

From such historical evidence, it becomes apparent that the construction of fixed, dichotomous sexualities is an extremely recent invention in the Western world, but one that has very real consequences for queer individuals. Similarly, the challenges to this rigid sexual structure are even more recent, and illustrate the ongoing sociopolitical attempts to define and redefine aspects of human identity and sexuality.[18] In particular, the range of nonheterosexual behaviors, or queer sexualities, labeled by medicine, the sciences, and other cultural groupings as illnesses or diseases, established a series of assumptions and scenarios for those who "suffered" from such afflictions.[19] Whether the cause of the unnatural sexuality was attributed to biological variation (for example, genetic mutation) or poor environmental conditions (for example, psychological disorders brought on due to a poor childhood), the status of queer sexuality as a disease necessitated some form of intervention to provide a "cure" for or abeyance of the behavior. This meant that those who "suffered" from such a disease could once again lead a normal, useful life only if they met the criteria of the modern-day heterosexual. Since the cause of homosexuality was expressed as a classic Western dualism—for example it was rooted in either nature (biology) or nurture (environment)—the possible remedies for the disease were also developed along this Cartesian either/or binary. For this reason, much of the research regarding homosexuality (and its cures) resides within two disciplines, biology and psychology.

In the field of psychology, homosexuality was a certified psychological disorder by virtue of the fact that it was registered as such in the Diagnostic and Statistical Manual of Psychiatric Disorders (DSM), the primary diagnostic manual for the American Psychological Association and the American Psychiatric Association. Homosexuality remained listed as a psychological disorder that could (and presumably should) be treated by mental health professionals until the American Psychiatric Association struck it from the DSM in 1973. The American Psychological Association affirmed this decision in 1975, when it passed a resolution supporting the removal of homosexuality from the DSM register.[20] More recently (in 1997), the American Psychological Association passed a resolution that reiterated its claim that homosexuality is not a mental illness and thus does not require "so-called conversion therapy," because such therapies "prey on prejudice and ignorance about sexual orientation."[21]

What changed in this timeframe? Why did homosexuality, or its conceptualization, shift from being abnormal to normal and unnatural to natural? One possible reason for the shift is that further research into sexuality highlighted that homosexuality was not a psychological disorder; rather, biological or genetic attributes contributed to or caused the condition. The American Psychological Association, for example, supports such an interpretation for the DSM change when it states that

> human beings can not choose to be either gay or straight. Sexual orientation emerges for most people in early adolescence without any prior sexual experience. Although we can choose whether to act on our feelings, psychologists do not consider sexual orientation to be a conscious choice that can be voluntarily changed.[22]

As a consequence, it was argued that psychology should not categorize the condition (or characteristic) as a mental disorder or illness. Instead, homosexuals, or those with queer sexualities generally, might require psychological counseling due to homophobia within society that places undue (and unjust) pressure on the individual, in turn creating psychological disorders such as anxiety, depression, and other conditions that remain in the DSM manual. Yet another possible explanation is that the removal of homosexuality from the DSM was a direct consequence of the ongoing political movement established by gays and lesbians worldwide, and particularly in the United States, for recognition of their human rights. Additionally, the fact that a number of practicing psychiatrists and psychologists are themselves gay, lesbian, or queer also contributed to the attitudes in, and politicization of, the discipline and clinical practice of psychology. In this sense, the redefinition of homosexuality may be a consequence of altered social, cultural, and legal contexts, as well as legislative and policy mechanisms based upon the recognition that homosexuals are entitled to the same respect and dignity as all other humans accorded protection under national and international law.

Nevertheless, individuals, groups, and organizations within the psychological profession, as well as in the wider sociocultural landscape, continue to regard homosexuality, and the range of queer sexualities, as a disorder that is abominable and requires treatment. Both the Internet and academic indices provide excellent examples of the ongoing (and prolific) debates regarding the causes and possible cures for homosexuality, as well as queer sexualities more generally. For example, a major counterforce to the American Psychological Association's stance on homosexuality comes from the National Association for Research and Therapy of Homosexuality (NARTH), founded in 1992. NARTH's home page on the World Wide Web provides further information for individuals who suffer from homosexuality and wish to be cured or "changed," in NARTH's terminology.[23] In addition to advocating possible alternatives to the gay lifestyle, NARTH's members include psychological practitioners who support and implement various forms of conversion and reparative therapies for homosexuals who wish to change from a homosexual to a heterosexual lifestyle. Such activity is underwritten by NARTH's statement of purpose, which notes that "NARTH's function is to provide psychological understanding of the cause, treatment and behavior patterns associated with homosexuality, within the boundaries of civil public dialogue."[24]

NARTH argues that change to one's homosexual behavior is possible with hard work, a supportive counseling environment, and self-reflection. Fundamentally, NARTH claims that homosexuality is not a direct inherited condition, that is, it cannot be explained as genetic, and thus it is justifiable (and prudent) to focus upon the environmental factors that contribute to homosexuality.[25]

Additionally, NARTH comments directly on the "abnormal" and "unnatural" aspects of homosexuality. Specifically, it argues that homosexuality is not "normal" because

> As clinicians, we have witnessed the intense suffering caused by homosexuality, which we see as a "failure to function according to design." Homosexuality distorts the natural bond of friendship that would naturally unite two persons of the same sex. It works against society's essential male/female design and the all-important family unit. In males, it is associated with [*sic*] poor relationship with father; difficulty individuating from mother; a sense of masculine deficit; and a persistent belief of having been different from, and misunderstood by, same-sex childhood peers. In adulthood we also see a persistent pattern of maladaptive behaviors in gay and lesbian life.[26]

Based upon these assumptions and premises, NARTH was instrumental in challenging the American Psychological Association's recent attempts at imposing a professional sanction on those who perform conversion therapies. Ultimately, the APA's resolution was to reemphasize its view of homosexuality (noted earlier) and state that all therapies used with and on homosexual clients must be carried out in an ethical and professionally appropriate manner, that is, with the client's consent. NARTH ensured that the more directive policy, namely the one disallowing conversion therapies altogether, did not become an APA resolution. This example also highlights that values and belief systems can become more entrenched despite (and because of) changes in professional communities or current research. Ultimately, these websites, and the views they present, illustrate that attitudes regarding homosexuality are not easily changed, despite their relatively recent introduction to the Western medical and psychological lexicon. Thus, the ongoing linguistic, cultural, professional, and legal battles surrounding homosexuality continue within and across the professional/public realms of discourse and politics in psychology.

Such battles and ongoing debates are also evident within the biological sciences where research is undertaken with regard to sexuality and sexual practices among humans, as well as across other species. Again, issues regarding what is "natural" and "normal" abound. As Bruce Bagemihl explains

> Homosexuality has a "natural history" in every sense of the term: that is, it has both biological ("natural") and social or cultural ("historical") dimensions that are interconnected and inseparable. It is not a uniform phenomenon in either animals or people: it takes many forms, and it exhibits numerous variations and idiosyncrasies. The interplay of biology and environment in shaping these features—and indeed the very definition of what is "cultural" as opposed to "biological"—is far more com-

> plex than polarized debates would have us believe. Because the discussion is often framed in terms of misleading dichotomies such as "nature versus nurture" or "genetics versus environment," the possibility that both are relevant (and can influence one another) is repeatedly overlooked, as is the possibility that sexual behavior in some animals has a significant sociocultural component.[27]

Bagemihl explores the idea that natural diversity within and across species contributes to the necessary variation of life on the planet. Moving beyond the now common discussions of biodiversity, as has become customary within ecological circles, Bagemihl addresses the diverse forms of sexuality evident across species by documenting hundreds of species and their homosexual proclivities. He does so with the intention of highlighting that biology can and does contribute to humankind's understanding of how the world works, both because of and irrespective of human prejudice and cultural predilections. This is because ultimately the binary structure of homosexuality depends upon "the eye of the beholder, rather than . . . any inherent quality or context of the phenomenon itself."[28]

Although such both/and constructions can yield far more engaging possibilities than the either/or binary noted earlier, most scientific research into sexuality, especially homosexuality, remains trapped within the hetero/homo binary dualism. This is evident in the way that recent biological and neuroanatomical research regarding homosexuality's possible contributing factors received media notoriety. Perhaps the most striking recent examples are Dean Hamer's "gay gene" and Simon LeVay's "gay brain" studies.[29] The "gay brain" became a frequently used term in 1991, after LeVay, a neuroscientist, published a study that showed a physical difference between heterosexual and homosexual brains.[30] Specifically, he cited a difference in the nucleus of the hypothalamus that appeared larger in straight (i.e., heterosexual) men than in gay men.[31] Although various problems can be attributed to the study, the media's desire to create a readable (i.e., saleable) story meant that the tightly defined scientific interpretations of the data had to be reinterpreted, resulting in the idea that gay men's brains are fundamentally different than straight men's brains, and this difference means that homosexuality, or at least gay male homosexuality, could no longer be discriminated against because it was innate, that is, genetic rather than the product of choice or "lifestyle."[32]

A more obvious example of the binary constructions and difficulties of articulating research on homosexuality is evident in Dean Hamer's "gay gene" studies. The "gay gene" was popularized when Hamer's research regarding genetic linkages on the X chromosome of gay brothers was published.[33] Hamer and his team spent considerable time ensuring their methodologies were followed with painstaking precision. The specific method used by Hamer's team, linkage analysis, is premised upon the assumption that "two genes near to each other in a parent's chromosome are more likely to be passed on to offspring together than two genes far apart."[34] The researcher must look for a marker—parts of DNA that are always similar and can be tracked—that fits with the phenotype they are investigating, in this case, gay males. Although this technique is painstaking and time consuming, it does work, and it led Hamer's team to conclude that a particular location on the X chromosome, Xq28, could be identified as a statistically significant "marker" for homosexuality—a heritable link for homosexuality was present. However, this does *not* mean that it is the only possible location for a gene that influences homosexuality; nor does it mean that other variables, such as hormonal influences during embryonic development, do not affect the expression of homosexuality. Indeed, a later study by Hamer, Pattatucci, and others confirmed that the linkage between Xq28 and homosexuality was evident in males but could not be linked with females.[35] Despite following the scientific community's established protocol when generating these findings, Hamer and his team still had to contend with the realities of cultural (re)interpretation of these particular scientific findings.

Hamer's research catapulted him into the media spotlight, with interviews on key U.S. news programs such as *NBC Nightly News, Nightline, World News Tonight,* and the *MacNeil/Lehrer News Hour.*[36] All of the programs ultimately confused the concept of the gene as a biological unit to one of metaphor, whereby the gene represented cultural and political preferences and issues. Here again is an example of old maps being transposed onto new ones, yielding poor and inaccurate information. Hamer's reflections of his encounter with the media offer some insight into the differing worldviews and frames of reference that are evident between society and scientific practice. Burr comments on Hamer's reflections in this manner:

> Hamer views his experience with the media with good-humored amazement. He recalls the CNN reporter who intoned solemnly before the camera that Hamer's possible finding of a gene "indicates homosexuality might not be a choice." Hamer sighs and then laughs. "It's the exact reverse. The phenotypic fact that homosexuality is *not* chosen was one of the mandatory biological preconditions to concluding there was a gene

> for this trait." . . . He pauses, incredulous. "Can you imagine any sane, reputable biologist spending years of their life and their resources looking through chromosomes for a gene for something that's *chosen?* I suppose you could do it, but you'd have to be a complete idiot, because it would be the genetic equivalent of staking your entire scientific career and reputation on finding the gene for . . . being a Methodist." He sits in his office, trying to imagine it.[37]

Such misunderstandings between the scientific world and the public occur every day. The life sciences are not just a matter of scientific method and pure objectivity; they also depend upon information dissemination via the media, and financial support through sales and the market. However, these three cultural systems of knowledge and meaning making operate under different assumptions, so that what drives one may yield problems, such as misinterpretation, in another cultural knowledge system. Although the consequences of such misinterpretation are often benign, they can also yield serious consequences. For example, for those whose DNA registers the Xq28 marker, possible consequences could be housing or employment discrimination based upon homophobia, despite the individual's not actually displaying "homosexual tendencies." And, in extreme cases, such DNA diagnostics could contribute to genocidal policies and activities.[38] Since this diagnostic tool would initially be specifically targeted at gay males, Jones's argument regarding gendercide is especially compelling here.

It should be noted, however, that gendercide could also be inflicted on female homosexuals (lesbians), transsexuals, intersexuals, and others identifiable under the "queer sexuality" label if a similar diagnostic were to be formulated for these characteristics. At this stage, the research on homosexuality and its genetic links has focused more upon male homosexuals. This is partly due to the general preponderance of biomedical research on male subjects, but it can also be attributed to the link between gay men and HIV/AIDS. Much of the HIV/AIDS research focuses upon gay male subjects, and the data from such studies are also used for other types of research.[39] For these reasons, it is highly likely that gay males will be the initial targets of such new technologies.

Nevertheless, the impacts upon lesbians and other queer populations should not be underestimated. Besides the possible diagnostic tools that could be used to screen for homosexuality, lesbians would also be directly affected by the ongoing changes within reprogenetics. The public's awareness of lesbian parenthood has increased over the past few years, particularly as a result of media attention to celebrity lesbians who choose motherhood, and this has not gone unnoticed by the biomedical and reprogenetic professions. The number of lesbians seeking "treatment" at fertility clinics in order to undergo insemination from sperm donors, IVF, or other reproductive techniques has increased and tested the ethical and legal mechanisms regarding gay women's right to procreate. In some cases, clinics deny lesbians access to sperm-donor facilities and reproductive technologies outright, due to the perceived immorality of enabling homosexuals to reproduce.

The recurring theme of homosexuality, and lesbianism more specifically, as immoral, unnatural, and abhorrent is evident in a variety of other strategies that work to reemphasize and perpetuate the belief that queer individuals deserve ill treatment and fewer rights than do other humans. Although the gendercide framing can certainly be applied to gay males, it can also be conceptualized with regard to women. Specific violence against lesbians has been documented and, as the following quote from an anonymous Peruvian witness indicates, lesbians as well as gay men are easily perceived and treated as "unnatural":

> In 1994 in Lima a very violent raid was carried out in the capital where about seventy-five lesbian women were beaten up and ill treated by the police. Prostitutes get a very rough time in jail. But the treatment of lesbians was even worse. Lesbians were beaten up because, however degrading prostitution can be, it is still regarded as normal behaviour, whereas lesbianism is seen as too threatening to the status quo.[40]

Similar attacks on, and abuse of, transvestites, transsexuals, and other queer-identified people have been documented by Amnesty International, as well as by local, regional, and national organizations. The violence is directed against all those who display differences from the cultural norms prescribed for sexuality. Such abuse can be, and is, directed at the complex *gender* identities of the individuals.

Gender identity in this sense encapsulates assumptions about biological "sex" as well as the culturally defined protocol of "gender" (and its performance). Since the seemingly fixed category of biological sex—that is, male or female—has become more fluid, due to the more detailed understanding of intersexuality and chromosomal differences, this category is no longer as useful or appropriate as it may once have been. Additionally, the many varied formations of "gender" (often regarded as versions of masculinity and femininity) that intersect with sexuality necessitate a more robust and diversified term. "Gender" here incorporates the variety of expressions within the rather artificial boundary between sex (biology) and gender (culture) to acknowledge and integrate the significant interplay between sex, gender, and sexuality. Such a reconceptualization is necessary in the light of ongoing developments in reprogenetics, because it is important to

> consider the politics at stake in the emergence of this latest biogenetic discourse. Like eugenics, the new genetic essentialism and the construction of the genetic subject, *homo geneticus,* is about genetic fitness, about good and bad genes. This introduces a whole new language about genetic defects, abnormal genes, genetic predispositions, genetic selection, genetic screening, genetic therapy, genetic counselling, etc. This is a language about the surveillance of individual pathology. It is a powerful and privileged language, produced and guaranteed by the authority of science and the expertise of the medical profession.[41]

For this reason, it is helpful to use Adam Jones's conceptualization of gendercide, because it allows for a more fluid and dynamic interpretation of specified forms of genocide. Nevertheless, the cultural reality is that many binary dualisms remain entrenched in social, political, legal, and biomedical practices. Thus, the use of the hetero/homo binary and hierarchy continues to have a dramatic effect upon the sociocultural landscape. This is the legacy within which contemporary biopolitics is situated, and with which it must contend.

Millenarian Eugenics: Biological and Social Realities

At this stage, it should be clear that the politics of sexuality, especially queer sexualities, is complex, politically charged, and highly relevant to biology, genetic engineering, and biotechnology. The future possibilities of mapping the human genome with greater precision and accuracy will be complemented by scientific studies of the causes and factors of homosexuality. These, in turn, will be combined with the ongoing political and professional battles amongst the psychological associations, creating a fraught and unstable sociopolitical decision-making context. This fluid and contentious environment also includes a relative dearth of protection for anyone claiming a queer identity. Although some countries do have laws that protect queers (usually with reference to homosexuality), many countries do not.

The realm of international law is even less clear and supportive of queer identities. For example, the Universal Declaration of Human Rights, drawn up after World War II in the face of genocidal atrocities that also involved the deaths of many homosexuals, did not specifically include gays and lesbians (or any other "queers," for that matter). When Amnesty International recently voiced its concerns for sexual minorities at the World Conference on Human Rights in Vienna, its request for provisions specifying protection for "vulnerable groups that require greater attention within the human rights programme including children, indigenous peoples, people with disabilities, religious, sexual, ethnic and linguistic minorities, and those afflicted with HIV and AIDS" was not adopted in the conference's final document.[42] This is but one example of the ongoing difficulties associated with protecting those with different sexual preferences and orientations.

Amnesty International's documentation of human rights abuses against queer individuals includes a variety of activities directed at queer individuals based upon their actual or perceived sexual preference. The types of abuses range from complaints of ill treatment while in police custody to rape, sexual abuse, sexual realignment surgery, extrajudicial executions and disappearances, and state-sanctioned execution.[43] The murder of gays and lesbians due to their sexuality, or to associated behaviors and illnesses (e.g., HIV and AIDS), not only means that the individuals are targeted, but also—due to the relatively small numbers of gays and lesbians—becomes tantamount to genocide and now, more specifically, gendercide. Although a full complement of the gay community is not murdered in such acts, the relatively small statistical populations of gays and lesbians overall means that the annual death toll of queer identities can be regarded as a genocidal act. For example, according to Luis Albert, a male prostitute in Colombia:

> For gays in Colombia, there is no rule of law. The only program the government has for people like me is a program to kill us. . . . There were a group of fifteen of us working the streets that were HIV positive and that the police knew about. . . . From January to May of this year (1993) five of us had been killed. Picked up in police cars, shot and dumped.[44]

Further statistics related to Colombia show that between 1986 and 1990, "328 gay men were murdered in the city of Medellin alone."[45] Such directed killings fit Mary Warren's definition of genocidal activity, which states that

> an action, law or policy should be regarded as genocidal if (1) it results in an absolute or relative reduction in the number of persons of a particular racial or cultural group; and (2) the means whereby this result is brought about are morally objectionable for independent reasons—e.g.,

> because they violate certain individuals' right to life, liberty or security against wrongful assault.[46]

The examples from Colombia, as well as others documented by Amnesty International, fall into both categories. It is evident that a form of gendercide is currently being perpetrated against gay men.

The current climate of anti-queer values and activities will continue as long as homosexuality, and the sexualities I described in my definition of queer sexuality earlier, remain unacknowledged in international conventions and charters, as well as in national and state laws. Clearly, the danger for current gay males (and all those of queer persuasion) is serious and real in many parts of the world. Overlaying the linguistic, technological and political quilt of the Human Genome Project, DNA diagnostics, and other forms of genetic engineering and biotechnology upon the current climate of anti-queer sentiment simply fuels the already tragic reality and conditions of many queers around the world.

The creation and perfection of some of the genetic and diagnostic technologies will increase the potential to reduce the queer population in part or in whole. If the research on the "gay gene" does become more precise—if a genetic marker or markers can be specified—then lab technicians using in vitro fertilization and preimplantation genetic diagnosis will be able to ascertain whether or not the preembryos are predisposed toward homosexuality (or other possible queer sexualities). With this information in hand, the parent(s) or the reprogeneticist will be able to select which preembryo will be chosen for implantation and birth. In this way, it would be possible to ensure that a gay man, or any other homosexual, would not be born, thereby removing the need to kill or murder groups of homosexuals. In this sense, the biopolitics of the future may require a further extension of Mary Anne Warren's already extended interpretation of genocide, which states that

> not all instances of genocide involve direct or deliberate killing. Deaths or cultural disintegration deliberately or negligently brought about through starvation, disease or neglect may also be genocidal. Indeed, some acts of genocide do not involve any deaths at all, but rather consist of the wrongful denial of the right to reproduce.[47]

Without a doubt, homosexuals primarily reproduce in one way at present —that is, culturally. They are "created" via the traditional method of procreation, but their subcultures, art, music, politics, and the like all necessitate cultural reproduction. Although homosexuals do have children—procreate—

their children appear to be just as likely to be "straight" in adulthood as children born to heterosexuals. Future technologies provide the opportunity for homosexuals to procreate sexually using such methods as IVF, potentially selecting the preembryos that *do* show signs of homosexual orientation. However, set within the social and biological context portrayed here, it is more likely that queer biopolitics in the future will also include incidents of genocide and gendercide, as Mary Anne Warren articulated these phenomena, through the outright denial of their birth. In doing so, the natural variation of a population can be affected, as can its psychological profile and sociopolitical standing. Ultimately, protection of queer individuals and communities requires a much more sophisticated way of understanding and challenging the contemporary forces that make up the realm of biopolitics. In order to avoid a eugenics of the twenty-first century, it is necessary to recraft the aging social maps in a manner that enables a queer cartography relevant to the Age of Biopolitics.

Notes

The chapter epigraph is from Lee M. Silver, *Remaking Eden: Cloning, Genetic Engineering, and the Future of Humankind?* (London: Phoenix/Orion Books, 1998), p. 13 (emphasis in original).

1. Nicholas Wade, "Scientists Complete Rough Draft of Human Genome," *New York Times,* 26 June 2000.

2. According to Chandler Burr, *A Separate Creation: How Biology Makes Us Gay* (New York: Bantam Books, 1996), p. 476: "Xq28 represents the twenty-eighth region of the q (long) arm of the X chromosome, where Dean Hamer discovered a genetic locus linked to homosexual orientation in some men." This is revisited in the latter stages of this chapter.

3. Selecting children based upon genetic profiles has already occurred and was first reported in the elite science journal *Nature* in 1990. See A. H. Handyside, E. H. Kontogianni, K. Hardy, and R.M.L. Winston, "Pregnancies from Biopsied Human Preimplantation Embryos Sexed by Y-Specific DNA Amplification," *Nature,* 344 (1990), pp. 768–70.

4. The term "biopolitics" is used here to encapsulate the complex and ever-changing dynamics within, and related to, the areas of genetic engineering, biological medicine (biomedicine), and the biotechnology industry. In this sense, biopolitics incorporates the multiple forms of human interaction (e.g., personal, professional, cultural, political, and financial) that address and drive such sectors of science and technology.

5. For a detailed timeline (from 1750 B.C. to the present) regarding some of this research, see "A Timeline of Biotechnology," compiled by the *New York Times*, *www.bio.org/timeline/timeline.html.*

6. The "Biotech Century" is a term used by many in the life sciences and business to describe the next century of progress with regard to genetic engineering and its commercialization. For further comments about the term and its relevance, see Jeremy Rifkin, *The Biotech Century: Harnessing the Gene and Remaking the World* (New York: Penguin/Putnam, 1998), pp. 1–36.

7. A recent collection of essays dedicated to genetic engineering and human rights addresses a variety of ethical issues regarding the science and technologies mentioned here. See Justine Burley, ed., *The Genetic Revolution and Human Rights: The Oxford Amnesty Lectures 1998* (Oxford: Oxford University Press, 1998).

8. For further discussions of these criticisms, see: Rifkin, *The Biotech Century;* Vandana Shiva, *Biopiracy: The Plunder of Nature and Knowledge* (Toronto: Between the Lines, 1997); T. J. Brown, "Spiritual and Ethical Considerations," in Ray Prebble, ed., *Designer Genes: The New Zealand Guide to the Issues and Facts about Genetic Engineering* (Wellington: Dark Horse Press, 2000), pp. 111–17; Bevan Tipene-Matua, "A Maori Response to the Biogenetic Age," in Prebble, *Designer Genes,* pp. 97–109; Peter R. Wills, "Disrupting Evolution: Biotechnology's Real Result," in Richard Hindmarsh, Geoffrey Lawrence, and Janet Norton, eds., *Altered Genes: Reconstructing Nature—The Debate* (St. Leonards, NSW: Allen and Unwin, 1998), pp. 66–80; Stephen Crook, "Biotechnology, Risk, and Sociocultural (Dis)order," in Hindmarsh et al., *Altered Genes,* pp. 132–44.

9. Matt Ridley, *Genome: The Autobiography of a Species in 23 Chapters* (London: Fourth Estate, 1999), p. 3.

10. Natalie Angier, "Reading the Book of Life: The Human Genome Abounds in Complex Contradictions," *New York Times,* 26 June 2000, *www.nytimes.com/library/national/science/062700sci-genome-nature.html.*

11. Wade, "Scientists Complete Rough Draft."

12. For another interpretation of the relevance of symbolism, metaphors, and discourse when applied to DNA and genetic engineering, see Dorothy Nelkin and M. Susan Lindee, *The DNA Mystique: The Gene As a Cultural Icon* (New York: W. H. Freeman, 1995).

13. The complexities and nuances of Judeo-Christian and premodern European assumptions regarding marriage, sexuality, and fidelity receive a detailed and thorough analysis by John Boswell, who challenges many modern religious assumptions about these topics in a thorough, scholarly historical narrative. See John Boswell, *Same-Sex Unions in Premodern Europe* (New York: Vintage Books, 1994).

14. Jonathan Ned Katz, "'Homosexual' and 'Heterosexual': Questioning the Terms," in Martin Duberman, ed., *A Queer World: The Center for Lesbian and Gay Studies Reader* (New York: New York University Press, 1997), pp. 178, 177.

15. Simone de Beauvoir, *The Second Sex* (New York: Vintage Books, 1989). The original 1949 publication of de Beauvoir's book was released in French as two volumes under the title *Le Deuxième Sexe: I. Les Faits et Les Mythes, II. L'Expérience Vécue.*

16. An articulation of the racial aspects of oppressive forces as related to genocide and gendercide is articulated elsewhere in this volume (see, for example, A. C. Del Zotto's contribution).

17. The 1999 film *Paragraph 175,* directed by Rob Epstein and Jeffrey Friedman, provides a documentary analysis of the homosexual experience in Nazi Germany through the living testimonials of ten of the twelve known remaining gay survivors of the Jewish holocaust. The directors follow historian Klaus Müller, project director for Western Europe at the U.S. Holocaust Memorial Museum, during his interviews with the survivors (nine men and one woman). The film is poignant, and provides the greatest amount of information available thus far regarding the treatment of homosexuals during the Nazi era in Germany. In so doing, the following critical information is documented:

> 100,000 men were arrested for homosexuality in Nazi Germany, half of whom were imprisoned. An estimated 10,000–15,000 were sent to concentration camps, where the death rate of homosexual prisoners was 60% (the highest among non-Jewish prisoners). By 1945, only 4,000 survived. . . . After the war, the persecution of male homosexuals, who were not seen as political prisoners but criminals under the sodomy law [Paragraph 175], continued. Some were even re-arrested and re-imprisoned after the war. In the 1950s and 60s, the number of convictions for homosexuality in West Germany was as high as under the Nazi regime. Gay male prisoners received no reparations by the German government and the sodomy law was not repealed until 1968 in East Germany and 1969 in West Germany.

This information, along with other relevant details about the homosexual experience of the Holocaust and the film itself, can be found at *www.popmatters.com/film/reviews/p/paragraph-175.html.*

18. The use of various postmodern insights and critiques of the sciences and social sciences has generated a large number of publications regarding biological essentialism, social constructionist views, and the tensions between these. A useful overview of these positions and their relevance for homosexuality and queer studies can be found in John P. De Cecco and John P. Elia, "A Critique and Synthesis of Biological Essentialism and Social Constructionist Views of Sexuality and Gender," *Journal of Homosexuality,* 24: 3–4 (1993), pp. 1–26.

19. The term "queer sexualities" is used here to incorporate a range of sexualities. The term "queer" was relatively recently reclaimed by gay and lesbian activists to signify a more political and militant force or movement for their own liberation and freedom. It became especially prominent with regard to AIDS activism in the United States. Since the late 1980s, the term has been extended to incorporate a variety of

sexualities and gender differences, and queer studies has become an academic field of inquiry and theoretical exploration. My use of the term is quite broadly construed and includes gays, lesbians, bisexuals, transsexuals, intersexuals, two-spirit persons, and those (heterosexuals included) who cannot procreate without medical intervention. The use of "queer sexualities" here encapsulates those who identify along the continuum of sexuality. This includes those who identify themselves as a social queer manifestation, that is, sexuality as a lifestyle choice; those who regard themselves as a biological or genetic manifestation, that is, sexual orientation; and those who see themselves influenced by a combination of biology and culture. The term also accepts that an individual can move between these sexuality categories; they need not be fixed in an individual or in society. As such, the use of "queer" here posits that sexuality is neither solely biological nor solely socially constructed. Rather, it implies that human behavior, including sexuality, incorporates biological variation that can be affected by the sociocultural environment. Individuals will have their own predilections, biologically and socially constructed, and from this a fluid landscape of sexuality can be exhibited, interpreted, and reconfigured. For further discussion and use of this term as defined here, see Stefanie S. Rixecker, "Exposing Queer Biotechnology via Queer Archaeology: The Quest to (Re)construct the Human Body from the Inside Out," *World Archaeology* 32: 2 (October 2000), pp. 263–74.

20. American Psychological Association, Answers to Your Questions about Sexual Orientation and Homosexuality, *www.apa.org/pubinfo/answers.html.*

21. "APA Passes Resolution on Homosexuality Conversion Therapy," *Behavioral Health Treatment*, 2 (September 1997), p. 5.

22. American Psychological Association, *Answers to Your Questions.*

23. National Association for Research and Therapy on Homosexuality (hereafter, NARTH), narth.com.

24. NARTH, "NARTH's Purpose," narth.com/menus/statement.html.

25. NARTH, "Is There a 'Gay Gene'?" narth.com/docs/istheregene.html.

26. NARTH, "NARTH's Purpose."

27. Bruce Bagemihl, *Biological Exuberance: Animal Homosexuality and Natural Diversity* (New York: St. Martin's Press, 1999), p. 80.

28. Ibid.

29. Regarding Hamer's "gay gene" study, see Dean H. Hamer, S. Hu, V. Magnuson, N. Hu, and A.M.L. Pattatucci, "A Linkage between DNA Markers on the X Chromosome and Male Sexual Orientation," *Science*, 261 (16 July 1993), pp. 321–27. For LeVay's "gay brain" study, see Simon LeVay, "A Difference in Hypothalamic Structure between Heterosexual and Homosexual Men," *Science*, 253 (30 August 1991), pp. 1034–37.

30. LeVay, "A Difference in Hypothalamic Structure."

31. The hypothalamus is located in the brain beneath the thalamus, which is a mechanism that relays information from the external world, that is, information

outside the body. The hypothalamus is a counter to the thalamus in that it acts as a mechanism that relays information regarding the inside of the body, for example, hunger, thirst, body temperature, and sex drive. Additionally, the hypothalamus has the job of "switching on" the pituitary gland, which regulates the hormones related to ovulation.

32. For discussions and critiques, see L. Allen, "Sex Differences in the Corpus Collosum of the Living Human Being," *Journal of Neuroscience*, 11(1991), pp. 933–42; Burr, *A Separate Creation*; W. Byne and B. Parsons, "Human Sexual Orientation: The Biological Theories Reappraised," *Archives of General Psychiatry*, 50 (1993), pp. 228–39.

33. Hamer et al., "A Linkage between DNA Markers."

34. Burr, *A Separate Creation*, p. 474.

35. Dean H. Hamer, Angela Pattatuci, et al., "Linkage between Sexual Orientation and Chromosome Xq28 in Males but Not in Females," *Nature Genetics* (11 November 1995), pp. 248–56.

36. Burr, *A Separate Creation.*

37. Ibid., p. 282 (emphasis in original). A book-length assessment of the research process according to Hamer himself can be found in Dean Hamer and Peter Copeland, *The Science of Desire: The Search for the Gay Gene and the Biology of Behavior* (New York: Simon and Schuster, 1994).

38. Dean Hamer offers a number of arguments against the future use of a diagnostic for homosexuality. In part, he does not foresee such a use, because even with improved technology "it still won't be possible to conclusively test every person's current or future sexual orientation. . . . Even with a test, parents could only be told the probability an unborn child would grow up to be straight or gay, a very weak statistic upon which to judge a human life." Although Hamer also acknowledges that the sociopolitical environment has often discriminated against homosexuals on the basis of far less biological knowledge, he argues that ultimately "biology is neutral" and gays and lesbians could just as easily choose to use the technology to abort heterosexual fetuses. Although there is some truth to this, Hamer's interpretation is overly sanguine in light of the historical and ongoing prejudice against queer people around the world. Hamer's comments and arguments can be found in Hamer and Copeland, *The Science of Desire*, p. 218.

39. For discussions regarding the link between HIV/AIDS and gay male subjects, including as a criticism of Simon Levay's "gay brain" studies, see Burr, *A Separate Creation.*

40. Amnesty International United Kingdom (hereafter, AIUK), *Breaking the Silence: Human Rights Violations on Sexual Orientation* (London: AIUK, 1997), p. 23.

41. Sarah Franklin, "Essentialism, Which Essentialism? Some Implications of Reproductive and Genetic Techno-Science," *Journal of Homosexuality*, 24: 3–4 (1993), pp. 37–38.

42. AIUK, *Breaking the Silence*, p. 8.
43. AIUK, *Breaking the Silence.*
44. Cited in ibid., p. 16.
45. Ibid., p. 17.
46. Mary Anne Warren, *Gendercide: The Implications of Sex Selection* (Totowa, N.J.: Rowman and Allanheld, 1985), p. 23.
47. Ibid.

8

Geno and Other Cides

A Cautionary Note on Knowledge Accumulation

Stuart Stein

Introduction

The core subject matter of the field of genocide studies is mass killing, supposedly mass killings of a particular kind.[1] There is, however, no agreement on the defining characteristics of this particular kind of mass killing. The definition of genocide included under Article II of the 1948 genocide convention has, in the absence of consensus on any other definition, been the anchor for the analysis of genocide-related case studies and comparisons. Because that definition cannot accommodate the empirical varieties of mass killings under consideration by regulators and scholars, it has spawned numerous variants. Gendercide is the latest addition. The discussion here is directed at charting the genocide-related conceptual field, situating gendercide, and addressing issues relating to the analytical viability and empirical status of gendercide and related concepts.

Gendercide: Introductory Comments

Mary Anne Warren introduced the term "gendercide" to designate killings directed at individuals because of their sex (or gender).[2] She was of the opinion that the terms and analytical frameworks then employed in the feminist literature to designate gender-motivated killings of women—femicide and gynocide—implied that only one gender category, women, were targets of gender-selective killings. The term "gendercide" was to be gender neutral. Having leveled the playing field, Warren reverted to concentrating on the analysis of killings relating to women—namely, witch burning, female infanticide, female genital mutilation, and suttee.

In all probability the concept would have languished there and then, had Adam Jones not employed it in attempting to account for what he perceived as an infrequently recognized and reported-on characteristic of some instances of mass killing, namely, their gender selectivity. The burden of his argument is that gendercide is a subcategory of genocide, that gender selectivity is a defining characteristic of much genocide, that it merits consideration, therefore, alongside other accepted subtypes. These include politicides and ethnocides. The end point of his analysis is a reworking of Steven Katz's definition of genocide, namely, "the actualization of the intent, however successfully carried out, to murder *in whole or in substantial part* any national, ethnic, racial, religious, political, social, gender or economic group, as these groups are defined by the perpetrator."[3]

In sum, Jones seeks two main objectives. First, recognition of the significance of gendered selection of victims in mass killing contexts, particularly genocides, by demonstrating the empirical viability and utility of the term "gendercide." Second, an extension of the scope of the concept "genocide" by the addition of gender as a dimension of group membership to which the term should be applied.

Accordingly, "gendercide" is to be added to those terms that are currently employed by authorities in descriptions and analyses of mass killing. To assess its analytical utility, it needs to be contrasted with other concepts currently being employed that purport to refer to the same or allied phenomena. In evaluating its empirical scope, on the other hand, it is necessary to examine those illustrations of mass killing adduced as evidence for its applicability.

The Conceptual Field of Genocide and Mass Killings

The terms employed by authors to refer to mass killings, particularly those whose work forms the core of the genocide studies field, abound. These cannot be ordered in terms of any single dimension, or by a factoring of dimensions. The phenomena they refer to cannot be arranged in terms of context of origin, the course of their evolution, the dynamics of sociostructural interaction, the sociostructural characteristics of the social systems in which they arise, the categories or volume of victims, the number of separate incidents that constitute the events to be explained, the time span of the total number of incidents associated with a particular cluster of mass killings, the categories of victims, the characteristics of perpetrators, or the outcomes of such mass killings.

Even a cursory examination of the terminology and its mode of deployment in the discourse of genocide studies and allied disciplines reveals that this is a somewhat disordered field, lacking any significant degree of consensus on relevant events or how to order them. The concepts that have been employed with some currency in the course of the description and analysis of mass killings, arranged alphabetically, are: communalism, cultural genocide (culturecide), democide, destructive program, ethnic cleansing, ethnocide, femicide, gendercide, gendered atrocity, genocidal killings, genocidal massacre, genocidal process, genocidal rape, genocidal society, genocidal state, genocide and genocide types, genocide/direct, genocide/indirect, genocide/selective, governmental crime, gynocide, Holocaust (destruction of European Jews), h/Holocaust (destruction excluding European Jews), infanticide, man-made deaths, massacre, mega murders, pogrom, politicide, relations of genocide, Shoah, state crime, state-sponsored mass murder, total war, and vigilantism. While other variants of these are also employed by authorities, those listed suffice to demonstrate that this is a somewhat crowded terrain.

Regarding that which they purport to designate, the overlap between many of these terms is extensive. Many of them are often employed simultaneously to designate the same sequence of events.[4] One author's genocide is another's state terrorism.[5] With the exception of culturecide, more frequently referred to as cultural genocide, infanticide, and *some* of the killings covered by femicide (gynocide), they all refer to the same *explicandum* (the *facts* to be explained): the killing of a sizable number of individuals on the basis of their membership in a group that is differentiated from other groups along one or more dimensions.[6] These killings are invariably carried out by individuals who are acting as members, or representatives, of groups.

In carrying out these killings, perpetrators are impelled by considerations that, from their perspective, single out the victim group as a suitable and justifiable target. Their cognitive focus is on one or more dimensions of group membership, real or imputed. The dimensions that have been singled out as having featured most prominently in mass killing events are ethnic status, race (color), religion, politics, socioeconomic status, nationality, and territory of habitation. In many specific instances these dimensions overlap.

The concepts, in contrast to the phenomena that they are directed at depicting, can be ordered on a number of dimensions. In terms of frequency of use in primary academic discipline of origin, there are four main clusters, as delimited in Table 1.

TABLE 1

I. Human Rights/Law	genocide, genocidal techniques, genocidal practices, cultural genocide, ethnocide, ethnic cleansing, genocidal rape, infanticide
II. History	genocide, Holocaust/Shoah/destructive program, total war, man-made deaths, genocidal killings, genocidal massacre, genocidal process, genocidal rape, genocidal state, genocidal society, genocide and genocide types, genocide/direct, genocide/indirect, genocide/selective, gendercide, H/holocaust, gendercide, ethnic cleansing, communalism, pogrom, massacre, vigilantism
III. Sociology and Social Psychology	gendercide, femicide (gynocide), gendered atrocity, massacre, genocidal rape, politicide
IV. Political Science	democide, mega murders, politicide, communalism, ethnic cleansing, state-sponsored mass murder, state crime, government crime, extra-judicial killings, vigilantism

I have attempted to list the concepts in each disciplinary cluster in terms of the scale of killings referenced. In some instances the volume of killings indicated is similar for adjacent terms (e.g., communalism/massacre, pogrom/communalism). The order of the scale of killings designated by the concepts in each disciplinary cluster listed in the table corresponds, in large measure, with the seriousness attributed to them by governments, academic authorities, legal and regulatory agencies, and commentators. Thus, in the human rights/legal cluster, genocides are considered more serious than ethnocides, and ethnocides more serious than ethnic cleansing.[7] Similarly, in the history cluster the order would be genocide, Holocaust (applied to the destruction of European Jewry), ethnic cleansing, communalism, pogrom, and massacre.

The hierarchical ordering of the left-hand column in the table corresponds to relative disciplinary influences in shaping contemporary approaches to analyzing and conceptualizing mass killings, particularly those large-scale mass killings termed genocides. Increasingly, the tendency has been to assimilate lesser-scale mass killings to the dominant human rights/juridical genocide paradigm.

Those working within the human rights/legal framework are principally oriented toward documenting and analyzing instances of mass killing in the service of control and punishment. This conceptual framework has two related sources. One is the definition of genocide provided for under Article II of the 1948 convention on the Prevention and Punishment of the Crime of Genocide. The other is the influence of Raphaël Lemkin, who originated the term in 1944.[8] The two are closely related because Lemkin was instrumental in ensuring that a proposal be put before the UN General Assembly affirming that "genocide is a crime under international law which the civilized world condemns," and calling on the Economic and Social Council to "prepare a report on the possibilities of declaring genocide an international crime and assuring international co-operation for its prevention and punishment."[9] He was also a member of a committee of legal experts that was asked to comment on the draft convention during its UN legislative history. Unfortunately, neither the views of Lemkin, nor Article II of the convention, are models of clarity.[10]

Although Lemkin apparently wrote voluminously on the subject of genocide,[11] the three main sources for information on his views that are referred to repeatedly in the literature on this question, both social scientific and legal, are: (1) his report and proposals to the Fifth International

Conference for the Unification of Penal Law, held at Madrid from 14 to 20 October 1933; (2) Chapter 9, "Genocide,"[12] of his book on the occupation policies pursued by the Axis powers in Europe;[13] and (3) his contribution to placing the issue on the agenda of the UN General Assembly, and in the drafting of the 1948 convention, as mentioned.

The most detailed source of Lemkin's views is his chapter on genocide, and the context provided by the rest of his lengthy monograph on Axis occupation policies. The main elements of his conception of genocide can be summarized as follows. Paradigmatic instances of genocide are various combinations of policies applied by Nazi administrators, principally between September 1939 and May 1945, in German-occupied countries. Genocide is viewed as a *composite* activity directed at the annihilation of groups by weakening, or destroying, the essential foundations of group continuity by systematically, almost scientifically, applying genocidal techniques. As discussed by Lemkin, genocide is clearly a policy that can be applied only by a modern bureaucratic state.[14]

In Lemkin's framework, genocide is accomplished by the application of what he refers to as genocidal techniques. By techniques Lemkin means policies. He collated those policies that he perceived as being "genocidal practices" under seven headings that correspond to seven fields of human and group existence: political, social, cultural, economic, biological, religious, and moral.[15] Lemkin provides no criteria for distinguishing genocidal techniques from other administrative policies. He includes no discussion concerning criteria for differentiating such policies from other oppressive measures applied by an occupying power. Although cogent arguments can be advanced to justify the fact that Lemkin identifies no particular cluster of specified techniques as genocidal per se, it is somewhat unsatisfactory that he appears to identify all clusters of genocidal techniques, that is, occupation policies, as genocides.

His discussion of the concept of denationalization, which he seeks to supplant with that of genocide, indicates that the composite of different actions that he seeks to classify as genocide overlaps with three policy clusters from which it is not clearly demarcated: (a) ethnic cleansing, in the sense of rendering an area ethnically homogeneous, or clearing it of one of the groups residing there; (b) denationalization; and, (c) oppressive occupation policies.[16]

As far as I am aware, no detailed historical study of the origins of the 1948 convention has been published, although some authorities have documented the drafting process.[17] In the convention, genocide is defined by Article II:

> Genocide means any of the following acts committed with intent to destroy, in whole or in part, a national, ethnical, racial or religious group, as such [by]
> a. Killing members of the group;
> b. Causing serious bodily or mental harm to members of the group;
> c. Deliberately inflicting on the group conditions of life calculated to bring about its physical destruction in whole or in part;
> d. Imposing measures intended to prevent births within the group;
> e. Forcibly transferring children of the group to another group.

In terms of detail and primary emphasis, the relationship between Lemkin's views as outlined in the sources mentioned earlier and Article II is somewhat tenuous. With the possible exception of (d), none of the acts listed requires "a *coordinated plan of different actions* aiming at the destruction of essential foundations of the life of national groups, with the aim of annihilating the groups themselves."[18] Under the terms of the convention, genocide is not necessarily a composite crime, although, if two or more of (a) to (e) be pursued simultaneously, it could be construed as such. Nor does the articulation of the concept "genocide" in Article II represent an "*elaborate, almost scientific, system* developed to an extent never before achieved by any nation."[19] Both of these factors were repeatedly emphasized by Lemkin as being defining characteristics of genocide.[20] The notion of genocide implicit in the convention is at once broader and less elaborate than that detailed by Lemkin in 1944. Also, while it is difficult to conceive of "a coordinated plan of different actions," constituting an "almost scientific, system" being implemented on a significant scale other than by a bureaucratic state, it is possible to envisage the concordance of the requisite intent and proscribed actions under the convention being applied at lower levels of organizational mobilization and control.[21]

Ever since the passage of the 1948 convention, authorities of various disciplinary persuasions have commented upon its alleged shortcomings. The two primary sources of concern have centered on the issue of intent, both its type and the difficulties involved in establishing its presence in specific instances of mass killing, and the scope of the groups included.[22] Criticisms that center on the type of groups referenced take the following form:

> Genocide, as defined under Article II, does not apply to political, economic, gender, cultural, and other groups. Yet, these groups may also be targeted by the same means, and with the same end goal, namely, their destruction, in whole or in part, as such. Moreover, the conditions that

> gave rise to the targeting of those groups referred to in Article II may be identical with, or similar to those that obtain in relation to those groups not included under the terms of the Convention. Accordingly, political, economic, gender, cultural, and other groups, should be brought within its purview.[23]

Despite the frequency with which both these alleged shortcomings have been aired, the definition of Article II has been retained, unaltered, in the Rome Statute of the International Criminal Court.[24]

The shortcomings of the convention singled out by specialists researching large-scale mass killings are less interesting than the fact that it has become the anchor of conceptual, typological, descriptive, and theoretical analyses. Few experts accept the Article II definition as adequate. Some others believe that despite its more obvious flaws, it should be retained in essential detail for purposes of comparative analysis or modified insubstantially.[25] Regardless of the position taken on these issues, the underlying orientation of many scholars is that it is a prerequisite for an explanation of such events that they be assimilated to the category "genocide," however defined.

Accordingly, analysis is often directed toward, or ends with, establishing that the mass killing cluster under consideration meets the definitional parameters of "genocide," however defined. This is not to say that these studies exclude very valuable and detailed information critically relevant to the development of etiological accounts of mass killings. What I wish to indicate is that establishing "genocidal credentials," or, in some cases their absence, is often considered to be of paramount importance, or necessary, by their authors.[26] The analyses of Huttenbach and Milton respecting Nazi policies toward Gypsies, Barta's discussion of the impact of colonization policies in Australia on the Aborigine population, and Churchill's extensive accounts of the impact of policies adopted by successive waves of settlers toward Native Americans are illustrative of excellent contributions that, nonetheless, ride this undercurrent.[27] Both Huttenbach and Milton seek to establish that policies toward Gypsies were no less genocidal than those applied to Jews, and Barta that genocides need not be confined to intended policies of group destruction but can inhere in certain forms of structural relations between groups. The end point of Churchill's exhaustively researched monograph is a proposal for a new convention on genocide that substantially broadens the Article II notion.

There are a number of reasons for this emphasis on establishing "genocide credentials" in the context of the analysis of particular case studies, and the assimilation of mass killings to some notion of genocide. First, and probably most significantly, the dominant cognitive paradigm of the most influential authorities in the genocide studies field is heavily skewed in the direction of a human rights/juridical perspective. The regulation of perpetrators of noncombatant mass killings, particularly those that occur on a vast scale, and the prevention of such events has been a major concern. I draw a distinction here between the genocide studies field on the one hand, and the literature on mass killings, both combatant and noncombatant, on the other. The latter is heavily weighted in the direction of the contributions of historians, with some important additions by political scientists, and is very substantially larger than the former.

Contributions by historians are of central importance to the field of genocide studies and provide the bulk of empirical data that can be employed in comparative analyses. However, such work is primarily directed at the *reconstruction* of the past. While its findings constitute invaluable and necessary source materials for genocide studies, if genocide is referenced at all, this is invariably only to establish that the case study concerned can be construed as an instance of genocide. The vast literature on the destruction of European Jewry, written largely by historians over the last six decades, illustrates this amply.[28]

The dominant influence of a human rights/juridical regulatory orientation on the part of genocide studies authorities can be demonstrated by reference to a number of key texts. The two most influential and useful compendiums of genocide case studies are Chalk and Jonassohn and Totten, Parsons, and Charny.[29] In the introduction to the former, having briefly elaborated on the importance of employing a suitable definition of genocide in order to facilitate the development of an adequate typology, the authors note that the identification of relevant parameters is "a first step in the prevention of future genocides." The introduction to the latter begins with the exhortatory questions: "Will the killing ever stop? Will the source of genocide ever be eradicated? Will humanity ever be wise enough to prevent the deaths of potential genocide victims before they occur?" The section headings in the introduction emphasize that more detailed and systematic information on genocides is a prerequisite for intervention and prevention and that there is a need for a well-organized, collective, and concerted effort to intervene in and/or prevent genocide; point to the desirability of developing genocide early warning systems; and stress the need for delivering widely a broadly based educational program about genocide. Leo Kuper, a sociologist, and widely acknowledged as a key early figure in the development of genocide studies, notes in the preface to his influential *Genocide: Its Political Uses in the Twentieth Century* that his work in this field has been impelled by the indifference of the United Nations to its prevention and punishment, and adds that it "would seem that it can only be recalled to its duty by the mounting pressure of international opinion."[30] Helen Fein, also a sociologist, in her judicious overview of genocide studies devotes the final section to social policy issues of punishment and prevention.[31]

It is not my intention to either deny or downgrade the importance of detection, prevention, and punishment, or to imply here any criticism of these authors' analyses. What I wish to stress is that this social-control, regulatory orientation has had important consequences in directing the focus of work in this field. First, it has encouraged case-study analyses at the expense of the development of micro- or macrocomparative frameworks. Despite the fact that the structure of Article II is an implicit recognition of the possibility of thirty-two different genocides in terms of the acts separately listed as genocidal, when combined with the requisite specific intent, the notion of genocide that dominates the literature is generally undifferentiated.[32]

The destruction of European Jewry is the paradigmatic instance of genocide, the analyses of which have significantly shaped our notions of what should be construed as genocide. Usually referred to simply by the shorthand "Holocaust," the term is entirely undifferentiated. It designates, depending on the authority one consults, a series of significantly different events between either January 1933 and May 1945, or September 1939 and May 1945, although sometimes November 1938 (*Kristallnacht*) and May 1945, or June 1941 and May 1945. In many cases it is not temporally delimited. It encompasses pogroms; ghettoization; discriminatory legislation; mass murders accomplished by *Einsatzgruppen* battalions, police battalions, and units of the *Wehrmacht;* extermination through slave labor, transportation, death marches, starvation and disease, concentration camp incarceration, and gas vans and chambers, perpetrated by professional killers, killing professionals, and others.[33] These killings have been carried out in the territory of the Third Reich and in German-occupied countries, by Germans and persons of many other nationalities, for varied reasons. While it is true that all this can be subsumed under "acts committed with intent to destroy, in whole or in part, a national, ethnical, racial or religious group, as such," that in itself does not tell us very much about similarities or differences, along various dimensions, relating to these varied killings, policies, and perpetrators. The accretion to our knowledge in the form of general propositions relating to genocides is negligible.

In like manner, authorities repeatedly make reference to the genocides of the Armenians, Cambodians (sometimes described as an autogenocide), Rwandans, Burundians, and others.[34] All of these are summary terms for very complex clusters of multiple events involving a diversity of mass killings, some of which may merit the designation genocide in the context of the presence of the required specific intent, but which also subsume other categories of mass killing.[35] It is hardly surprising that there are few generalizations that can withstand close scrutiny in relation to the origins, processes of development, perpetrators of, or conditions leading to the closure of such clusters.[36]

The social control/juridical orientation leads easily to the assimilation of all instances of mass killings to the category genocide, as a fundamental preoccupation with the equal worth of all human life underlies the concerns of both scholars and practitioners. Israel Charny notes that although the Jewish "Holocaust" is in some ways unique, this "actually underscore[s] that much more how capable human beings and society have been—and still are—of destroying different peoples en masse."[37] Elsewhere he has advocated a "simple commonsense definition" of genocide, namely, that "whenever a large number of people are put to death by other people, it constitutes genocide," and that the "generic meaning of genocide" is "mass murder or massacre."[38] When primary orienting concerns are focused on prevention, regulation, and punishment of mass killings, there is no rationale for not assimilating all forms of these to the category genocide, particularly as doing so is often politically, personally, and organizationally expedient as well.

Equally, there is no obvious rationale for restricting the application of the term "genocide" to those groups specified in the convention. Huttenbach suggests that we define "genocide" as "the destruction of a specific group within a given national or even international population" and reasons that the "precise character of the group need not be spelled out. . . . Since, by definition, the list can never be complete, it is best not appended, not even for purposes of illustration."[39] Huttenbach couches the argument at its most abstract. Others have reasoned along similar lines to advocate the assimilation of political, economic, social, and gender groups to those mentioned in Article II of the convention, and to equate physical and cultural destruction.[40]

There have been other reasons prompting the dissolution of boundaries between those groups specified in the convention and those excluded.

Among these the issue of empirical comparability has been an important consideration. Many of the factors that have been singled out as being causally implicated in the destruction of groups covered by Article II have been shown to be identical with those that apply with respect to excluded groups; not infrequently both types of group are singled out for destruction within the same social system. During the period of Khmer Rouge rule in Cambodia, certain ethnic and religious groups were targeted for destruction by the same leadership that targeted individuals because of their real or imputed past economic status, or their political affiliations or allegiances.[41] If Jews, Gypsies, the mentally and physically impaired, and Russian commissars were targeted for different reasons by the Nazi regime, the social system and ideological complex that facilitated their annihilation was common, as were many other factors associated with these destructive programs. As Staub has noted in relation to the deliberate annihilation of individuals on the basis of their real or imputed political group membership, there is "no reason to believe that the types of psychological and cultural influences differ in political and other group murders."[42]

Historians have written the bulk of the literature pertaining to genocide. Invariably, they draw on comparative findings rather than direct their research efforts toward the development of general theoretical frameworks or models. Their work has consistently demonstrated that as far as issues relating to the origins, processes of development, and involvement of various categories of actors in large-scale mass killings are concerned, there are few grounds for differentiating between those groups included and those excluded under the terms of Article II.

The issue of empirical comparability constitutes in some measure a common link between the regulatory human rights/juridical orientation toward genocide studies, and that which I refer to as the comparative analytical perspective. It is easier to postulate the divide between the two than to illustrate it, because many sociologists, social psychologists, and political scientists straddle the two positions. There are some pure cases. Both Rummel and Elliott are more concerned with exploring those factors responsible for twentieth-century large-scale mass killings and their interrelationship, than with issues pertaining to social control.[43] Among social psychologists and psychologists, Kelman and Hamilton, Staub, Baumeister, and Du Preez are examples of those that also fall into this category.[44]

There are two directions, therefore, that research directed at the development of explanatory models of genocide can take. All mass killings directed at the destruction of groups, as such, can be assimilated to the concept "genocide," as defined by Article II. This approach is largely deductive in orientation. It is based on an a priori assumption, namely, that *the intention* to destroy a group, when married to the means specified under the terms of Article II, isolates a behavioral complex that is differentiated from other behavioral clusters involving mass killings in terms of relevant analytical dimensions. A variant of this approach is that which drops the intent requirement of Article II, emphasizing consequences in place of intent.[45] The notion that destructive processes associated with groups are differentiated on the basis of relevant analytical dimensions is retained. The mirror image of this approach is that no distinctions should be drawn between variants of mass killings, all of which should be classified as genocide.[46] Here the a priori is that all mass killings share some commonalities that justify designating them by the same concept, "genocide," and these are more significant than any dissimilarity.

An alternative approach starts out from the assumption that genocide, as defined under Article II, with the addition of groups targeted on the basis of dimensions additional to those included in 1948, *may* constitute a specific variant of mass killing. This, however, cannot be established on the basis of definitional parameters alone. The development of explanatory models of mass killing requires isolation of their distinguishing characteristics, through comparative analysis and theoretical modeling that draws upon it. The unit of analysis is mass killing. This approach is inductive and the element of discourse is a unit of behavior, namely, mass killing. There are no a priori assumptions underlying this orientation, other than that mass killing constitutes a meaningful unit of analysis for comparative purposes.

The magnetic pull of the Article II construction on genocide, or its mirror image, has been so overwhelming that few authors have resisted the temptation of employing the concept "genocide," or one of its derivatives, in the context of accounting for extensive mass killings. As noted earlier, and in line with the provisions of Article II, episodes or event clusters that do not involve any killing at all are also assimilated to the category genocide.[47]

The objective, and practice, of subsuming all group-targeted and other mass killings under the umbrella concept "genocide" partly accounts for some of the basic misunderstandings that prevail concerning the content of the convention and its role in the international regulatory framework. A not infrequent refrain is that the exclusion of certain groups from the provisions of Article II, especially political groups, is due to "cynical political manipulation" and the political self-interest of those involved in the drafting process.[48] Presumably, no expert on international relations would consider raising such comments. International agreements are concluded on the basis of compromises between the negotiating parties. In the absence of the ambiguities of phrasing that it included, and the exclusion of particular groups, the 1948 convention was unlikely to have been concluded.[49]

The impetus to classify all instances of group-targeted mass killing as genocides, regardless of whether they meet the criteria of Article II, also accounts for some of the flawed arguments advanced on occasion in support of the classification of particular instances, or clusters, of mass killing as genocide. Thus, Schaack contends: "Even though the Cambodia massacre is widely considered as a paradigmatic case of genocide, a close reading of the Genocide Convention leads to a surprising and worrisome conclusion," namely, that it "does not cover a significant portion of the deaths in Cambodia."[50] It follows as a matter of logic, that if "genocide" is defined in terms of the convention, and the Cambodian mass killings do not meet the criteria it sets forth, then the Cambodian mass killings cannot conceivably be considered to be a paradigmatic case thereof.

To some degree such arguments obtain their resonance because of the heavy loading of moral opprobrium attached to the concept "genocide." As Lang notes, the term "has come to be used when all other terms of opprobrium fail, when the speaker or writer means to indict a set of actions as extraordinary in their malevolence and heinousness."[51] Classifying a case study as an instance of genocide has implications concerning both its moral and academic importance. Hence the degree of resoluteness with which some scholars have argued for the classification of particular instances under one heading or another.[52]

Returning to Table 1, which I have slightly modified and reproduce below as Table 2:

In Table 2, the terms in [ ] brackets either predated the 1948 convention or apply to the destruction of European Jewry, which is universally accepted as a paradigmatic instance of genocide.[53] I have omitted genocide and infanticide, the latter because it is very rarely employed in the genocide-related literature. The terms in { } brackets depict extensive mass killings but are not employed frequently in the genocide-related literature, other than to imply a distinction of scale between a *genocide* and other mass killings.

All the terms in Table 2 outside of brackets have been introduced subsequent to the passage of the 1948 convention. They have been employed

TABLE 2

I. Human Rights/Law	[genocidal techniques,] genocidal practices, cultural genocide, ethnocide, ethnic cleansing, genocidal rape
II. History	[Holocaust/Shoah/destructive program], {total war, man-made deaths,} genocidal killings, genocidal massacre, genocidal process, genocidal rape, genocidal state, genocidal society, genocide and genocide types, genocide/direct, genocide/indirect, genocide/selective, H(h)olocaust, gendercide, ethnic cleansing, {communalism, pogrom, massacre, vigilantism}
III. Sociology and Social Psychology	gendercide, {femicide (gynocide)}, gendered atrocity, {massacre}, genocidal rape, politicide
IV. Political Science	{democide, mega murders,} politicide, {communalism, ethnic cleansing, state sponsored mass murder, state crime, government crime, extrajudicial killings, vigilantism}

primarily to incorporate into analyses mass killings that, on empirical grounds, have significant resemblances to those that are considered to comply with the parameters of the Article II definition. All of them depict some aspect of mass killing. They can be subdivided into four classes on the basis of whether they amplify the meaning of "genocide" in terms of scale, type, social system characteristics, or groups targeted, as represented in Table 3.[54]

Gendercide

Although gendercide parallels politicide in the sense that both terms designate dimensions of group classification that are not accommodated under Article II, mass killing that constitutes an instance of gendercide differs in one important respect from those that are instances of a politicide, as well as

TABLE 3

Scale	genocidal killings, genocidal massacres
Type	direct, indirect, selective, ethnic cleansing, ethnocide, cultural genocide, genocidal rape, genocidal types included in genocide typologies[a]
Social system characteristics	genocidal state, genocidal relations, genocidal processes, genocidal practices
Group	politicides, gendercides

[a] Chalk and Jonassohn in 1988 classified genocides into "genocidal killings that are committed in the building and maintaining of empires" and those "that are committed in the building and maintaining of nation states." Frank Chalk and Kurt Jonassohn, "The History and Sociology of Genocidal Killings," in Israel W. Charny, ed., *Genocide: A Critical Bibliographical Review* (London: Mansell, 1988), p. 40. In 1990, they distinguished genocides on the basis of motive, in *The History and Sociology of Genocide* (New Haven: Yale University Press, 1990), p. 29. Du Preez differentiates between ideological genocides, subcategorized into progressive and reactionary, and pragmatic genocides, subcategorized into developmental, retributive, and hegemonic (see *Genocide: The Psychology of Mass Murder* (London: Boyars/Bowerdean, 1994), pp. 77–78). Harff and Gurr develop a typology on the basis of the position of the victim group vis-à-vis the state and the policy objectives of its ruling groups, in Barbara Harff and Ted R. Gurr, "Toward an Empirical Theory of Genocides and Politicides: Identification and Measurement of Cases since 1945," *International Studies Quarterly,* 32 (1988), p. 363.

those group-based mass killings that are referenced by the convention. As Jones notes in Chapter 1 in this volume, in referring to gendercide: "We are not . . . talking about an abstract 'hatred of men' [or women] as lying at the root of these genocides and genocidal massacres, in the way that Nazi mass murder was clearly founded on an ideological hatred of Jews (and others)." This is an important distinction, because it signifies the omission of the qualification, *as such,* which applies to those groups referenced under Article II. The Nazi authorities, in their mass killings of Jews, Gypsies, the mentally and physically impaired, and political commissars, were killing them *as such,* as representatives of groups that were perceived as being organized in terms of a particular dimension (religion, way of life, physical or mental imperfection, political affiliation).

With few exceptions, most of the examples cited by Jones, although they illustrate the singling out of persons of a particular gender, do not demonstrate that selection was undertaken on the basis of gender per se. The exceptions mentioned are suttee, female infanticide, and witchcraft. With the possible exception of female infanticide, their occurrence was never particularly extensive compared to the mass killings currently subsumed under genocide or its amplifying extensions.[55]

Leaving these illustrative instances aside, the others cited confuse, in my opinion, certain issues relating to notions of social role and gender.[56] Gender is invariably regarded as a socially created construct that involves "the social or cultural and psychological aspects linked to males and females through particular social contexts. What a given society defines as masculine or feminine is a comment on gender."[57] "Role" is a concept with a narrower focus than that of "gender." Although it is not uncommon in the social science literature to find references to gender or sex roles, these are generally understood to apply to behaviors in a wide variety of contexts, whereas the term "role," as understood in the context of role theory, designates a particular set of behaviors, expectations, and beliefs associated with the occupancy of a particular status, it being understood that each individual, of whatever sex/gender, will usually occupy numerous status positions. As Goffman formulates this:

> A *status* is a position in some system or pattern of positions and is related to the other positions in the unit through reciprocal ties, through rights and duties binding on the incumbents. *Role* consists of the activity the incumbent would engage in were he to act solely in terms of the normative demands upon someone in his position. Role in this normative sense is to be distinguished from *role performance* or role enactment, which is the actual conduct of a particular individual while on duty in his position.[58]

In his chapter "Gendercide and Genocide" in this volume, Jones seeks to illustrate that gender-selective mass killing and "disappearance" of males, especially "battle-age" males, remains "a pervasive feature of contemporary conflict [that] is not open to dispute." He does so by citing supporting sources relating to recent conflicts in Kosovo, Bosnia-Herzegovina, Jammu and Kashmir, Colombia, Sri Lanka, Rwanda, Iraqi Kurdistan, Peru, and India. Many more could be added to this list. It is noteworthy, however, that in many of these conflicts both males and females were targeted and killed, although frequently in different proportions relative to their base populations.[59] The selection process is in most cases gender/(sex) related, but not gender/(sex) specific. Another problem is that we very often do not have adequate information concerning the extent of mass killings, or the proportion killed by age or sex.[60]

Jones himself notes that the reasons for a disproportionate emphasis on the killing of males in many conflict situations, particularly of battle-age males, are "fairly intuitive," namely, the destruction of those who are considered to pose the greatest continuing and potential threat to the perpetrators. It is relatively clear, therefore, that they are frequently selected out, not because of a hatred of "maleness" along the lines of "Jewishness" or "blackness" or nationality, but because in most cultures men of a certain age bear arms in conflict situations; are most likely to join guerrilla organizations and more likely to resist occupying forces, passively or actively; and are considered to pose potentially a greater economic or political threat to those occupying positions of power than are females, largely because of the ascriptive roles that they each perform in *patriarchal-type* social systems. The dimension of primary significance here is not gender, but current and imputed role and status.[61] This is apparent also from the intersection of age with imputed status position, which is noted by Conquest in connection with Stalinist purges, whom Jones cites at length.[62] If "maleness" were the only consideration that dictated selection, there would be no need to qualify gender selectivity by reference to age, or "battle-age." In many of the conflict situations cited by Jones, those clearly no longer of "battle-age" were less likely to be noncombatant victims.

This argument applies equally to the selection of females. In connection with the Rwandan mass killings of 1994, Newbury noted, "women were not killed simply as a 'by-product' of war, as 'collateral damage'; instead, targeting women was a policy specifically encouraged and directed to further the goal of the leaders of the genocide," that is, to destroy all Tutsi as a social group.[63]

Many of the examples singled out by Jones as demonstrating the influence of gender are open to alternative interpretations:

Russian prisoners of war. Approximately 3.3 million of the 5.7 million Russian POWs who fell into the hands of the Germans or their allies died in captivity.[64] Jones, in Chapter 1 of this volume, quoting Bartov, notes that this policy was directly related to "the ideological concepts of the Nazi regime, which strove physically to eliminate the 'Bolshevik *Untermenschen*.'" He concludes, therefore, that this was an "outright genocidal *and gendercidal* assault."

It is, of course, widely accepted that German conduct of warfare on the eastern front was impelled and shaped by ideological considerations, that it was waged essentially as a *Vernichtungskrieg*, a war of extermination, by the Nazi and military elite.[65] However, as Bartov notes, the brutalization of warfare was shaped by other factors as well: "[It] was the result of three major factors: the conditions at the front; the social and educational background of junior officers; and the political indoctrination of the troops."[66] Moreover, the continuation of Bartov's earlier quotation points to another consideration that impacted significantly on the fate of the Russian POWs, namely, "Hitler's fear that the economic burden of caring for millions of prisoners would bring about unrest among the German population or even cause a collapse of the 'civilian morale.' . . . In late 1941 it was realised that the best way to avert just such a disaster would be to mobilize the Russian POWs and civilian population to the German war effort. Throughout this period the army collaborated with the regime in implementing these policies, both by making use of the POWs for its own purposes at the front and by sending them as forced labour to the Reich."[67] There were additional factors that were responsible for the huge losses of Russian POWs, including inadequate ordinance, manpower, provisions, and preparations for handling the large numbers that fell into German hands, particularly during the first months of Operation Barbarossa.[68]

In "Gendercide and Genocide," Jones gives a different meaning to the term "gendercidal assault" in the case of Russian POWs than he does in connection with the other illustrative case studies that he mentions. Gendercide is defined as "gender-selective mass killing," which invariably involves "the physical act of separating men from women as a prelude to consigning men to death." Earlier, Jones stresses the purposefulness of gender selectivity in an analogy heavily laden with genocidal meanings:

> If gendercide and mass killings of males are to some degree definitional of modern conflict, we may also be able to isolate an essential if not universal ritual of gendercide against men. *It is the physical act of separating men from women as a prelude to consigning men to death.* The ritual is enacted with great frequency the world over, although it is not always

> explicit in [particular cases]. Nonetheless, as Hochschild likened the evidence of gendercide in the grotesquely misnamed Congo Free State to the "ruins of an Auschwitz crematorium," we should see in our minds the camp commander and his henchmen on the platform, systematically and dispassionately culling part of a group (here, the male part) and consigning those selected to rapid extermination.

This analogy is, to my mind, misleading. Russian POWs were not selected out in the same sense that the men of Srebrenica or Kosovo were.[69] Red Army POWs fell into German hands in the course of military operations; they were not selected out from among the population of males and females. Furthermore, there is at present very little evidence that suggests that Russian POWs were treated significantly differently on the basis of gender. This applies also to German operations against alleged partisans. In any event, the statistical information that is currently available does not, as Erickson notes, permit comprehensive comparisons on the basis of gender.[70]

The destruction of the Armenians during World War I and of European Jewry during World War II. In connection with both of these clusters of mass killings, which are regarded by most authorities as paradigmatic examples that qualify as genocides, in "Gendercide and Genocide" Jones singles out "a little-noticed gendering," namely, the differential treatment meted out on the basis of gender at different phases of their genocidal cycles.[71] It is clear that in both clusters of mass killings, gender selection was entirely subordinate to the broader goal of group destruction. Inasmuch as differential treatment existed in the case of the Armenians, this selectivity was itself a consequence of the perceived significance of males and females for the continuity of an Armenian presence in Turkey. The goal of the killings and the deportations was to ensure that there would no longer be a significant presence of Armenians there. Moreover, differences in treatment were only gender related, not gender specific. Different proportions of males and females, and young and old, may have been killed, deported, or forced to convert at different phases of the killings, but all of these policies were directed toward the same end.[72]

A similar argument applies respecting the destruction of European Jewry. As I noted earlier, this destructive program included many different types of action. Ghettoization began in 1939, with the invasion of Poland. Hilberg noted that more than 500,000 Jews died from starvation and disease in the ghettos, 30,000 before the start of Operation Barbarossa.[73] No gender selectivity was evident. Browning considers that many of these pre–June

1941 deaths resulted from the indifference of the ghetto managers and others to the plight of their inhabitants, in much the same way as senior officers of the *Wehrmacht* were indifferent to that of Russian POWs. In Browning's view, the change to a policy of deliberate liquidation of the ghettos and their inhabitants followed from a decision made by Hitler in July or August 1941 to solicit "a plan for the systematic mass murder of the European Jews. . . . [The] components of such a plan—deportation to camps equipped with gassing facilities—were agreed upon by the end of October 1941, when construction of the first two death camps at Chelmno and Belzec began."[74] It should be noted that there are some authorities that dissent from Browning's interpretation.

Jones suggests that a gender-selective policy existed as far as the early phases of the *Einsatzgruppen* operations were concerned, in that Jewish males were originally singled out as targets, whereas women were not. This was certainly the case. But gender was not the operative variable. As Christian Streit, one of the leading authorities on this issue, notes, Reinhard Heydrich, head of the Reich Security Main Office and the SS functionary directly responsible for overseeing the activities of the *Einsatzgruppen,* was careful not to exceed in his directives the demands of the Commissar Order and the Barbarossa Directive in essential points: "All party functionaries of higher, middle and 'radical lower' rank were to be executed, as well as all other 'radical elements' and 'all Jews in state and party positions.' "[75] Jews featured in the directives by virtue of their political and radical status, not their gender, essentially because they were perceived as an immediate threat. This is not very surprising given the close association in Nazi ideology between Bolshevism and Jewishness. However, as Streit emphasizes: "The target group of these orders was, in the first place, the Communist functionaries and in a wider sense all those who did not want to bow to German rule. There was no mention of the Jews," in the original Commissar Order and Barbarossa Directive.[76]

Many of the *Einsatzgruppen* clearly started interpreting these orders as they saw fit and executed all demographic categories of Jew, though in different proportions relative to gender at different phases. SS *Standartenführer* Jäeger, commander of SD *Einsatzkommando* 3, reported figures for executions up until 1 December 1941. From the outset both Jewish males and females were executed. Up until 18 August 1941, the number of males executed was proportionately higher, at times exceedingly so. From then on, proportionately more females were executed.[77] As Gilbert notes, the slaughter in the East began from *the first day* of the invasion: "at the frontier village of Virbalis, Jews 'were placed alive in anti-tank trenches about two kilometres long and killed by machine guns. . . . Only the children were not shot. They were caught by the legs, their heads hit against stones and they were thereupon buried alive.'"[78] Furthermore, the *Einsatzgruppen* were not the only units involved from the outset in the killing of Jews, or German the sole nationality of perpetrators.

These issues, however, are extremely difficult to unravel and have been points of contention for more than two decades among historians researching the Jewish Holocaust.[79] My own reading of the weight of evidence is that gendercidal selection was, if of any significance at all in the context of the initial onslaught of Operation Barbarossa, of very minor importance during a temporal phase of five or six weeks from June to August 1941. Whatever the orders were, and whoever was responsible for initiating this or that policy, from the outset of Barbarossa, Jews in all demographic categories were slaughtered on a massive scale. There was nothing in Nazi ideology that suggested that Jews were to be treated differently according to gender; in that bible of National Socialism, *Mein Kampf*, no such distinction is drawn.[80]

Conclusion

The issue of gender has not generally featured as a prominent parameter in studies of mass killings, including those referred to as genocidal. Jones has drawn attention to this neglect and has suggested its relevance for characterizing a variety of conflict situations. Gendercide is envisaged as a policy implemented by perpetrators whereby they select out persons for killing on the basis of their gender. As currently developed, the term is largely a means of naming or characterizing instances of, or clusters of, mass killings. Although in both his original article, and in his analysis of the impact of gender on the Rwanda 1994 killings (Chapter 4 of this volume), Jones refers to the need to draw out the "analytical and policy-relevant insights" associated with the term, this is not done. Moreover, I would argue that as presently conceived, it would be very difficult to do so.

In his, as with many studies in this field, a dominant imperative is to assert the significance of a chosen parameter in the overall framework of mass killings, largely on the basis of incomplete information and the absence of a discussion of methodological issues. The size of the population, in the statistical sense, of this field of inquiry is unknown but known to be very extensive. In a 1983 report that dealt only with political killings, Amnesty International noted that hundreds of thousands of people had been killed in the previous ten years by political authorities. Such killings occurred in virtually all regions of the world, in a very substantial number of countries.[81] Attempts to quantify the total number of victims of mass killings that have occurred in various contexts this century are beset with numerous difficulties. Few estimates place the figure at less than 120 million.[82] They represent hundreds of thousands of separate incidents. On methodological grounds alone it is difficult to justify the deduction that gendercide "is a frequent and often defining feature of human conflict . . . a regular, even ubiquitous, feature of contemporary politicomilitary conflicts worldwide."[83] While gender may be an important variable in some mass killing situations, its significance needs to be established, and the parameters of its influence identified.

The tendency to view gender as a sufficient and necessary dimension prompting certain instances of mass killing is liable to lead to the neglect of other interacting influences. In many of the case studies advanced as evidence for the impact of gender, other factors were exerting an effect simultaneously, being potentially of equal or greater importance. It is frequently impossible to disentangle the ethnic dimension from the political. In the case of the Rwandan genocide, ethnicity, political affiliation, and gender, inasmuch as these exerted an influence, interacted with each other, as they have done in many instances of mass killing.

As with many of those analyses that focus on other genocide-related terms, such as "politicide," "ethnocide," and "culturecide," there is a danger that demonstrating equivalence with a paradigmatic instance of large-scale mass killings, especially an instance of genocide, becomes a major imperative. Thus, Jones is led to assert that the "gendering of genocide in Rwanda bears comparison with many of the worst atrocities of the twentieth century."[84] Probably, but what are the dimensions on which they are being compared: the number of lives lost, the proportion of the population annihilated, the ruthlessness of the perpetrators, the indifference of bystanders, the intensity of prejudice on the part of specific segments of the population, a background of previous violent incidents, or the reaction of the international community? Moreover, would it not be more accurate to substitute "the ethnicizing" for "the gendering"?

The single most important influence on shaping approaches to the study of large-scale mass killings has been cognitive representations of genocide, framed largely in terms of the Jewish "Holocaust," the destruction of

European Jewry. Although not the paramount concern of Raphaël Lemkin, it has been interpreted widely as constituting the template of Article II of the 1948 convention on genocide. To play in the genocide studies league, authors of case materials need to ensure that the instances they document meet the requirements of Article II. As the real world of mass killings is far too complex and varied to produce a comfortable fit, this leads rapidly to conceptual modification and accretion. Such conceptual slippage is characteristic of the field, and is observable frequently within the pages of a case study or article. What starts out as gendercide becomes "gendercidal assault," or "gendered atrocity," when the scale of the phenomenon does not fit the cognitive representation of what a genocide should be.

The most important by-product of this crowded conceptual domain is that it is very difficult, if possible at all, to compare findings from studies of mass killings. Many of these studies are methodologically deficient. Frequently the terms that nominally designate variables are not defined.[85] These matters are not entirely unrecognized by others. Churchill, for whose thoroughness I have great admiration, devotes a chapter to considering the problems associated with "defining the unthinkable." But after expounding at length on the difficulties, he concludes that, on the whole, the "motif employed by the framers of the Genocide Convention is best" and proceeds to modify its framework.[86]

The concepts that I have been referring to in this chapter, as well as others, would, in a mature disciplinary field, represent components of a classification system. As Hempel points out: "A classification . . . divides a given set or class of objects into subclasses. The objects are called *elements* or *members,* of the given set; the set itself will also be referred to as the *universe of discourse* especially when it is assumed to contain as its elements all the objects with which a given investigation is concerned."[87] Genocides are a subclass of the universe of discourse whose elements are mass killings. The *differentia specifica* of that subclass can, in my view, only be established following detailed empirical investigations and theoretical modeling focused on mass killing in its varied manifestations. Assimilating cases studies to the Article II definition by conceptual modification and accretion is an analytical cul-de-sac, one that over the last four decades has paid few dividends, other than in the many excellent case studies that constitute the raw materials for a more comparative approach.

On the matter of gendercide, therefore, I draw a distinction between gender and gendercide. Gendercide is potentially a subclass of mass killings that needs to be defined by the specification of necessary and sufficient conditions of membership in it. Gender is one of a range of variables that may be of etiological consequence in a proportion of mass killings. Holter, in the first paragraph of his conclusion to his chapter "A Theory of Gendercide" in this volume, draws attention to some other variables of established or potential etiological relevance. In this, as in other contexts, detailed specification of the gender component is likely to be a complex affair. As a component of the *explanans,* gender can have coefficients of variable value. In some mass killings, whether of males or females, whether perpetrated by males or females, its value is high. In others, it is, as I have argued here, low. In some instances it may have no bearing at all. The same applies, in my view, to other variables. That gender may be a relevant variable in some instances of mass killings is, to my mind, established.

Notes

1. Killing members of the group is only one of five acts potentially indicative of genocide under Article II of the 1948 *Convention on the Prevention and Punishment of the Crime of Genocide.* In practice, acts (d) and (e) do not feature prominently in contemporary conflicts potentially classifiable as genocides, and (b) and (c) are invariably closely linked with killing members of the group (a).

2. Mary Anne Warren, *Gendercide: The Implications of Sex Selection* (Totowa, N.J.: Rowman and Allanheld, 1985).

3. Katz quoted in Adam Jones, "Gendercide and Genocide," Chapter 1 in this volume.

4. For instance, L. Piyadasa, *Sri Lanka: The Holocaust and After* (London: Marram Books, 1984), described an incident that occurred in July 1983: "Remand prisoners and political detainees . . . being *massacred.* The armed forces joining in and sometimes organising this *pogrom.* . . . The Sri Lanka *holocaust* demonstrates . . . the dangers" (p. 5, emphasis added).

5. Erwin Staub classified the Argentinean disappearances as genocide in *The Roots of Evil* (Cambridge: Cambridge University Press, 1993). Most authorities on terrorism and Latin America classify the same event as either state terrorism or government crime. See, for example, Michael Stohl and George A Lopez, eds., *Government Violence and Repression* (Westport, Conn.: Greenwood Press, 1986). In the framework developed by Harff and Gurr, it would be classified as a politicide; see Barbara Harff and Ted R. Gurr, "Toward an Empirical Theory of Genocides and Politicides: Identification and Measurement of Cases since 1945," *International Studies Quarterly,* 32 (1988). Hitchcock and Twedt note that "examples of *genocidal actions* against Native American populations include . . . systematic *extrajudicial killings* of dozens of Oglala Lakota" (emphasis added). Robert K. Hitchcock and Tara M. Twedt, "Physical

and Cultural Genocide of Various Indigenous Peoples," in Samuel Totten, William S. Parsons, and Israel W. Charny, eds., *Century of Genocide: Eyewitness Accounts and Critical Views* (New York: Garland, 1997), p. 380.

6. "Culturecide" and "ethnocide" are sometimes employed interchangeably, as by Leo Kuper in *Genocide* (Harmondsworth: Penguin, 1994), p. 31. Some authors define ethnocide to include physical destruction of members, as well as the destruction of their "way of life," making it virtually impossible to distinguish these from each other or from genocide. See Monroe C. Beardsley, "Reflections on Genocide and Ethnocide," in Richard Arens, ed., *Genocide in Paraguay* (Philadelphia: Temple University Press, 1976).

7. These rankings are impermanent due to definitional changes and the application of established terms to new episodes or clusters of mass killings. For example, the Commission of Experts on the former Yugoslavia so redefined ethnic cleansing as to grant it coequivalence with genocide. See the section "Ethnic Cleansing," *www.ess.uwe.ac.uk/comexpert/I#II-IV_D.htm#III.B,* and Robert M. Hayden, "Schindler's Fate: Genocide, Ethnic Cleansing, and Population Transfer," *Slavic Review,* 55: 4 (1996), p. 732.

8. Vahakn Dadrian notes that the notion of race murder, *Völksmord,* was employed earlier by a Swiss authority to characterize World War I mass slaughters. Dadrian, "The Convergent Aspects of the Armenian and Jewish Cases of Genocide: A Reinterpretation of the Concept of Holocaust," in *Remembering for the Future: The Impact of the Holocaust on the Modern World* (Papers to be Presented to an International Scholar's Conference to be held in Oxford, 10–13 July 1988, Preprints, Theme II [Oxford: Pergamon Press, 1988]), p. 1981.

9. Matthew Lippman, "The Drafting of the 1948 Convention on the Prevention and Punishment of Genocide," *Boston University International Law Journal,* 3: 1 (1985), p. 5; Beth Van Schaack, "The Crime of Political Genocide: Repairing the Genocide Convention's Blind Spot," *Yale Law Journal,* 106, p. 2263.

10. The absence of published research on the origins of the convention, and the discrepancy between Lemkin's views that have appeared in print and the content of Article II, have not prevented assertions concerning Lemkin's influence. Thus, Helen Fein notes, "Lemkin was the guiding legal hand and lobbyist for the United Nations Convention." Fein, "Genocide: A Sociological Perspective," *Current Sociology,* 38: 1 (1990), p. 1. Lemkin was only one of a number of legal experts whose views were sought on the content of the convention during one phase of its passage from General Assembly resolution to agreed convention. Of course, his behind-the-scenes influence may have been very significant, but this has not yet been documented.

11. Most of this is unpublished. Fein noted in 1990 that Lemkin's writings were then being edited by Rabbi Steven L. Jacobs of Birmingham, Alabama. Rabbi Jacobs informed me some ten years later that this work was still in progress. My discussion of Lemkin's views, here and elsewhere, is based on the material he published in English up until 1948. Whatever his subsequent views may have been, those that he

expressed up to this point are those that were most likely to have had a bearing on the content of the 1948 Convention. Fein, "Genocide," p. 12 (note 1).

12. This chapter is reproduced at *www.ess.uwe.ac.uk/genocide/Lemkin.htm.*

13. Raphael Lemkin, *Axis Rule in Occupied Europe: Laws of Occupation, Analysis of Government, Proposals for Redress* (Washington, D.C.: Carnegie Endowment for International Peace, 1944). See also Lemkin, "Genocide as a Crime under International Law," *American Journal of International Law,* 41 (1947).

14. I discuss Lemkin's approach in greater detail in Stuart D. Stein, "Conceptions and Terms: Templates for the Analysis of Holocausts and Genocides," *Journal of Genocide Research,* forthcoming 2004.

15. Lemkin, *Axis Rule,* pp. 82–90.

16. Ethnic cleansing does not necessarily destroy the "essential foundations of the life of national groups." Lemkin assumes, a priori, that removal has this consequence. He also assumes that change is necessarily undesirable. The Jewish populations of the Yemen and Iraq, to cite some examples, were rescued and moved to Israel in the late 1940s and early 1950s, as were the Benei Israel from India in the 1960s, and Ethiopian Jews in the 1980s. Members of these groups did not necessarily view the fundamental changes thus wrought as undesirable. In the literature on genocide, particularly that segment of it focused on indigenous peoples, there tends to be, as in Lemkin's analysis, an implicit assumption that the restructuring of group culture is always genocidal, even though in some instances no change would be more likely to lead to nonretention of significant components of group culture than would change.

17. Lippman, "The Drafting of the 1948 Convention"; Schaack, "The Crime of Political Genocide"; United Nations, Economic and Social Council, *Study of the Question of the Prevention and Punishment of the Crime of Genocide,* Document No. E/CN.4/Sub.2/416 (1978).

18. Lemkin, *Axis Rule,* p. 79 (emphasis added).

19. Ibid., p. 90. The reference, of course, is to Nazi Germany.

20. Consequently, I find that Kuper's contention that the convention "incorporates the original concept of Raphael Lemkin" true only to the extent that it proscribes the destruction of certain groups, as such. Lemkin's conception of genocide and that implicit in the convention are, however, radically different. Kuper, *Genocide,* p. 31.

21. I believe that Levene is mistaken in asserting that Lemkin did not properly address the fact that "the perpetrators of genocides are states, or state-sanctioned bodies"; these were in fact the only entities that he took cognizance of in this context. Mark Levene, "Is the Holocaust Simply Another Example of Genocide?" *Patterns of Prejudice,* 28: 2 (1994), p. 4.

22. For a recent discussion and review of the issue of intent, see Alexander K. A. Greenawalt, "Rethinking Genocidal Intent: The Case for a Knowledge-Based Interpretation," *Columbia Law Review,* 99 (1999). For a detailed proposal for modi-

fying the convention on the basis of types of intent, see Ward Churchill, *A Little Matter of Genocide* (San Francisco: City Light Books, 1997), pp. 431–37. For a countervailing argument based on the notion of specific intent, see Hugo Adam Bedau, "Genocide in Vietnam," *Worldview*, 17 (1974).

23. Katherine Bischoping and Natalie Fingerhut, "Border Lines: Indigenous Peoples in Genocide Studies," *Canadian Review of Sociology and Anthropology*, 33: 4 (1996); Frank Chalk and Kurt Jonassohn, *The History and Sociology of Genocide* (New Haven: Yale University Press, 1990); Churchill, *A Little Matter of Genocide;* Fein, "Genocide"; Jones, "Gendercide and Genocide"; Kuper; *Genocide;* Totten et al., *Century of Genocide.*

24. *Rome Statute of the International Criminal Court*, U.N. Doc. A/CONF. 183/9 (17 July 1998). Reproduced in Theodor Meron, *War Crimes Law Comes of Age* (Oxford: Oxford University Press, 1998), pp. 310–17.

25. "Many social scientists have accepted the UN 1948 Convention on Genocide definition of genocide explicitly or implicitly or a broadened version thereof, including political and social groups." Fein, "Genocide," p. 12.

26. Bauer has repeatedly sought to rank certain mass killings by a process of exclusion. See Yehuda Bauer, "Holocaust and Genocide: Some Comparisons," in Peter Hayes, ed., *Lessons and Legacies: The Meaning of the Holocaust in a Changing World* (Evanston, Ill: Northwestern University Press, 1991), p. 43; Bauer, "A Past That Will Not Go Away," in Michael Berenbaum and Abraham J. Peck, eds., *The Holocaust and History: The Known, the Unknown, the Disputed, and the Reexamined* (Bloomington: Indiana University Press, 1998), p. 14; Bauer, *The Holocaust in Historical Perspective* (Seattle: University of Washington Press, 1978), pp. 35–38.

27. Henry R. Huttenbach, "The Romani Porajmos: The Nazi Genocide of the Gypsies in Germany and Eastern Europe," in David M. Crowe and John Kolsti, eds., *The Gypsies of Eastern Europe* (London: M. E. Sharpe, 1991); Sybil Milton, "Holocaust: The Gypsies," in Totten et al., *Century of Genocide;* Tony Barta, "Relations of Genocide: Land and Lives in the Colonization of Australia," in Isidor Wallimann and Michael N. Dobkowski, eds., *Genocide and the Modern Age* (Westport, Conn.: Greenwood Press, 1987); Churchill, *A Little Matter of Genocide.*

28. Christopher Browning's contributions to our understanding of the Final Solution and its perpetrators are universally acknowledged as among the most significant and profound. One of his important monographs is *The Path to Genocide,* which includes a section entitled "The Prelude to Genocide" and an essay, "Genocide and Public Health." The term "genocide" is nowhere defined, nor is it mentioned in the index, and to the best of my knowledge it is not mentioned in the text. The term is so closely linked to the Jewish holocaust that no elaboration is required, and Browning's discussion makes it clear that genocide, the Final Solution, the deliberate mass murder of the Jews, and deaths through ghettoization can all be taken as synonymous with it. A similar lack of attention to definitional parameters, the absence

of a listing in the index, and the lack of a comparative research framework characterizes Daniel Goldhagen's influential *Hitler's Willing Executioners.* Goldhagen does employ the term frequently in the text, as well as "genocidal killing," "genocidal slaughter," "genocidal executioners," and "genocidal motivation," none of which is defined. The implied meaning of the genocide prefix parallels that of Browning. Christopher R. Browning, *The Path to Genocide: Essays on Launching the Final Solution* (Cambridge: Cambridge University Press, 1992); Daniel J. Goldhagen, *Hitler's Willing Executioners: Ordinary Germans and the Holocaust* (London: Little, Brown, 1996).

29. See Chalk and Jonassohn, *The History and Sociology of Genocide;* Totten et al., *Century of Genocide.*

30. Kuper, *Genocide,* p. 9.

31. Fein, "Genocide"; Bischoping and Fingerhut, "Border Lines," p. 482.

32. Some authors have proposed typologies of genocide. As I refer to such typologies at greater length elsewhere, here I note just three relevant considerations. First, the types listed are generally undifferentiated relative to that which they purport to depict: retributive, internal, colonial, economic exploitation, and so on. The likelihood that anything meaningful can be said by lumping together all mass killings that can be subsumed under economic exploitation, colonialism, or retribution is small. Second, there is usually no attempt to delimit their dimensional parameters. It is assumed that terms such as "exploitation," "colonialism," "pragmatic," and so forth pose no interpretative problems. Third, often what is designated a type of genocide is in fact a cause of genocide. See Stein, "Conceptions and Terms."

33. The distinction between professional killers and killing professionals was introduced by Robert J. Lifton in *The Nazi Doctors: Medical Killing and the Psychology of Killing* (New York: Basic Books, 1986).

34. I have refrained from providing a lengthy list of relevant materials relating to these genocides, as the issue is hardly contentious.

35. There is no formula for deciding when a series of killings of a particular type, combined with a specified volume of deaths, in the context of specified group relations, and so on, should be construed as a genocide, rather than a massacre, a pogrom, or a gendered atrocity. Designations are invariably entirely arbitrary. Two very good examples of this are Anthony James Joes, "Insurgency and Genocide: La Vendée," *Small Wars and Insurgencies,* 9: 3 (1998), which does not bother to define genocide or make reference to any authority on the subject in the bibliography; and Jaroslava Colajacomo, "Guatemala. The Chixoy Dam: The Aya Achi Genocide. The Story of a Forced Settlement," *IWGIA* [International Workgroup for Indigenous Affairs] *Newsletter,* 3–4 (1999), pp. 64–79.

36. One obvious example concerns the protracted debate relating to the moral/psychological status of persons involved as perpetrators of the Jewish holocaust. The dominant consensus has now settled on the normality-banality thesis.

From the hundreds of thousands of killing contexts, authors select out a few instances from which to arrive at conclusions, invariably providing no methodological justification respecting their choices. It is quite clear that much of the debate and the conclusions deduced have little application to many instances of twentieth-century mass killings, not least those that have occurred recently in Africa and the Balkans. See Stephen Ellis, "Liberia 1989–1994: A Study of Ethnic and Spiritual Violence," *African Affairs*, 94 (1995); Roy Gutman, *A Witness to Genocide* (Longmead: Element Books, 1993); Mary Kaldor, *New and Old Wars: Organized Violence in a Global Era* (London: Polity Press, 1999), esp. ch. 3; Scott Peterson, *Me against My Brother: At War in Somalia, Sudan, and Rwanda* (London: Routledge, 2000).

37. Quoted in Totten et al., *Century of Genocide*, p. xv.

38. Israel W. Charny, "The Study of Genocide," in Charny, *Genocide*, pp. xii, 358 (note 2). Of course, there are no settled means for inferring "generic meanings" other than by reference to the views of the author.

39. Henry R. Huttenbach, "Locating the Holocaust on the Genocide Spectrum: Toward a Methodology of Definition and Categorization," *Holocaust and Genocide Studies*, 3: 3 (1998), p. 295.

40. Churchill, *A Little Matter of Genocide.*

41. David Chandler, *Brother Number One: A Political Biography of Pol Pot* (Boulder, Colo.: Westview Press, 1992); *Voices from S-21: Terror and History in Pol Pot's Secret Prison* (Berkeley: University of California Press, 1999); David Hawk, "The Cambodian Genocide," in Totten et al., *Century of Genocide;* Ben Kiernan, *The Pol Pot Regime: Race and Genocide in Cambodia under the Khmer Rouge, 1975–1979* (New Haven: Yale University Press, 1996).

42. Staub, *The Roots of Evil*, p. 8.

43. R. J. Rummel, *Death by Government* (New Brunswick, N.J.: Transaction, 1995); Rummel, *Democide: Nazi Genocide and Mass Murder* (New Brunswick, N.J.: Transaction, 1992); Gil Elliott, *Twentieth-Century Book of the Dead* (London: Allen Lane, 1972).

44. Herbert C. Kelman and V. Lee Hamilton, *Crimes of Obedience* (New Haven: Yale University Press, 1989); Staub, *The Roots of Evil;* Roy F. Baumeister, *Evil: Inside Human Violence and Cruelty* (New York: W. H. Freeman, 1999); Wilhelmus Petrus Du Preez, *Genocide: The Psychology of Mass Murder* (London: Boyars/Bowerdean, 1994).

45. Barta, "Relations of Genocide"*;* Jean-Paul Sartre, *On Genocide* (Boston: Beacon Press, 1968).

46. Charny, "The Study of Genocide," p. xii; Israel Charny, *How Can We Commit the Unthinkable? Genocide: The Human Cancer* (Boulder, Colo.: Westview Press, 1982), p. 358, footnote 2.

47. "The term cultural genocide . . . is an extension of the original idea of genocide." Uriel Tal, "On the Study of Holocaust and Genocide," *Yad Vashem Studies*, 13 (1979), p. 15; Beardsley, "Reflections on Genocide and Ethnocide," p. 87.

48. Levene, "Is the Holocaust," p. 92.

49. Fred C. Ikle, *How Nations Negotiate* (New York: Harper and Row, 1964), p. 15.

50. Schaack, "The Crime of Political Genocide," p. 2261.

51. Berel Lang, "The Concept of Genocide," *Philosophical Forum,* 16 (1984–85), p. 1; Tal, "On the Study of Holocaust," p. 21.

52. See, for instance, Bauer's arguments relating to the mass killings of Armenians during the First World War, and Gypsies and Jews during the Second. He is led to postulate a continuum "on which we find mass murder, genocide and Holocaust." However, as he has rejected the possibility of differentiating between mass killings on the basis of absolute numbers killed, or the proportion of the base population killed, this is a continuum without any dimension that permits the absolute or relative situating of these terms, in fact no continuum at all. Bauer, "Holocaust and Genocide," p. 43.

53. Strictly speaking, the term "ethnocide" also predates the Convention. Lemkin noted: "Another term could be used for the same idea (of genocide), namely, ethnocide, consisting of the Greek word 'ethnos'—nation—and the Latin word 'cide.'" Lemkin, *Axis Rule,* p. 79 (note 1). As far as I am aware, no one has drawn attention to this use of the term by Lemkin or currently employs it in this way. As Fein has noted, the "deliberate destruction of the culture of a distinct group without physical annihilation of its members is most often termed ethnocide now." Fein, "Genocide," p. 10.

54. I have omitted *gendered atrocity,* which is a scale variable relative to gendercide.

55. See the articles in Jill Radford and Diana E. H. Russell, eds., *Femicide: The Politics of Woman Killing* (Milton Keynes, UK: Open University Press), 1992.

56. There is also a subsidiary confusion between "sex" and "gender." Sex refers to the biological status of the individual, whereas gender refers to socially learned behaviors and expectations. As far as selection of individuals in the situations depicted by Jones are concerned, differences between sex and gender are unlikely to be taken note of by perpetrators, selection being made on the basis of sex. To be strictly accurate, therefore, the selectivity that Jones refers to should be designated sexcide.

57. Linda L. Lindsey, quoted in Ian Marsh, *Sociology,* 2d. ed. (Harlow, UK: Pearson Education, 2000), p. 329.

58. Erving Goffman, *Encounters* (New York: Bobbs-Merrill, 1961), p. 85; Michael A. Hogg and Graham M. Vaughan, *Social Psychology* (Hemel Hempstead, UK: Prentice-Hall, 1995), pp. 243–44; Thomas P. Wilson, "Normative and Interpretive Paradigms in Sociology," in Jack D. Douglas, ed., *Understanding Everyday Life* (London: Routledge and Kegan Paul, 1971), pp. 59–60.

59. This also characterized witch-hunts in early modern Europe. As Levack has noted, the figures available on persons prosecuted indicate that "witchcraft was a sex-related but not a sex-specific crime. Women . . . were more readily suspected of and prosecuted for witchcraft by virtue of their sex, but they had no natural monopoly of the crime. There was nothing in the definition of a witch that excluded males. Men

could, just like women, practise harmful magic, make pacts with the Devil, and attend the Sabbath." Brian P. Levack, *The Witch-Hunt in Early Modern Europe* (London: Longman, 1993), p. 124.

60. See John Erickson, "Soviet War Losses," in Erickson and David Dilks, eds., *Barbarossa: The Axis and the Allies* (Edinburgh: Edinburgh University Press, 1994), in connection with the killings on the eastern front during World War II, probably the most extensive mass killings of the twentieth century that were genocidal in character.

61. This was clearly the case in relation to many massacres during World War II. See also Erickson, "Soviet War Losses," p. 271; Peter Padfield, *Himmler: Reichsführer SS* (London: Macmillan, 1990), p. 387, in connection with the Lidice reprisals. Equally, however, there were many thousands of instances of mass killings when no distinction was drawn on the basis of gender/sex when it came to selecting victims. This applies to many contemporary conflicts as well. Moreover, if, following Jones, "Gendercide and Genocide" and "Gender and Genocide in Rwanda," in this volume, certain types of rape are included, the gender balance is evened out further.

62. Jones recognizes the problematic status of "gender-selectivity" in relation to Stalin's purges, the political status of the victims being the primary variable determining selection for one or other of the purge-related programs being pursued. This, however, appears in a footnote, whilst the burden of the text leaves the impression that gender was of preponderant influence. See Jones, "Gendercide and Genocide," note 12.

63. David Newbury, "Understanding Genocide," *African Studies Review,* 41: 1 (1998), p. 92. In other words, gender selectivity there was, but its objective in all cases was destruction of the group, the Tutsi, not the gender. Moreover, this policy toward women was pursued at the same time as males were being slaughtered.

64. Although Russian sources have recently released new, more reliable and detailed statistical information relating to Soviet losses during World War II, most figures still need to be regarded as of uncertain reliability. Vladimir Andrle, *A Social History of Twentieth-Century Russia* (London: Edward Arnold, 1994), p. 211, suggests that as many as 4.5 million Russian POWs might have died in captivity, whereas John Barber and Mark Harrison, *The Soviet Home Front 1941–1945* (London: Longman, 1991), p. 41, mention a figure of 4.7 million. See also Erickson, "Soviet War Losses."

65. See K.-J. Müller, "The Brutalization of Warfare: Nazi Crimes and the Wehrmacht," in Erickson and Dilks, *Barbarossa,* pp. 230–31; Jurgen Förster, "The German Army and the Ideological War against the Soviet Union," in Gerhard Hirschfeld, ed., *The Policies of Genocide* (London: Allen and Unwin, 1986); Martin Gilbert, *The Holocaust: The Jewish Tragedy* (London: Collins, 1986), pp. 159–60.

66. Omer Bartov, *The Eastern Front, 1941–45* (London: Macmillan, 1985), p. 5.

67. Ibid., pp. 107–8.

68. Barber and Harrison, *The Soviet Home Front,* p. 41, note that "according to

German sources, 3.35 million Soviet soldiers had fallen into German hands by the end of 1941," that is, less than five months from the start of the Eastern Campaign.

69. Jan Willem Honig and Norbert Both, *Srebrenica: Record of a War Crime* (London: Penguin, 1996), pp. 28–29, 48–66; Tim Judah, *Kosovo: War and Revenge* (London: Yale University Press, 2000), p. 180.

70. Erickson, "Soviet War Losses," p. 259. According to Barber and Harrison, *The Soviet Home Front,* pp. 41–42, the total number of male casualties attributable to the war may be put at 20 to 20.5 million, and female deaths at 7 to 7.5 million. These deaths are attributable to multiple causes: direct military casualties, civilian casualties due to bombing, military assaults, antipartisan measures, starvation, slave labor, and disease attendant to war conditions. There is, however, "only fragmentary information about the composition of this large number."

71. Jones, "Gendercide and Genocide," Chapter 1 of this volume.

72. Vahakn N. Dadrian, *The History of the Armenian Genocide* (Oxford: Berghahn Books, 1995); Richard G. Hovannisian, ed., *The Armenian Genocide in Perspective* (New Brunswick, N.J.: Transaction, 1986); S. J. Karijian, "An Inquiry into the Statistics of the Turkish Genocide of the Armenians, 1915–1918," *Armenian Review,* 25 (1972).

73. Gilbert, *The Holocaust,* p. 154.

74. Christopher R. Browning, "Nazi Ghettoization Policy in Poland, 1939–1941," in Browning, *The Path to Genocide,* p. 54.

75. Christian Streit, "The German Army and the Politics of Genocide," in Hirschfeld, *The Policies of Genocide,* p. 5.

76. Ibid., p. 8.

77. The Jäger Report, available at *www.netbistro.com/electriczen/jager.html*; summary figures in Gita Sereney, *The German Trauma: Experiences and Reflections, 1938–2000* (London: Allen Lane, 2000), p. xvi.

78. Gilbert, *The Holocaust,* p. 155.

79. Among the many imponderables that are relevant in the context of Jones's discussion of the destruction of European Jewry, and one which he links with the "gendercidal assault" on Soviet POWs, is the change in killing tactics in the East from execution squads to gas vans and chambers. Jones suggests in Chapter 1 of this volume that the "very infrastructure and techniques of the death camps were originally developed to enslave and exterminate Soviet POWs, not Jews." There is, however, a substantial body of opinion that traces the link to the euthanasia campaign, mediated perhaps by the "psychological pressures" experienced by members of the *Einsatzgruppen.*

80. Adolf Hitler, *Mein Kampf* (Boston: Houghton Mifflin, 1943).

81. Amnesty International, *Political Killings by Governments* (London: Amnesty International, 1983).

82. Rummel, *Death by Government;* Elliott, *Twentieth-Century Book of the Dead.*

83. Jones, "Gendercide and Genocide."

84. Jones, "Gender and Genocide in Rwanda."

85. A recent example of this is an edited volume by Mark Levene and Penny Roberts, *The Massacre in History* (New York: Berghahn Books, 1999). Although it includes an introduction by Levene, and a section entitled "Defining Our Terms: Extending the Debate," no definition is provided. It is assumed that the *generic* meaning of the term will somehow erupt into consciousness through the mention of Dresden, Hiroshima, Guernica, and St. Bartholomew (pp. 5–7). A similar reluctance can be found in Eric Carlton, *Massacres: An Historical Perspective* (Aldershot, UK: Scolar Press, 1994).

86. Churchill, *A Little Matter of Genocide,* p. 431.

87. Carl G. Hempel, "Fundamentals of Taxonomy," in *Aspects of Scientific Explanation* (New York: Free Press, 1965), p. 137.

9

Beyond "Gendercide"

Operationalizing Gender in Comparative Genocide Studies

R. Charli Carpenter

Introduction

The new attention to gender in comparative genocide studies is among the most promising trends in the subfield. This is so both because gender is ubiquitous in social life and because theoretical knowledge of how gender operates is still underdeveloped. Feminist scholars of world politics have long said that gender dynamics underpin and enable violent conflicts of all types, but their work has typically focused on women as a disadvantaged group.[1] Until very recently, the only writing on gender and genocide focused primarily on rape and sexual atrocity against women and girls in contemporary genocides.[2] The failure of mainstream political scientists and international relations scholars to engage with gender as an analytical category has resulted in a body of research and policy making on gender that primarily reflects feminist normative concerns.

Adam Jones sought to address this issue in 1996, when he argued that gender analyses should not be built upon gender stereotypes, including the passivity, pacifism, or innate victimhood of women, and that they should seek to explain sex-specific outcomes pertaining to men as well.[3] This work was later expanded to intersect with comparative genocide studies through the "gendercide" framework.[4] Drawing on Mary Anne Warren's work on sex-selective mass killings of women, Jones argued that sex-selective killings of men as well as women should be analyzed by scholars of armed conflict, and recognized by policy makers in strategies regarding when, how and on whose behalf to engage in organized rescue.[5]

Jones's seminal article swiftly generated a body of genocide research that specifically focuses on sex selectivity in patterns of mass killing, with an emphasis on genocide: the March 2002 issue of the *Journal of Genocide Research,* from which this volume derives, was devoted entirely to the topic. The articles cut at the problem of sex-selective killing from a variety of directions, but all share two commonalities. First, they focus on the practice of targeting members of one or another sex as a crucial site around which gender dynamics manifest in genocidal atrocity. Second, they seek to balance the emphasis on women's human rights with analysis of the extent to which males are targeted on the basis of gender.

This inclusive approach to sex-selective killing corrects for much of the feminist bias in earlier literature, while contributing critically to our understanding of gender and genocide. However, there are limitations to the "gendercide" concept that must be addressed in the course of further developing gender as a framework for analysis in comparative genocide studies. "Gendercide" has so far been defined as "gender-selective mass killing."[6] The criteria for the definition is the biological sex of the dead, rather than the beliefs about gender, that generate those outcomes. Besides producing some conceptual inconsistency in the literature, this definition excludes sex-inclusive targeting for reasons that are gender related.

Moreover, as so defined, while "gendercide" is a component of many genocides, it does not map neatly onto or encompass problems of gender and genocide. "Gendercide" is a broader concept than "genocide," because many varieties of mass killing may be sex selective (gendercidal), and only when other components are brought to bear does a genocide occur.[7] Gendercide as defined by Jones may indeed be a tactic of genocide, but it is not in itself genocide. Only the targeting of gender groups as such would qualify under the Convention on the Prevention and Punishment of the

Crime of Genocide, and as I will demonstrate, this need neither be sex selective nor involve mass killing.[8]

"Gendercide" is also a narrower concept than "gender and genocide," because sex-selective mass killing is not the only manifestation of gender in genocide, nor may it be the most important in terms of an agenda for prevention. To make gendercide the focus of an agenda to bring gender into comparative genocide studies is either to ignore a vast range of analytical categories and topics that are relevant or, as some have done, to incorporate these other gendered aspects under the same framework, which reduces the analytical precision of the gendercide concept itself.

Jones is entirely correct to demand a more inclusive agenda, and a recognition of men as victims. But the concept of gendercide may constitute too limited a framework to be useful in promoting this agenda. In this respect, I share some of Stuart Stein's skepticism in "Geno and Other Cides," Chapter 8 in this volume, on the conceptual approach employed, when he argues for distinctions between sex-selective and sex-specific killings, or points out some problems with the conflation of "gender" and "sex." However, I do not agree with Stein that the study of sex-selective massacre as a gendered component of ethnic conflict is a dead end for genocide scholarship. Rather, we can develop clearer concepts, more precise vocabulary, and an agenda for incorporating the gender variable that goes beyond sex-selective massacre. Gendercide is a good beginning but should not be the ultimate focus of scholarship on gender in the field of comparative genocide studies.

I will make my case in three parts. First, I argue for conceptual labels that better capture the concepts at hand and their subdistinctions. I emphasize the need both to clearly differentiate sex and gender and to generate a typology of gender effects. Second, I argue that while sex-selective mass killing needs to be analyzed in genocide studies, it is a mistake to equate it with genocide itself. Third, having recast gendercide as a component of gender-in-genocide, rather than an overarching research agenda, I conclude with suggestions for research in areas still underdeveloped in this emerging field.

Sex, Gender, and "Gendercide": Some Remarks on Theory Building

A problem with the concept of gendercide as a research framework rather than a political label is that it confuses biological sex and social gender. In

"Gendercide and Genocide" in this volume, Jones defines "gendercide" as "gender-selective mass killing" and specifically claims that gender "can be defined primarily, if not exclusively, in terms of biological sex." To his credit, Jones recognizes as an aside that this is not necessarily the only usage of "gender," but he claims that "for present purposes" it is the best usage. I disagree and will therefore bracket "gendercide" in quotes to refer to the scholarship on the subject and use the more accurate term "sex-specific massacre" to describe what Jones has labeled "gendercide."

The term "gendercide" is not without its political advantages. In terms of capturing the attention of policy makers and activists, Jones could not have been more clever in turning Warren's label into a political catchphrase for sex-specific massacre. "Gendercide" appropriates the colloquial usage of the term "gender" (indeed we do see it used to code biological sex on census forms and in much international discourse pertaining to women); it also creates an obvious semantic corollary to the much-abused term "genocide."[9] No wonder writings and commentary in the mainstream have been so provocative; no wonder the Gendercide Watch website, *www.gendercide.org.*, has received so much traffic and acclaim since its establishment.

It is when we attempt scholarly explanation of the phenomenon that the term "gendercide" begins to create problems. On the one hand, gender is defined as *bodies,* as in David Buchanan's "gender-selective human rights violations" in "Gendercide and Human Rights" in this volume. On the other, it is defined as *ideas,* as in Øystein Gullvåg Holter's "masculinization of the enemy" in "A Theory of Gendercide," also in this volume: not as brute facts of human biology, but as social kinds such as ideologies, norms, and intersubjective ascriptive characteristics. This makes for terribly confusing scholarship replete with analytical inconsistencies, enabling Jones, for example, to make the extraordinary statement that since Jews of both sexes died, "gender was far from a dominant consideration in the holocaust."[10] It also renders scholars incapable of distinguishing varieties of sex (biological and performative) and varieties of gender (structural, ascriptive-ideology, prescriptive ideology, and individual), to say nothing of capturing the interplay between them or identifying pressure points where political leverage could be brought to bear to create change.

Gender must be distinguished from sex in order to build good theory. I would go so far as to say this is *especially* true for the study of "gendercide" if we are going to test *whether* (rather than assume *that*) sex-specific outcomes are the result of social beliefs rather than of biological necessity. For present purposes, I follow Robert Connell's 1987 description of gender as a social process whereby divisions of labor, power, and emotion, as well as modes of dress and identity, are differentiated (and the differences naturalized), among as well as between men and women.[11] Much of this has very little to do with biological sex.

Gender refers, variously, to social beliefs and institutions that direct our awareness to sex differentiation and regulate human interaction on that basis. *Gender identities* at the individual level regulate a person's sense of what sort of man or woman they are, and how thus to act in a given situation.[12] *Gender discourses* both ascribe certain attributes to men and women respectively (men *are* aggressive, women *are* nurturing) and generate principled *gender ideologies* that govern behaviors and configurations based on these attributes (men *should be* soldiers, women *should be* mothers). Gender discourses also contain prescriptive or proscriptive *gender norms,* such as "spare the women and children" or "women and children first," that govern action in specific cases where individuals must make policy choices.[13] *Gender structures* are created by the social channeling of men and women disproportionately into different institutions, such as the military, the national security establishment, or the nursing profession, such that outcomes pertaining to those locations become sex specific. The experiences and lifeworlds of such men and women develop differently, and their presence naturalizes the supposed masculinity or femininity of the institutions themselves. All of these social impacts help create and sustain the myth that women and men are fundamentally different.

Sex inheres biologically rather than being socially ascribed. The sex/gender dichotomy maps onto Searle's famous distinction between "brute facts" (objects which exist in the real world, such as tanks, nuclear weapons, or people with uteruses) and "social facts" (such as money, Christmas, marriage, or misogyny, which require intersubjective agreement on their existence and constitution).[14] Brute facts "exist whether or not there is agreement that they do."[15] It is an empirical fact that human beings are divided into roughly two categories based on reproductive biology; this would still be true even if it had no impact on human social order.

Of course, there is something to arguments that the very categories "men" and "women" are themselves socially constructed. Postmodern scholars in particular claim that the category of "male" or "female" is more a social than a biological reality, and thus to define sex as biological and only gender as social is to ignore an important role gender plays: the construction of male/female difference.[16] For example, "it is the firmly held belief that there are two and only two sexes that explains the relative ease with which initial sex assignment is achieved."[17] It is certainly true that an observer alien to human culture might not consider the biological distinctions between sexes a significant means of categorizing human beings: it is the sociocultural milieu of gender that makes these distinctions decisive. Nonetheless the distinctions are also *real* in that they exist independently of humans noticing them or making them the bedrock of social differentiation. Most human beings can indeed be coded as male or female.[18]

It is coding for male and female that tells us we are dealing with sex. There are two ways to code for male and female; both are practices in which people engage constantly and with little reflection. First, one can look for the brute bodily differences that sex engenders: Does this person have the look of a woman, and how do we know? Are there breasts, for example? Abundant facial hair? What is the vocal pitch? Teaching a child how to distinguish types of people using biophysical cues is a crucial component of language acquisition and socialization. Where there is doubt, as in Rwanda when the *génocidaires* would undress infants to determine which were boys to kill, external genital differences constitute the indicator.[19] Most of the time such extreme measures are unnecessary because people beyond a certain age also *perform* their sex identities: Women and men wear their hair differently, dress differently, use various coding mechanisms as indicators of what kind of human being—male or female—they are underneath. Because performing one's sex is a social act, and because many people rely upon performative sex as an indicator of biological sex, males or females can make themselves appear as the opposite in certain cases. Women (females) have often posed as men throughout history in order to gain access to militaries and other male-dominated institutions, and as Jones reports, men have often hidden among women to escape sex-selective massacre.[20]

Performing one's gender is different from performing one's sex. Performing gender is not about whether I am male or female, but which form of masculinity or femininity I enact: What *kind* of a woman do I think I am, and how does that sort of woman behave in a given context? Gender performances do not necessarily correspond to sex, nor are they generally disruptive of the capacity to distinguish sex: Anyone can tell the difference between a "woman" and a "man acting feminine." Males and females are coded dichotomously, even if the coding is sometimes wrong. But because masculinity and femininity (both roles and attributes) are continuous, highly contextual variables, gender cannot be coded dichotomously, as in "gender-selective massacre."

The "gendercide" literature confuses these two phenomena by locating "gender" in the sex disparity of atrocity itself rather than in the sociocultural structures and discourses that make those sex disparities seem natural and necessary.[21] Jones identifies with the theoretical framework advanced by Joshua Goldstein's recent "mainstream" contribution to the literature on war and gender. According to Goldstein: "The sex/gender discourse constitutes a false dichotomy between biology and culture which are actually interdependent and mutually constitutive; . . . social and gender roles are not so separate from the bodies that perform them."[22]

It is true that sex and gender overlap empirically. We cannot understand the masculinization of politics without understanding women's systematic exclusion from citizenship and public life.[23] The sex-specific distribution of labor in the international political economy is caused by and reinforces gendered stereotypes about women's suitability for certain jobs.[24] Moreover, a major contribution of feminist theory has been to identify that, given prevailing gender constructs, sex-specific environments and institutions are gendered, rather than gender neutral: Millman and Kanter point out, for example, that "when men look at a meeting of a board of trustees and see only men, they think they are observing a sexually neutral or sexless world rather than a masculine world."[25] Sex-specific distributions are thus related to gender constructions that justify and naturalize those distributions.

And yet, although these phenomena are related, they are still *different*, and their relationship is not unilinear. Goldstein, who wishes to determine how culture and biology work together to create the male predominance in the military, emphasizes the mutual constitution of social attitudes and biological differences. But attempting to capture this interplay requires differentiating the two to begin with. In fact, Goldstein's analysis can be divided into "biological factors" and "cultural factors." The fact that he does not make this distinction semantically is a source of confusion in his work and makes it difficult for him to support his causal argument.

Recalling the sex/gender distinction enables us to establish cases where gender is a cause and sex-specific outcomes an effect. But it also helps us distinguish between *different* gendered causes of sex-specific outcomes. Returning for the moment to sex-specific massacre, gender can operate indirectly, as a cultural schema which channels men and women into separate spaces where they are at risk for different types of harm; or directly, as a conscious ideology of actors who may use sex as a proxy variable for socially constructed attributes.

A preexisting *gender structure* can generate sex-specific outcomes without any gender selectivity on the part of particular policy makers. If in any particular case we wish to explain sex-specific killing, one hypothesis is that men are disproportionately killed just because men happen to occupy the social roles that perpetrators consider threatening.[26] If the target is not *adult males* but *everyone in the military and political elite* (institutions that just happen to be male dominated), then men will die more frequently. To use the converse example, where villages are attacked indiscriminately, women, children, and the elderly are often the primary casualties because many adult males have either been conscripted or killed or have fled.[27] In such cases, it is not that women and children are being targeted as such, as many humanitarian commentators like to claim: They simply happen to occupy the targeted location in greater numbers. Although gender ideology on the part of the perpetrators is irrelevant in these cases, it is still true that *gender* (as a preexisting cultural system that has created sex disproportionality in social institutions) has played a role in generating these outcomes.

Where *gender ideology* is the key factor, however, men may be specifically targeted because of perpetrators' conscious beliefs regarding ascriptive characteristics of men.[28] This was clearly the case in the Rwandan genocide, where even small boys were killed lest they grow up to be RPF soldiers, while their sisters were spared as chattel for the Hutu militias.[29] This can be a deliberate and self-reflexive act. (There is a story from Croatia about Serb soldiers arguing in front of a widow and her children about whether to kill only the boys or also the female family members.)[30] Thus, killings may not be merely sex specific, where men happen to be killed because of the social roles they inhabit, but sex *selective:* Men of a group are consciously targeted because of the assumption that they may possibly inhabit those roles, now or in the future.[31] Gender structures may create sex-specific outcomes regardless of conscious thought on the part of actors; gender ideology operates consciously in the decision-making process of those actors themselves.

Gender ideology and gender structure can be mutually reinforcing. However, gender ideologies can remain robust even where the gender structure has changed. In the United States, the movement of women into previously male-dominated institutions such as the military has arguably done little to immediately change the masculinism of these institutional cultures.[32] Even if women in a particular ethnic conflict are as equally well armed and as likely as men to serve in rebel armies, the perception that it is men who are combatants may result in gender-selective atrocity and gender-motivated interventions by third parties under the assumption that "women and children" are innocent and vulnerable.[33]

For researchers, distinguishing between gender structure and gender ideology will not always be easy. In many contexts it may require extensive interviewing of perpetrators who may have no reason to honestly admit the rationale behind their action; or it may require access to political documents that are not available. Investigative tribunals have set some precedent in generating data on perpetrator decision making as described by witnesses. Regardless of the methodological constraints, making these distinctions is important not only for analysts, but also for policy makers. Reducing targeting of civilians, male or female, will require different gender policies depending on whether structure or ideology is the key problem in a particular context. It also matters greatly in assigning penalties for particular categories of war crimes. Ultimately, we must be open to developing and testing alternative hypotheses for the role gender plays: "Gender matters" is no longer by itself a novel argument. The question is, "How, precisely?"

"Gendercide" and Genocide

Beyond fuzzy conceptualization, the key problem with the "gendercide" concept is the manner in which is has been equated with genocide. This is due to a false analogy in Warren's book and a misappropriation of her concept by Jones. In Warren's pathbreaking book, she writes that, "genocide [is defined as] 'the deliberate extermination of a race of people.' By analogy, gendercide would be the deliberate extermination of persons of a particular sex (or gender)."[34] Of course, the actual analogy would be the deliberate extermination of *a particular sex:* the *Oxford Dictionary* defines "genocide" as extermination of a race, not just of some persons of that race. If any attack on mere persons of a particular race were genocide, regardless of the reason or the connectedness to a policy to destroy the whole group as such, then any racial killing would be genocidal. Likewise, to be genocidal, attacks on men or on women must be connected to an intent to destroy men as a group or women as a group to be analogous to racial or ethnic genocides.

Warren concludes that "genocide," for her purposes, means "wrongfully killing or otherwise reducing [either] the relative [or the absolute] number of persons of a particular race," a definition which can apply to any one person's death for any reason.[35] By substituting "sex" for "race," Warren effectively claims any act of murder is "gendercide." This is not her intent, however, and she is careful to distinguish killing as such from killings motivated by hatred of a particular group. Yet in the end, her "gendercide" definition, far from being analogous to genocide, boils down to any acts of homicide that are intentionally sex selective.

However questionable Warren's interpretation of the genocide convention, she goes no further than to draw an analogy. She does not define "gendercide" as genocide in itself.[36] Jones makes this move when he expands on Warren's female-centered analysis to include sex-selective targeting of males: "Gendercides against men and women—but particularly men—may be seen in this light as one of the more common forms of genocide." Steven Katz's list of groups against which the intent to commit genocide may be enacted includes "gender groups," by which Katz apparently means homosexuals as well as "women" (but not men), but which Jones appropriates as synonymous with biological sex: Gender groups are either men or women. Thus, "mass purges and 'politicides' weighted disproportionately . . . against males" and "militarized genocides carried out against a backdrop of heavily masculinized dissidence" constitute gendercide as genocide, along with "female infanticide," "rape-killings of women through history," and "mass murders for witchcraft."[37]

Contributors to this volume have echoed this use of the term. For example, Lindner identifies "gendercide" as "gender-selective killing of others" (versus "suicide: gender-selective killing of oneself").[38] This usage highlights the fact that if we extend "gendercide" to *any* killing rather than *mass killing*, while simultaneously ignoring the question of perpetrator intent, all killing becomes gendercidal: any individual victim is one sex or another. It also showcases the slipperiness of the term, as currently conceived, and how arbitrarily and inconsistently it can be applied without seeming to raise eyebrows.

It is true that sex-specific massacres figure prominently in many ethnic genocides. But that "gendercide" is a type of genocide in itself is conceptually inaccurate on two counts. Neither women nor men constitute a group that, as a whole, has been targeted for extermination by another group (members of the opposite sex); nor have sex-selective or sex-related atrocities generally been directed against men or women *as such*.[39] Jones insists that sex-selective massacre of males is analogous to the witch-hunts against women, a "paradigmatic instance of genocide against women."[40] He is correct that they are analogous, but wrong to accept that either of these cases is genocide.

First, as Stein has correctly pointed out, it is not men *as such* but men *of particular groups* who are targeted in the sex-selective massacres to which the "gendercide" literature refers. This point, made in reference to targeting civilian males, also applies to most of Warren's cases of "gendercide." Witch-hunts were not a genocide against women; they were a genocide against "witches," in the same way as Stalin's purges were a genocide against the "enemies of the people."[41] Being female was not by itself enough to be accused of witchcraft; not all women were accused, nor were all the accused women.

Nor were all the accusers men, which brings up the second point: "Gendercide" as conceptualized in this literature usually involves individuals of the same sex within both perpetrating and victimized groups, while defining the sex as such as the victimized group. For example, A. C. Del Zotto discusses white males killing black males as a gendercide against males rather than a genocide against blacks by whites.[42] But genocidal acts are undertaken by members of one group *against members of another.* Thus, both the witch-hunts and sex-selective massacre à la Srebrenica make no sense as genocides against women or men as such, but only as genocides against *witches (*the perpetrating women saw themselves as *not witches* rather than as fellow women) or against *Bosniaks* (it was not fellow men that General Mladic massacred, but Muslim men who were "the other").

Jones anticipates this objection in his original article, but his preemptive defense proves the point: "it can be countered that the Hutus who slaughtered Tutsis in Rwanda were also 'other blacks.'"[43] But of course, no one is arguing that the genocide in Rwanda was a genocide "against blacks." It was a genocide by certain blacks against certain other blacks; and we define the genocide in terms of the perceived otherness of the groups from one another. This is why we cannot say Srebrenica was a genocidal slaughter against men. It was a genocidal slaughter conducted by Bosnian Serbs against Bosnian Muslims.

In the case of mass hate killings of women by men (or of men by women—though cases do not spring to mind, surely they are conceivable), the perpetrators define the otherness of their victims on the basis of sex.[44] It seems that this is the key factor that would justify Katz's/Jones's emphasis on biological sex as a basis for extermination in their reworked genocide definitions.[45] But this is not borne out in most of the cases the "gendercide" literature cites.

Were there a case of women or men targeted because of their femaleness or maleness as part of an attempt to wipe out women as women or men as men, in whole or in substantial part, that would be genocide: "the actualization of the intent, however successfully carried out, to murder in whole or in substantial part, a . . . gender . . . group," under Jones's definition. Since technology could well provide the means of enacting a true genocide against either men or women as such on this basis, it is important not to dilute the concept of genocide against a sex by applying it to cases (such as sex-selective killing of a non-sex-based target group) that are of a fundamentally different character.

Such actual "gendercides" are without historical precedent. Crucially however, they are not beyond the range of plausibility. What woman hasn't joked with her girlfriends about a world where there were no men, if only women could find a way to reproduce without them; similar themes run through radical feminist thought.[46] And no one who has studied history doubts the capacity of men to organize hatred of women into destructive policies in which even the well intentioned may be complicit.[47] Although these "gendercidal" tendencies routinely find expression in patterns of rape, hate killings, lesbian fiction, and the capacity of political institutions to organize misogyny for their own ends, what has always stopped such antipathy short of the desire to destroy the opposite sex as a group (what has made it possible to joke about such things) has been men's and women's utter biological interdependence. At this historical juncture, however, thinking through "genocide on the basis of sex" as a real political possibility casts new light on ethical debates in biotechnology.[48]

There is thirdly the question of what constitutes "mass killing" in this literature. I will not digress too far in exploring whether or not cumulative cases of murder, such as individual witch burnings, lynchings, or even "domestic abuse," once added up over time and space, can be discussed as mass murder in the same way as can the simultaneous organized slaughter of eight thousand men and boys at Srebrenica, the mass-produced death of the Nazi camps, or the hate-based execution of a dozen women in Montreal.[49] There is, admittedly, a potential argument to be made here regarding structural violence. My only point is that this argument should at least be made and defended; but so far, "gendercide" scholars have simply assumed these are the same kind of phenomenon.

Two things are certain. First, if we call cumulative murder per se "mass murder," then *all* murder is "mass" and the term loses its meaning. Second, there are certainly qualitative distinctions between individual killings for whatever reason, individual killings that are part of a broader historical pattern of killings, and large-scale massacres. However one may attempt to situate phenomena such as infanticide or bride burning, one should at least take note of these important conceptual distinctions rather than simply subsuming such diverse phenomena under the same label.

There is the further complication in the use of the term "killing" to describe sex-selective abortion. It is interesting that Warren's work on sex-selective abortion and Rixecker's work on genetic screening for homosexuality come very close to meeting the criteria of targeting gender groups as such. But is mass *killing* involved when the targets are fetuses? If so, it will be hard not to take seriously claims that *all* abortion is genocide against the unborn.[50] We cannot have our cake and eat it too on this moral issue.

On the other hand, if we recall that not all acts of genocide involve killing, we may view the abortion of certain fetuses as "prevention of births" under Article II(d) of the Genocide Convention. This speaks to the limitations of defining "gendercide" as "mass killing." In fact, several other possible forms of genocide against gender groups are imaginable: As Rixecker explains, since homosexuals reproduce wholly through culture, simply impeding this social reproduction could constitute genocide.[51] Warren's suggestion that sex-selective abortion of males could constitute "new modes of rebellion against male domination" may also be interpreted as a call for genocide against men in this vein.[52] Since men (at least in the current precloning era) rely upon women to reproduce themselves, refusing to bear sons would constitute "prevention of births" under Article II(d). The current definition of "gendercide" as mass killing would miss the mark in such cases.

To avoid the risk of being misinterpreted, let me reiterate the two crucial points I wish to convey through this critique. First, Jones's attempt to incorporate sex into the definition of genocide, and to do so inclusively, is valid. He has simply situated "gendercide" incorrectly. Adjusted to include *only* genocide against both sex *and* gender groups *as such* and expanded to include *all* genocidal acts against such groups, the concept of "gendercide" becomes far more radical than Jones may have even intended. Precisely because such forms of genocide have not yet been enacted and are in fact barely conceivable to most people, the analysis of the social and technological conditions under which they could occur could be the single most preemptive research agenda for genocide studies as a discipline. Precisely because both the social and technological conditions for such a disaster could very well be nascent, taking Jones's prescription with the utmost seriousness, seen for what it really implies, will be pivotal. I thus advocate *neither* watering down the gravity of genocide against gender/sex groups by including sex-selective killings of other types, *nor* disposing of the concept because of its alleged inconceivability.

Second, my argument that sex-specific massacre is not by itself genocide does not mean sex-specific massacre need not be studied by genocide scholars. On the contrary, Jones has demonstrated that this phenomenon is a vital component of genocide that the field cannot keep ignoring. But we do not need to call sex-selective massacre "genocide" in order to legitimize its study by genocide scholars.[53] Instead, this phenomenon should be a jumping-off point to noticing and analyzing the gendered character of all genocides—in more ways than one.

This ties back into my overall argument about the term "gendercide" itself as a way of situating "gender in genocide studies." I have so far raised issues of the consistency of the label in theory building, and of the problems of treating it as a variety, rather than a strategy, of genocide. But I am equally concerned that by making "gendercide" per se the focus of gender research in our discipline, we unnecessarily narrow our knowledge of gender. The project must be broader. The remainder of the paper will flesh out this point.

Gender beyond Gendercide

The argument for preventing "gendercide" from becoming the sole focus of gender analysis in comparative genocide studies can be summed up by the following three propositions.

All gendered outcomes are not sex selective. Elsewhere in this essay I have argued that many sex-specific outcomes are artifacts of a preexisting gendered social structure, rather than conscious gendered policy on the part of actors. In "Gendercide and Genocide," Jones has defined "gendercide" as (sex)-*selective* mass killing, emphasizing the segregation of men from women and children before execution: Presumably, sex-*specific* killing does not count the same way. Stein too, in "Geno and Other Cides" in this volume, bases part of his critique of "gendercide" on this point, and it is a valid one: For example, "Russian POWs were not selected out [for massacre] in the same sense that the men of Srebrenica or Kosovo were." Instead, they were killed because they were POWs, not men, but they happened to be men because it was men who were conscripted. In such cases, however, the fact that killers may not consciously employ gender ideologies in their decision-making processes does not mean gender does not matter: Gender was responsible for placing men and women disproportionately into targeted spheres to begin with. Understanding this process must be at least as integral to our analysis as is the conscious decision making of war criminals.

Similarly, Stein suggests in the same essay that where outcomes are merely "sex related" rather than purely sex specific, gender is not at work. Any disproportionality relative to base population of men and women deserves attention, however. Moreover, even when killing is equally distributed across the sexes, patterns of abuse may be sex *distinctive:* Women and men may experience different fates. For example, women may be raped before death; men may be at greater risk of sexual mutilation. Men and women are also indirectly victimized by harm to loved ones of the opposite sex, a point which should not be invalidated in attempting to define who the "true victims" are. For example, Anne Goldstein writes,

> men too are injured by the sexual assault of women for reasons untainted by offensive, antiquated notions of chivalry and ownership. To watch helplessly as someone you love is tortured may be as bad or worse than being tortured yourself, and international law should be able to reach and punish such harms.[54]

Additionally, where women and men are given the same objective treatment, gender confers qualitative differences in the meaning of the experience. Rape of a male prisoner carries a different meaning than rape of a female.[55] Forcing a father to rape his daughter has multiple gendered components, although the act simultaneously victimizes both a male and a female.[56]

Finally, gendered outcomes can actually be *sex inclusive:* They can have identical effects on persons of either sex, because gender creates certain categories having nothing to do with one's sex, but having instead to do with one's relationship to a gender regime's definition of male/female relations more generally. Consider the maltreatment of children born of genocidal forced maternity. The tactic of forced maternity has become increasingly common in contemporary ethnic warfare and is predicated on at least two gendered notions: (1) ethnicity is patrilineal, so a child fathered by a Serb rapist on a Bosnian Muslim woman is ethnically "them" rather than "us"; (2) women are the property of men, and so pregnancy as evidence of rape constitutes an attack on the woman's male family and community.[57] Thus through a convergence of gender and race, forced maternity is highly disruptive to ethnic communities, as well as to the women on whom it is imposed. However, forced maternity also victimizes children born of such rapes, who are typically neglected, stigmatized, or even killed.[58] Although gender beliefs (internalized by the target community, as well as by the perpetrators) account for the reprisals against children of rape, the reprisals themselves are sex inclusive: Male and female infants are similarly at risk. Gender is also implicated in the persecution of homosexuals of both sexes.[59]

All sex-selective outcomes are not gendered. The "gendercide" framework assumes that if sex selection is occurring, it happens because of gender beliefs that are mutable. This is a hypothesis for which in many (if not most) cases there is excellent supporting evidence. However, it remains a hypothesis, which should always be tested against the null (that biological sex rather than social gender determines the selection) in each particular case. In most cases, as Joshua Goldstein has shown, sex and gender combine to produce such outcomes: "Biology provides diverse potentials and cultures limit, select and channel them," so that understanding the relationship between the two is critical.[60] In some cases, gender beliefs trump perceptions of empirical reality regarding peoples' capacities, regardless of sex. For example, despite the fact that Somali females and children were armed combatants, their killing by UN forces was treated as a "massacre" because of the gendered assumption that women and children are by definition innocent bystanders.[61]

In other cases (fewer perhaps, but we should still be alert for them), biological factors determine sex selectivity, even where gender determines the milieu in which sex selection may take place. One example is the sex specificity of forced pregnancy. Women are not selected to be impregnated (versus men) because of a gender ideology regarding women as mothers. Women rather than men are subjected to this form of abuse because they are biologically female.[62] As noted earlier, gender discourses and ideologies are responsible for the use of forced pregnancy as a strategy, and for its success rate in splintering communities. But we do not need "gender" to explain why it is women and not men who are targeted.

All gendered aspects of genocide are not "mass killing." Previously I discussed the fact that even in the specific category of "genocide against gender groups," mass killing was only one genocidal strategy among several. This is also true of the impact of gender in genocides against racial or ethnic groups. Warren is aware of this, and her book focuses less on actual killing of women than on sex-selective abortion of female or male fetuses, which she does not consider "mass killing," although it is gendercidal in reducing the relative number of persons of one sex. For Jones, "gendercide" is limited to acts of mass murder.

Yet gender provides a social system in which cultural continuity can be attacked through less overt means. Genocidal rape, for example, is not necessarily "gendercidal"; it may or may not involve killing of rape victims.[63] What makes rape of women genocidal is the cultural effect it has on a target community's ability to reproduce. Rape is effective as a tool of genocide where preexisting gender structures mitigate against future reproduction with raped women.[64] Rape may also result from gender ideologies inherent in militaries, but it is the gender structure of the target community itself that makes rape genocidal.[65] This is an important point, because it may well be easier to change the gender structure of a target community (encouraging men to accept their raped wives, for example, or providing and validating opportunities for women outside of reproductive roles) than to change the misogynistic tendencies of paramilitaries. This change would not reduce cases of rape that stem from sheer misogyny, but it would reduce the genocidal effect of mass rape on groups; and to the extent that mass rape is a calculated strategy of genocide, reducing its effectiveness could reduce its prevalence. At any rate, looking at gender structure and gender ideology separately would enable analysts to suggest best practices in particular contexts.

The foregoing examples demonstrate that gender can facilitate human rights abuses that are either sex specific or sex inclusive. But gender can also be an important variable when the *explanandum* is the overall political environment, rather than specific human rights abuses. Individuals' sense of their own masculinity or femininity can be manipulated by commanders, policy makers, or relief workers to bring about positive or negative outcomes. A literature on the relationship of states to political constructions of individual masculinity and femininity has much to offer comparative genocide studies. For example, Koontz has described the importance of specific configurations of masculinities in the social construction of Nazi executioners.[66] Even where the state does not deliberately construct such identities for genocidal purposes, the relationship between economic structures and gender identities can provide a context which can later be exploited, as Jones has described in "Gender and Genocide in Rwanda" in this volume: "for younger Rwandan males, the [economic] crisis was additionally an *existential* one. . . . When the genocide erupted, the temptation for Hutu men to kill their Tutsi counterparts and seize their land, cattle, money, and belongings must have been irresistible." Mueller has also emphasized the deftness with which génocidaires can mobilize masses of otherwise ethnically ambivalent young men simply by framing killing as a site of masculine camaraderie, drink, and looting without sanction.[67] Michael Ignatieff draws on concepts of gender in his pessimistic account of the decline of military ethics among the world's killers: "In most traditional societies, honor is associated with restraint, and virility with discipline; . . . the particular savagery of war in the 1990s taps into another variety of male identity—the wild sexuality of the adolescent male."[68] It is not surprising that grassroots initiatives to promote awareness of international humanitarian law in war-affected areas now focus on redefining "acceptable" masculinity through appeals to "warrior codes."[69]

Thus Holter is right to call for deeper analyses of the devaluation of nonviolent masculinity—or, at least, forms of masculinity that restrain violence.[70] Peace efforts and peace-building scholarship must direct more attention to the creation of meaningful nonmilitarized identities and occupations for men and boys. This literature needs to be complemented by value-neutral analysis of initiatives to bring women and girls more fully into the peace-building process. Such research should be careful not to assume that women are inherently more peaceable than men or that their gender identities are any less problematic or malleable.

Conclusion

To sum up, "gendercide" works better as a political catchphrase than as a theoretical framework for understanding sex-selective massacre. As an analytical concept, it confuses sex and gender and obscures rather than illuminates the variation within these concepts. As a framework of analysis in comparative genocide studies, it has been offered as a type of genocide, rather than as a modality of genocide, which is both conceptually and factually problematic. Moreover, to the extent that the study of gender and genocide is conveniently limited to "gendercide," we are missing vast insights regarding the role of gender in mass killing.

Yet Jones and others are correct to have identified sex-selective massacre of males as a crucial site around which gendered cultures and structures are reified, reproduced, and, during genocides, destroyed. We *do* need to study and to understand sex-selective massacre—not merely as advocates of gender equality, but as analysts of political violence. My caveat is that sex-selective massacre should neither encompass the definition of "gendercide," nor necessarily be the defining location around which gender-and-genocide studies should focus. I can suggest three additional research avenues, underdeveloped both in feminist literature and the new "gendercide" scholarship, for which a gender approach could yield important insights in the field of comparative genocide studies.

First, we must better conceptualize the interrelationship between gender and age. Too much gender theory has treated males and females as oppositional categories, assuming that gendered power has a static, unidirectional flow. Investigations of how this intersects with race and class have not been adequately supplemented with corresponding analyses of the gender/age nexus. In truth however, age categories (child, youth, adult, elder) intersect and even constitute gender categories (woman, women and children, battle-age male, woman of childbearing age). With this in mind, sex disparities in power become highly contingent. As Gruenbaum describes in her analysis of gender dynamics in societies that practice female circumcision, "females [dominate] over children, older women over younger women, older children over younger children; . . . even in the most strongly male-dominated culture, young men often do not feel that they have power."[71] Moreover, age categories frame our understanding of gender in multifaceted ways. It is interesting to note, for example, how often the term "men and boys" is juxtaposed to "women and children" in depictions of the civilian/combatant divide. This should lead us to wonder both why older boys are not also defined as children, and why older children in that category do not include girls. This is a critique for gender theory at large, rather than genocide studies specifically, but it is a flashpoint around which genocide analyses could be very relevant.

A second highly neglected issue that is particularly crucial for genocide studies is homosexuality and the state. Too frequently, "gender issues" are defined as women's issues; Jones's having "brought males in" has done nothing to destabilize the assumption of heterosexuality that the gender/sex conflation leaves us with. Indeed, one of the most persecuted gender categories may not be women or men but homosexuals of both sexes. An analogy to women's issues should suggest what a critical point of inquiry this needs to be. Much core work in feminist theory on the state and international relations has aimed at exposing the state as a gendered (meaning masculinized) entity, predicated in large part on masculinist ideology and harnessing women in the service of its nationalist doctrines as a routine practice of statecraft.[72] As Holter argues in "A Theory of Gendercide," gender ideologies pertaining to women provide the permissive cultural structure in which genocide against groups can take place. At least as crucial has been the construction of the modern state as heterosexual. Thus there are important links between battles over gay participation in state militaries, which are seen not just as fighting machines but as institutional symbols of masculinized civic participation; the targeting of homosexuals under fascism and the links between homophobia, misogyny, and racism; and the abject lack of a norm humanizing homosexuals in international law.[73]

Finally, the role of gender identities and ideologies in local genocidal contexts has been examined to the exclusion of analyses of how gender governs the moral dialogue of the international community in regards to halting ethnic cleansing. Some normative cries have been put forth, especially regarding the framing of human rights discourse, but what is required is systematic analysis, and an incorporation of gender as a variable into scholarship on the role of norms in international affairs.[74] Lindner's discussion in "Gendercide and Humiliation," in this volume, of the distinction between human rights and honor-based societies is meant as a comparative analysis across states, but it may also be relevant to examine the tension between overlapping moral regimes within international society. In some ways, the state system itself could be conceived of as an "honor system," taking as it does ownership over "its" citizens, and the use of "women and children" as symbols of the nation, as a defining feature of sovereignty. On the other hand, the new doctrine of universal human rights stands counterpoised to this, and much of the seeming inconsistency in international moral discourse may stem from this tension.

At any rate, an examination of gender norms at the international system level will surely provide insights into patterns of response to ethnic conflict and genocide. To give one example, the term "women and children" as a rhetorical flourish is omnipresent in international condemnation of war crimes, calls for action, justifications for intervention, and media portrayals of humanitarian emergencies. This term is used in a highly gendered way with little situational regard for the actual context, behaviors, or needs of those "civilians" in question. Feminists have at times pointed out how this term defines women as mothers and subjects rather than agents;[75] Jones has argued that it also elides civilian men from the category of those entitled to our moral concern;[76] and surely children's human rights are not facilitated by being defined as appendages of their female parents rather than as ontological beings. The effect of the combined gendered discourses embedded in international society surely has a direct bearing on the propensity to intervene and on specific modalities of intervention in genocidal conflicts. Are we in fact serving the most needy when we evacuate "women and children first"? What is the net effect of attempts at gender mainstreaming in international organizations that continue to reproduce traditional gender conceptions?[77] What does the tendency of Western publics to react only when slaughter sweeps up "women and children" mean for early prevention? And perhaps most importantly, how do war criminals exploit gender norms in international society for their own nefarious ends? These questions require rigorous explanatory analysis of discourse and policy at the interstate level.

In short, sex-selective massacre is an excellent starting point for an incorporation of gender in comparative genocide studies, but it also illustrates the importance of more systematic means of employing abstract concepts like "gendercide." To make useful comparisons of "gendercides," we must at the very least make a coherent distinction between sex and gender and between different types of gender effect (structure vs. ideology, norm vs. identity, and how these relate). However, inclusive analyses of gender should not be limited to the topic of massacre: Much terrain exists to be charted in the process of delinking gender from the monopoly of women's issues. This includes examining gender assumptions that operate in social systems at all levels of analysis, developing research on the construction of gender as heterosexual, and examining children's concerns through the lens of patriarchy. All of these factors combine with issues of race, class, and status in the world system to generate patterns of genocide and ethnic conflict.

Notes

1. Cynthia Enloe, *Bananas, Beaches and Bases: Making Feminist Sense of International Politics* (London: Pandora, 1989); J. Ann Tickner, *Gender in International Relations: Feminist Perspectives on Achieving Global Security* (New York: Columbia University Press, 1992); Francine D'Amico and Peter Beckman, eds., *Women, Gender, and World Politics: Perspectives, Policies, and Prospects* (Westport, Conn.: Bergin and Garvey, 1994).

2. Most of this work began to appear as evidence mounted of the mass rapes of Bosnia and Rwanda. For example, Alexandra Stigalmeyer, ed., *Mass Rape: The War against Women in Bosnia-Herzegovina* (Lincoln: University of Nebraska Press, 1994); Beverly Allen, *Rape Warfare: The Hidden Genocide in Bosnia-Herzegovina* (London: University of Minnesota Press, 1996); Bianfer Nowrojee, *Shattered Lives: Sexual*

Violence in the Rwandan Genocide and Its Aftermath (New York: Human Rights Watch Africa, 1996). Some earlier work had also addressed this topic: Susan Brownmiller, *Against Our Will: Men, Women, and Rape* (New York: Bantam, 1975).

3. Adam Jones, "Does 'Gender' Make the World Go Round? Feminist Critiques of International Relations," *Review of International Studies,* 22: 4 (1996), pp. 405–29.

4. See Adam Jones, "Gendercide and Genocide," Chapter 1 in this volume, for the revised article.

5. See Mary Anne Warren, *Gendercide: The Implications of Sex Selection* (Totowa, N.J.: Rowman and Allenheld, 1985).

6. Jones, "Gendercide and Genocide."

7. Warren, *Gendercide,* p. 2.

8. Article II of the Convention on the Prevention and Punishment of the Crime of Genocide defines genocide as "any of the following acts committed with intent to destroy, in whole or in part, a national, ethnical, racial, or religious group, as such: a) killing members of the group; b) causing serious bodily or mental harm to the group; c) deliberately inflicting on the group conditions of life calculated to bring about its physical destruction in whole or in part; d) imposing measures intended to prevent births within the group; e) forcibly transferring children of the group to another group."

9. This is probably why Warren coined the term, since she otherwise uses "sex" and "gender" consistently. "Sexcide" just isn't as catchy. However, Warren's definition also focused on the social targeting of gender groups, rather than merely the reduction of sexed bodies, so her use of the term could have reflected that. On the uses and abuses of "genocide," see Frank Chalk and Kurt Jonnasson, *The History and Sociology of Genocide: Analyses and Case Studies* (New Haven: Yale University Press, 1990).

10. See Jones, "Gendercide and Genocide." The work of Claudia Koontz on the centrality of Nazi gender manipulation in generating the Jewish holocaust suggests otherwise: see Koontz, *Mothers in the Fatherland: Women and the Family in Nazi Politics* (New York: St. Martin's Press, 1981); see also Mary Daly, *Gyn/Ecology* (Boston: Beacon, 1978), and Judith Baumel, *Double Jeopardy: Gender and the Holocaust* (London: Valentine Mitchell, 1998). Mark Mazower, among others, has commented that Nazi gender ideologies probably cost Germany the war, as it prevented mass mobilization of women for the war effort on par with the other great powers. See Mazower, *Dark Continent: Europe's Twentieth Century* (New York: Knopf, 1999), ch. 5.

11. Robert Connell, *Gender and Power: Society, the Person, and Sexual Politics* (Stanford: Stanford University Press, 1987).

12. See Stephanie Rixecker, "Genetic Engineering and Queer Biotechnology: The Eugenics of the Twenty-first Century?" this volume. "Gender identity" is similar to Sandra Harding's concept of "individual gender." See Harding, *The Science Question in Feminism* (Ithaca, N.Y.: Cornell University Press, 1986).

13. The norm against killing "women and children" is probably the most robust, in terms of both lip service and actual compliance, in all the practices of armed conflict. For examples, see David Grossman, *On Killing* (New York: Back Bay Books, 1996). The corollary, of course, is that in the absence of other defining criteria, "adult male" is a legitimate proxy variable for "combatant," as articulated by such authoritative sources on ethics in warfare as Michael Walzer: "a soldier who, once he is engaged, simply fires at every male villager between the age of 15 and 50 . . . is probably justified in doing so, as he would not be on an ordinary battlefield." See Walzer, *Just and Unjust Wars* (New York: Basic Books, 1997), p. 192. On norms, see James Coleman, *Foundations of Social Theory* (Cambridge: Belknap Press, 1990), ch. 10.

14. John Searle, *The Construction of Social Reality* (New York: Free Press, 1995), p. 2.

15. John Ruggie, "What Makes the World Hang Together? Neo-utilitarianism and the Social Constructivist Challenge," *International Organization,* 52 (1998), p. 886.

16. Christine Sylvester, *Feminist Theory and International Relations in a Postmodern Era* (Cambridge: Cambridge University Press, 1994); Marianne Marchand and Anne Sisson Runyan, *Gender in Global Restructuring: Sightings, Sites, and Resistances* (London: Routledge, 2000), p. 8.

17. Candace West and Sarah Fenstermaker, "Power, Inequality, and the Accomplishment of Gender: An Ethnomethodological View," in Paula England, ed., *Theory on Gender, Feminism on Theory* (New York: Aldine de Gruyter, 1993), p. 155.

18. The very ability to identify the genetic distinction in fetuses is what makes sex-selective abortion a possibility, at a stage of life when social gender is irrelevant.

19. See Jones, "Gender and Genocide in Rwanda," in this volume.

20. Joshua Goldstein, *War and Gender* (Cambridge: Cambridge University Press, 2001); Jones, "Gender and Genocide in Rwanda."

21. Some feminist literature does this too, and it is equally problematic there. For example, the term "gendered" is simultaneously used to describe beliefs (militaries are "gendered" because they rely on hyper-masculinized belief systems, symbolism, and codes of conduct) and sex distributions (militaries are "gendered" because they are composed mostly of men); or the term "feminization" of a sphere means both the movement of embodied women into it, and its social devaluation relative to male-dominated spheres.

22. Goldstein, *War and Gender,* p. 2.

23. Jan Pettman, *Worlding Women* (New York: Routledge, 1996); Jean Bethke Elshtain, *Women and War,* 2d. ed. (Chicago: University of Chicago Press, 1995).

24. Enloe, *Bananas, Beaches and Bases.*

25. Marcia Millman and Rosabeth Moss Kanter, "Introduction to Another Voice: Feminist Perspectives on Social Life and Social Science," in Sandra Harding, ed., *Feminism and Methodology* (Bloomington: Indiana University Press, 1987), p. 34.

26. See Stuart Stein, "Geno and Other Cides," in this volume.

27. Julie Mertus, *War's Offensive on Women: The Humanitarian Challenge in Bosnia, Kosovo, and Afghanistan* (Bloomfield, Conn.: Kumarian Press, 2000).

28. Jones has emphasized the perception that men are combatants, but the notion that it is men rather than women who carry and transmit ethnicity also plays a role; and the belief that men are human while women are property explains the ancient practice of killing men and appropriating women. To this Lindner has added the belief that men are "worthy of death" under honor systems. See Evelin Gerda Lindner, "Gendercide and Humiliation in Honor and Human Rights Societies," in this volume.

29. See African Rights, *Rwanda: Death, Despair, and Defiance* (London: African Rights, 1995).

30. Steven Riskin, ed., "Three Dimensions of Peace-building in Bosnia: Findings from USIP-Sponsored Research and Field Projects," Peacework no. 32, U.S. Institute of Peace, December 1999, *www.usip.org/pubs/peaceworks/pwks32.pdf.*

31. Conversely, there are cases where only men are spared, on the assumption of their utility as laborers. See Eugen Kogon, Hermann Langbein, and Adalbert Ruckerl, eds., *Nazi Mass Murder: A Documentary History of the Use of Poison Gas* (London: Yale University Press, 1993), p. 153.

32. Cynthia Enloe, *Maneuvers: The International Politics of Militarizing Women's Lives* (Berkeley: University of California Press, 2000).

33. Charli Carpenter, "Women and Children First: Gender, Norms, and Humanitarian Intervention in the Balkans, 1991–1995," *International Organization,* 57: 4 (fall 2003), pp. 661–94.

34. Warren, *Gendercide,* p. 22. In this respect it is unfortunate that Warren relies upon the incomplete Oxford definition of genocide rather than on the Genocide Convention's itself.

35. Ibid., pp. 22–23.

36. In ibid., page 2, in fact, she emphasizes that what makes sex-selective massacre of males genocidal is precisely the extent to which they are targeted as members of a racial group.

37. Jones, "Gendercide and Genocide." Katz does not mention men as a gender group, for which Jones rightly corrects him (ibid.). Presumably, for Jones, rape-killings of men do not count.

38. Lindner, "Gendercide and Humiliation."

39. I borrow the term "sex-related" from Stein, "Gender and Other Cides," to convey killings that are disproportionately, but not wholly, sex specific.

40. Jones, "Gendercide and Genocide."

41. On the perpetrator's role in defining the target group, see Chalk and Jonassohn, *History and Sociology of Genocide,* p. 30, and Frank Chalk, "Redefining Genocide," in George Andreopoulos, ed., *Genocide: Conceptual and Historical Dimensions* (Philadephia: University of Pennsylvania Press, 1994). The witch-hunts were not entirely sex selective, and the extent to which they were likely varied cross-nationally.

42. Augusta C. Del Zotto, "Gendercide in a Historical-Structural Context: The Case of Black Male Gendercide in the United States," in this volume.

43. Jones, "Gendercide and Genocide."

44. I am thinking here of cases such as the Montreal Massacre at the Ecole Polytechnique. See Buchanan, "Gendercide and Human Rights," and *www.gendercide.org/case_montreal.html* for case details. But even such a case lacks the scale and the intent to destroy the entire group as such, as required for making a claim of genocide.

45. Indeed, sexist motivations constitute a key component of the "gendercides" Warren discusses, enabling her to distinguish between sex-selective abortion of male fetuses at risk of genetic deficiency and of female fetuses only because they are female.

46. Daly, *Gyn/Ecology;* see Warren's analysis of these cultural themes in *Gendercide,* pp. 56–77.

47. Warren doubts, however, that men would ever commit genocide against women because they are too dependent on women's social labor, in addition to the many cultural barriers to such changes in the species. See Warren, *Gendercide,* pp. 57–61.

48. As long ago as 1982, Sally Miller Gearhart suggested the use of ovular merging, then used on mice, to enable women to reproduce without male sperm. See Gearhart, "The Future—If There Is One—Is Female," in Pam McAllister, ed., *Reweaving the Web of Life: Feminism and Nonviolence* (Philadelphia: New Society, 1982), p. 252. Human cloning could have similar uses, as Warren discusses in *Gendercide.* The use of prenatal biotechnology to eradicate other gender groups such as homosexuals and hermaphrodites is even more likely given the prevailing social climate in advanced countries. See Rixecker, "Genetic Engineering and Queer Biotechnology."

49. On witch burnings, see Warren, *Gendercide;* on lynchings, see Del Zotto, "Gendercide in Historical-Structural Context"; on domestic abuse, see Jones, "Gendercide and Genocide."

50. William Rubenstein, "Genocide Surveyed," *International Journal of Human Rights,* 5 (2001), p. 122.

51. Rixecker, "Genetic Engineering and Queer Biotechnology."

52. Warren, *Gendercide,* p. 26.

53. Additionally, there are other international legal concepts that could be used to advance gender equity for men, as well as for women. For example, the emerging norm of "gender persecution" ought to be applied to men who escape conscription, as well as to women who escape mutilation.

54. Anne Tierney Goldstein, "Recognizing Forced Impregnation as a War Crime" (New York: Center for Reproductive Law and Policy, 1994). The same point is often made regarding wives, mothers, and sisters of dead males.

55. Dubravka Zarkov, "War Rape in Bosnia: On Masculinity, Femininity, and the Power of Rape Victim Identity," *Tijschrift voor Criminiologie* 39: 2, pp. 140–51.

56. See Buchanan, "Gendercide and Human Rights."

57. Goldstein, *War and Gender;* Siobhan Fisher, "Occupation of the Womb: Forced Impregnation as Genocide," *Duke Law Journal,* 46 (1996); Lindner, "Gendercide and Humiliation."

58. Charli Carpenter, "Surfacing Children: Limitations of Genocidal Rape Discourse," *Human Rights Quarterly,* 22: 2 (2000), pp. 428–77.

59. Richard Plant, *The Pink Triangle: The Nazi War against Homosexuals* (New York: Holt, 1996); Frank Rector, *The Nazi Extermination of Homosexuals* (New York: Stein and Day, 1981).

60. Goldstein, *War and Gender,* p. 2.

61. Art Pine, "UN Forces Fire on Somali Crowd, Fueling US Debate," *Los Angeles Times,* 10 September 1993.

62. Not all women are subjected to forced pregnancy, for only those capable of gestating a pregnancy can be forcibly impregnated; however, all people subjected to forced pregnancy are women.

63. According to Beverly Allen, a typology of mass rape existed in Bosnia, including public rape, abduction-rape-murder, and detention rape/forced impregnation/enforced pregnancy. See Allen, *Rape Warfare.*

64. Paul Salzman, "Rape Camps as Means of Ethnic Cleansing: Religious, Cultural, and Ethical Responses to Rape Victims in the Former Yugoslavia," *Human Rights Quarterly,* 20 (1998), pp. 348–78.

65. Much has been written on the relationship between militarism and misogyny. In the context of the Bosnian rapes, see Catherine MacKinnon, "Rape, Genocide, and Women's Human Rights," in Stigalmeyer, *Mass Rape.*

66. Koontz, *Mothers in the Fatherland.*

67. John Mueller, "The Banality of Ethnic War," *International Security,* 25 (2000); see also Gerard Prunier, *Rwanda: History of a Genocide* (New York: Columbia University Press, 1995).

68. Michael Ignatieff, *The Warrior's Honor: Ethnic War and the Modern Conscience* (New York: Metropolitan Books, 1997), p. 127.

69. Marion Harroff-Tavel, "Promoting Norms to Limit Violence: Some Original Initiatives," *International Review of the Red Cross,* 322 (1998), pp. 5–20.

70. Holter, "A Theory of Gendercide."

71. Ellen Gruenbaum, *The Female Circumcision Controversy: An Anthropological Perspective* (Philadelphia: University of Pennsylvania Press, 2001), p. 41.

72. Tickner, *Gender in International Relations;* Jill Steans, *Gender and International Relations: An Introduction* (New Brunswick, N.J.: Rutgers University Press, 1998), pp. 60–80; Pettman, *Worlding Women,* pp. 3–24; Enloe, *Maneuvers;* F. Anthias and N. Yuval-Davis, eds., *Woman-Nation-State* (London: Macmillan, 1989).

73. Elizabeth Kier, "Homosexuals in the US Military: Open Integration and Combat Effectiveness," *International Security,* 23 (1998), pp. 4–39; Chip Berlet, ed.,

Eyes Right: Challenging the Right-Wing Backlash (Boston: South End Press, 1995); Debra DeLaet, "Don't Ask, Don't Tell: Where Is the Protection against Sex Orientation Discrimination in International Human Rights Law?" *Law and Sexuality,* 7 (1997), p. 31.

74. On the framing of human rights discourse, see, for example, Adam Jones, "Genocide and Humanitarian Intervention: Incorporating the Gender Variable," *Journal of Humanitarian Assistance,* February 2002, *www.jha.ac/articles/a080.htm;* Buchanan, "Gendercide and Human Rights," in this volume; D.W.L. Jarvis, *International Relations and the Challenge of Postmodernism: Defending the Discipline* (Columbia: University of South Carolina Press, 2000).

75. Tickner, *Gender in International Relations;* Enloe, *Maneuvers.*

76. See also Jarvis, *International Relations.*

77. Mertus, *War's Offensive on Women;* Donna Marshall, "Women in War and Peace: Grassroots Peacebuilding," Peaceworks no. 34, U.S. Institute of Peace, 2000, *www.usip.org/pubs/peaceworks/pwks34.pdf.*

10

Problems of Gendercide

A Response to Stein and Carpenter

Adam Jones

In the very process of defending the viability of our criteria . . . we have already hinted at its limitation, which is its schematism. Such schematism has its place in any comparative science of history and society, and I make no apology for it. It is the essential heavy plow that must first clear the ground, turn the rough soil, and demarcate the boundaries.

—Orlando Patterson, *Slavery and Social Death*

Stein's "Geno and Other Cides"

At the heart of Stuart Stein's insightful critique of my work (Chapter 8, this volume) is skepticism that the term "gendercide" can be applied in cases where gender is combined with, or apparently subsumed by, other causal variables. I think it is noteworthy that the exceptions he allows to the gender framing—that is, killings where "selection was [indeed] undertaken on the basis of gender per se"—are those that overwhelmingly or exclusively target women ("suttee [widow-burning], female infanticide, and witchcraft"). But other causal variables also seem profoundly relevant in understanding these gender-selective atrocities against women. An age variable, for example, is relevant in all the cases cited, as it is in most gendercides against men. Female infanticide targets infant girls, and both *suttee* and witchcraft seem closely correlated with older women. But in the case of women and girls, this age variable does not seem to preclude, for Stein, a legitimate focus on gender.

Similarly, if one wanted to split hairs, one could construct exactly the kind of argument in these cases that Stein advances for mass killings of males: namely, that it is not women per se being targeted, but women who are believed to represent a particular "threat" to the killers. Widows, for example, are seen as "extraneous" members of society—a drain on the community—by virtue of their loss of a male spouse and supporter.[1] Girl children are killed because they represent the need to feed an "extra mouth" when resources are scarce; because they will be less able to supplement those resources in the future through wage labor; and because their future dowry requirements will impose an onerous material burden on the family. Female witches, of course (apart from often being widows), are killed because they are presumed to be in league with the forces of evil and perpetrating all manner of dastardly and destructive crimes. Thus, in none of these cases are females necessarily targeted on the basis of an "abstract hatred" of females *as a group;* important additional variables determine *which* females will be killed and *when.* But few people, I think, would contend that gender, and gender discrimination, are not indispensable to an understanding of what is taking place.

Likewise, in the case of gendercides against men and boys, it seems to me accurate—but of secondary relevance—to state, as Stein does, that males are targeted "because in most cultures men of a certain age bear arms in conflict situations; are most likely to join guerrilla organizations and more likely to resist occupying forces, passively or actively; and are considered to pose potentially a greater economic or political threat to those occupying positions of power than are females, largely because of the ascriptive roles that they each perform in *patriarchal-type* social systems." By the same reasoning, females may be murdered because they are exclusively or generally the widows, dowry-bearers, and "useless mouths" in patriarchal systems. If these ascriptive roles do not rule out genuinely gender-selective killings of females in Stein's formulation, then why adopt a different standard for gender-selective atrocities against men and boys?[2]

Stein's analysis of the Armenian and Jewish holocausts is very well informed. His call for attention to the policy of ghettoization in the Nazi-occupied territories between 1939 and 1941, and his emphasis on the importance of the "euthanasia" campaign to the strategies of mass killing that the Nazis developed, are especially well-taken. But I differ with his contention that "in both clusters of mass killings, gender selection was *entirely subordinate* to the broader goal of group destruction" (emphasis added). A more accurate statement, I think, would be that "gender selection was *both integral and subordinate to* the broader goal of group destruction," something that I readily acknowledged in my original article.[3] Gendercide against out-group males is frequently a subordinate and/or preliminary strategy in root-and-branch genocides. It is also regularly a sufficient end in itself in more limited, *but still genocidal,* campaigns of mass killing—as in Bosnia-Herzegovina or Bangladesh (1971).

Stein's comments about Nazis targeting members of the Jewish (and Soviet) elite who happened, overwhelmingly, to be male, is amply in keeping with the link I proposed in my original article between gendercide and eliticide. "Since most elites are to most appearances mostly male," I wrote, "it is not a great leap to the proposition that male equals elite—just as men's 'potential' as combatants may be enough to secure them death in a typical counterinsurgency sweep."[4] Stein's framing does little justice to the "spillover" aspect of these eliticides: the way out-group males per se come to be perceived as an elite, regardless of their objective status. There seems to have been no serious attempt to distinguish among the thousands of Jewish men rounded up by the Nazis for incarceration in concentration camps (after the *Kristallnacht* of 1938) or mass execution (after the invasions of Poland and the Soviet Union).[5] A demonstrably elite/Bolshevik/oppositionist Jewish male might have been best; but in a pinch, any Jewish man would do. Equally indiscriminate were the "reprisal" killings carried out by the Nazis, as at Lidice in Czechoslovakia (to which Stein makes passing reference) or Kragujevac in occupied Yugoslavia.[6] If the men massacred in such circumstances had been considered genuine "threats," one presumes they would have been rounded up earlier. What appears to have predominated in such instances is simple revenge, *limited to acceptably gendered targets* by codes of "chivalry" and "civilized behavior." As Leo Kuper noted in his classic book, it is often the case that "while unarmed men seem fair game, the killing of women and children arouses general revulsion"—even among the most hardened killers.[7]

Stein's chapter (and the UN Genocide Convention) place considerable stress on the targeting of groups "as such" (per se) as a definitional element of genocide. I am not sure the phrase deserves such a significant place in the analysis. Can we say, for example, that Jews were targeted "as such" by the Nazis? In one sense, the answer is surely yes. But if we analyze the Nazis' stated *rationale* for targeting the Jews, we see that it revolved around a close identification between Jews and a whole range of other groups: capitalist exploiters and rapacious elites, Bolsheviks, subversives, traitors and backstabbers, enemies of the faith, spreaders of disease, and so on ad nauseam.[8] Whatever the perverted rationales and broader group identifications offered by the killers, however, we have little difficulty perceiving the common (though not exclusive) element of Jew-ness that runs through these depictions. Thus, the Jews were indeed targeted *as such*—and as many other things besides.[9]

There should be no greater difficulty in recognizing the gender variable that operates to consign men to genocidal slaughter, blended with the oppositionist, subversive, or elitist/exploitative tendencies that the *génocidaires* impute disproportionately to out-group males. Theorizing genocides need not be a zero-sum game in which one ascriptive trait necessarily cancels out all others. In my view, a given campaign of mass killing can easily be labeled as genocidal, democidal, politicidal, eliticidal, and gendercidal all at once—with each of these designations representing an analytical cut that exposes one aspect of the campaign and serves to buttress comparative studies of a particular "cide."[10] Stein himself notes that genocidal killers' "cognitive focus is on *one or more* dimensions of group membership, real or imputed" (emphasis added). If the génocidaires do not feel constrained by mutually exclusive categories, I see no reason why the analyst of their actions should be. My intention in "Gendercide and Genocide" was simply to focus on a variable that seemed to me powerfully significant, and one that, at least in the case of mass killings of men, had never received sustained scholarly attention.

A note on the "selection" process that I isolate as central in gendercidal killings. Stein is quite right that the process need not directly resemble that of the Auschwitz camp commander on the railway siding.[11] But the broader argument-by-analogy seems reasonably valid. If males are overwhelmingly selected from a targeted community to serve as forced laborers, for example, and then are killed by the thousands or millions in the corvée, gender selection for genocidal killing *does* seem to me to have occurred, albeit less directly. In the case of the Congo "rubber terror," to cite just one case, slaughter occurred on a scale fully comparable to the Jewish holocaust, such that Adam Hochschild—surveying the catastrophic gender disproportion in local census figures after the terror—likened the experience to "sifting the ruins of an Auschwitz crematorium."[12] As for the "selection" in the case of the Soviet POWs, Stein does not mention the evidence I cited that Nazi commanders had orders to round up *all Soviet males* (but not females) between the ages of fifteen and sixty-five and incarcerate them as POWs, whether they had seen military service or not.[13]

Finally, Stein claims that "although . . . Jones refers to the need to draw out the 'analytical and policy-relevant insights' associated with the term [gendercide], this is not done." I would agree that I have not yet carried this project very far. But I believe I have made a start, as with my suggestion in "Gendercide and Genocide" that "one line of investigation that offers real promise is the notion of gendercide as a tripwire or harbinger of fuller scale root-and-branch genocides," which would presumably be vital to the development of effective genocide early-warning systems;[14] and in the conclusion of my Rwanda chapter in this volume.[15] Most of the other contributors to this book have also sought to make practical suggestions aimed at blunting the gendercidal impetus. Certainly, a great deal more remains to be done in order to "operationalize" the gendercide theory for purposes of analytical reflection, humanitarian intervention, and genocide prevention. But I do not think it will necessarily "be very difficult to do so," as Stein asserts—or that the task should be shirked in the face of whatever difficulties may present themselves.

Carpenter's "Beyond 'Gendercide'"

It is worth stressing, at the outset, how much Carpenter's approach shares with my own. She, too, criticizes the application of "gender" frameworks to women and girls alone, calling for "a recognition of men as victims." She accepts the validity of a focus on "sex-selective killing [that] corrects for much of the feminist bias in earlier literature, while contributing crucially to our understanding of gender and genocide." It is heartening to see my analysis validated in these key respects. I will limit myself here to exploring some of the areas of difference and disagreement between Carpenter and myself.

Carpenter makes a strong case for distinguishing between "sex" and "gender," a hallmark of her own research and that of many feminist scholars (especially, as she notes, postmodern feminists).[16] She feels that what I call "gendercide" would better be referred to as "sex-selective massacre." I believe, by contrast, that there are solid grounds for using "gender" as shorthand to designate a continuum of biologically given and culturally constructed traits and attributes. I offer three justifications for this approach. First, as Carpenter notes, the blurring of sex and gender is common in "colloquial usage," as well as in "much international discourse pertaining to women." Second, distinguishing in an analytically rigorous way between biological sex and culturally constructed gender seems to me, *pace* Joshua Goldstein's analysis, to preempt a debate over the influence of biology and physiology on gender constructions.[17] Third, my use of the term "gendercide" is broadly in keeping with Mary Anne Warren's original usage, which defines the concept as "the deliberate extermination of persons of a particular sex (or gender)." Deploying "gendercide" allows the analyst, and the activist, to exploit Warren's felicitous vocabulary, which like Raphael Lemkin's original term "genocide" has the advantage of describing a particular phenomenon or set of phenomena "as shortly and as poignantly as possible."[18] Carpenter herself notes that the term "is not without its political advantages," as it "creates an obvious semantic corollary to the much-abused term 'genocide'" and helps to advance the political-activist component of the research (as reflected most obviously in the Gendercide Watch website that Carpenter mentions). This utility should not be lightly abandoned, in my view.

Thus, much may be gained in terms of nomenclatural convenience, and little analytical force surrendered, if the term "gender" is employed but its specific context borne in mind throughout. When I talk, for example, about the "gendering" of the victims of a mass grave (or a campaign of sexual assault, or a military press-gang), it can be assumed that I am concerned with the fate of "embodied" (biological) males and females, rather than to—or prior to—more subtle elements of cultural conditioning. "Gendercide" similarly refers to the deaths of "embodied" males and females—or rather, violently disembodied ones. In gendering social phenomena and historical events, meanwhile, I should be understood as seeking to discern the explanatory power of the gender variable (the continuum of biology and culture) in the political and sociological equation. Issues of "gender structure" and "gender ideology," as defined and explored by Carpenter, can usefully be factored into this level of analysis.

As an aside, even those who feel that the "gender" prefix is unduly stretched in the gendercide framework should acknowledge that "genocide" has proved similarly malleable. In most applications, at least in scholarship that seeks to transcend the language and limitations of the Genocide Convention, the term has moved beyond the ethnic connotations of "genos" (Greek: "race, tribe") to encompass other groups, particularly those designated by common political affiliation. In the convention itself, as Carpenter notes, "genocide" also encompasses acts that fall well short of the literal "-cide" (killing) of human beings (under the convention, genocide can also include "causing serious bodily or mental harm to members of the group," "imposing measures to prevent births within the group," "forcibly transferring children of the group to another group," etc.).

I should emphasize, however, that I do not consider Carpenter's own approach to the sex-vs.-gender debate to be misguided. There is room for different analytical and rhetorical strategies; I hope only that my own will be seen as also valid. Moreover, Carpenter is right when she suggests that it would be disastrous for studies of gender and genocide to become preoccupied with the theme of gendercide (or "sex-selective massacre") to the exclusion of all else. Her specific recommendations for building on the existing gendercide literature—such as further exploring the age variable, destabilizing heterosexual assumptions, and examining gendered discourses of humanitarian intervention—strike me as highly persuasive. Indeed, I believe I can claim to have traveled some analytical distance in all three areas: by emphasizing the particular vulnerabilities of "battle-age" males to gendercidal massacre; by commissioning an article for the special gender-and-genocide issue of the *Journal of Genocide Research* on the theme of biotechnology and potential gendercide against gays and lesbians, reproduced in this book (Rixecker, "Genetic Enginerring and Queer Biotechnology"); and by exploring discourses of humanitarian crisis and intervention, both in my chapter "Gender and Genocide in Rwanda" and in a more recent piece, "Genocide and Humanitarian Intervention: Incorporating the Gender Variable."[19] Clearly, however, more research into these and other aspects of gender and genocide is urgently required.

Gendercide, then, should not be *the* focus of gender-and-genocide research. In my view, though—and apparently in Carpenter's as well—it should remain a legitimate focus of such research. And perhaps the case can be made that gender-selective mass killing is one of the most *urgent* subjects for investigation, given that this phenomenon has not, until now, been framed inclusively, analyzed within its comparative and global-historical framework, and integrated with the policy and humanitarian agenda.

In the activist context, in which "issues" must be carefully defined and energetically lobbied, the validity of a focus on gender-selective mass killing becomes clearer still. Primary attention to the most atrocious real-world reflections of gender bias can create the kind of cognitive "shock" that is vital to establishing phenomena as issues and problems. It is especially vital to draw attention to male victims, since the culture's prevailing obliviousness to this category of victims means that only the worst abuses have a chance of being viewed as morally problematic and worthy of policy concern.

The real world changes far more slowly than does scholarship. One can be reasonably sure that if one advances theory X in the social sciences and succeeds in finding an audience for it, a year or two later one will be reading an article entitled "Beyond X." Activism, on the other hand, often involves *decades* of patient and insistent work before one even begins to see one's framings and arguments reflected in the policy sphere—if one ever does. The question, then, is whether "gendercide" is nothing more than a political "catchphrase," as Carpenter suggests (that is, something gimmicky and disposable); or whether it serves instead as a *catalyzing idea,* without which no meaningful "principled-issue network" can develop. I believe strongly that it can succeed as the latter.[20]

Carpenter, like Stein, devotes considerable attention to the phrasing of the UN Genocide Convention, which defines genocide as the destruction "in whole or in part" of group members "as such." Two points can be made here. First, if we base ourselves on the Genocide Convention, we cannot discuss genocide against gender or sexual groups at all. The convention limits itself to "national, ethnical, racial, or religious" groups, allowing no room for such a framing. Thus, any attempt to conceptualize gender- and sex-related mass killing necessarily adopts a different definition of genocide, one that cannot be ruled out simply because it does not conform to the strict tenets of the convention. (My own definition, derived from but adapting the one put forward by Steven Katz, is: "the actualization of the intent, however successfully carried out, to murder in whole or in substantial part any national, ethnic, racial, religious, political, social, gender, or economic group, as these groups are defined by the perpetrator, by whatever means.")

One useful way of integrating the different variables that may operate in a particular case of gendercide/genocide is to isolate the decision chain that results in the gendercidal targeting, for example, of "battle-age" males, in a broader context of ethnic, political, or religious conflict. The decision chain here is standardly as follows:

Ethnicity/
religion/
political affiliation/
social class ⟶ Gender ⟶ Age

That is, a target group is isolated, commonly on the basis of ethnicity, religion, political affiliation, or social class (usually the group is bounded geographically as well, as we will see). Then the male segment of this group is singled out for especially unsympathetic attention. Of this subgroup, males of "battle age" are isolated as *primary or preliminary* targets, and perhaps also as *sufficient* ones, as far as the actual campaign of mass killing is concerned.[21]

This last point pertains to Carpenter's contention, which I think is unjustified, that members of a definable group (for example, the gender/sexual group "men") have to be targeted "as a whole . . . for extermination" in order for the campaign to qualify as genocide. This is not a standard that we apply in most other cases of genocide—perhaps not even in the case of the Jewish holocaust (it remains an open question whether Hitler envisaged the extermination of all Jews everywhere, or only in the territories designated for the Nazi *Lebensraum*). Consider the 1994 carnage in Rwanda. Hutu *génocidaires* clearly targeted Tutsis on ethnic grounds—and also on political grounds, since to be "Tutsi" was to be deemed oppositionist. But they targeted Tutsis *only in Rwanda*—there was never an intention of extending the campaign to Tutsis in neighboring Burundi, Uganda, and Zaire, for example. So those designated for extermination were not all Tutsis "as such," but *Rwandan* Tutsis. Likewise, in the case of gendercides against males, it seems natural that the gender variable will be accompanied by others, as I have regularly stressed in my writings. The gendercidal massacres at Srebrenica in 1995 did not target males as a global gender (or sexual) group, nor all males in the vicinity. They clearly *did* target "battle-age" Bosnian Muslim males; and the gender variable was just as clearly decisive, in that others who shared every ascriptive trait but maleness (i.e., younger Bosnian Muslim women) were generally spared outright murder.

A similar argument could be made in the case of Saddam Hussein's Anfal Campaign against Iraqi Kurds in 1987 and 1988.[22] There, the targeted population was not Kurds as a whole, but exclusively *Iraqi* Kurds (their ethnic counterparts in Turkey and Iran were of no real interest or concern to the Iraqi government). This targeted group was then broken down, first by geographical location—the "mountain" Kurds of the north were targeted, while the urban Kurds of Baghdad and other cities were not—and then by gender. Thus, in the final accounting, the core element of mass murder was focused overwhelmingly upon: (1) northern/rural; (2) Kurdish; (3) males; (4) of a battle age. Despite these crucial geographical and gender limitations on the

Iraqi campaign, however, most observers accept that Anfal constituted a "crime of genocide" against the Kurdish people as a whole.[23]

This argument is relevant to Carpenter's claim that gendercide can never be seen as *coterminous* with genocide. I have tried to demonstrate in my research that gendercide against battle-age males may be seen as a tripwire or harbinger of a broader root-and-branch campaign of mass killing against all members of the targeted group. The three "classic" genocides of the twentieth century, Armenia, the Jewish holocaust, and Rwanda, fit this pattern. In many other cases, however—Bangladesh in 1971, Anfal in 1987 and 1988, Bosnia-Herzegovina from 1992 to 1995, and Kosovo in 1999, to cite just a few examples—the gendercidal component was *sufficient,* and marked the limits of the genocidal campaign, at least as far as mass killing was concerned. (Other gendered groups, such as children and women, were of course exposed to a host of different and less lethal but no less "gendered" measures, notably rape and mass expulsion.) In such cases, I think the gendercide *is* largely coterminous with genocide—or at least with its murderous component, which by my own definition is the essential one.

In sum, let me emphasize that I view my work in this volume and elsewhere as an extended "plausibility probe" for future research. Many readers, like Carpenter and Stein, will find aspects of my analysis *im*plausible. I hope those who differ with elements of the framing or its exposition will nonetheless find the broader endeavor worthwhile.

Afterword

On 7 December 2000, during the closing stages of working on the special gendercide issue of the *Journal of Genocide Research,* a message arrived from one of the contributors to this volume, Stefanie Rixecker. It seemed to put a finger on elements of the gendercide framework, and its policy relevance, that I had been trying to articulate for some time. Rixecker questioned

> the assumption that highlighting different aspects of genocide waters it down and removes the serious aspects of the act itself. I do not think this is true at all. If anything, addressing contributing factors is essential if humankind wishes to preempt such atrocities. The more we understand of the different means of labelling hate—and perpetrating violence based upon these labels—the better off we will be in ensuring future genocides do not take place. I would have thought this was the ultimate goal—and the ultimate policy outcome.

I regard your original gendercide piece, and this [volume], as fundamental lynchpins in constructing and extending policy mechanisms that can recognize the various aspects of genocide. This is essential, especially from the perspective of minorities—the customary targets of such violent acts—because without addressing the complex (and often entrenched, yet ignored) forms of discrimination, it is impossible to properly mediate and resolve the underlying reasons for genocide and other atrocities. How can we ensure civilian men are *not* regarded as fodder for death programs if we do not publicly discuss these issues? How is it possible for us to create organizations and watchdogs if we do not pressure for their realization?

In the case of homosexuality, it was only in the early 1990s that Amnesty International *finally* agreed that sexuality could be regarded as a factor in human rights abuses. Policy-wise, violence against gays/lesbians/queers was not regarded as having status, because it was not recognized by an organization as being a form of abuse—or at least not one that could be equated with the abuse other people suffered for their personal, political and religious beliefs. The *only* reason AI and others changed their approach and understanding was because individuals, and their groups, lobbied, argued, and demonstrated that they had legitimate issues. In turn, the queer community can now better monitor and act upon human rights abuses based upon or framed around sexuality issues. This is a powerful policy consequence, arising from a trajectory similar to the one you have established with regard to gendercide. . . . I think you have already made considerable headway in analyzing policy mechanisms and consequences. And I am certain more will come.

Notes

The epigraph is from Orlando Patterson, *Slavery and Social Death: A Comparative Study* (Cambridge: Harvard University Press, 1982), p. 332.

1. For a fine analysis of the plight of widows in the Third World, see Margaret Owen, *A World of Widows* (London: Zed Books, 1996).

2. Stein also argues against labeling "recent conflicts in Kosovo, Bosnia-Herzegovina, Jammu and Kashmir, Colombia, Sri Lanka, Rwanda, Iraqi Kurdistan, Peru, and India" as gendercidal, because "in many of these conflicts both males and females were targeted and killed, although frequently in different proportions relative to their base populations." But in the Nazi-occupied territories during World War II, many other groups were killed besides Jews and Roma (Gypsies), "albeit in different proportions relative to their base populations." Does this belie the reality of the genocides against Jews and Roma, or the centrality of ethnicity in the holocausts inflicted upon them?

3. For example, with the statement that "although the element of 'gendercide' in the Armenian holocaust is important . . . it is far less significant in describing or explaining the broader exterminationist impulse toward ethnic Armenians," which was "generalized"; and the acknowledgment that "gender was far from a dominant consideration in the [Jewish] holocaust overall." Jones, "Gendercide and Genocide," this volume.

4. Ibid.

5. One source refers to "the systematic slaughter of most young men of Jewish origin" in the early weeks of the invasion. "In the large cities, those capable of military service were interned during the first days of the occupation; Jews were usually separated from the rest, and, as a rule, executed soon afterward (Minsk, Kiev). In the smaller towns, Jewish men were rounded up—ostensibly for forced labor, but in reality to be put to death." See "Jewish History of the Russian Federation," *www.heritagefilms.com/RUSSIA2.htm.* To cite a handful of instances drawn from Christopher Browning's book *Ordinary Men: Police Battalion 101 and the Final Solution in Poland* (New York: HarperPerennial, 1998): Białystok, where on 27 June 1941 "Major Weis . . . ordered his battalion to comb the Jewish quarter and seize male Jews" (p. 11); the order issued on 11 July by "Colonel Montua of the Police Regiment Center . . . [that] 'all male Jews between the ages of 17 and 45 convicted as plunderers are to be shot according to martial law'" (p. 13; Browning adds on p. 14: "There was, of course, no investigation, trial, and conviction of so-called plunderers. Male Jews who appeared to be between the ages of seventeen and forty-five were simply rounded up and brought to the stadium in Białystok on July 12"); Narevka-Mala on 15 August 1941, where "All male persons between 16 and 65 years of age were shot" (p. 15, citing the testimony of Lieutenant Riebel).

6. In 1941, "in response to a Chetnik [Serb partisan] ambush, Nazi commander Major König rounded up the entire male population of Kragujevak, including several hundred schoolboys from grade five and up. 7,000 men and boys were gunned down by machine guns in a field just outside of town." Kurt Jonassohn with Karen Björnson, *Genocide and Gross Human Rights Violations* (New Brunswick, N.J.: Transaction, 1998), p. 285. Harald Turner, a Nazi military administrator in Yugoslavia, stated on 26 October 1941: "It is a matter of principle . . . to put *all* Jewish men and male Gypsies at the disposal of the troops as hostages." Cited in Christopher R. Browning, *The Path to Genocide: Essays on Launching the Final Solution* (Cambridge: Cambridge University Press, 1992), p. 136, emphasis added. Of the massacre at Lidice, Henri Michel writes: "After the assassination of [Reinhard] Heydrich [in 1942], Hitler gave orders that 30,000 Czechs should be put to death at once. Frank, Heydrich's successor, decided on 'a special repressive action to give the Czechs a lesson in propriety.' His choice fell upon the little town of Lidice because two of its inhabitants had left the country in 1939 and were serving in the RAF. The day after the 'Protector's' funeral a convoy of trucks arrived; the town was cordoned off and all exits barred. The inhabitants were then assembled in the square and lined up, men

on one side, women on the other. The men were shot in groups of ten, while the houses were blown up. . . . The dreadful scene was filmed to lend weight to the lesson." Michel, *The Shadow War: European Resistance, 1939–45* (New York: Harper and Row, 1972), pp. 352–53.

7. Leo Kuper, *Genocide; Its Political Use in the Twentieth Century* (London: Penguin, 1981), p. 204. A Russian soldier in Chechnya told the *Los Angeles Times:* "I killed a lot. I wouldn't touch women or children, as long as they didn't fire at me. But I would kill all the men I met during mopping-up operations. I didn't feel sorry for them one bit. They deserved it. I wouldn't even listen to the pleas or see the tears of their women when they asked me to spare their men. I simply took them aside and killed them." Maura Reynolds, "War Has No Rules for Russian Forces Battling Chechen Rebels," *Los Angeles Times,* 17 September 2000. As this example suggests, an element of gender hatred may well be a factor in gendercides against males, even if it does not predominate. Consider the propaganda barrage directed at German Jews under the Nazi regime. If one thinks of the typical Nazi caricature of the "dirty" "cosmopolitan" Jew, what comes to mind? Surely it is the hook-nosed, skulking, threatening figure of the *male* Jew that overwhelmingly dominated the Nazi discourse. Joan Ringelheim notes: "Legitimation for targeting Jewish men was plentiful in Nazi anti-Semitic and racist propaganda and, more to the point, in Nazi policy. The decision to kill every Jew did not seem to demand special justification to kill Jewish men. They were already identified as dangerous. This was not so for Jewish women and children." Ringelheim, "Genocide and Gender: A Split Memory," in Ronit Lentin, ed., *Gender and Catastrophe* (London: Zed Books, 1997), p. 19. Such visceral and deeply gendered hatred may help to account for the gratuitous brutality meted out to many "out-group" males, who are prone to be not simply annihilated but humiliated, tortured, castrated, raped, or forced to rape each other—acts that are familiar from the Bosnian genocide, among others.

8. See, for example, Henrich Himmler's comments to a gathering of SS officers in Poznan on 4 October 1943: "We know how difficult it would be for us today—under bombing raids and the hardships and deprivations of war—if we were still to have the Jews in every city *as secret saboteurs, agitators, and inciters.*" Quoted in Israel W. Charny, ed., *Encyclopedia of Genocide* (Santa Barbara, Calif.: ABC-CLIO, 1999), p. 241, emphasis added. Stein, too, notes "the close association in Nazi ideology between Bolshevism and Jewishness."

9. Even stronger arguments could be made in the case of the genocides in Armenia, Bangladesh, Rwanda, and Kosovo, where the targeted populations (unlike the Jews of the Nazi-occupied territories, at least until the holocaust descended with full force) gave support and sustenance to militarized resistance movements that exacted at least a limited toll on government forces. In the Armenian case, the prevailing view among Ottoman authorities was "that Armenians in particular were the perpetrators of 'depraved,' that is, tyrannical behaviour, and thus deserved severe punishment." Ottoman propaganda served to depict Armenians as belonging en

bloc to "a 'terrorist' culture," much as "battle-age" males (and frequently older men and young boys) among the designated out-group are depicted as uniformly subversive and dangerous. Quotes from James Reid, "Conservative Ottomanism as a Source of Genocidal Behavior," in Levon Chorbajian and George Shirinian, eds., *Studies in Comparative Genocide* (New York: St. Martin's Press, 1999), p. 61.

10. Stein writes, "If 'maleness' were the only consideration dictating selection," as if I had suggested that this was the defining feature of anti-male gendercide; but I do not believe that I did.

11. I hoped this was implicit in my phrasing of the selection process as "essential if not universal" and "not always explicit"—I should perhaps have written "essential *though* not universal," which was my intended meaning. Jones, "Gendercide and Genocide."

12. Adam Hochschild, *King Leopold's Ghost* (Boston: Houghton Mifflin, 1998), p. 232.

13. Jones, "Gendercide and Genocide." It is impossible to determine how many civilian Soviet males were swept up in the holocaust, but the number may have been very substantial indeed, especially if the even more massive estimates of murdered POWs that Stein cites are accurate.

14. Jones, "Gendercide and Genocide." See also Adam Jones, "Genocide and Humanitarian Intervention: Incorporating the Gender Variable," *Journal of Humanitarian Assistance,* February 2002; *www.jha.ac/articles/a080.htm.*

15. For example, this passage: "Feminist and human rights scholarship has done much to draw our attention to the gender-specific needs and concerns of women survivors, but it has standardly ignored or skated over the gendercides against males that produce such situations. Systematic attention to the male experience is clearly called for and seems no less policy relevant. Humanitarian interventions, for example, must supplement their attention to the special vulnerabilities of women and girls with a recognition of the particular vulnerabilities of men and boys."

16. Stein does the same in passing: see "Geno and Other Cides," note 56.

17. "Many scholars use the terms 'sex' and 'gender' in a way that I find unworkable: 'sex' refers to what is biological, and 'gender' to what is cultural. We are a certain sex but we learn or perform certain gender roles which are not predetermined or tied rigidly to biological sex. Thus, sex is fixed and based in nature; gender is arbitrary, flexible, and based in culture. This usage helps to detach gender inequalities from any putative inherent or natural basis. The problem, however, is that this sex-gender discourse constructs a false dichotomy between biology and culture, which are in fact highly interdependent. More concretely, the conception of biology as fixed and culture as flexible is wrong. . . . Biology provides diverse potentials, and cultures limit, select, and channel them. Furthermore, culture directly influences the expression of genes and hence the biology of our bodies. No universal biological essence of 'sex' exists, but rather a complex system of potentials that are activated by various internal and external influences. I see no useful border separating 'sex' and 'gender' as

conventionally used. I therefore use 'gender' to cover masculine and feminine roles and bodies alike, in all their aspects, including the (biological and cultural) structures, dynamics, roles and scripts associated with each gender group." Joshua Goldstein, *War and Gender* (Cambridge: Cambridge University Press, 2001), p. 2.

18. Lemkin quoted in Samantha Power, *"A Problem from Hell": America and the Age of Genocide* (New York: Basic Books, 2002), p. 42.

19. Adam Jones, "Gender and Genocide in Rwanda," this volume; Jones, "Genocide and Humanitarian Intervention."

20. Carpenter might agree, since she notes that the gendercide framework has "swiftly generated a body of genocide research that specifically focuses on sex selectivity in patterns of mass killing," succeeded in disseminating "provocative" writings to the mainstream, and drawn "much traffic and acclaim" to the Gendercide Watch website since its founding.

21. Carpenter also criticizes my use of the term "mass killing" as being somewhat woolly. I agree that it has imprecisions, as does virtually all terminology in these subject areas. In common parlance, a mass killing is "any killing of four or more victims at one time and place" (the American FBI definition; see *jove.prohosting.com/~mclough/massmurder.htm,* which includes the author's discussion of definitional problems). I believe, however, that "mass killing" can also be used to describe large-scale killings that may, at ground level, be carried out by individuals against individuals, with the acts removed from one another in time and space—but territorially and temporally bounded nonetheless and linked to a larger plan, strategy, *or institutionally patterned behavior.* If every willing and unwilling executioner in Rwanda, for example, had killed just one Tutsi or oppositionist Hutu—800,000 perpetrators killing 800,000 victims in twelve weeks—could we not speak of the "mass killing" of Tutsis and oppositionist Hutus? Note also the common usage of "mass rape" to define widespread sexual assault in the Balkans, Bangladesh, Japanese-occupied China, and other conflict areas. Does this phenomenon require that women be brought together in a confined physical space and then raped all together and at once? Or does "mass rape" instead generally consist of the *repeated, systematic* sexual assault of individual women on separate occasions? I do not think, in other words, that calling cumulative murders of this type "mass" murder means that "*all* murder is 'mass' and the term loses its meaning," as Carpenter claims.

22. See the Gendercide Watch case study at *www.gendercide.org/case_anfal.html.*

23. See, for example, Human Rights Watch, *Iraq's Crime of Genocide: The Anfal Campaign against the Kurds* (New York: Human Rights Watch/Yale University Press, 1995). I am reminded also of the brief but highly suggestive passage in Daniel Goldhagen's *Hitler's Willing Executioners* that refers to the early days of gender-selective mass killing of (male) Jews on the eastern front in 1941. See Jones, "Gendercide and Genocide," note 65.

11

Men and Masculinities in Gendercide/Genocide

Terrell Carver

"Gender" in Context

Feminists have put gender on the map in society and academic life. The concept has a history rooted in social science and psychoanalytic explorations of sex and sexuality from the 19th century onward, but postwar feminism's usage has served as a signal that sex and sexuality have become problematic and political, rather than unproblematic and "natural." Feminists have not agreed on exactly what gender means, nor exactly how it relates to sex and sexuality. Nor, indeed, has anyone else—though many, to their credit, have tried, including the contributors to this volume.

In challenging the link between sex and sexuality and the "natural" (which is guarded by the "scientific"), feminists have added far more than "woman" to the discussion of gender. The most interesting and convincing use of gender to signal discussions of sex and sexuality has been, and continues to be, in feminist (rather than non-feminist) thought and practice, and in thought and practice that locates itself critically but supportively with respect to these achievements. Marking off feminist thought as "normative" or "prescriptive" (as opposed to "analytical" or "value-neutral"), or "biased" or "one-sided," is not in my view a positive start to considering men and masculinities in any context—especially the present one.[1]

While the history of post-war feminism is too large a topic to summarize here,[2] suffice it to say that a central concern was validating "woman" as object of study, and women as qualified "to speak" about that and, in principle, any other topic in intellectual life. Given that feminism is above all a movement to liberate women from the oppressions of marginalization, exclusion, silencing and erasure, it is unsurprising that feminists have not been anxious to continue centering men as object of study, and as qualified (indeed, particularly qualified) to speak. By definition, feminists sought to decenter and deflect previous practice. In that respect, the present volume is necessarily somewhat controversial regarding feminism, though by no means instantly anathema. On the contrary: In my view, it is in principle worthy of support.

Men have already figured prominently in feminist thought, particularly as objects of critique. "Malestream" thought is now a recognized descriptive category in intellectual life, rather than a mere slogan. The term refers to thought that marginalizes, excludes, silences and erases "woman" and thus women, and does the same for experiences commonly coded as feminine. In examining and criticizing malestream thought, feminists have studied men, masculinity, male violence, the "man" question in various guises, structural masculinism, militarism, international relations as a mirror to masculinity, masculinized political theory and philosophy, rationality as a masculine preserve and strategy, and other areas too numerous to mention.[3] What they have not done, unsurprisingly, is men's history—that is, critical reflections on men's experience as experienced by men. Nor have they engaged in consciousness-raising auto-critique—that is, setting out to reform men by reformulating masculinity.

The men's studies and masculinities literature has arisen self-consciously within a feminist frame. Moreover, it self-consciously distinguishes itself from mythopoetic evocations of manhood or essentialized masculinity, and from "recovery" literatures and therapies that seek to unite contemporary men with "their" manhood. Indeed, from the point of view of the men's studies and masculinities literatures, those ideas, movements and groups are all objects for study and critique, rather than an "applied" or political wing of a presumed intellectual movement.[4]

The feminist frame is crucially important in defining the men's studies and masculinities literatures, for two reasons. The first is overtly political. It concerns an acknowledgement of women's oppression (along with oppressions based on race/ethnicity, class, and other ascribed categories, as feminists frequently aver). The second is a recognition that feminist thought has crucially exposed the male representation of "man" as supposedly universal and gender- or sex-neutral—but in fact as a masculinized figure, certainly not a woman. Joan Wallach Scott, the feminist historian and historian of feminism, writes

> One of the important effects of feminist activism and scholarship has been to point to the ways in which seemingly neutral categories are in fact sexed. Thus the abstract individual, the foundation of liberal democracy, has been revealed to be male.[5]

The apparently de-gendered, "abstract" individual was thus conceptualized as "public man" by men, evincing all the virtues that are coded "masculine," and none of the lesser-valued "feminine" ones. Yet that figure was held up as the generic human—the "everyman" citizen, the arbiter of what is reasonable, rational, and "normal." For most women, most of the time, that masculinized figure did not fit comfortably; indeed, he ground women down.[6]

The men's history and masculinities literatures, while aligned in a feminist frame, developed from the conviction that although "generic man" was certainly not a woman, he was not really a man, either. This was because the limited range of "public" experiences that he embodied and expressed did little justice to the frustrations, oppressions, and struggles that many men have faced in becoming men and achieving some measure of masculinity, or achieving some alternative identity in practice.[7] As with Simone de Beauvoir's famous comment about women, so with men: They are not born, but made. Sociologists and occasionally historians had in pre-feminist times (viewed from their perspective) interested themselves in men's experiences, and in characteristically masculine behaviors, whether self-consciously or not. But the political context was usually that of social class, whether conceived as a point of radicalizing difference, or as an issue in larger schemes of social integration. The sex war, and gender politics, had not yet (formally) begun in the "public" world of social science and political institutions.

Marginalized, "deviant," troubled and troublesome men—whether individually in memoirs and personal history, or collectively in class terms—have thus been objects of study. Those studies have exposed the numerous and pervasive masculinizing institutions in societies that have historically selected some men, excluded others, and then produced men in a variety of formats, at a significant human cost. Armies, sports, workplaces, sexualities and subjectivities have all been explored and exposed, though these explorations have yet to reach a wide audience, despite the current world-weary claims of a surfeit of masculinity studies. Overwhelmingly, the academic reaction to men's studies and masculinities is an understandable one: "But men were always representing themselves in histories and literatures that excluded, devalued, or misrepresented women. What's the difference?" The difference is that a universalized but masculinized "humanity" is now only a first step in an analysis that subsequently works to make problematic men's representations of themselves as "the norm." A second step is to reconsider men's representations of themselves that are overtly masculine and specifically male, with a view to analyzing their variety, political import and reform.

While the more self-conscious evocations of masculinities as troubled and multi-formed sites of construction and rebellion may or may not speak to feminist issues, it is undeniably the case that those counter-hegemonic activities and representations are contrasted with "normal" man and his allegedly universal masculinity. While accounts of marginalized men in the men's studies and masculinities literatures are cross-cut with considerations of race/ethnicity, class, and other factors of exclusion and devaluation, it is also the case that hegemonic masculinity itself is not an unproblematic and untroubled experience. Men's histories show this, and masculinity studies have reflected it. Highly advantaged males are also produced, not born; and it is in understanding those processes that men's studies and masculinities have the most to offer. Put very simply, they have the power to expose the workings of masculine domination from the inside that feminists have identified (variously) as patriarchy and male power.[8] Victims need publicity, but perpetrators should have it in spades.

There is thus considerably more involved in inserting men's studies and masculinities into current forms of social science and critical politics than merely drawing attention to male bodies, men's activities, and masculinized hierarchies in which some men dominate others (and women).[9] The sociology of masculinities, in particular, has highlighted the extent to which hierarchies feature strongly in men's experiences of one another, and in masculinized power structures generally. While from the feminist perspective men appear to share a kind of equality as perpetrators of patriarchy, and beneficiaries of its structural oppressions, further analysis has revealed the structures of competition and exclusion, reward and punishment, within the masculine power structure as a whole. This is a structure in which women have a "role" as counters or markers in men's power struggles *with each other;* it is one in which most men are oppressed by a few, both in objective practice and subjective experiences.[10]

It is possible to explore these analytical points without losing a focus on the feminist framing of male oppression. In fact, such a focus offers a closer and more persuasive account of how that oppression is organized, and why it is so tenacious. While men benefit in general from the patriarchal oppression of women, they do not necessarily have to do much to keep it in place. Symbolic structures and "public" institutions do it for them, albeit at a price that most of them are willing to pay—the price exacted by knuckling under to structures of hegemonic masculinity. Most will never measure up to this ideal, which in practice delivers huge benefits to a few; but the ideal still provides some benefits to all (at women's expense).[11] Michael S. Kimmel summarizes as follows:

> All masculinities are not created equal; or rather, we [men] are all created equal, but any hypothetical equality evaporates quickly because our definitions of masculinity are not equally valued in our society. One definition of manhood continues to remain the standard against which other forms of manhood are measured and evaluated. Within the dominant culture, the masculinity that defines white, middle-class, early middle-aged, heterosexual men is the masculinity that sets the standards for other men, against which other men are measured and, more often than not, found wanting . . .
>
> This is the definition that we will call "hegemonic" masculinity, the image of masculinity of those men who hold power, which has become the standard . . .[12]

Evidently the balance suits most men well enough—with notable exceptions, where the politics has centered around issues of race/ethnicity and sexuality that are "other" to the dominant white, heterosexual ideal. While those movements have destabilized masculine ideals and hierarchies somewhat, their relationship to feminism and women generally is questionable. The feminist framing of the men's studies and masculinities literature is intended to address this:

> Men's dominance over women is also related to the dominance of some men over other men. The hierarchy between men means that some men are also disadvantaged by the existing system of gender relations. These men may choose to struggle against the dominant model of gender relations and be open to forming alliances with women to bring about change.[13]

Perhaps even more subversively, David Gutterman has suggested that profeminist men who *do* fit dominant stereotypes of hegemonic masculinity, and who *do* already benefit from patriarchal and masculinist oppressions, might be especially "slippery" and thus effective in dismantling existing power-structures of privilege across both the masculine and feminine arenas of ascriptive markers:

> Indeed, rather than creating new categories of masculinity and femininity, or heterosexuality and homosexuality, at their best profeminist men challenge the "naturalness" of these divisions. Profeminists are often most effective when they use their culturally privileged status as men as a platform from which to disrupt categories of sexual and gender identity. (The privileges of race, class, education, etc., of course, also provide some profeminist men with access to other platforms.) . . . Much as transvestites and macho gay men are especially disturbing to normative standards of masculinity, the slipperiness of profeminist men provides them with opportunities to be extraordinarily subversive. Thus, whereas women and gay men often are forced to seek to dismantle the categories of gender and sexuality from culturally ordained positions of the "other," profeminist men can work to dismantle the system from positions of power by challenging the very standards of identity that afford them normative status in the culture.[14]

More than any other theoretical contribution, feminist thought has drawn attention to power as an effect of gender, however "gender" is defined. Locating that power involves exploring sex and sexuality. In what follows, I try to make a virtue of the indeterminacy of "gender" as a concept: its inability to tell us exactly what sex and sexuality are or must be, and how they are related to one another and to the bodies and activities they supposedly describe and explain. Many "gender issues" do not appear as such, especially to many men—most of whom are hardly conscious that they have any "gender," or a role in "gender relations" and "gender studies" at all![15] One way to keep trouble at bay, after all, is to deny that it exists.

Gender in the Present Volume

Judith Butler put the trouble with gender very succinctly: it's "gender trouble."[16] In considering gender in the context of the present volume, then, my strategy will be to explicate it as a term of contestation, and inevitably a term that is itself contested. Rather, though, than operate as the conventional tidy-minded and helpful philosopher, concerned to obviate discord, create agreement and put people to rights, I will instead suggest that we approach this volume as a celebration of diversity, and that therefore, unsurprisingly, its authors employ a diverse range of meanings when deploying the term "gender." What they understand by gender depends on their particular project, and therefore on what understandings they are trying to create (as ever, against a background of what it is that they are trying to "trouble," and what they seek to leave untroubled).[17] Interestingly, the common project here is to state and explore a view of men and masculinity/ies that is "gendered," and then to use that "to gender" the study of genocide, in terms of its victims, perpetrators, and processes.

I am hopeful that this way of explicating gender will minimize the difficulties of miscommunication and "talking past one another" that notably occur when people use the same word, unknowingly, in different ways (and then feel frustrated when the "other" in the debate never seems to make any sense, or find any common ground). I am not promising to create such common ground. Rather, I am attempting to defuse some of the frustrations that might arise by suggesting where the different parties "are coming from," particularly with respect to the way that they use the term "gender." This has already been identified as an area of crucial difficulty, and the work here builds in various ways on work carried out elsewhere, in diverse quarters. So, again resisting the urge to homogenize, I shall try to draw out these differences in aid of illumination, rather than agreement. As a goal, "agreeing to disagree" is not all that bad, and there may be various minimal levels of such consensus through which some of the politics proposed in this volume could actually operate.

Any negotiation of a term like "gender" is going to run straightaway into a dichotomy: that between common usage (constantly changing, rarely more so than in the present case), and more philosophical or technical usages that represent "terms of art," developed by some writer or school of thought as a "solution," based on the theory that clarity is obtainable and agreement is good. Philosophically, this is an old and important issue: Does the meaning of a word lie in its use (so what people generally say is right, because that is what they say—and mean)? Or does it lie in its (relative) correspondence to some ideal of logic or perfect "form"? No one is going to resolve this issue, either; the dichotomy is probably presupposed by any concept of language. I merely flag it here to remind readers that the issues involved are not simple and straightforward, given the history of debate.

In social scientific and feminist work generally, "gender" has usually signalled that cultural stereotypes and individual behaviour vary with respect to bodily sex (presumed to be dichotomous and opposite). That is, men have varying ways of being masculine across and within cultures, as women have varying ways of being feminine. At another level of dislocation, what is feminine may be associated, at times, with men, and vice-versa. Most other writers in this volume would like that distinction, contrary to ordinary usage, to remain in place and to retain its explanatory force. The problem, then, is which explains which. The usual and traditional view is that bodily sex tends to explain why men are masculine—without then examining why a supposedly universal notion of bodily sex should "give rise" to different forms of masculinity (of course, the same process, and the same question, obtain in the case of femininity). In this view, bodily sex would also obviously explain heterosexuality, given that sex is defined in reproductive terms in the first place. How it explains homosexuality, or how homosexuality is to be explained otherwise, are—following this line of thought—still mysterious. Is "it" a gene, or something learned, or something chosen? Given that it violates the (supposed) reproductive determinism of bodily sex, how are appropriately sex-related (and "opposite") behaviors then said to follow? Early theories of "inversion" (i.e., homosexual men would be "feminine" in some sense, and the reverse for lesbians) did not seem to fit descriptively, and with more recent changes in gay male "style," these stereotypes are far less easy to map onto a gay/straight boundary. Clearly, gender as behavior has become rather too dislocated from sex as bodily/reproductive difference to make the rather neat dichotomy of culture/behavior vs. body/biology very persuasive anymore, given that our own observation and usage does not map masculine and feminine neatly onto men (only) and women (only). Nor can we map variants in sexuality neatly across a gay/straight binary, which in any case intersects with the original male/female binary of bodily sex.

One solution to this has been Butler's radical reversal: Gender does not "flow" dichotomously from sex (as male/female bodily difference). Rather, concepts of sex as dichotomous difference flow from gendered thinking. Gendered thinking, on this view, employs a pastiche of binary and hierarchical concepts, which are then mapped onto bodies. The identification of bodies as different—not just from each other, but in certain stereotypical ways—is presented as a dichotomy, and maintained as such through disciplinary medical and social practices. It follows that familiar stereotypes of masculinity and femininity are but further binary and hierarchical effects of the same kind of thinking, and the institutionalized disciplines that create and enforce them. Obviously it takes more than thinking to produce effects like sexual difference and masculine/feminine stereotypes. Indeed, it is repetition and citation of the stereotypes that create the patterns of thought and behavior that render sexual difference, masculinity/femininity, and the gay/straight binary so solidly "normal" and familiar. Thus, the "facts" of the world are such because discursive practices cite them repetitiously, not because language merely describes what is already the case in social realities that seem "natural."[18] This is generally known as a post-structuralist or post-modern view, distinguished from a cultural or "constructionist" view by its thoroughgoing critique of any view of sex and sexuality as "natural" and as dichotomous, because "biological" and therefore "grounded" in reproduction as "fact."[19]

Scott has discussed the recent history of the concept of gender, tracing its troubling quality in feminist and gender-studies debates concerning the nature/culture problem and the way that human attributes, namely those thought to create a binary and "opposite" sexual difference, can be attributed to supposedly fixed biological facts, on the one hand, and fungible norms and roles in the domain of culture, on the other. Quoting (now amusing) exchanges from the time of the French Revolution between Condorcet and Chaumette, Scott argues deconstructively that the nature/culture dichotomy is itself a malleable notion that arises, and is successively redefined and reprojected, to make some human attributes factual and fixed and others flexible and alterable:

> Why should those exposed to pregnancies and other passing indispositions, not be allowed to exercise rights that no one imagines denying to those who have gout all winter or who catch cold quickly? [Condorcet]
>
> Since when is it decent to see women abandoning the pious cares of their households, the cribs of their children, to come to public places, to harangues in the galleries, at the bar of the Senate? Is it to men that nature confided domestic cares? Has she given us breasts to feed our children? [Chaumette].[20]

Scott's view is that gender will never be successfully distinguished from sex; nor will the two ever be successfully conflated. Rather, there is a continuing dialectic between the two in terms of distinction and conflation (witness all the different views on sex/gender and on conflation/distinction of the two in this volume). This signals the impossibility of locating sex as bodily difference always and forever in the realm of culture, as we have too much *desire* to place this in the "natural," where it will be fixed and therefore universalized. And it will signal the contrary desire to find gender, as malleable meaning and behavior, residing in the differentiating realm of culture, and therefore impossible to locate in "nature." Intriguingly, Scott suggests that the ambiguous synonymy, and thus apparent but unsuccessful conflations of sex and gender, signals a realization that both are really linguistic markers for our uncertainties about what is universal and fixed, and what is differentiated and malleable. Moreover, they are the counters we use in our stubbornly recurring efforts to fix some things as "natural," and to release other things as "cultural." Denominating something as "natural" does not actually remove it from language to a non-linguistic realm of materiality and certainty; things in language will always stay in language. Pulling at "sex" in some or all respects in order to make it "gender," and thus to unfix some things from the "natural" and so make them political, is therefore precisely what the two terms sex and gender signify *together*.[21]

Those in this volume who want to hold some attributes of "woman" or "man" as biological referents, inalterable at least for the time being, or untroubled by any "intermediate" or "minority" forms, will want to be aware of the position that Scott is expounding. Nonetheless, given that common usage does attribute fixity to nature, and a Darwinian universality to human reproductive biology, it may be that for some projects a "troubling" of those points for political departure might be counter-productive. Where there are political projects, proponents are going to have to choose. Numerous feminists, for instance, have argued passionately, politically, and successfully for naturalized conceptions of sex (or for "strategic essentialism"), in particular of the markers (if not the actual realities) of female reproductive experience. Conversely, and rather regrettably, considerations of the male side of sex, in the reproductive and biological sense just mentioned, have been profoundly unfeminist (and mostly overtly anti-feminist) in intent and import.[22]

In terms of sexuality, rather than markers for sex as reproductive biology, contributors to this volume are again divided collectively and uncertain individually about sexuality's relation to gender. Are homosexuality and heterosexuality "genders" that "gay people" and "straight people" belong to (because of same-sex or opposite-sex "object-choice")? Or are they sexual identities that men and women "have" differently as men and as women (because biology—or culture—has created the man/woman binary sexual difference in the first place)? Does the commonplace gay/straight binary actually exhaust the possibilities? Is deliberately non-reproductive sex valid as a sexuality at all? Or is sex almost extraneous to contemporary conceptualizations of reproduction, given the bio-technologies available? And, importantly for the contributors to the present volume, what is the downside of sexuality (and particularly heterosexuality) as abuse, rape, forced pregnancy, castration and so on? Do some or all of these fall into place with respect to "people" (irrespective of the "reproductive" sex-binary of male and female), or do most of these constitute different phenomena for men and women precisely because the sex-binary is so crucial (so we tend to think) to individual subjective experience, and to dichotomized collective experience? These are issues that are important to raise, and on which we can expect disagreement, and indeed diversity with respect to different political projects. However, I am hopeful that if we expect diversity and disagreement at the outset, then readers will be less likely to interpret what they find in these debates as confusion or error. This volume should therefore "trouble" readers—but productively.

Overall, then, gender signals projects in the realm of sex and sexuality, and debates over the meanings and referents of all these terms. It does this not simply within a descriptive realm, taking a fact/norm or nature/culture dichotomy for granted, but within a complex realm in which those terms and binaries are themselves made problematic. As I say, some of those problems can be set to one side, though preferably self-consciously, in order to get on with a (political) job. But readers should be aware where lines are being drawn and who is, and is not, troubled by these bones of contention. In much simpler terms, then, I offer a brief account of the "working" understandings of gender, sex and sexuality that are variously, and contrastingly, deployed throughout this volume, together with some sense of the political projects that are here "on the go," through which these different strategic moves are elaborated.

Projects and Definitions

Most importantly, overall, there is the project of making younger adult males visible as victims of mass killing, for which they have been targeted despite their non-combatant status (Lindner, Holter, Buchanan, Jones, Stein, Carpenter). Some contributions then pursue the gendercide/genocide analogy both ways—exploring targeting of males for oppression short of killing (Del Zotto), and targeting of a "gender" for total annihilation (Rixecker).

Jones uses sex and gender as synonyms, since he says (accurately) that in common usage this is increasingly the case. Both assume a binary (that is two, and only two, terms) and a dichotomy (that is, the two terms of the binary exhaust the possibilities). Physical markers commonly taken to distinguish one sex from the other (typically visible at birth), and the biology of reproduction in the species (if not the mechanics today, nor its applicability to every adult), are then a widely-recognized baseline from which to work. While there may be minority variants and individual eccentricities, ordinary people and ordinary governments in practice operate with an ordinary distinction relating to ordinary bodies and ordinary subjectivities. This is perhaps not uniform in all cases, but it certainly operates with great predictive force and with generalizing confirmations. The issue, here, is not the categorizing and normalizing practices of governments, but rather the ordinariness of the indifference between the terms sex and gender.[23] Philosophers and social scientists, dedicated to conceptual clarity and clear definitions, may find it opportune to lecture the rest of the world, but their chances of being effective are slight. Ordinary usage is unashamed by ambiguous synonymy (Do the two terms mean the same thing? Or different things?), as apparently is Jones.[24]

Other writers are more concerned to maintain, or seem to maintain, a sex/gender distinction in nature/culture terms (Holter, Buchanan, Stein and Carpenter), or at least not to drive the two terms towards synonymy or conflation.[25] Del Zotto is concerned with race and class in relation to "males," and does not address the sex/gender distinction directly. None of the present contributors adopts a radical Butlerian position, namely that gendered thinking (as stereotypical binary and hierarchical terms) itself creates a dichotomous and hierarchical notion of sexual difference, which is then naturalized conceptually as sex in (supposed) biological fixities of reproduction. Those who come the closest are perhaps Lindner and Rixecker. In Lindner's chapter, cultural constructions ("honor society") do almost all the explanatory and, more importantly, definitional work, telling us who is a man (and who therefore is a woman). There is comparatively little interest in conventional notions of bodily difference as dichotomous sex. Rixecker, for her part, openly pushes biology itself, and its conceptions of dichotomous sexual difference, into the cultural realm. She incorporates highly variable sexualities into gender as well, making it less and less dichotomous, as it less and less mirrors the male/female difference that we supposedly know and accept in advance:[26]

> Gender identity in this sense encapsulates assumptions about biological "sex" as well as the culturally defined protocol of "gender" (and its

> performance). Since the seemingly fixed category of biological sex—that is, male or female—has become more fluid, due to the more detailed understanding of intersexuality and chromosomal differences, this category is no longer as useful or appropriate as it may once have been. Additionally, the many varied formations of "gender" . . . that intersect with sexuality necessitate a more robust and diversified term. "Gender" here incorporates the variety of expressions . . . to acknowledge and integrate the significant interplay between sex, gender and sexuality.[27]

In practice, and in this volume, there is not a lot of difference between regarding gender as masculine/feminine behaviors loosely deriving from the (presumed) sexual binary of male/female, on the one hand, and as a discursive practice producing a wide variety of diverse effects (and sexualities), on the other.[28] Once we have a notion of "warrior masculinity" (Holter) or "honor society" (Lindner) in play, then it is up for grabs who is masculine, and what they do. That they will generally be men (on commonplace understandings) is no surprise. But then again, the link between the naturalized properties of "the male sex" and either of these "gender" categories ("warrior masculinity" and "honor society") is never really discussed or made problematic by cultural constructionists in this volume (as opposed to postmodernists, who do situate bodily sex wholly in relation to culture).

Contributors to this volume are thus tracing the dialectic between conflation and distinction across the (presumed) nature/culture divide that Scott has identified. At this point, though, a certain confusion sets in.

Gendering Explanation

This confusion is between "the thing to be explained" (*explanandum*) and "the thing that does the explaining" (*explanans*), and the role of gender (however interpreted) as identifying something as either. The "thing to be explained" in the chapters in this volume tends to be the mass killing of males (whether because they are "military age," male homosexuals, or for some other purported reason), or other phenomena said to fall within the rubric of "gendercide." While "battle-age men" are (as a result of work done in conjunction with some of the political interests expressed here) now made visible as males, and are therefore "the thing to be explained," it is never the case that maleness is the only thing visible. Nor is maleness in the victims the thing that does "the explaining" (despite a prevalent *desire* to make *gender* do *both* at once). After all, as Carpenter points out, no one is trying to exterminate all males as such—and indeed, even if they were, the maleness of the victims would not in itself explain why they (presumably females, in theory) were doing it.[29] Much the same is true of Rixecker's speculations about genocide perpetrated on gays through genetic screening and institutionalized surveillance, presumably instituted by (some) straights.[30] While we may presume that mass killers, the more usual subject here, are males "looking for males" (rather than females—for some purposes), their mindset is not explained by the victims' maleness, nor indeed by their own maleness (female *génocidaires* are thus an example that bolsters this argument). Some construction within the mass killers' minds does the explaining for us—that is, some cultural and/or political construction of an "enemy" group that is so "other" that mass killing is justified and normalized (at least to a degree and for a time). Certainly, maleness in these mindsets is central to, but does not exhaust, what defines the group selected for slaughter—those who are the result of the thing to be explained (i.e., mass killing). Rather what seems to be involved is a construction of a group as not just male (obviously), *but marked in other ways as dangerous and threatening* (e.g., for reasons of race/ethnicity/religion/age) in the minds of the perpetrators. This seems commonsensical, after all, as "battle-age males" is a readily understandable term (as is "black-male-as-criminal" in Del Zotto's context, or "male homosexual" in Rixecker's).[31]

The further issues, as discussed in the present volume, tend rather to be concerned with why the mass killing of such groups is not reflected in the press, or is not *sufficiently* reflected there, or why humanitarian agencies have not considered such groups to be a category of persons particularly at risk and have therefore not taken appropriate (or sufficient) action on their behalf.[32] What does the explaining here are the same "cultural" concepts of masculinity/manhood that assign the potential for violence and fighting exclusively, or at least disproportionately, to males of a certain age-range, rather than to "women and children." (Note that some of latter are obviously male, and also that "old men" beyond "battle-age" are an ancillary.) Both killers and humanitarians can be complicit with this stereotype of masculinity in complex ways, and the strength of some contributions is in tracing this out (e.g., Lindner).[33] There are then a variety of theories as to why killers and aid agencies are alike the victims of this stereotype, which runs counter to other international definitions of the combatant/non-combatant distinction. The least persuasive explanation, for me, is that the non-visibility of male victims in the press and in humanitarian efforts is the result of a feminist "taboo" on making men visible as victims, as Jones has suggested.[34] There are in my view sufficient "taboos" within stereotypical concepts of man-as-warrior (and therefore *not* as victim) to account for this, without ascribing to feminists an undue influence in the world's media or over largescale humanitarian agencies.[35]

Thus, given what has been said earlier about conflation/distinction debates on this supposed binary, it would seem that not a lot turns on whether we are looking at "*sex*-selective" mass murder (Stein, Carpenter), or "*gender*-selective" mass murder (Buchanan, Lindner, Rixecker, Del Zotto), or "*gender or sex*-selective" mass murder (Jones, Holter). Nor does a lot turn on whether one thinks that sex is a "brute fact," whereas gender is a (merely) cultural construction.[36] Whatever anyone's position on these issues in the present volume, it is the case that no one is offering explanations for murder (or silence) that are rooted in naturalized concepts of (biological) sex. Nor, protestations to the contrary, is anyone really offering explanations rooted in cultural constructions that somehow *flow* from sex as a natural dichotomy. That is, no one is saying either that mass murders are committed by hyper-masculine males, who target other males because the sex of hyper-masculine males has somehow produced that cultural construction; or that female *génocidaires* do what they do because of some cultural construction of femininity that flows from their—hyper? hypo?—femaleness. Put plainly, sociobiological explanations would have to flow from universal categories of maleness to mass murder (implausible, as not all men inflict these atrocities, and some women do). Cultural explanations that presume a link between behavior and sex, meanwhile, cannot find a grounding in "sex" itself on either side of the supposed "biological" binary that refines the perpetrator group sufficiently in relation to the target group (or vice-versa), with sex as the determinant.

It follows that what is doing the explaining here are cultural constructions delinked from bodily sex in terms of the *actions* of the perpetrators (even if only members of one sex do the perpetrating), and rooted instead in stereotypes of masculinity and femininity that are complex pastiches of apparently objective categories (age, strength) and apparently ascriptive ones (extreme danger and otherness). These cultural constructions, delinked from the *bodies* of the perpetrators, then account for what happens. The link to the *bodies* of the victims is really in the perpetrators' *minds.* What happens is certainly not explained by the sex of the victims' bodies; that belongs in the thing to be explained.

Carpenter's claim that women's "sex" makes them open to impregnation, and that this explains the actions of male rapist/impregnators in choosing them (rather than males) for attack, rather misses the point. The relevant concept of "open to impregnation" is the one in the perpetrators' minds—not the one in the gynecologists textbooks, or in commonplace notions of the female role in reproduction.[37] Women may (or may not) understand their own fertility and fertility cycle and use this knowledge, if they have it, in various ways. Males who rape specifically to impregnate have their own indiscriminate concepts of what rape and possible impregnation mean. It is that concept which tells them what the target is ("woman") and makes impregnation a desired but not certain consequence. A cultural construction of "warrior masculinity" does the explaining, not the sex of the bodies involved, given that "warrior masculinity" is a complex narrative about bodies, victims, shame, hurt, and so on that *includes* "biological" presumptions and "knowledge" about men and women. The explanation here must be rooted in the perpetrator's mindset. Why should the victim's *body* be complicit in *somehow* explaining such vile actions, just because the body is (naturally or culturally) marked with sex as some "brute" fact (or with gender thought to be rooted in sex)?

I suspect that there is a lingering desire in Carpenter's argument for the (supposedly) indisputable "material" and "factual" qualities of "sex." It is that which produces these rather symptomatic confusions between explanans and explanandum, and the need to assert the existence of "brute facts" that are independent of human experience (and indeed existence) in the first place. Insofar as present contributions to this volume employ "gender" in both explanandum and explanans, then, gender neither stands in for sex, nor refers to behaviors that somehow derive from sex. Rather it signals an intent to find sex, and sometimes sexuality, wherever it figures in *both* the thing to be explained (explanandum), and in the thing that does the explaining (explanans). However, finding "gender," as it were, in one or the other, does not ipso facto make it the explanans in a "gendered" explanation; nor does "gender" exhaust the "gendered" explanandum (which is really killing, albeit of a certain sort). Gender is therefore not a thing, but is better conceptualized as a strategy of making sex and sexuality visible in both the explanandum and the explanans, *without therefore defining the one exhaustively and making the other causal.* Whether this is best done within a "gendercide" framing, given its publicity value, or within a more tightly defined "mass killing" framework focusing on "battle-age males" (and possibly other male and/or other gender-related groupings), is another question. The important point is that gender as a way of making sex and sexuality visible should not produce confusions between *explanans* and *explanandum*. Nor should it produce unnecessary line-drawing debates over conflation/distinction issues between sex and gender, and thus between the fixed/natural and the malleable/cultural. Some positions on these terms and issues are doubtless relevant to anyone's project at hand; but no project at hand contains or presupposes all research questions, such that its solutions in this regard are the mirror and model for all further work.

Men, Masculinities, and Gendercide/Genocide

Where, then, does this leave studies of men and masculinities? Insofar as this volume highlights the overtly gendered character of men (as they live their lives as fathers, husbands, lovers, sons, boys, etc.), rather than as normalized and overlooked ciphers for the apparently de-gendered "abstract citizen" or "generic human," then the inquiries are all to the good. That is, men gain many advantages from being "unmarked" as such in gender terms and so standing in for anyone and everyone, even though living their lives through masculinized values and practices. But not always—once the "marking" is that of "warrior masculinity" (through conscription into armed forces, and ascription of "battle-age" status), then the tables are turned, and warrior masculinity takes its toll—of men. If warriors are honored and valued as top-class citizens and virile heroes (and, famously from Greek history, as dutiful sons), then they risk death as combatants or as (supposedly) would-be fighters, and so the slaughter continues.[38] Any analytical strategy that highlights the conceptual slippage between male and warrior (that is, not all males are even suitable for this role, let alone armed, while some females are ready, willing and equipped), and the conceptual slippage between female and victim/vulnerability/powerlessness (for the same reasons), is all to the good. Huge economic and emotional resources in the contemporary world are invested in warriordom and its associated myths of "women and children" as helpless victims.[39] The more that this is practically deconstructed, as it is by all the contributions in this volume, the better.[40]

Men's studies and studies of masculinities were founded on a distinction between men as apparently de-gendered, and men as overtly gendered, taking the position that the former was both a source of power and at odds with much male experience marked by supposed fixities of sexual difference.

Moreover, men's overtly gendered experience has been rather selectively sentimentalized (and demonized) in narrative and representation—rather than exposed, evaluated, and revisioned in theory and in practice. Contributors to this volume, in deploying concepts of sex and gender, speak to the same considerations, even if not in the same way, or as yet fully informed by the available literatures. This chapter has attempted to make the men's studies and masculinities literatures both more visible and more accessible to other communities of scholars and researchers than has previously been the case. In particular, it has sought to separate men's studies and studies of masculinities from any intrinsic association with writing and practice that romanticizes and excuses men in dubious ways.

Men's studies and studies of masculinity have a track record in documenting and analyzing masculine vulnerabilities and victimhood in ways that do not necessarily eclipse or prejudice feminist analyses of female marginalization and powerlessness. In the same way, men's studies and studies of masculinities have mounted fierce criticisms of characteristically masculine practices of violence, including mass murder and the mass murder of males (the war literatures, especially those on World War I, provide a good example).[41] Warrior masculinity has made men cannon fodder, and virtually no one would say that men have anybody to blame for that but themselves (as it were). It is in these areas that the present contributors find men a matter of concern, and are concerned for men. Making this an issue requires a recovery of men-as-men from within the disguise of man-as-anyone, which itself effectively dilutes the specificity through which these potent forms of masculinity actually operate. To do this is also to question the ghostly feminine ('man-as-*anyone,*' now seen in female combat soldiers), and so to disarm the questionable linkage between maleness and warriorhood.

By scrupulously researching the phenomenon of mass killing, contributors to this volume, and to the genocide literature more generally, are making an important contribution to an understanding of masculinities in politics. It is important, however, that such analyses seek out sex and sexuality —incorporated in contingent and complex categories like "battle-age male"—as a matter of course, and in a supportive encounter with feminist work. It is equally vital that they do not relapse into unspecified de-gendered (and de-gendering) conceptions of "the human condition," or into presumptions that maleness in and of itself is an unproblematic explanans or explanandum. Feminists have exploded that myth, and made men and masculinities visible, at least in principle. For obvious reasons, they have not done *all* the work themselves; but they, and scholars of men and masculinities, have charted a course for future exploration. In my view, the gendercide/genocide debates constitute a further very important step, both in their methodological pluralism and in their global political salience.

Notes

1. R. Charli Carpenter, "Gender Theory in World Politics: Contributions of a Nonfeminist Standpoint?" *International Studies Review,* 4:3 (2002), pp. 153, 165; Carpenter, "Beyond 'Gendercide': Operationalizing Gender in Comparative Genocide," this volume; Adam Jones, "Does Gender Make the World Go Round?" *Review of International Studies,* 22: 4 (1996), p. 424; Jones, "Gendercide: A Response to Carpenter," *International Journal of Human Rights,* 7:1 (2003), p. 141. Evelin Gerda Lindner ("In Honor and Human Rights Societies," this volume) has unfortunately repeated only Jones's rejoinders to me on the subject of feminism and his work, giving the impression that I am antifeminist because of my critical remarks about his work. She has not quoted from my comments about feminism, Jones, and myself in Terrell Carver, Molly Cochran, and Judith Squires, "Gendering Jones: Feminisms, IRs, Masculinities," *Review of International Studies* 24:4 (1996), pp. 299–303, so that readers of the present volume might evaluate her judgment for themselves. While opinion about our work (Jones's and mine), our views of each other, and the relationship between each of us and feminism will surely differ, it seems that each of us feels he has a positive and constructive relationship with this movement.

2. For a synoptic introduction and readings on postwar feminism, see Judith Squires and Sandra Kemp, eds., *Feminisms* (Oxford: Oxford University Press, 1997).

3. See, for example, Cynthia Cockburn, *Brothers: Male Dominance and Technological Change* (London: Pluto, 1983) and *In the Way of Resistance: Men's Resistance to Sex Equality in Organizations* (Basingstoke, UK: Macmillan, 1991); Lynne Segal, *Slow Motion: Changing Masculinities, Changing Men* (London: Virago, 1990). On masculinity: Wendy Brown, *Manhood and Politics: A Feminist Reading in Political Theory* (Totowa, N.J.: Rowman and Littlefield, 1988); Christine di Stefano, *Configurations of Masculinity: A Feminist Perspective on Modern Political Theory* (Ithaca, N.Y.: Cornell University Press, 1991); Jean Bethke Elshtain, *Meditations on Modern Political Thought: Masculine/Feminine Themes from Luther to Arendt* (New York: Praeger, 1986). On male violence: Wendy Brown, *Manhood and Politics: A Feminist Reading in Political Theory* (Totowa, N.J.: Rowman and Littlefield, 1988); Christine di Stefano, *Configurations of Masculinity: A Feminist Perspective on Modern Political Theory* (Ithaca, N.Y.: Cornell University Press, 1991); Jean Bethke Elshtain, *Meditations on Modern Political Thought: Masculine/Feminine Themes from Luther to Arendt* (New

York: Praeger, 1986). On the "man" question: Kathy E. Ferguson, *The Man Question: Visions of Subjectivity in Feminist Theory* (Berkeley, Calif.: University of California Press, 1993); Marysia Zalewski and Jane Parpart, eds., *The "Man Question" in International Relations* (Boulder, Colo.: Westview, 1998); Jean Bethke Elshtain, *Private Man/Public Woman: Women in Social and Political Thought* (Oxford: Martin Robertson, 1981). On structural masculinism: very recent studies by Charlotte Hooper, *Manly States: Masculinities, International Relations, and Gender Politics* (New York: Columbia University Press, 2001); R. Claire Snyder, *Citizen-Soldiers and Manly Warriors: Military Service and Gender in the Civic Republican Tradition* (Lanham, Md.: Rowman and Littlefield, 2000). On militarism: Jean Bethke Elshtain, *Women and War* (Chicago: University of Chicago Press, 1995); Cynthia Enloe, *Bananas, Beaches, and Bases: Making Feminist Sense of International Politics* (Berkeley, Calif.: University of California Press, 1990) and *Maneuvers: The International Politics of Militarizing Women's Lives* (Berkeley, Calif.: University of California Press, 2000). On international relations as a mirror: J. Ann Tickner, *Gender in International Relations: Feminist Perspectives on Achieving Global Security* (New York: Columbia University Press, 1992); V. Spike Peterson, *Gendered States: Feminist (Re)visions of International Relations* (Boulder, Colo.: Lynne Rienner, 1992); V. Spike Peterson and Anne Sisson Runyan, *Global Gender Issues* (Boulder, Colo.: Westview, 1993). On masculinized political theory and philosophy: Diana Coole, *Women in Political Theory: From Ancient Misogyny to Contemporary Feminism*, 2d. ed. (Brighton: Harvester/Wheatsheaf, 1992); Moira Gatens, *Feminism and Philosophy* (Cambridge: Polity, 1991); Susan M. Okin, *Women in Western Political Thought* (Princeton, N.J.: Princeton University Press, 1979). On rationality as a masculine preserve and strategy: Genevieve Lloyd, *The Man of Reason: "Male" and "Female" in Western Philosophy* (London: Methuen, 1984); Raia Prokhovnik, *Rational Woman: A Feminist Critique of Dichotomy*, 2d. ed. (Manchester, UK: Manchester University Press, 2002).

4. See Michael Kimmel, *The Politics of Manhood* (Philadelphia: Temple University Press, 1996); Michael A. Messner, *Politics of Masculinities: Men in Movements* (Thousand Oaks, Calif.: Sage 1997); Bob Pease, *Men and Gender Relations* (Melbourne: Tertiary Press, 2002).

5. Joan Wallach Scott, *Gender and the Politics of History*, rev. ed. (New York: Columbia University Press, 1999), p. 211. I am grateful to Helen Kinsella for bringing Scott's new concluding chapter, "Some More Reflections on Gender and Politics," to my attention.

6. See the classic study, Carole Pateman, *The Sexual Contract* (Cambridge: Polity, 1988). For an exploration in relation to men and masculinities, see also Terrell Carver, "'Public Man' and the Critique of Masculinities," *Political Theory*, 24 (1996), pp. 673–86.

7. For the classics of men's studies and masculinities literatures, see R.W. Connell, *Masculinities* (Cambridge: Polity, 1995); Harry Brod, ed., *The Making of Masculinities:*

The New Men's Studies (Winchester, Mass.: Allen and Unwin, 1987); Arthur Brittan, *Masculinity and Power* (Oxford: Blackwell, 1989); David H. J. Morgan, *Discovering Men: Sociology and Masculinities* (London: Routledge, 1992). For recent studies, see Judith K. Gardiner, ed., *Masculinity Studies and Feminist Theory: New Directions* (New York: Columbia University Press, 2002); Michael S. Kimmel, *The Gendered Society* (Oxford: Oxford University Press, 2000); Stephen M. Whitehead, *Men and Masculinities: Key Themes and New Directions* (Cambridge: Polity, 2002). For a comprehensive overview, see *The Men's Studies Bibliography* at *www.xyonline.net/mensbiblio/*.

8. See, for example, Sylvia Walby, *Theorizing Patriarchy* (Oxford: Blackwell, 1990); Jeff Hearn, *Men in the Public Eye: The Construction and Deconstruction of Public Men and Public Patriarchies* (London: Unwin Hyman/Routledge, 1992).

9. See David T. Evans, *Sexual Citizenship: The Material Construction of Sexualities* (London: Routledge, 1993).

10. For a defining discussion, see Connell, *Masculinities,* pp. 76–81.

11. For the "patriarchal dividend," see R. W. Connell, *Gender* (Cambridge: Polity, 2002), pp. 5–6, 112–13, 142–43.

12. Michael S. Kimmel, "Masculinity as Homophobia: Fear, Shame, and Silence in the Construction of Gender Identity," in Stephen M. Whitehead and Frank J. Barrett, eds., *The Masculinities Reader* (Cambridge: Polity, 2001), pp. 271–72.

13. Bob Pease and Keith Pringle, "Introduction: Studying Men's Practices and Gender Relations in a Global Context," in Bob Pease and Keith Pringle, eds., *A Man's World? Changing Men's Practices in a Globalized World* (London: Zed Books, 2001), p. 8; see also Michael S. Kimmel, "Global Masculinities," in the same volume, pp. 21–37.

14. David Gutterman, "The Interrogation of Masculinity," in Whitehead and Barrett, *The Masculinities Reader,* p. 65. See also Bob Pease, *Recreating Men: Postmodern Masculinity Politics* (London: Sage, 2000).

15. For discussion on this point, see Terrell Carver, *Gender Is Not a Synonym for Women* (Boulder, Colo.: Lynne Rienner, 1996). See also Stephen M. Whitehead, "Man: The Invisible Gendered Subject," in Whitehead and Barrett, *The Masculinities Reader,* pp. 351–68.

16. Judith Butler, *Gender Trouble: Feminism and the Subversion of Identity* (London: Routledge, 1990).

17. This theme is developed in Terrell Carver, "Men in IR/Men and IR," in Louiza Odysseos and Hakan Seckinelgin, eds., *Gendering the "International"* (Basingstoke, UK: Palgrave, 2002), pp. 86–105.

18. Butler, *Gender Trouble,* pp. 1–34.

19. For a typology of gender theories, see Carver, "Men in IR/Men and IR," pp. 87–89.

20. Scott, *Gender and the Politics of History,* pp. 208–9.

21. Ibid., pp. 200–202.

22. See the discussion in Connell, *Gender,* pp. 30–33.

23. For an important analytical discussion of governments' practices, see Jacqueline Stevens, *Reproducing the State* (Princeton, N.J.: Princeton University Press, 1999).

24. Jones himself suggests a "conceptual laziness" here; Adam Jones, "Gendercide: A Response to Carpenter," p. 141.

25. Holter responds: "I disagree. Carver seems to have missed the central distinction in my chapter—not between nature/culture or biological/social elements of gender, but between inequality structure (patriarchy) and gender. The point is not that gender is partly biological—if I leave that impression, sorry, my text needs clarification!—but that (1) gender structures and (2) inequality structures are different *social* patterns. This is quite a new thought for many people, which might be relevant to Carver's misinterpretation. My point is that these two are changing sociohistorical formations, and precisely the fact that they are different creates the ground for a 'theory' of gendercide. So certain 'mobbing formations' of society, including strong gender-reactive elements, create genocide/gendercide. I can't see that this has anything at all to do with an essentialist or naturalistic gender/sex analysis." Personal communication to editor, April 2003.

26. Joshua S. Goldstein does this as well in his recent study, *War and Gender: How Gender Shapes the War System and Vice Versa* (Cambridge: Cambridge University Press, 2001), p. 2.

27. Stefanie Rixecker, "Genetic Engineering and Queer Biotechnology: The Eugenics of the Twenty-first Century?" this volume.

28. Among these are concepts of biology, reproduction and sex that instantiate the binary between male and female, and the hierarchy of male over female.

29. Carpenter, "Beyond 'Gendercide.'"

30. Rixecker, "Genetic Engineering."

31. Jones, "Gender and Genocide in Rwanda," this volume; Augusta C. Del Zotto, "Gendercide in a Historical-Structural Context: The Case of Black Male Gendercide in the United States," this volume.; Rixecker, "Genetic Engineering."

32. Adam Jones, "Of Rights and Men: Towards a Minoritarian Framing of Male Experience," *Journal of Human Rights* 1: 3 (2002), pp. 387–403; Carpenter, "Gender Theory in World Politics," pp. 154, 159–60; Carpenter, "Beyond 'Gendercide.'"

33. Carpenter makes a similar point about cultural concepts in relation to Jones and Goldstein, but criticizes both for mishandling the sex/gender distinction, as she sees it; "Gender Theory in World Politics," pp. 161–62; also Carpenter, "Beyond 'Gendercide.'"

34. Adam Jones, "Gendercide and Genocide," *Journal of Genocide Research* 2:2 (2000), pp. 185–86, 197, 198.

35. Dubravka Zarkov, "The Body of the Other Man: Sexual Violence and the Construction of Masculinity, Sexuality, and Ethnicity in Croatian Media," in

Caroline O. N. Moser and Fiona C. Clark, eds., *Victims, Perpetrators, or Actors? Gender, Armed Conflict, and Political Violence* (London: Zed Books, 2001), pp. 69–82.

36. Stuart Stein, "Gender and Other Cides," this volume, and Carpenter, "Beyond 'Gendercide.'"

37. Carpenter, "Beyond 'Gendercide.'" Presumably, the same argument and critique hold for castration.

38. A Spartan mother is reported to have said laconically, "either with this [shield] or on it." Plutarch, *Sayings of Spartan Women*, 241F #16, *omega.cohums.ohio-state.edu:8080/hyper-lists/classics-1/99–03–01/0287.html*

39. Children are a category deserving special and careful discussion; the emphasis here is on the use of "children" as a marker to designate women as juvenile and helpless.

40. For an in-depth discussion of the history and structure of the combatant/noncombatant distinction, see Helen Kinsella, "Securing the Civilian," paper presented at the International Studies Association Annual Convention, Portland, Ore., 26 February–1 March 2003.

41. Brod, *The Making of Masculinities;* see also *The Men's Studies Bibliography.*

About the Contributors

David Buchanan is a human rights activist and writer living in Vancouver, BC. He holds a baccalaureate in natural science from the University of Guelph and is writing a book on the topic of male vulnerability. E-mail: *dbuchana@vcn.bc.ca*

R. Charli Carpenter has recently completed a Ph.D. in political science at the University of Oregon, and currently holds a grant from the MacArthur Foundation to conduct research on children born of genocidal rape. She has published articles on gender and ethnic conflict in *Human Rights Quarterly, International Studies Review,* and *International Organization.* Her current research interests include sex-selective mass killing, children's human rights, and gender as a category of analysis in international relations theory. E-mail: *charli.carpenter@drake.edu*

Terrell Carver is professor of political theory at the University of Bristol. He has published extensively on gender, masculinity/ies and feminist theory, particularly in the field of international relations. He is author of *Gender is Not a Synonym for Women* (Lynne Rienner, 1996), and was awarded a grant from the Arts & Humanities Research Board of the UK to finish his book *Men in Political Theory* (Manchester University Press, forthcoming). E-mail: *tfcarver@earthlink.net*

Augusta C. Del Zotto is a doctoral fellow at Syracuse University's Maxwell School of Public Admistration. She serves as commissioner for the City of San Francisco's Mental Health Board, where she established the Children and Youth Violence Prevention Program and is executive director of Pursestrings, an economic literacy program for women leaving the US welfare system. She has lectured at numerous universities, government agencies, and NGOs on violence prevention and community renewal. E-mail: *DelZottoA@aol.com*

Øystein Gullvåg Holter, Ph.D., is Researcher 1 at the Work Research Institute in Oslo, Norway. He has written several books on gender and equality issues, most recently *Can Men Do It? Men and Gender Equality—The Nordic Experience* (Copenhagen: TemaNord, 2003). E-mail:*oeholter@online.no*

Adam Jones is professor of international studies at the Center for Research and Teaching in Economics (CIDE) in Mexico City. He holds a Ph.D. in political science from the University of British Columbia and is executive director of Gendercide Watch (*www.gendercide.org*), a web-based educational initiative. He is the author of *Beyond the Barricades: Nicaragua and the Struggle for the Sandinista Press, 1979–1998* (Ohio University Press, 2002), and editor of *Genocide, War Crimes, and the West: History and Complicity* (Zed Books, 2004). Most of his published articles on gender and international politics can be found on his website at*adamjones.freeservers.com/scholar.htm*. Email: *adamj_jones@hotmail.com*

Evelin Gerda Lindner, M.D., Ph.D., is a cross-cultural social psychologist and physician. In 1996, she designed a research project on the concept of humiliation and its role in genocide and war. From 1997–2001, she carried out this research, interviewing more than two hundred people regarding the genocides in Rwanda, Somalia, and Nazi Germany. Affiliated with the Department of Psychology, University of Oslo, she works with the Maison des Sciences de l'Homme, Paris, and the International Center for Cooperation and Conflict Resolution at Columbia University, New York. E-mail: *e.g.lindner@psykologi.uio.no*

Stefanie S. Rixecker is director of the Environment, Society and Design Division at Lincoln University, Aotearoa, New Zealand. She has contributed to academic, governmental, and global policy initiatives in the areas of biodiversity, biotechnology, ecological gender analysis, cultural risk assessment, and environmental justice and human rights. The author of numerous book chapters and articles in journals such as *Policy Sciences,* the *Canadian Journal of Environmental Education, World Archaeology, Women's Studies Journal,* and *Journal of Genocide Research,* she has been active in the Aotearoa branch of Amnesty International, especially with regard to queer human rights, and is working on a book on biopolitics and the queer community. E-mail: *Rixeckes@lincoln.ac.nz*

Stuart Stein is director of the Web Genocide Documentation Centre (*www.ess.uwe.ac.uk/genocide.htm*) and visiting research fellow at the University of the West of England. He holds a Ph.D. in sociology and an M.Sc. in social psychology from the London School of Economics. He is the author of six books, including *International Diplomacy, State Administrators, and Narcotics Control* (Gower, 1985). E-mail: *Stuart.Stein@uwe.ac.uk*

Index